Ronald R. Rindfuss · Minja Kim Choe
Editors

Low Fertility, Institutions, and their Policies

Variations Across Industrialized Countries

Korea Institute for Health and Social Affairs
www.kihasa.re.kr

EAST-WEST CENTER

Springer

Editors
Ronald R. Rindfuss
Department of Sociology
University of North Carolina
Chapel Hill, NC
USA

and

East-West Center
Honolulu, HI
USA

Minja Kim Choe
East-West Center
Honolulu, HI
USA

ISBN 978-3-319-32995-6   ISBN 978-3-319-32997-0 (eBook)
DOI 10.1007/978-3-319-32997-0

Library of Congress Control Number: 2016936655

Printed on acid-free paper

This Springer imprint is published by Springer Nature
The registered company is Springer International Publishing AG Switzerland

Foreword

Over the past half century, countries in many parts of the world have experienced rapid economic growth along with far-reaching changes in social and political conditions. In many countries, these developments have been accompanied by fertility declines to very low levels. In 2013, the average total fertility rate (TFR) was 1.8 children per woman in North America, 1.5 in East Asia, and 1.6 in Europe.

Within the general trend toward lower fertility, the pace and extent of fertility decline have been widely diverse, resulting in very different effects on population age structure and population growth, as well as important implications for institutions and policies. As a result, there is an urgent need for a comprehensive review of fertility levels and trends across low-fertility countries.

Early in 2013, the Korea Institute for Health and Social Affairs (KIHASA) and the East-West Center agreed to collaborate on a project to improve understanding of the patterns and causes of fertility decline in various social, economic, cultural, and political settings and to consider the associated policy implications. The project identified 18 low-fertility countries with varying fertility levels and trends, cultural backgrounds, social patterns, and economic conditions. For each country, an expert scholar was invited to write a country paper and participate in a series of workshops for discussions with experts from other countries.

These papers are being published in two volumes. The first, published in October 2015, includes revised versions of the papers presented at the first workshop, held at the East-West Center in December 2013 and addressing the fertility situation in Australia, China, Hong Kong, Japan, South Korea, the Netherlands, Singapore, and the United States. The chapters in this volume discuss the factors that are influencing fertility in Austria, Canada, the Czech Republic, France, Hungary, Italy, Norway, Spain, Taiwan, and the United Kingdom. They are revised versions of the papers presented at the second workshop on low fertility, held at the East-West Center in August 2014. It is hoped that the collection of papers presented in these two volumes will serve as an important reference point for all those interested in fertility variation across economically advanced countries.

The Ministry of Health and Social Affairs of the Government of the Republic of Korea provided generous funding for the project. Thanks are due to East-West Center's Research Program for project coordination and institutional support. On behalf of KIHASA, I am grateful to East-West Center Senior Fellows Minja Kim Choe, Sang-Hyop Lee, and Ronald R. Rindfuss for coordinating project activities, to Sidney B. Westley for expert editorial management, and to Ki-Tae Park for research assistance.

Sangho Kim
President
Korea Institute for Health and Social Affairs

Contents

Diverse Paths to Low and Lower Fertility: An Overview 1
Ronald R. Rindfuss and Minja Kim Choe

Not so Low Fertility in Norway—A Result of Affluence, Liberal Values, Gender-Equality Ideals, and the Welfare State 13
Øystein Kravdal

The Influence of Family Policies on Fertility in France: Lessons from the Past and Prospects for the Future 49
Olivier Thévenon

Fertility and Population Change in the United Kingdom 77
Wendy Sigle

Canadian Fertility Trends and Policies: A Story of Regional Variation 99
Sarah R. Brauner-Otto

The European Middle Way? Low Fertility, Family Change, and Gradual Policy Adjustments in Austria and the Czech Republic 131
Tomáš Sobotka

Fertility Decline and the Persistence of Low Fertility in a Changing Policy Environment—A Hungarian Case Study 165
Zsolt Spéder

The Policy Context of Fertility in Spain: Toward a Gender-Egalitarian Model? 195
Pau Baizan

Aging Italy: Low Fertility and Societal Rigidities 221
Maria Letizia Tanturri

Transition from Anti-natalist to Pro-natalist Policies in Taiwan 259
Meilin Lee and Yu-Hsuan Lin

Governmental Support for Families and Obstacles to Fertility in East Asia and Other Industrialized Regions 283
Anne H. Gauthier

Diverse Paths to Low and Lower Fertility: An Overview

Ronald R. Rindfuss and Minja Kim Choe

Abstract All the countries represented in this volume have fertility below the replacement level, with some well below. Low fertility leads to population aging and issues of labor-force size and the provision of welfare benefits to the elderly. This introduction previews chapters that describe the situation in Austria, the Czech Republic, Hungary, Italy, Spain, and Taiwan, all with a total fertility rate (TFR) below 1.5 children per woman, and France, Norway, and the United Kingdom, where fertility is close to the replacement level of 2.1. The final country is Canada, which has a TFR between these two country groups, reflecting generous childcare and maternity-leave policies in Québec and considerably less generous policies in the rest of Canada. The discussion focuses on common features across the countries as well as distinctive cultural, institutional, and policy features of each country that might affect fertility levels, either deliberately or inadvertently. Such features include flexibility of the labor market, the link between marriage and childbearing, factors that help or hinder parents in balancing work and family obligations, gender equity, education systems, the housing market, and government subsidies for the cost of childrearing.

Keywords Fertility · Work · Childcare · Education · Housing · Gender

As the number of countries with very high fertility diminishes and the number with very low fertility increases, researchers that examine fertility, its causes, and consequences, have been turning their attention to the issue of low fertility. The countries with low fertility tend to have advanced economies and high education levels. Within the low-fertility group, however, there is considerable variation in

R.R. Rindfuss
Department of Sociology, University of North Carolina, Chapel Hill, NC, USA
e-mail: ron_rindfuss@unc.edu

R.R. Rindfuss · M.K. Choe (✉)
East-West Center, Honolulu, HI USA
e-mail: mchoe@hawaii.edu

R.R. Rindfuss and M.K. Choe (eds.), *Low Fertility, Institutions, and their Policies*, DOI 10.1007/978-3-319-32997-0_1

fertility level—some countries have a total fertility rate (TFR) just below the replacement level of 2.1 children per women, while others have fertility 50–75 % below that level. That such diversity exists among developed countries on something so fundamental as how many children people have suggests that country-level factors are operating—factors that tend to affect everyone within a country but vary across countries. Such factors include institutions, policies, culture, and history.

This is the second volume in a project examining fertility trends and the factors shaping fertility in 18 diverse countries. This volume includes chapters on Austria, Canada, the Czech Republic, France, Hungary, Italy, Norway, Spain, Taiwan, and the United Kingdom (UK), plus a chapter that examines fertility levels and government support for families across a variety of countries. The first volume (Rindfuss and Choe 2015) included chapters on Australia, China, Hong Kong, Japan, South Korea, the Netherlands, Singapore, and the United States. Together these two volumes cover countries with widely different geographies, histories, political systems, institutional arrangements, and fertility regimes.

Figure 1 shows the trend in TFRs from 1981 to 2012 for the 10 countries in this volume. France, Norway, and the UK have had the highest TFRs since 2001, with France above 2.0 since 2008. The UK had a TFR of 1.63 in 2001, but then recovered to TFRs approaching 2.0. Norway has had a TFR of 1.75 or higher since 1988. By contrast, six countries have had TFRs at or below 1.5 since 2001—Austria, the Czech Republic, Hungary, Italy, Spain, and Taiwan. Taiwan has shown the most interesting trend during this period. In 1981, Taiwan had the highest TFR of any of these countries—at 2.46 children per woman—as it was still completing the demographic transition from high to low fertility. By 2010, it had reached a low of 0.90[1]—the lowest fertility recorded for any of these countries. Since 2001, Canada has been between the high- and low-fertility countries. This is the result of pro-natalist fertility policies introduced in Québec but not in the rest of Canada. Note that none of these countries currently has a TFR above the replacement level of 2.1. Only Taiwan was above 2.1 at any point since 1981, and it was last above 2.1 in 1983.

Below-replacement fertility, especially for the countries below a TFR of 1.5, implies an aging population and eventually a shrinking population. The prospects of population aging and shrinking are typically greeted with alarm, but not universally so. Some environmentalists welcome the prospect of fewer people—in Taiwan (this volume) this view has led environmentalists to oppose policies under consideration to increase fertility. Feminist groups in Taiwan have also voiced objections to proposed pro-natalist policies because they worry that such policies would work against efforts to promote gender equality. And in Italy (this volume), the legacy of Fascism makes it very difficult to have a policy discussion about the "problem" of

[1]2010 was the Year of the Tiger in the Chinese Zodiac. Many Taiwanese believe that children born in the Year of the Tiger will question authority and at some point cause trouble for themselves, their family, or their employer. By contrast, 2012 was the Year of the Dragon, thought to be an auspicious year. Note that Taiwan's TFR jumped to 1.27 in 2012.

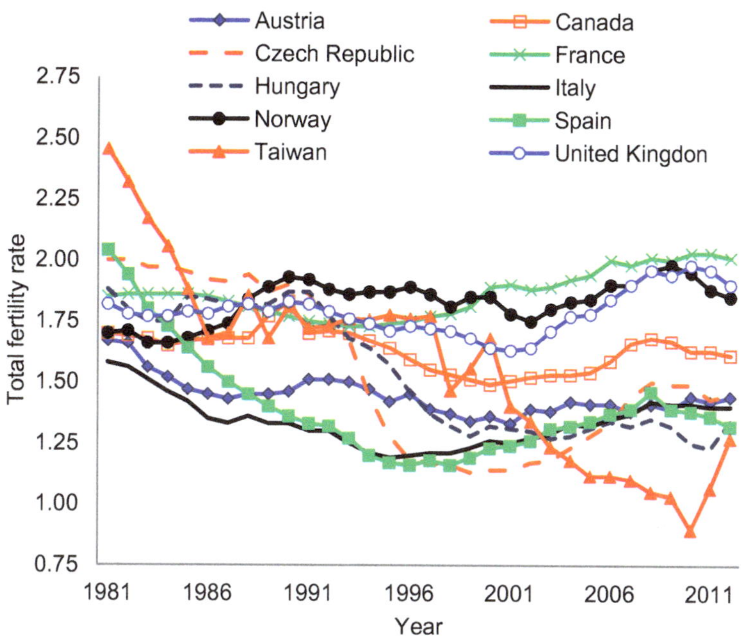

Fig. 1 Trends in period total fertility rate (TFR) in 10 countries, 1981–2012 (World Bank 2013)

low fertility. Instead, public discourse has to be framed in terms of reconciling work and family responsibilities.

Nonetheless, the majority of interest groups and decision-makers in countries with very low levels of fertility are concerned about aging and shrinking populations. Their concerns include loss of nationalistic pride, a declining number of consumers purchasing the country's goods and services, and a declining number of young adults to serve in the military. An aging population—that is, a population in which the proportion at older ages is increasing—also has implications for various welfare policies. Most countries have pay-as-you-go programs to support the elderly with taxes received from those at working age. As the elderly become a larger fraction of the population and those at working age a smaller fraction, politically painful adjustments need to be made, such as increasing retirement ages, decreasing benefits, and/or raising taxes. Norway is unique with a cushion of more than US$900 billion in assets in its Sovereign Wealth Fund derived from oil revenue; the other countries do not have this luxury.

This volume had its beginning at a conference where the chapters were presented as papers. Authors were asked to identify the institutions, history, culture, and policies of their countries that might affect fertility levels and patterns. They were asked not only to consider institutions and policies that might be intentionally affecting fertility, but also those that might inadvertently affect fertility, negatively or positively. Considerable time was allocated for discussion, which allowed questions about each country's institutions, policies, culture, and history. The chapters in this volume, including this introductory chapter, were revised to take into account the rich discussion that took place.

In this introductory chapter, we begin by explaining a few technical terms that are used in the various chapters. We then highlight some of the commonalities and differences across the countries. Throughout this introduction, with one exception, we use country names to refer to the chapters that follow. The exception is the chapter by Anne Gauthier that examines governmental support across a variety of countries; we refer to that chapter as Gauthier.

First, Some Definitions[2]

We begin by noting a few issues of definition that permeate the chapters. We address these issues in non-technical language. Readers interested in technical details are urged to consult standard demographic texts (such as Preston et al. 2001 or Wachter 2014) or journal articles on specialized topics (such as Bongaarts and Feeney 1998 on tempo distortion in period total fertility rates).

The period total fertility rate, commonly indicated as TFR, is a measure of fertility for a particular time period, usually a year. It has the useful property of not being distorted by the age structure of a population in a particular year. The TFR is the number of children a woman would have in her lifetime if she experienced the age-specific fertility rates that existed in the year for which the TFR was calculated. As such, it is expressed in an easily understood metric: number of children per woman. The cohort TFR is the average number of children per woman that a cohort of women would have in their lifetimes.

Replacement-level fertility is the TFR that would produce a population growth rate of 0.0 if it were experienced for a long time and there were no change in mortality and no in- or out-migration. For most purposes, 2.1 is a reasonable approximation of replacement-level fertility. It is larger than 2.0 because some female births do not survive to childbearing age.

Tempo distortion occurs whenever women are having children at either earlier or later ages than they had previously. If births are occurring earlier, tempo distortion will result in a higher TFR even if women are not having more births throughout their lives. And conversely, if women are postponing births, the TFR will be lower even if women are having the same number of births as previously. To intuitively see this, imagine one year for a population where all women had twins at age 25 and no other children year after year—the TFR in that population would be 2.0. If for some reason these women postponed having their twins until age 26, during the postponing year the TFR would drop to 0.0 even though the actual number of children that women in this population were having over their lifetimes would not change.

---

[2]This section is reproduced, with permission, from Rindfuss and Choe (2015) with some additional material.

Although the language of causality is frequently used in these chapters, the papers do not represent empirical tests of causal hypotheses. Rather, the authors were asked to describe the institutions, history, culture, and policies that might be affecting fertility. As such, it is important to recognize that what is being presented is a series of hypotheses rather than causal analyses.

Postponement of Childbearing

Over the past two or three decades, women in all 10 countries described here have been postponing the start of their childbearing. The mean age at first birth in most of these countries is now about 28. Italy (this volume) has the latest mean age at first birth at 30.6 (excluding women who were born outside Italy). This postponement has meant that period TFRs are lower than the underlying cohort measures. The influence of postponement on the period TFR was most dramatic in the Czech Republic (this volume) where the period TFR fell from 1.87 in 1990 to a low of 1.13 in 1999, then increased to just below 1.5 recently. In contrast, the TFR adjusted for this tempo effect (specifically TFRp*, see Bongaarts and Sobotka 2012) gradually declined from 2.0 in 1990 to just below 1.8 in 2009–2012.

Postponement is related to increased educational attainment in all 10 countries, with women having achieved higher attainment than men. Basically, it is difficult to combine the student and mother roles, and so fertility is delayed, although the degree of difficulty varies and appears to be lowest in Norway (this volume). Not only does increased educational attainment take time, it also raises occupational and career expectations, further delaying motherhood. High levels of young-adult unemployment in Spain and Italy (this volume) also contribute to postponement, as does the economic uncertainty that emerged after the fall of communism in the Czech Republic and Hungary (this volume).

Postponement of childbearing is related to rising childlessness in some countries. In Italy (this volume) childlessness is approaching 30 % among the better educated, and childlessness among the better educated has also been increasing in the UK (this volume). In Austria (this volume), voluntary childlessness is now considered more acceptable than it was in the past. This may be related to seeing, evaluating, and possibly emulating the emergence of a childless lifestyle, as Lutz et al. (2006) have argued.

Labor-Market Factors

There are substantial structural differences in the labor markets of these 10 countries, and the differences likely affect fertility. The general expectation is that the easier it is to combine the worker and mother roles and the easier it is to re-enter the labor market after staying home to care for a child, the higher the fertility. In two of the three higher-fertility countries, the labor market shows these favorable features. Norway (this volume) has very low unemployment rates allowing easy re-entry into the labor market, a high share of part-time jobs, and relatively short work days. The UK (this volume) has an unregulated and fluid labor market that offers mothers easy re-entry into the labor force and widely available part-time opportunities. This is especially the case for those in low-skill jobs, and it has led to higher fertility among those with lower human capital. While part-time jobs are not as available as in some other countries and the labor market is not quite as flexible as in the UK, France (this volume) has a stay-at-home allowance for mothers taking care of young children, and this allowance appears to have had a positive effect on childbearing, especially among those at the lower end of the occupational hierarchy.

Among the remaining countries, Italy (this volume) has a labor market structure that is perhaps the least favorable to fertility. There are few part-time jobs, and full-time employees are expected to work relatively long hours in comparison with other European countries. Unemployment rates are high for young adults, and entry-level salaries are low. Traditionally, the labor market was a structured "insider-outsider" market, so that those with jobs were legally protected and difficult to fire, making employers hesitant to add new employees. This also made it difficult for mothers who had left their jobs to re-enter the labor market later. In an effort to make Italy more economically competitive, some of these regulations have been relaxed, but the result has been to create precarious jobs, that is, jobs where employees do not receive benefits and can easily be fired. In a country long used to having job security, women may be reluctant to marry or have a child with a man who has a precarious job. And finally, it is known that some Italian employers, when hiring a woman of childbearing age, will force her to sign an undated letter of resignation to be used if she becomes pregnant. Even though firing a pregnant woman is illegal, the practice of using undated resignation letters is not.

Some of these labor-market features are also found in other countries with relatively low fertility. Spain (this volume) has long work hours for full-time employees, an insider-outsider labor market, high young-adult unemployment rates, and some recent restructuring leading to an increase in precarious jobs. Taiwan (this volume) has long work hours for full-time workers. With the transition to capitalist systems, the Czech Republic and Hungary (this volume) have considerable uncertainty in the labor market—something that did not exist under the communist regime. The Czech Republic also has rigid work hours for full-time workers and few part-time jobs.

Marriage-Childbearing Link

For most of these countries, the link between marriage and fertility has been weakening. In France and Norway, more than one-half of all births occur outside marriage, although frequently within long-term cohabiting relationships. In Austria, the Czech Republic, and Hungary approximately two-fifths of all births are non-marital. Even in Italy, the site of the Vatican, approximately one-quarter of births are non-marital. Taiwan is an exception to this trend, with only 4 % of births occurring outside marriage. In fact, non-marital fertility rates are low throughout East Asia.[3]

It is unclear to what extent the relaxation of the link between marriage and childbearing affects fertility. If the marriage-fertility link is weak, women (and couples) have more flexibility in their childbearing decisions. But, if there is an effect, we expect it to be relatively small compared with other factors, such as the structure of the labor market and the availability of high-quality, government-subsidized childcare.

Childcare and Paid Leave

The incompatibility between most jobs in modern economies and care for a child is well known. This incompatibility is greatest in the first days, weeks, and months of a child's life. It is somewhat reduced if a new mother can take leave from her job with a guarantee that she can return to the same job at the end of the leave. If the leave is paid, the incompatibility is further reduced. And if affordable, high-quality childcare is available when the mother wants to return to work, then the incompatibility is again reduced, especially if the childcare facility is open during the full hours that the mother works and commutes.

From this perspective, Norway (this volume) likely has the lowest incompatibility. Parental leave, primarily taken by mothers, is available at full pay for 49 weeks or at 80 % pay for 59 weeks. After that, government-subsidized, high-quality childcare is widely available during the usual working and commuting hours. Eighty percent of children age 1–2 are in childcare, and this rises to 97 % for children age 3–5. It should be noted that these policies were developed to facilitate women's participation in the labor force rather than to increase fertility.

France (this volume) takes quite a different approach compared with Norway. In France, parental leave can be as long as three years after the birth of a child, with the right to return to the same job or a similar job with the same employer. This coupled with a stay-at-home allowance reduces the incompatibility between work and parenthood during the child's first three years. If both parents work, childcare options are available, although not as readily available as in Norway, and kindergarten is available for children after their third birthday.

In the other countries, the situation is less favorable, and the incompatibility between work and parenthood (most often motherhood) is higher. In the UK, the third country with relatively high fertility, 3- and 4-year-olds have the right to attend early-education programs, but the programs are only for 15 h a week. Maternity (unpaid) leave is 52 weeks, but mothers retain the right to return to the

[3] In Singapore, South Korea, and Japan only about 2 % of all births occur outside marriage and in Hong Kong about 5 %. See relevant chapters in Rindfuss and Choe (2015).

same job for only 26 weeks. Private childcare is available, but since it is expensive, it is essentially only available for those with higher-paying jobs. Some of the need for childcare is met by welfare programs that provide financial assistance, so that low-income mothers of young children can stay at home. Perhaps as a result, women without the skills to obtain higher-paying jobs tend to have more children and to have them earlier in their lives.

In Taiwan, less than 1 % of young children are in childcare, and the preference is for mothers to stay at home to care for their children. Similar preferences are found in Austria and the Czech Republic. Within Europe, Eastern European countries generally have the lowest proportion of young children in childcare (Gauthier this volume). In Italy and Spain, most 3–5-year-olds are in educational programs, but relatively few childcare places are available for children age 0–2. In Italy, grandparents are expected to play an important role in providing childcare—in some municipalities, the child is not given a place in a public childcare center if the grandparents live nearby.

Canada presents an interesting case in that there are large differences between Québec and the rest of the country. In the late 1990s, the Québec government was concerned about low fertility and decided to implement more generous family policies. Government-subsidized childcare was greatly expanded and very reasonably priced. The daily fee per child now ranges from CAD7.30 (US$5.18) to CAD20.00 (US$14.19) depending on family income. To put this in perspective, the hourly minimum wage is CAD10.15 (US$7.20). Québec's parental leave policy is also more generous than that of the rest of Canada—a parent (usually a mother) can receive up to 12 months of leave, paid at 70 % of what her earnings were before the birth of the child, up to a maximum of CAD59,000 (US$47,890) per year.

Primary and Secondary Education Systems

While not normally considered as such, schools perform a childcare role, and schooling costs are also a consideration in fertility decisions. In Italy (this volume), children are in school for a relatively short time—mornings only for secondary school. Places in after-school programs are difficult to obtain, and for secondary-school children, parents, rather than schools, are responsible for organizing extracurricular activities. Such a situation makes it difficult for mothers to have full-time jobs, likely reducing fertility for some. There is also limited availability of after-school programs in Austria. In Taiwan (this volume), as in other East Asian countries, children need to prepare for important entrance exams for secondary school and university. Most parents send their children to after-school "cram" programs designed to prepare them for these exams. Not only does this involve considerable expense, but also mothers are generally responsible for getting information about the best cram schools, taking children to and from classes, providing them with meals, and helping with homework.

France and Norway (this volume) provide a contrasting structure for primary and secondary schools—a structure that reduces the incompatibility between employment and parenthood. School hours are relatively long, lunch is provided, and after-school programs are available. And the Norway chapter makes the point that crime is low and parents are more willing than in many other countries to leave children on their own after school.

Immigration

Austria, Canada, France, Italy, Norway, Spain, and the UK all have positive net immigration. Since immigrants tend to be young adults, the inflow of immigrants partially offsets the aging concerns associated with below-replacement fertility. This is especially important in countries such as Austria, Italy, and Spain that have very low fertility levels. Further, in some of these countries, the immigrants arrive from countries with higher fertility and thus tend to have somewhat higher fertility than the native-born population. The effect on overall fertility can be quite small, however, as shown for Spain (this volume, Fig. 2 in chapter "The Policy Context of Fertility in Spain: Toward a Gender-Egalitarian Model?").

The fertility behavior of Polish migrants in the UK provides an illustration of how institutions and policies can affect fertility. Polish women who migrate to the UK now have higher fertility levels than Polish women who remain in Poland. Qualitative research in London and Krakow (Marczak 2012, reported in the UK chapter in this volume) suggests that better government support for children in the UK and better compatibility between parenting and work are responsible for this fertility difference. This finding is consistent with the broad arguments in this volume: Country-level factors, including institutions and policies, have a major effect on fertility behavior.

Housing

In most developed countries, with the exception of some in East Asia, the expectation is that young couples, whether married or cohabitating, will live in their own dwelling unit rather than with either sets of parents. Thus, other things being equal, the easier it is to obtain a dwelling unit, owned or rented, the earlier childbearing is likely to occur and the more children couples are likely to have.

Italy and Spain (this volume) are examples of countries where it is difficult for young couples to obtain their own housing, and this most likely leads to lower fertility levels. The proportion of housing units that are available for rent is low; there is little public (social) housing; lenders require large down payments to secure a mortgage; and lenders are also reluctant to lend to young adults, especially if they do not have a secure job. In Taiwan, the price of dwelling units has been rising rapidly in recent years.

A number of government policies affect the availability of housing for young people wishing to start a family. Mortgages with relatively low down payments are available in Canada and Norway. In France, about 20 % of the housing units are public housing. In the UK, it is easier to obtain a public housing unit if a couple has one or more children. In Norway, housing allowances are available for university students. Austria provides financial support for low-income households who are renting their dwelling unit.

Gender Considerations

A more equal division of domestic tasks between women and men is expected to be associated with higher fertility (Esping-Anderson 2009; McDonald 2006; Goldscheider et al. 2015). The basic logic is that women want to work outside the home, and if they also have to do all or most of the domestic work, including caring for children, then they are likely to be reluctant to have children, especially if they have a job that is well remunerated and enjoyable. While comparable measures were not available for all 10 countries, it appears that the household division of labor (including childcare) is most equal in Norway, which also has a relatively high level of fertility, as theory would predict. Austria, the Czech Republic, Italy, Spain, and Taiwan all appear to have a very unequal division of domestic labor, as well as quite low fertility. Within Canada, Québec has a more equal division of domestic labor, and higher fertility, than the rest of the country.

Discussion

Reading across the fertility situations in 10 countries, one thing that stands out is the diversity of factors that seem to lead to fertility either near or far below the replacement level. One general principle is that women, and their partners, will have children when they see a clear path in other life-course domains, including schooling, establishment in the labor force, setting up an independent household, and achieving reasonable compatibility between family and work roles. Women are also more likely to have children when they feel confident about the future and when there is a reasonable level of gender equity in domestic work. By contrast, there are some commonalities across the countries with the lowest fertility levels: relatively high incompatibility between work and family roles; aspects of the education system that make it difficult for parents to work full time; and relatively high levels of gender inequity in domestic labor including childcare. Similar associations between very low fertility and high levels of gender inequity in domestic labor have been observed in China, Hong Kong, Japan, and South Korea

(Rindfuss and Choe 2015). Other factors appear to affect fertility in some countries only, such as the sudden introduction of employment insecurity that arose in Hungary and the Czech Republic after the fall of communism.

The countries with higher fertility appear to have achieved these levels through different routes. In recent years, Norway and the UK have had very similar fertility levels, and yet many of their policies are quite different. This diversity of factors that are likely to affect fertility makes it difficult to evaluate the effectiveness of various policies (see chapter on France in this volume) or to advise policymakers who wish to increase fertility in their countries.

The chapters in this volume also suggest that inadvertent policies, that is, policies that were instituted for some purpose other than affecting fertility, can play a large role. Norway, for example, instituted a variety of policies with the aim of increasing women's labor-force participation, but many of these policies also led to fertility levels close to replacement. Or to take another example, many countries have policies for primary education that inadvertently make it difficult for mothers of primary-school-age children to have a full-time job.

References

Bongaarts, J., & Feeney, G. (1998). On the quantum and tempo of fertility. *Population and Development Review, 24*, 271–291.

Bongaarts, J., & Sobotka, T. (2012). A demographic explanation for the recent rise in European fertility. *Population and Development Review, 38*(1), 83–120.

Esping-Andersen, G. (2009). *The incomplete revolution: Adapting to women's new roles.* Cambridge: Polity Press.

Goldscheider, F., Bernhart, E., & Lappegård, T. (2015). The gender revolution: A framework for understanding changing family and demographic behavior. *Population and Development Review, 41*(2), 207–239.

Lutz, W., Skirbekk, V., & Testa, M. R. (2006). The low-fertility trap hypothesis: Forces that may lead to further postponement and fewer births in Europe. *Vienna Yearbook of Population Research, 4*, 167–192.

Marczak, J. (2012). *Transnational groups of reference and intentions for the second offspring among Poles living in Poland and the UK.* Paper presented at the British Society for Population Studies Annual Conference, Nottingham, September 10–12, 2012.

McDonald, P. (2006). Low fertility and the state. *Population and Development Review, 32*(3), 485–510.

Preston, S. H., Heuveline, P., & Guillot, M. (2001). *Demography: Measuring and modeling population processes.* Oxford: Blackwell Publishers.

Rindfuss, R. R., & Choe, M. K. (2015). Diversity across low-fertility countries: An overview. In R. R. Rindfuss & M. K. Choe (Eds.), *Low and lower fertility: Variations across developed countries* (pp. 1–13). Cham, Switzerland: Springer International Publishing.

Wachter, K. W. (2014). *Essential demographic methods.* Cambridge: Harvard University Press.

World Bank. (2013). *Data: Indicators.* http://data.worldbank.org/indicator/SP.DYN.TFRT.IN. Accessed March 21, 2014.

Not so Low Fertility in Norway—A Result of Affluence, Liberal Values, Gender-Equality Ideals, and the Welfare State

Øystein Kravdal

Abstract In Norway, the total fertility rate over the years 2000–2013 averaged 1.86 births per woman. Women born in 1968, which is the youngest cohort that has completed their reproductive period, had 2.03 children on average. Only 13 % of that cohort remained childless, and 83 % of those who became parents had at least two children. This chapter discusses possible reasons for this high fertility compared to that of most other rich countries. Norway's advantaged economic position is probably one ingredient. There is little income insecurity for individual families, and the state can afford to be generous with parents, not least with respect to daycare and parental leave. The willingness to prioritize such spending does not reflect concern about below-replacement fertility, but rather the social-liberal or social-democratic ideas about public responsibility for individual well-being that are strongly rooted in Nordic societies, accompanied by widely accepted ideals of gender equality. It is possible that these ideals also affect fertility positively by promoting men's involvement with children and in housework. Another explanation for Norway's high fertility may be that, although the retreat from marriage has been as least as pronounced as in most other rich countries, this has been counteracted by widespread cohabitation and a large number of births among cohabiting couples—probably reflecting in part their trust in the welfare state and liberal values. The chapter ends with a discussion of whether lower fertility would, in fact, be a problem for Norway.

Keywords Affluence · Norway · Fertility · Gender equality · Policies

Almost all "more developed countries" have a total fertility rate (TFR) below replacement level, which is 2.08 births per woman in populations with very low mortality. In the long run, below-replacement fertility leads to a shrinking population

Ø. Kravdal (✉)
Department of Economics, University of Oslo, Oslo, Norway
e-mail: okravdal@econ.uio.no

R.R. Rindfuss and M.K. Choe (eds.), *Low Fertility, Institutions, and their Policies*, DOI 10.1007/978-3-319-32997-0_2

size in the absence of immigration. Furthermore, the proportion of elderly in the population will increase particularly rapidly when fertility is very low. The TFR is below 1.5 births per woman in several countries, as low as 1.1–1.2 in some, and even lower in a few countries consisting of only a large city. This very low fertility has led to concerns, primarily about the economic and welfare consequences of an aging population. On the other hand, among countries with below-replacement fertility, there is also a quite large group with TFR above 1.75. Norway is in this category, with a TFR of 1.78 in 2013—down from 1.90–1.98 in 2006–2009—and an average of 1.86 over the years 2000–2013 (Statistics Norway 2014). Norwegian women in the youngest birth cohort that has reached the end of the reproductive period (born in 1968) have had 2.03 children on average.

Additionally, Norway has for some years had very high net in-migration (43,700 annually as an average over the past five years, which is 0.9 % of the population size), so the annual population growth rate is currently about 1.3 %—slightly above the world average of 1.2 %. Immigrants from high-fertility countries and Norwegian-born individuals with parents from such countries still constitute only about 5 % of the country's population, however, and thus contribute little to the national TFR. In fact, if immigrants are excluded from the calculations, Norway's TFR is only 0.07 lower (Aase and Kaldager 2014). According to Statistics Norway's medium projection, which assumes that TFR will continue at about 1.8 and that net immigration will remain high for several years, the population size will increase from 5.1 million today to 5.9 in 2030, 6.6 in 2050, and 7.7 in 2100. The proportion above age 70 will increase from the current 11 % to 19 % in 2060 (Tønnessen et al. 2014).

The first part of this chapter gives a short description of Norway's fertility trends and patterns. Next, possible reasons for the country's relatively high fertility are discussed. Obviously, knowledge about the factors underlying the relatively high fertility in Norway and some other rich countries is potentially valuable to countries concerned about low fertility, as it may inform discussions about steps they could take to raise fertility. More specifically, some of the policies that have probably led to high fertility in Norway—although this was never the explicit intention—might be adopted with some revision by other countries. Other fertility-stimulating factors, however, are rather unique and may not be "transferable" to the same extent.

The chapter ends with a discussion of whether the concern about low fertility is actually justified—in other words whether it would have mattered if Norway's fertility had not been so high. While meeting the needs of an older population clearly presents challenges, there are also advantages from having a smaller and older population. It is also far from obvious how a small family size affects the well-being of the family members themselves—both parents and children as well as childless adults. These aspects of the low-fertility issue have not received much attention in the public debate.

Fertility in Norway in International Perspective

The TFR in Norway fell from about 4.5 births per woman in the late 19th century to 1.7 in the 1930s, increased to 3.0 as of 1965, and then fell again. Fertility reached a record low of 1.66 in 1984 and then increased. It has been above 1.80 every year since 1988 except 2001, 2002, and 2013, when it was 1.75–1.78. Indeed, Norway's TFR exceeded 1.9 in seven of the years since 1988. The average over the period 2000–2013 was 1.86.

Over the past quarter century, the Norwegian TFR has been higher than the Nordic average. In Denmark and Finland, TFR was about 0.1 below that of Norway throughout the period, while the Swedish TFR was below through most of the period, but above in the early 1990s and slightly above over the past few years (Fig. 1). Iceland's TFR has been consistently about 0.2 above the Norwegian level.

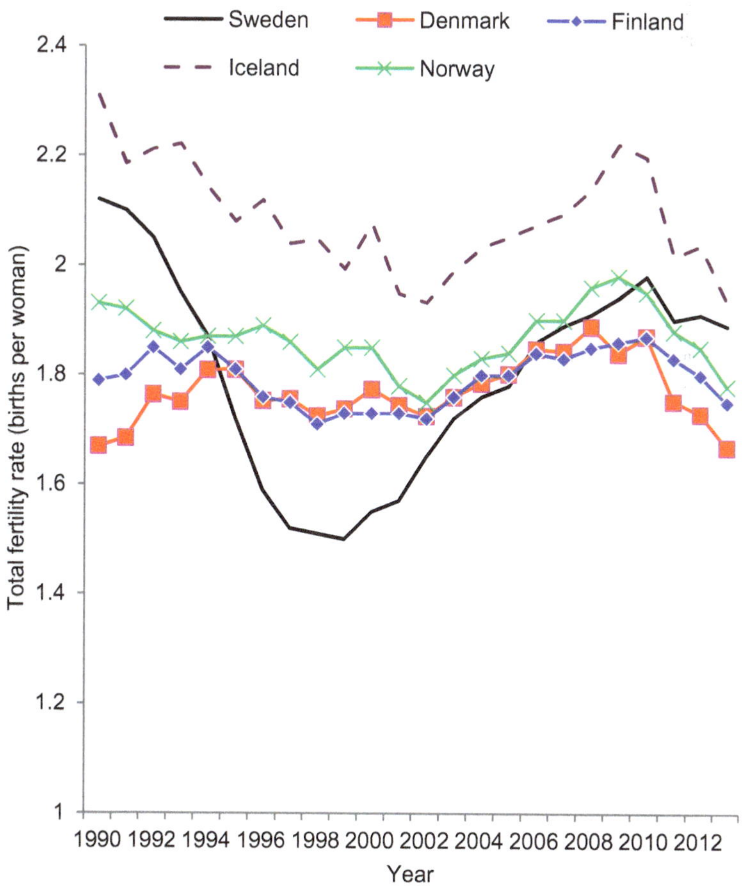

Fig. 1 Total fertility rates (TFR) in Nordic countries, 1990–2013 (Aase and Kaldager 2014)

Among other European countries, only France (TFR of 2.0), Ireland (2.0), and the United Kingdom (1.9) were above Norway in 2013 (Population Reference Bureau 2014). Fertility was also higher in two English-speaking countries outside Europe, New Zealand (2.0) and the United States (1.9), and in another more-developed country, Israel (3.0), where the situation is in many ways extraordinary. In comparison, the TFR is very low in some countries in Central Europe (Germany 1.4, Austria 1.4), Southern Europe (Portugal 1.2, Greece 1.3, Spain 1.3, Italy 1.4), and Eastern Europe (Poland 1.2, Hungary 1.3, Romania 1.3). Even lower levels are seen in East Asia (Taiwan 1.1, South Korea 1.2), and in the second-largest country in that region, Japan, the TFR is only 1.4.

In periods during which mother's average age at childbirth is increasing, the average number of children born to cohorts of women ("cohort fertility") of reproductive age is higher than the TFR (often also referred to as "period TFR" to avoid misunderstanding). The youngest cohort of Norwegian women that can be observed up to age 45—those born in 1968—have had, on average, 2.03 children. The women born in 1972 had 0.05 fewer children at age 40 than those born in 1968 (1.95 as opposed to 2.00). In comparison, Norwegian women born in the 1930s had 2.5 children.

According to figures for the 1972 cohort, based on forecasting for ages above 40, the other Nordic countries have a completed cohort fertility similar to that of Norway or somewhat lower. It is 1.99 in Denmark, 1.97 in Sweden, and 1.90 in Finland (Vienna Institute of Demography 2014; for trends over time, see Max Planck Institute for Demographic Research 2013). Only Iceland has higher cohort fertility, at 2.31. Among the other Western European countries, Ireland is highest at 2.1, followed by France at 2.0 and the United Kingdom at 1.9. Within Eastern Europe, where very low period fertility is a rather recent phenomenon, some countries have cohort fertility above 1.8, but there are also some that are below 1.6. In many of these countries, cohort fertility is on its way down. The lowest figures are found in Germany (1.5), Italy (1.5), and Spain (1.4). Among the large more-developed countries outside Europe, cohort fertility in the United States is 2.2, and it is also above 2.0 in New Zealand and Australia, while it is well below 2.0 in Canada and only 1.4 in Japan (see also Max Planck Institute for Demographic Research 2013).

The decline of Norwegian cohort fertility from 2.5 for those born in the 1930s to the current level slightly below replacement has to a great extent been the result of a larger proportion of women stopping childbearing after having two children. The proportion childless has only increased a few percentage points. In the 1968 cohort, 13 % were childless at age 45. Among those in that cohort who had a first child, 83 % also had a second child, and among those who had a second child, 43 % proceeded to have a third child. Thus, 31 % ended up with at least three children. Eight percent had at least four.

Figure 2 shows parity-specific birth rates relative to those in 1976 (see note to Fig. 2 for a more detailed explanation). The decline in second- and higher-order birth rates started in the mid-1960s and lasted for about one decade, after which the rates stabilized or increased, except for a small decline in 2000–2002 and a

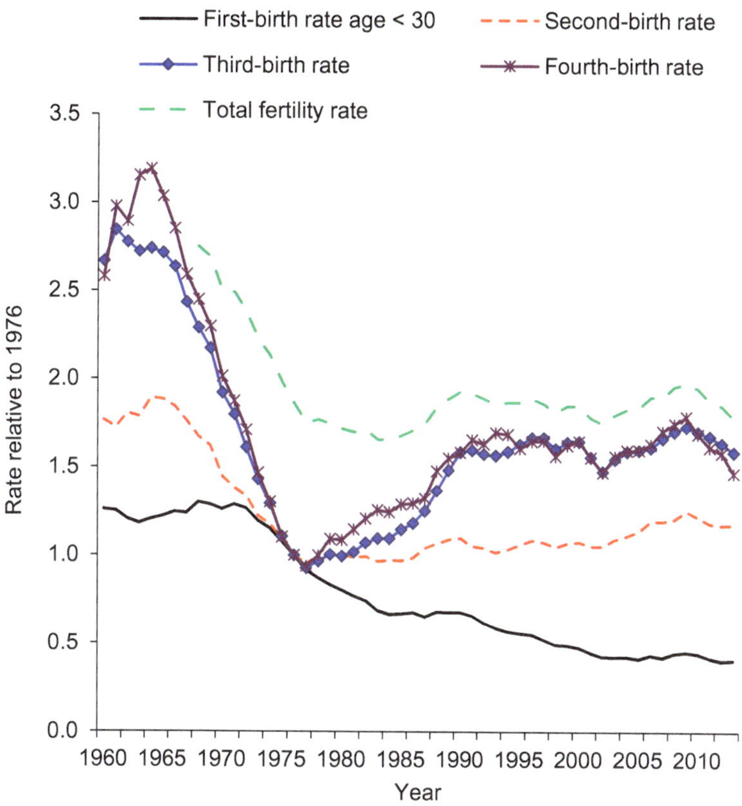

Fig. 2 Period effects on parity-specific birth rates, controlling for age and time since last birth, and total fertility rate. *Note* Discrete-time hazard models were estimated from register data including all Norwegian women and extracted by Astri Syse of Statistics Norway. In the analysis of first-birth rates, childless women were followed from age 17 (but not before 1960) until they reached age 29, emigrated, died, or had a first child, or the end of the observation period was reached (2013), whichever occurred first. The models included age and period. In the analysis of second-birth rates, one-child mothers were followed from first birth (but not before 1960) until they reached age 39, emigrated, died, or had a second child, or the end of the observation period was reached. The models included age, time since previous (i.e., first) birth, and period. Similar models were estimated for third- and fourth-birth rates. The graph shows the period effects in these models, using 1976 as the reference year. In other words, for each parity transition and each year, the rate relative to the corresponding rate (i.e., for that particular transition) in 1976 is shown. Results were very similar when the foreign-born were excluded or when individuals were left out during periods of temporary residence outside Norway between 1986 and 2013

somewhat sharper decline after 2009. First-birth rates below age 30 started to fall in the early 1970s, giving period TFR an extra push downward above and beyond the effect of the lower cohort fertility (which was closely related to a stronger inclination to stop after two children). The first-birth rates below age 30 were stable during the last half of the 1980s, went down slightly in the 1990s and the first years of the new millennium (so that cohort fertility was still higher than period TFR), went slightly up over the years 2005–2009, followed by yet another dip downward. First-births rates at ages above 30 (not shown in Fig. 2) have increased, which of course accords well with the fact that there has been only a modest increase in the proportion remaining childless.

Other Nordic countries have also seen an increase in second- and higher-order birth rates from the mid-1970s or early 1980s, although in Sweden the rates fell again in the first part of the 1990s (Andersson 2004). Similar measures are not available for other countries, but according to studies of parity progression ratios from a cohort perspective (which blurs any sharp period turning points), there were increases across cohorts from the 1950s in the proportion of one-child mothers having a second child in France and increases in the proportion of two-child mothers having a third child in France, the Netherlands, and the UK (Frejka 2008). A French analysis taking a period perspective showed that progression ratios to the higher parities increased a little or were stable after the mid-1970s (Toulemon et al. 2008), in spite of higher average age at first birth, which means that with controls for age as in the Nordic analyses, there would have been a sharper increase in the progression ratios.

The overall conclusion is that a relatively large proportion of Norwegians have at least one child, although figures are even higher in some Eastern European countries. Childlessness is more widespread in the other Nordic countries, except Iceland (Andersson et al. 2009). In addition, it is more common for parents with one child to have a second child in Norway than in most other rich countries (Frejka 2008). Similarly, a larger proportion of Norwegian women move on to higher parities, although transitions beyond the third child matter little for differences in total fertility because so few women have this many children.

The average age at first birth is lower in Norway than in many other rich countries, but higher than in many Eastern European countries (Thévenon 2011). In 2013, it was 28.6 years for women. This relatively low age at first birth contributes to Norway's relatively high cohort fertility, because at the individual level, a later first birth reduces the likelihood of having a second or third birth (although in Norway, there appears to be a pronounced effect only when the age at first birth exceeds about 30 years (Kravdal 2001)). The discussion below will therefore deal both with factors affecting quantum (completed fertility) directly and with timing determinants of fertility.

A Theoretical Framework

This section reviews briefly the kind of factors that determine a woman's chance of having a child, with inspiration from the Easterlin and Crimmins (1985) framework. In subsequent sections, the discussion will turn to similarities and differences between Norway and other countries with respect to each of these main determinants of fertility.

Obviously, in order to have a child, the woman must be *sexually active and physiologically able to conceive*, as must her partner, and also be able to bring the pregnancy to term. The chance of being sexually active depends, of course, on whether the woman is involved in a *relationship*, which also—along with the *type* of relationship—has implications for other main fertility determinants. The chance of entering into and remaining in a relationship, and the type of relationship it is, in turn, depend on individual economic potentials, other factors that make a person attractive, values, and how easy it is to meet potential partners. Making this even more complex, actual fertility or childbearing plans may be involved in building and maintaining a partnership, thus producing a two-way association between partnership and fertility.

Assuming that the woman lives in a partnership, the couple's *childbearing desire* depends partly on their *purchasing power* and the expected *costs of childbearing*. The latter include foregone income if a parent stays at home with the child (still largely the mother) and more "direct" costs of, for examples, clothes and food, plus childcare expenses if a parent does not stay at home to care for the child. Another determinant of fertility desire is the couple's "*preferences,*" i.e., their ideas about the emotional benefits from having and rearing children compared with the satisfaction one might derive from an alternative use of time and money. In reality, there is, of course, more complexity involved. Recent literature deals with how desires are formed and lead to intentions, how they change over time, and possible discrepancies in desires and intentions between partners (e.g., Bachrach and Morgan 2013). From the comparative perspective of this paper, however, these issues may not be very important, and only the possibility of different desires between partners is touched on briefly.

Arguments with respect to purchasing power and costs vary depending on whether it is the number of children or the timing of the (first) birth that is considered. In addition, fertility desires and the way they are influenced by expected childrearing costs and the couple's purchasing power likely depend on whether the partners are married or only cohabiting. Cohabiting partners are perhaps more likely to anticipate that the relationship might be disrupted, after which there may be less involvement and economic contribution from the father. A single woman is typically less likely to want a child than a woman who is married or cohabiting, and it would obviously only be relevant for her to take her own resources into account in her economic considerations.

Furthermore, people may feel some social pressure, if they are married, to have at least one and preferably two children. Conversely, many of those who are not married may feel subjected to expectations about avoiding childbearing, especially, of course, if they are not even cohabitants. One may consider such norms about the number of children—or about the appropriate timing of childbearing—to be another determinant of childbearing desires, or they could be considered a separate additional factor. (In addition, there are normative influences on important determinants of fertility desires, such as mothers' work activity, and other factors of importance for fertility.) Norms reflect to some extent current actual behavior. Thus, in countries where it is common to have few children, it may also be more accepted to remain childless or have only one child. The low "ideal fertility" in Central Europe has been interpreted as an indication of such a mechanism (Goldstein et al. 2003). Other authors have described European countries as being caught in a "low-fertility trap" (Lutz and Skirbekk 2005). Conversely, one could argue that the rather high fertility level in Norway tends to further promote high fertility.[1]

Finally, another main determinant of the chance of having a child is the *access to and acceptance of abortion and various types of contraception.*

Fecundity and Partnership

There is no evidence to suggest that sub- or infecundity is less common in Norway than in other rich countries, thus contributing to the relatively high fertility level. In principle, it is possible that widely accessible infertility treatment through Norway's public healthcare system could contribute positively to fertility. This is not likely to matter very much, however. It has been estimated that assisted-reproduction technology was involved in 3 % of births in Norway in 2009, while the contribution from intrauterine inseminations was very small (Ferraretti et al. 2013). More careful estimation based on Danish data showed a similar contribution from assisted-reproductive technology (Sobotka et al. 2008). Some figures indicate that this technology is only one-half as commonly used in some other European countries (Ferraretti et al. 2013), but such a difference would only correspond to about 0.03 births per woman.

Is the high fertility in Norway a result of a relatively large proportion marrying and remaining married? No, on the contrary, Norway has experienced a massive retreat from marriage: There has been a sharp increase in the proportion who never marry, those who marry do so at a later age, and divorce rates are higher than ever —changes that probably are driven not least by women's economic independence, a generous welfare system, and generally liberal values (as well as a snow-ball effect in the sense that further changes in these directions may be produced by an increasing proportion unmarried). Crude marriage rates are not particularly high in Norway by European standards, and crude divorce rates are not particularly low (Eurostat 2014a). Thus, the proportion married at any given age is probably not relatively high either. This situation is compensated for by informal cohabitation to a larger extent than elsewhere, however, and many cohabitants have children. Indeed, out-of-wedlock fertility is very high, as in the other Nordic countries.

[1]In principle, a preference for having at least one boy will increase fertility in settings with generally low or moderate fertility and where the alternatives to achieving such a goal—sex-specific abortion or excess female mortality—are deemed unacceptable. However, sex preferences are typically weak in rich countries outside Asia (Andersson et al. 2006). Also, the "insurance effect," "replacement effect," and other effects of mortality on fertility that are important in many parts of the world have little relevance in more-developed countries, given their very low infant and child mortality.

In 2014, cohabiting mothers accounted for 44 % of all births in Norway, and single mothers for 13 %.

The relatively high fertility among Norwegian cohabitants reflects, of course, the same factors that generally stimulate fertility in the population. In addition, it is possible that factors that tend to depress fertility among cohabitants compared to the married are weaker in Norway than in many other countries. There is probably a weaker normative pressure to restrict childbearing to formal marriages, given the generally liberal values, and women may not fear to the same extent being left alone with many of the economic and emotional burdens of childrearing. Even if a relationship is dissolved, the father may contribute substantially through shared custody or child-support payments (see Skevik 2004 for a discussion of the demands placed on fathers and the rights they have). Besides, Norwegian women have good earning potential, and there is a welfare state to rely on (NAV 2014).

In addition to the normal annual allowance of 11,600 NOK (equivalent to US $1535 as of 16 January 2015) per child, a single parent in Norway is entitled to an extra 11,600 NOK per year. Single parents also receive a child allowance supplement for infants of 6700 NOK (US$887) per year and special tax benefits corresponding to about 15,000 NOK (US$1985) per year. In addition, two-thirds of childcare costs are covered, corresponding to up to 17,600 NOK (US$2329) per year for the youngest children. At the lowest ages, this adds up to about 10 % of the average earnings of a full-time worker age 30–34 and should cover a substantial part of the costs of having a young child. In addition, a special allowance is given to single parents who work or study at least half-time. It is 195,000 NOK (US$25,805) per year, for 2–6 years, for those who have earnings below 45,000 NOK (US $5955) per year. The amount is reduced proportionally as an individual's income exceeds this level. Some of these entitlements are generous even by Nordic standards (Rønsen and Skrede 2008). Finally, children with a single parent are not likely to feel especially stigmatized—nor are their parents—in Norway's liberal society, particularly as the situation is so common. Some of the factors that may affect fertility among cohabiting couples may also contribute to the relatively high fertility of single women, of course, and they could, in principle, have a positive impact on the fertility of married couples concerned about the quality of their relationship and the possibility of divorce.

The issue has so far to a large extent been seen from the woman's perspective. Another question is why men agree to have children in relationships that they should realize are potentially unstable, so that they run quite a high risk of having little contact with their child. The discussion will return briefly to this issue below.

This discussion of fertility among cohabitants builds on the assumption that such relationships are more unstable than marriages, and that those involved are conscious of this relative instability and take it into consideration in their decision-making. Indeed, the lack of stability in consensual unions is well documented in Norway as in other countries (Manning et al. 2004). Cohabitants with children have much higher disruption rates than parents who are married (Jensen and Clausen 2003; Texmon 1999), presumably reflecting a combination of a more tenuous relationship (Wiik et al. 2009) and lower practical and normative burdens associated with disruption. If such disruptions or the underlying parental discord are harmful to children—contrary to what the parents who decide to have a child in such a relationship perhaps believe—then this aspect of Norway's high fertility may be seen as constituting a potential child-welfare problem. Such concerns are voiced in, for example, the United States, where more of the out-of-wedlock births are to single mothers and the chance of falling into poverty is high (Sigle-Rushton and McLanahan 2002), but they are rarely heard in Norway.

Effects of Earnings and Earning Potentials

Earnings and earning potentials are not only key determinants of the (potential) purchasing power of prospective parents, but also influence their costs of raising children. In the discussion of these factors, a quantum perspective will be taken first, and it will be assumed that the woman is the primary caregiver.

A reasonable starting point is that, with a high income for the man, the couple can afford more children, given the costs of childrearing. If the man's income is high, however, the couple may also feel that they should spend a lot on each child, and they may attach more value to the material luxuries that compete with the costs of childrearing. Thus, those with a stable high income do not necessarily have more children than those with a stable low income. However, a sharp *decline* in income, for example as a result of unemployment, is likely to depress fertility, because the couple's material aspirations may reflect the higher income they enjoyed in earlier years and they may need time to adjust to a lower income level (Kravdal 2002a). In other words, the low unemployment rates among men in Norway, and the low *fear* of unemployment or of an income drop for other reasons, may have contributed to Norway's relatively high fertility. To elaborate, Norway's per capita gross domestic product (GDP) is one of the highest in the world, there is low income inequality, very few are considered poor, and the overall unemployment rate has not exceeded 4 % during most of the period since the Second World War. Oil revenues have been used to build up a fund corresponding to three times the annual GDP, and prospects for the future also look good for many other reasons (Olsen 2013).

If a *woman's* earning potential is high, similar mechanisms may operate. There is an additional effect, however. High wage potential for her means that more is foregone (i.e., higher opportunity costs) for each time unit she spends at home caring for a child. These higher costs of childrearing may prompt a woman and her partner to want fewer children. Possibly, it is not the woman's wage potential in an absolute sense, but rather her wage potential relative to the man's income that matters in such considerations. In Norway, this type of argument has become less relevant over time, however, as women with young children tend to spend less time out of the labor market without payment because they are entitled to a fully paid one-year maternity leave and because they are making greater use of childcare outside the home (as described below). Indeed, the employment rate for Norwegian women aged 15–64 is higher than in almost all other European countries and close to the rate for men (Eurostat 2014b).

To conclude, it is not obvious how unemployment or fear of unemployment among women should be expected to affect fertility. On the one hand, there is an effect similar to that of men's unemployment, though with a little twist: If there is a risk of unemployment, the woman may not be able to find or return to a job after the intense childcare period, and this lack of contribution to the family income may reduce the chance of wanting a(nother) child. On the other hand, there is a woman-specific argument that is of diminishing relevance: Unemployment reduces opportunity costs and thus increases fertility. To spell out this argument in more detail, a couple may find it particularly attractive to have a child, after which the woman may have to stay at home for some time after the maternity leave, if the woman would not have been able to work during this period anyway. In a Norwegian study, a weak positive association between women's recent unemployment experience and their first-birth rate appeared, while other relationships between fertility and women's or men's unemployment were negative (Kravdal 2002a). For similar reasons, it is hard to predict the fertility implications of high wages for women relative to men. Anyway, the gender wage gap in Norway is not particularly high or low. Rather, it is close to the European Union (EU) average (Eurostat 2014c).

Special arguments pertain to the timing of a birth and are thus particularly relevant for a discussion of the chance of having a first child, which to a large extent is a matter of when rather than whether to give birth. A fundamental idea (see, e.g., Happel et al. 1984) is that if childbearing costs are independent of the timing of the birth and of the parents' wages, and if borrowing money is costly, then it would make sense for a couple to postpone the first birth until their purchasing power has increased and the reduced consumption of other goods because of childrearing expenses therefore matters less (given a diminishing marginal utility of consumption). This strategy would be particularly relevant if childrearing costs are high or if the couple's income is currently low (in absolute terms or relative to earlier levels that may be of importance for material expectations).

In reality, however, the situation is more complex. First, there are typically opportunity costs of childrearing, which are linked especially to the mother's wage, although, as mentioned, the argument has become less relevant in Norway. If the mother's opportunity costs are high, there would be a particularly strong motive for postponing childbearing—provided that these costs will not be even higher later. On the other hand, there are direct costs of having a child that go far beyond the time when the woman might be losing income because she is staying at home with the child, and the higher her earnings, the weaker the reason for postponing childbearing because of these costs. An additional complication is that wages *do* tend to increase, so that the opportunity costs become higher if the couple waits to have a child. Thus, the conclusion would be similar to that obtained from a quantum perspective: Low unemployment for men probably contributes positively to first birth rates, while the effects of low unemployment (or high relative wages) for women are less obvious.

A second fundamental idea in the literature on first-birth timing is that childrearing costs are likely to depend on the timing of the birth not only because wages increase over time. In particular, having a child while still a student may increase the risk of never completing one's education, with economic and other long-term consequences (see elaboration on that argument in the next section). Also, to the extent that there are long-term wage penalties for leaving the workforce for a period to care for a child, it is possibly that these penalties depend on whether the period out of the workforce comes early in a woman's career or after she has become more established (or on what the couple making a decision about fertility anticipates in terms of long-term wage penalties). In other words, it is possible that some work experience would increase the likelihood of having a child sooner rather than later. An additional argument for such an effect, which indeed has been seen in Norway (Kravdal 1994), is that a woman with some work experience may have been able to save, thus making it less necessary to wait for a higher income before having a child. Accumulated income and work experience may be relatively high among young people in Norway, at least among those who have completed their education, because of the country's low youth unemployment rate—reflecting not only a generally low unemployment rate, but also the fact that the educational system prepares students reasonably well for vocations (Rindfuss and Brauner-Otto 2008).

The country's economically advantaged position not only prevents individual families from being hit by unemployment and feeling economic insecurity; it also makes possible the government's generous policies and welfare arrangements, which probably affect fertility positively. A much poorer country would find it problematic to finance these arrangements.

Other Factors Affecting Childbearing Costs

The next step is to discuss factors that affect the costs of raising children more specifically. These costs probably vary widely across rich countries (DiPrete et al. 2003), which likely contributes a great deal to the observed differences in fertility. This discussion implicitly builds on two fundamental ideas already mentioned. First, when costs are high people may not want so many children, and it makes particularly good sense to have the next child later rather than sooner. Second, the costs may depend on the timing of the birth.

Factors affecting childrearing costs are grouped into three categories: (1) Factors that make it easier to resume employment or otherwise maintain an income after childbearing, thus reducing opportunity costs, which have indeed been shown to be low in Norway compared to other countries (Sigle-Rushton and Waldfogel 2007); (2) Factors affecting the short- and long-term economic implications of having a child while studying, which have special relevance for the timing of first births; and (3) Other types of factors. The first and last categories are relevant both for the quantum and timing of fertility.

It should be noted that none of the policies that have probably influenced these factors has been implemented specifically in response to concerns about low fertility. Rather, the main motivations have been to improve the well-being of families, strengthen women's position in society, and add to the country's supply of labor—by reducing the conflicts experienced by working mothers. In addition, it is also often argued that being in a daycare center benefits children socially and intellectually, except perhaps the very youngest.

Factors Reducing the Loss of Income Due to Childrearing

The parental leave in Norway has been gradually extended from 12 weeks in 1956 to 20 weeks in 1987 and 42 in 1993. It currently stands at 49 weeks with full wage compensation or 59 weeks with 80 % compensation (NAV 2014). A minimum of 10 weeks is reserved for the father and 10 for the mother. This parental leave period is longer than in most other countries. For example, the average among members of the Organization for Economic Cooperation and Development (OECD) in 2007 was the equivalent of 32 weeks with full compensation (Thévenon 2011). In Norway, those who have not become entitled to parental leave by having earned an income during 6 of the 10 months before the birth receive a modest cash amount, currently about 39,000 NOK (US$5159), which is close to the average monthly earnings for women aged 30–34 who work full-time. Not surprisingly, some studies—including one from Norway (Rønsen 2004)—have suggested positive effects of parental leave on fertility, but on the whole the evidence for such effects is not very strong (Kalwij 2010).

Norwegians also have relatively good access to part-time work (Kalleberg 2000), which means that those who for various reasons cannot or do not wish to work full time when they have young children can earn at least some income. This also has implications for later wages, as these are influenced by accumulated work experience and the signals of work commitment that are shown. About 40 % of Norwegian women age 15–64 work part-time, which is higher than the European average. Only a handful of countries are at the same level, and only Switzerland and the Netherlands are higher (Eurostat 2014a).

Furthermore, employees are allowed to stay home with a sick child under 12 years old for up to 10–15 days per year with full wages (Barne, likestillings, og inkluderingsdepartementet 2012). The relatively few women who work full time with a child under one year old are also entitled to one hour of fully paid time off each day to breastfeed. These rights may make it more attractive to go back to paid work quite soon after giving birth.

Access to high-quality childcare also helps parents resume work after completing parental leave. In Norway, 80 % of children age 1–2 and 97 % of children age 3–5 are in public or private daycare centers, which are open during usual working hours every day. In contrast, almost no children age 0–6 were in daycare in the mid-1970s, and only about 40 % were in daycare in the late 1990s. Daycare is subsidized directly by keeping prices low and indirectly through tax deductions. According to a comparison made in 2010, the proportion of children younger than three who were enrolled in formal daycare on a full-time basis was higher in Norway than in almost any other European country (European Commission 2014). (Such comparisons are difficult, however, because the parental leave period, when daycare centers are not needed, differs among countries.) Norway was also well above average for daycare use among older children. The implications for fertility have been assessed by Rindfuss et al. (2010), who compared birth rates in Norwegian municipalities with high and low daycare coverage and concluded that without the expansion of daycare since the early 1970s, the country's fertility would have been one-fourth child lower.

Some parents also make use of other childcare services. Most commonly, they may pay a neighbor to look after the child, or there may be family members who can assist. Very few employ an *au-pair*. The price of these services may well be approximately the same as for a daycare center, but there is often less flexibility in terms of "open hours," the service may not be available when the caregiver is ill, and the adults providing care may be less qualified than a daycare worker.[2]

Since 1998, a cash-for-care benefit of 72,000 NOK (US$9395) per year has been offered to those who have a child age 13–23 months and who cannot find or do not want a place in institutional daycare. This amount is about twice the average monthly earnings for women age 30–34 who work full time. On the whole, this benefit reduces the cost of childrearing. For those who do not wish to work while their child is young (and therefore have opportunity costs not incurred by those who work and have a child in daycare), the cash benefit simply constitutes an additional subsidy. For those who use other childcare options, such as a neighbor or grandparent, the benefit also constitutes a subsidy. A third group of women may switch from daycare to using other types of childcare or may even stop working in order to receive the benefit, and they presumably do this because they think they are better off (although some might argue that this strategy is not really in their own economic interest in the long term). Finally, such a switch may free up slots in daycare for others, as there still is excess demand in some municipalities. In other words, another option that many would consider better is opened up for other parents. A positive association between taking up the cash benefit and subsequent fertility has been observed (Aassve and Lappegård 2009; Vikat 2004), but interpretation is difficult as it is not obvious what such an indicator really captures.

Yet another factor that helps parents combine childrearing and employment is the fact that children are kept in school during lunch breaks—rather than being sent

[2]Some parents might have returned to work immediately after the leave period regardless of the right to breastfeed or stay home with a sick child and regardless of whether they found a slot for their child in a daycare center or had to make use of other childcare services. In other words, they would have had no opportunity costs of childbearing even with a less generous system. However, such parents might see the generous policies and good access to high-quality daycare as making childrearing more convenient, thus strengthening their childbearing preferences (to be discussed further below).

home to eat as in many other countries—and after-school care is offered to the youngest (typically, 1st to 4th grade). Furthermore, one might speculate that Norwegians might be more comfortable than parents in other countries in allowing their young children to go home from school alone, to be alone at home, or to spend time in parks or other places outside the home without adult supervision (Rindfuss and Brauner-Otto 2008). The country has a low crime rate, and while the proportion living in urban areas is as large as in other rich countries, the cities tend to be smaller, with less intense traffic and good access to green areas.

It is possible that the generally family-friendly environment in Norway has contributed to diminishing the socio-economic differences in fertility. In particular, when childcare is available at a price that depends little on family income, the opportunity costs—which traditionally have been highest among the better-educated and others with a high wage potential—are substituted with direct costs that vary much less. Put differently, the efforts to help parents resume work quickly after birth have probably made Norwegian fertility higher than it would otherwise have been, and especially among the better educated.

The arguments above are implicitly based on the assumptions that most women would want to work if they did not have a young child (otherwise, there would be no opportunity cost) and that those who have a young child would want to work if other qualified persons were available to take care of the child. These assumptions should be reasonable enough. As already mentioned, Norwegian women have a generally high employment rate, and it is also widely accepted that children may be cared for by persons outside the family. In fact, there is hardly any European country where this is more accepted (European Commission 2014). One of the reasons for this attitude may be that the average work week in Norway—at 37.5 h—is quite short, implying that parents who work are still able to spend considerable time with their children.

Factors Improving the Compatibility Between Enrolment in Tertiary Education and Childrearing

A large proportion of young Norwegians are enrolled in college or university. In fact, the proportion of young adults expected to complete tertiary education is somewhat higher than the OECD average (OECD 2013). It may be relatively easy for female (and male) students in Norway to complete their education even if they have a child, thus weakening their incentive to postpone childbearing. One reason is that Norway has a flexible educational system that allows students to leave and re-enter schooling. Furthermore, students have quite good access to daycare, so they are less compelled to quit school to care for a child. Also, it may be relative easy for Norwegian students to finance their studies in spite of direct and other costs of childrearing because there are no tuition fees, except in a few private schools, and educational loans are available.[3] On the other hand, a woman must have worked 6 out of the previous 10 months before giving birth in order to be entitled to Norway's generous maternity leave, and except at the Ph.D. level, students often do not meet this qualification. This policy could have the effect of discouraging students from having children.

If the first mechanisms dominate, the effects of school enrollment on fertility may be weaker in Norway than in most other countries. This could contribute to relatively early first births and therefore high cohort fertility. If the increase in the number of years at school in Norway has not led to the same increase in the age at first birth as elsewhere, the gap between period TFR and cohort fertility (which is determined by *changes* in women's age at birth) would not be so large either.

Other Reasons for Relatively Low Childrearing Costs

In Norway, childrearing is subsidized through child allowances that are not related to income (NAV 2014). One would expect such a cost reduction to increase fertility, and indeed some studies (Gauthier and Hatzius 1997; Milligan 2005), but not all (Kalwij 2010), have shown fertility effects of child allowances. The amount received (11,600 NOK equivalent to US$1535, per year per child) until a child attains age 18 corresponds to about one-fifth of childrearing costs up to that age (see "standard budget" published by SIFO 2013). Child allowances are smaller in most other rich countries, but several countries also offer more generous tax benefits to parents, which closes a substantial part of the gap (Bradshaw and Finch 2002).

Housing prices are another relevant issue, because when a couple has a first or an additional child they may wish to have a larger house or apartment (e.g., Clark 2012). Statistics from the Federal Reserve Bank of Dallas (2013) show that housing prices, measured relative to personal consumption expenditure, are higher in Norway than in any other OECD country. It is possible to borrow up to 85 % of the purchase price of a house, however (i.e., a down payment of only 15 % is required), while some other countries require down payments of up to 50 % (Rindfuss and Brauner-Otto 2008). Also, mortgage interest (at a current rate of about 3 %) can be deducted from income, which essentially means that 28 % of the interest is paid by the state.

Finally, there is one component of the costs of childrearing—very broadly defined—that is lower in Norway than in most other rich countries: High-quality tertiary education is largely free. Many (especially well-educated) parents in countries such as the United States plan to help their children with college costs,

[3]In addition, students who do not live with their parents receive about US$500 per month as a housing subsidy. While this may not be seen as reducing the costs of childrearing in situations where a union has been formed, it facilitates the formation of a union among young students who otherwise would have lived with their parents.

and they may take these anticipated costs into account in decision-making about fertility. Free university education may also be one reason why the educational gradient in fertility is relatively small in Norway.

Preferences and Gender Equity in the Family

Is it possible that Norwegians have stronger preferences between countries than others in favor of having children in the sense that, given the costs of childrearing, they tend to prefer having children rather than spending their resources on alternative sources of satisfaction? This would have implications both for the quantum and timing of fertility. Do Norwegians, for example, have more tolerance than others for seeing the house messed up with toys or being kept awake at night by babies who cry? Does responsibility for children to a lesser extent than in other countries reduce the time parents have available for their own leisure activities (without children)? Or are Norwegian parents less distressed about having to forego some of their own leisure activities because of children? Such questions are very difficult to answer, but time-use surveys provide some indications. For example, Norwegian men, but not women, are *above* average in Europe when it comes to allocation of time to children (Gauthier and DeGusti 2012). On the other hand, the loss of leisure time as a result of childrearing is perhaps seen as a relatively serious disadvantage because Norwegians (in a broad age group), to a larger extent than people in other countries, reported in the World Values Surveys (2014) that leisure is "very important." Such results are problematic to interpret, however, because there is always doubt about the extent to which time with children is seen as "leisure time." Obviously, more explicit information about the pleasures derived from family life, compared with alternative sources of satisfaction, would be very welcome. While such studies have been undertaken in some countries (Crimmins et al. 1991), multi-country studies based on comparable data are lacking.

Fathers' involvement in childcare and housework is a relevant issue when discussing possible differences in childbearing preferences, in addition to having implications for other fertility determinants. To start with the latter, if men's contribution to work at home is relatively large, it is possible that the parents may be able to work more in total and thus incur lower opportunity costs. If a man makes a larger contribution at home, it is also possible that the couple will forego more of his earnings (while he is at home or works reduced hours plus a possible long-term penalty) and less of hers. The total costs may not necessarily be different, and as long as the union is intact and the partners have a joint economy, it is the total costs that matter. However, the distribution of earnings between a couple becomes an issue if the union is disrupted and could therefore have implications for whether and how fertility desires differ between the partners (in addition to any differences that may arise because they simply evaluate any given economic situation differently). These types of considerations are at the heart of much of the fertility literature on gender equality, such as McDonald's (2000) paper on how lack of equality in the family sphere may lead to very low fertility in settings where there is high equity in "individual-oriented institutions," so that paid work to a large extent is seen as an option for women.

Returning to the issue of preferences, fathers' involvement probably affects both partners' ideas about the non-economic benefits and burdens of childrearing, and also *reflects* especially the father's attitudes in these matters and his values more generally, depending on the extent to which his involvement is freely chosen. To spell this out in more detail, fathers who are strongly involved in housework and childcare and are happy about it may be inclined to want more children than fathers who are not so involved. It is also likely that the partners of such men have relatively positive attitudes toward childrearing. They may be pleased about sharing the joys and concerns of parenthood with the father as well as getting more leisure time because they can spend less time than they otherwise would on childcare and the additional housework that typically follows from having children.

If, on the other hand, the father is involved but *reluctantly*—having been pushed by modern norms about active fatherhood or requirements from his partner—the implications for fertility desires are less obvious. The father may well have relatively little desire for more children, given childbearing costs and purchasing power, while the mother may have a more positive attitude, and the balance could tip either way.

In support of these ideas, a European study showed a positive association between fathers' egalitarian attitudes about gender roles, the number of children they have, and the number they desire (Puur et al. 2008). Some studies of the association between fathers' time use and fertility have also been carried out, although not knowing how satisfied the fathers (and mothers) really are about their time use makes it difficult to interpret the associations. Besides, a rather diffuse empirical picture has appeared in these time-use studies. For example, an American study by Torr and Short (2004) showed the highest second-birth rates among the most traditional couples (where the woman had the greatest responsibility for childcare and household tasks) as well as the most modern couples (who shared the tasks more equally). In an analysis based on Italian data, Mencarini and Tanturri (2004) found that the chance of having another child was relatively high if the father helped with childcare or housework, but the effects differed between one- and two-child couples. It is also difficult to draw clear conclusions from the fact that fathers' share of the time spent on "physical" (Hook and Wolfe 2012) or "interactive" (see review by Gauthier and Philipov 2008) childcare appears to be higher in Norway than in other European countries, and that Norway has smaller differences between women's and men's unpaid work than other OECD countries (World Economic Forum 2014). What we can say is that, if Norwegian fathers' involvement indicates truly child-friendly attitudes, this could boost fertility, both because of their own childbearing preferences and because the mothers may see childrearing as more of a pleasure and less of a burden in such a situation. As pointed out earlier, fathers' participation at home could also contribute positively to fertility by lowering the couples' total opportunity costs of childrearing.

Given the high fertility among Norwegian cohabitants, men may be quite willing to have children in unions that they should realize have a large chance of being dissolved, after which they may have relatively little contact with their children. This may be seen as running counter to the idea that Norwegian men want a strong involvement with their children. However, many cohabitating men may not take such possible long-term consequences much into account in their considerations, and many children are also born to cohabitants without the fathers (or mothers) having definitely wanted a child.

In Norway, since 1993, some part of the parental leave (currently 10 weeks) has been reserved for fathers (i.e., not transferable to mothers), and many fathers have taken this leave (Haas and Rostgaard 2011). Some of the parental leave is also reserved for fathers in other Nordic countries. The intention has been to strengthen fathers' practical and emotional involvement with children, but it remains to be seen whether a few weeks alone (perhaps) with the child at this stage actually matters much in the long run. Attempts have been made to estimate the effect on fertility, but the higher fertility that has sometimes been observed among men who have used the "daddy leave" (Lappegård 2010; Olah 2003) could well be just a reflection of the general attitude of men in this category. In an econometrically more advanced study by Rege and Solli (2013), it was found that men who took the parental leave had lower incomes in the long run, which suggests that taking parental leave may have a lasting effect on men's participation at home, with further implications for their earnings.

Contraception, Abortion, and Unwanted Births

It is hard to imagine that Norway's high fertility can be attributed to a larger number of unwanted births than in most other countries because of poorer access to or acceptance of contraception or abortion. Many pregnancies in Norway are unintended, resulting in many abortions (245 abortions per 1000 births), and a large proportion of births are reported as "mistimed" or "unwanted" (about one-third among cohabitants according to a survey in 1996 (Kravdal 1997) and one-third of all births according to personal calculations from the 1988 Family and Occupation Survey (Statistics Norway 1991)). These proportions are probably not particularly high by European standards, however. The abortion rate is not far from the average for Western and Southern Europe (Sardon 2004), so unless a particularly small proportion of unintended pregnancies end in abortion, Norway's birth figures are not to a greater extent than elsewhere "blown up" by unwanted or mistimed births. Moreover, modern contraception is used by a larger proportion of women than in most other countries (United Nations 2012) in spite of apparently high fertility desires.

Summarizing the Fundamental Forces Behind Norway's High Fertility

To summarize, Norway is in an advantaged position economically, which probably contributes to the country's relatively high fertility. Individuals, including young adults, face a low risk of unemployment, and the state can afford to be generous with parents, not least with respect to daycare and parental leave. In addition, there is a political willingness to spend some of Norway's wealth on such policies, which is motivated by an intention to help families economically and strengthen women's position in the family and in society. This political willingness may stem from ideas about public responsibility for individual well-being that are strongly rooted in Nordic societies (Esping-Andersen 1999), accompanied by widely accepted ideals of gender equality. Indeed, the Nordic countries score at the highest level on a very broad gender-gap index developed by the World Economic Forum (2014). It is possible that Norway's gender-equality ideals also affect fertility positively through men's involvement with children and housework. Another explanation for Norway's high fertility may be that, although the retreat from marriage is at least as pronounced as in many other developed countries, this is counteracted by widespread cohabitation and a large number of births among cohabiting couples—probably reflecting in part their trust in the welfare state and liberal values.

Some Comments on Fertility Changes Over Time

This discussion has focused on possible reasons for Norway's generally high fertility level, but changes over time also deserve comment. Norway's fertility decline from the mid-1960s was probably driven by the same factors that were responsible for the decline in many other countries. First, the opportunity costs of childbearing were rising, reflecting the fact that women were increasingly likely to work and that they had the potential to earn higher wages than in the past. Second, there was a strong expansion of education, especially among women, which was responsible for women's wage increase and also contributed to delaying first births simply through the longer period of school enrolment. (A persistent desire to accumulate work experience before embarking on parenthood probably strengthened the fertility implications of the longer enrolment.) Third, there were later and fewer marriages and more divorces, driven not least by the development in education and other structural and ideational changes. Fourth, new contraceptive technologies were introduced. There may, of course, also have been a shift in preferences in favor of activities and goods that compete with childrearing and in norms with direct implications for fertility (Crimmins et al. 1991; Lesthaeghe and Surkyn 1988), although the evidence for this is not strong.

Reductions in the opportunity costs of childrearing—because of expansion of daycare and other increasingly generous family policies—may be an important factor behind the levelling out and increase in second- and higher-order birth rates from the mid-1970s, which has also been seen in some other countries with similar policy changes (Andersson 2004; Toulemon et al. 2008). Furthermore, the contraceptive "revolution" had to a large extent run its course by then, and there are some indications in other countries that the movement towards more liberal family values had come to a halt (Lesthaeghe and Moors 1995). Finally, the positive trend in higher-order birth rates may be partly a result of a selection effect, as explained in Kravdal (2002b). More specifically, when estimating time trends in birth rates, it makes good sense to control for current age and time since previous birth, which essentially means that one compares among women who had their most recent birth at the same age. One reason why mothers who, for example, had their first child at age 25 in 1975 had lower second-birth rates than those who had their first child at age 25 in 1995 may be that first births tended to occur later in the more recent period, so that becoming a mother at the early age of 25 was more indicative of characteristics leading to generally high fertility. Similarly, having a first child at, for example, age 30 in 1975, when many entered parenthood in their early or mid-20s, may indicate characteristics leading to low fertility to a larger extent than would a first birth at age 30 in 1995.

The fact that first-birth rates began declining later than higher-order birth rates may be due to increased sexual activity among young people in the late 1960s and early 1970s. It is far from obvious, however, why the decline in first-birth rates continued through the 1970s and the first half of the 1980s, and a new decline began about 1990, while higher-order birth rates have been largely stable or increasing since the mid-1970s. Possibly, the opportunity-cost argument matters less for decisions on timing than it does for quantum decisions (also consistent with the fact that second-birth rates increased less than third-birth rates since the mid-1970s). Furthermore, the continued expansion of education is likely to have had a particularly strong effect on first births.

The fertility trends have probably not—at least until recently—been strongly influenced by economic cycles, which have been rather moderate in Norway. In the mid-1990s, the first-birth rate and to lesser extent the second-birth rate declined, and the upturn in the third-birth rate stopped. This could be partly a result of unemployment, which was high in those years by Norwegian standards.

From 2002 to 2007, the total fertility rate increased by 0.2, and it fell by just as much from 2009 to 2013. Similar trends are also seen in the parity-specific birth rates. This development is not easy to understand. In 2003, the annual growth rate of per capita GDP was relatively low and the unemployment rate relatively high, which was followed by three to four years of stabilization or improvement. This might have contributed to the fertility upturn. Furthermore, there was an unusually low (actually negative) growth rate in 2009, but not a particularly high unemployment rate, and economic growth *increased* over the next three years (Norway being much less influenced by the financial crisis than most other countries), while fertility *declined*.

With respect to the other factors discussed above, there has not been any documented change that could contribute to the upsurge and subsequent downturn of fertility during the past 10 years. There has been considerable media attention on the busy lives of Norwegian women and men outside the work and family spheres, which in theory could contribute to a fertility decline. According to anecdotic evidence, young people are increasingly eager to spend time on physical exercise and sophisticated food-making, to be active with friends, and to have a nice home (and to document their success in these areas through social media). How widespread these attitudes really are, and whether there has been much of a *change* during the past half decade or so, remains to be seen. It would also be relevant to ask whether any such change—or other changes—have taken place in other Nordic countries, since they have all experienced a fertility decline recently (although it has not been quite as sharp in Sweden and Finland as in Norway, Denmark, and Iceland).

Should Norwegians Be Concerned if Fertility Were Much Lower?

There are two main reasons why one might be concerned about low fertility. The most widely discussed concern is that low fertility may have adverse consequences for society because it slows population growth or even makes it negative, and—more importantly—it increases the proportion of elderly people in the population. Another possible reason for concern is that adults who have no or few children could be disadvantaged in the long term, and children could experience adverse effects from growing up with no or few siblings.

Potential Adverse Effects of Low Fertility at the Aggregate Level

Particular attention has been devoted to the economic consequences of increasing old-age dependency ratios. For example, it has been argued that it may be difficult to sustain commonly used pay-as-you-go pension systems in populations with a large proportion of elderly (Blake and Mayhew 2006). A government may have to reduce pensions, increase taxes on workers, or take up loans abroad, with possibly increased dependence on other countries. In Norway, concern about the sustainability of the pension system has led to pension reform aimed at delaying retirement.

In addition, if a higher proportion of the population is elderly, health expenditures will be high (Dormont et al. 2006). This also may contribute to higher taxes or fiscal deficits, or there may be lower-quality medical care, which is not generally regulated by law to the same extent as pensions (Gerdtham et al. 2005). These concerns are, of course, relevant for Norway, and plans have been made to meet the challenges, for example regarding cancer treatment and care (Norwegian Ministry of Health and Care Services 2013). With a relatively small proportion of the population in the working ages, even finding the workers to provide healthcare for the elderly may be difficult.

Another type of argument is that population aging may have consequences for the welfare system. On the one hand, young people may want to downsize the welfare state, given the increasing challenges of supporting the old members of the population. On the other hand, there will be a larger proportion of old voters, who may want to maintain the current system or at least the parts from which they benefit (Galasso and Profeta 2007).

Yet another issue is that an older workforce might have lower productivity. There is much uncertainty about this, however, as older workers probably have both characteristics that tend to reduce productivity and characteristics with the opposite effect (Tang and MacLeod 2006; Skirbekk 2008; Disney 1996; Van Dalen et al. 2010).

The impact of a possibly smaller total population size that may follow in the wake of low fertility has been much less analysed, perhaps partly because there are still so few countries that have actually experienced declining population numbers. One issue is that a country may have less military power and less international political influence if its population, and therefore the absolute size of its economy, is shrinking. This “nationalistic” argument is an old one. It motivated, for example, the early French pro-natalist policies, but it may still have some relevance today (Demeny 2003; Grebenik 1989; Jackson and Howe 2008). Another possibly harmful effect, relevant for some countries, is that reduction in the size of the population may make it difficult for some sparsely populated regions to survive because there are too few people to share the expenses of basic infrastructure (Felmingham et al. 2002). Further, it is possible that a shrinking domestic market undermines entrepreneurial optimism and the willingness to take risks (Jackson and Howe 2008). The argument about populous countries having an advantage through possibilities for specialization and efficiencies of scale may be less relevant than in the past due to the globalized economy.

Certain steps can be taken to ameliorate some of the consequences of population aging. A government may, for example, increase the age at which workers become eligible for retirement pensions or initiate life-long learning programs to improve the productivity of older workers (who tend to be healthier than ever before). In many countries, efforts to increase women’s participation in paid work could also balance the decline of the working-age population, although in Norway there is limited scope for this approach because most women are already working. Furthermore, a government may try to prepare people to enter the workforce at younger ages through more efficient educational programs. Another alternative would be to admit more skilled, working-age immigrants (Cangiano 2014; Rand 2004; Blake and Mayhew 2006). Finally, it would be helpful to achieve cost savings in healthcare, but this is not a sector where it is easy to make large efficiency gains.

To the extent that population aging or decline actually has adverse social or economic effects and the mentioned possible remedies are seen as unsuitable or insufficient, attempts to raise fertility might be justified. Various schemes to subsidize childrearing would be natural ingredients. An obvious prerequisite, however, would be that the costs of such schemes do not exceed the gains. These gains include not only aggregate factors such as those mentioned, but also the advantages for individual families who, given positive incentives, presumably make childbearing decisions that give them a higher level of well-being than they otherwise would have had. To put it differently, one could certainly convince many people of reproductive age to have another child if—very hypothetically—not only were most expenses covered, but they were actually *paid*, and even generously. But would it be worth it? It will always be hard to know whether a pro-natalist policy is economically sound, as both the costs of increasing fertility and the benefits for society are very difficult to assess.

Potentially Positive Effects of Low Fertility at the Aggregate Level

Low fertility may also have aggregate-level effects that are positive. If these are dominant, the motive for trying to increase fertility for externality reasons would be undermined.

One relevant issue is that low fertility contributes to reduce the proportion of children in a population. If the total allocations to education are fixed, fewer children means a larger educational investment in each child, which will increase laborforce productivity later. Under some conditions, this effect may more than outweigh the costs of supporting a larger elderly population, so that—at least within a certain band of fertility—the countries with lower fertility would be better off economically (Lee and Mason 2010).

Another possible advantage is that as the workforce shrinks, a lower saving rate is needed to maintain the same capital-labor ratio. A related issue is that a country with a stable or declining population size faces fewer challenges than a country with a growing population in terms of expansion of infrastructure (e.g., increasing transportation capacity).

Furthermore, a smaller population may cause less environmental damage. An over-simplified version of this argument is that, if all types of environmental imprints from each individual are fixed, fewer persons means less emission of greenhouse gases, less air pollution in general, less waste production, less deforestation, and less soil degradation due to food production (McNeill 2006). The reality is more complex, of course, because changes in population size may lead to changes in income-generating and leisure activities, in technology, and in policies, with implications for how each individual influences the environment. For example, should population decline somehow lead to higher average incomes, the outcome may be an *increased* pressure on the environment. This seems a bit far-fetched, though. Just as environmental concerns are reckoned among the strongest arguments against high population growth in poor countries (Cleland et al. 2006)—though the exact effect certainly depends on a number of economic and political factors (e.g., Panayoutou 1994)—a population decline in rich countries should be welcome on environmental grounds. Population aging may also be beneficial from an environmental perspective because old people's consumption is probably less damaging to the environment than consumption by younger people (McDonald et al. 2006).

Finally, a crowded environment (which is not the same as environmental degradation) could have adverse psychological and health effects. There has not been much research on such crowding effects, although for some discussion and analysis of related issues, see Chaix et al. (2006) and Solari and Mare (2012). Arguments about environmental pressure and crowding are perhaps more relevant in countries that are more densely populated than Norway.

Individual-Level Effects of Fertility

Some of the consequences for parents of bearing and rearing children are broadly considered as positive, some may be seen as negative, and there may be widely different opinions about others. Moreover, some of the consequences can be foreseen and, therefore, presumably taken into account in decision-making about whether to have a child, while other consequences are unexpected. The different types of consequences are reviewed below. Next, the discussion touches on whether low fertility may be considered a "problem" for potential parents, which could be a rationale for policy interventions. Finally, the discussion moves to how the number of siblings may influence the well-being of children and whether there could be a low-fertility "problem" from that perspective.

Potentially Positive Social Effects for Adults Who Have Children

Researchers have described a number of positive benefits from having children (Eibach and Mock 2011; Nelson et al. 2013; White and Dolan 2009). Children may show affection, they may help their parents feel that life has a purpose, they may be seen as giving the parents adult status (relevant only for the youngest parents), parents may enjoy engaging in various activities with children, and it may be rewarding to see children develop. Children's contribution to family income is an important issue primarily in poor settings (Caldwell 1976), but it may also matter in some more-developed countries (Council of Europe 1996). In addition, financial support from adult children may be important to the poorest segments of the elderly population, especially in countries where public support systems are not well developed (Rendall and Bahchieva 1998). Adult children may also provide practical assistance when parents are old or sick (Antonucci et al. 2003; Barefoot et al. 2005; Lusyne and Page 2008). Possibly, such financial or practical help from children may become more important in the future because of strains on public support systems in populations with an increasing proportion of old people.

Research has shown that parents tend to be less inclined to take risks than the childless (Wang et al. 2009), they tend to be subjected to stronger social control at home (Joutseneemi et al. 2007; Kendig et al. 2007), and they are often better socially integrated into the community (Knoster and Eggebeen 2006; Bühler 2008; Nomaguchi and Milkie 2004). While these consequences of parenthood may not necessarily be deemed particularly positive or negative in themselves, they probably contribute positively to parents' health.

Other Social Effects on Parents' Well-Being and Physiological Consequences

Obviously, parenting also brings expenses and burdens. A child needs food, clothes, and equipment for leisure activities. In addition, parents may forego some income because one of them (typically the mother) may withdraw from the laborforce to care for a young child, or they must pay others for childcare. One or both parents may be able to put in extra hours of gainful work to compensate, but the family may still end up with reduced financial resources (Aassve et al. 2006). Withdrawal from the labor market may be a loss not only economically, but also because of the possible satisfaction and social interaction enjoyed at the work place.

Furthermore, while the intense involvement with a young child is probably seen as rewarding by many parents, others may consider it largely as a burden (Poortman and van der Lippe 2009). There may be a period when parents get little sleep while a child is young (Dørheim et al. 2009), and there typically will be less time for adult leisure activities for many years. Some parents may see these issues as major disadvantages, while others may be less concerned (Bittman and Wajcman 2000). Also, parents may experience distress because of worries about a child's well-being.

The number of pregnancies—and the age at which the first occurs—may affect the mother's chance of developing cancer through hormonal changes or other physiological mechanisms (Salehi et al. 2008; Russo and Russo 2007). There may also be biological effects on the likelihood of a mother coming down with other diseases (Fletcher et al. 2002; Skilton et al. 2009).

The observed positive relationship between parity and health, and the corresponding negative relationship between parity and mortality (Grundy and Kravdal 2010), reflect a combination of the mentioned social advantages and disadvantages of having children plus the physiological effects, which are relevant only for women, of course. Additionally, the relationships reflect selective influences.

Can Low Fertility Be Considered a "Problem" for Adults?

To the extent that low fertility in a more-developed country is a result of sub- or infecundity among couples who want to have children, one could argue that attempts should be made to increase the couples' well-being by supporting the relevant treatment. Yet there is always the possibility that the money could have more beneficial effects if used elsewhere. As argued above, however low fertility in rich countries probably largely reflects the fact that many people really *want* no or few children. They believe this is best for themselves—or perhaps for the children.

Obviously, the effects of having children cannot be perfectly foreseen by the parents. For example, couples (or individuals) may decide to have a child because they assume that the emotional rewards will more than outweigh the economic disadvantages and practical burdens associated with childrearing, and they may take into account other types of possible implications as well, but the child may for various reasons cause them much more worry than they expected, or their economic situation may be more strained than anticipated. Conversely, some people may, for example, be overly pessimistic about the care burdens in the first years of a child's life or they may underestimate the long-term health benefits of having children as old-age support, or they may be unaware of the physiological advantages (for women) of having children.

It only makes sense to consider the fertility level as a "problem" for individual adults if the unexpected benefits and burdens of parenthood tend to go in one direction, so that, by and large, people do not make fertility decisions that are in their own best interest. In other words, low fertility would be a "problem" only if adults, on the whole, chose to have no or few children out of ignorance of the advantages they would have derived from having a larger family, given their actual circumstances. There is at present little evidence of such a situation, but the issue has not attracted much research interest. To the extent that such evidence is ever established—or if evidence suggesting that people would be better off with *fewer* children should materialize—information about it should, of course, be disseminated to the public.

In contrast, it can hardly be considered a "problem" if fertility desires fall short of the number of children people consider "ideal" or would, in theory, have liked to have if they were richer or healthier or had better access to childcare, as argued in some grey literature and policy reports (Commission of the European Communities 2006; Fahey and Spéder 2004), although less often in scholarly journals. As mentioned also by Lutz (2007), we all have unsatisfied dreams. Some people would have taken great pleasure in driving a Rolls Royce, but do not have the money to buy one, while others would ideally have wanted an annual eight-week vacation. The key issue must be whether the obstacles to childbearing are "avoidable" or "unreasonable," in the sense that they could be removed without taking too much away from others. In principle, if there are laws, for example, that make it extremely inconvenient to have a second child, but that have no favourable impact on anything else, they may be abolished. This is far-fetched, however. More realistically, if there are economic or practical obstacles to having children, these most likely can only be removed by using resources that could otherwise be used to help people in other ways.

Effects of Low Fertility on Children's Well-Being

The number of children in a family may also affect the *children's* well-being in a number of ways. In particular, it is widely believed that children benefit from having at least one sibling—a notion perhaps underlying the two-child norm that has probably affected fertility in rich countries for a long time (Blake 1968). In support of such a notion, several (but not all) studies have shown that children with siblings tend to have well-developed social skills (e.g., Downey and Condron 2004).

There are potentially negative effects of having (many) siblings as well, however. In particular, there may be fewer economic resources available to children in large families, both during childhood and later (Keister 2003), and they may get less attention from their parents. In part because of such effects, one might expect a negative association between sibship size and children's education, and this has indeed been shown in some Western countries (Booth and Kee 2009; Conley and Glauber 2006; Downey 1995; Goux and Maurin 2005; Jæger 2008; Kuo and Hauser 1997). On the other hand, many of the more recent investigations, some of which have used twin births to deal better with the selection problem, have reported little or no effect (Angrist et al. 2010; Åslund and Grönqvist 2010; Black et al. 2005; Cáceres-Delpiano 2006; De Haan 2010). In addition, low fertility has longer-term implications for kinship size. The children of parents who have no or few siblings will have no or few aunts, uncles, or cousins, and this might also have an effect on their well-being.

Parents are likely to take expectations about such implications for their own children's well-being into account in their fertility decision-making. They may, for example, want two children even though they expect that they would be happier themselves with only one, because they think it is good for a child to have a sibling. Alternatively, perhaps they have a single child because this is in their own best interests and they do not see a significant disadvantage for the child. To expand the idea mentioned earlier, a family-level low-fertility "problem" arises if the parents want and have, for example, one child while they and their child on the whole—and contrary to the parents' beliefs—would have been better off if more children had been born. That said, it is not obvious how one should summarize aspects of well-being across individuals and especially when some of them only exist potentially. A somewhat different issue is that parents, in principle, may make fertility decisions that are good for themselves, but bad for their children, because they do not care so much about their children's well-being. From society's point of view that could also be consider a "problem".[4]

[4]It was assumed above, for simplicity, that low fertility can affect the lifestyle and well-being of individual families and also have societal effects through population growth and structure.

Tying the Pieces Together

To conclude, Norway has higher fertility than most other rich countries, which probably is a result (though unintended) of a good economic situation, gender equality ideals that are deeply rooted in society, and generally liberal values. These factors are not easily transferable to other countries. Norwegian society is also characterized by strong political agreement about a public responsibility to support individual families—for example, through daycare services and other arrangements that reduce the costs and burdens of having children. Countries concerned about low fertility could, in principle, decide to give higher priority to these kinds of initiatives.

That said, it is not obvious that Norway's relatively high fertility is particularly enviable, except that it signals a favorable economic situation. Low fertility exacerbates population aging and exerts a downward pressure on population growth, which may cause certain societal-level disadvantages—for example related to the financing of pensions and healthcare for the elderly. Yet there may also be adverse societal consequences of relatively *high* fertility. In particular, a younger and more rapidly growing population (although admittedly, in Norway, primarily a result of massive immigration) will intensify pressure on the environment. This argument, which is even more relevant for countries that are poorer or have higher population densities, has not received much attention in the political debate. Obviously, childbearing also has effects at the individual level (with further implications for society), but we are not in a position to say whether relatively high fertility tends to be better for adults and children than low fertility. Stated differently, it is possible that families in Norway would have been just as well off if the parents—given their circumstances—instead had decided to have as few children as, say, the Italians. Besides, even if there are no clear individual-level advantages or disadvantages associated with the current fertility level, one might ask whether childbearing *in unstable relationships*—which is quite common in Norway and contributes to the country's high fertility—could have some adverse implications for those directly involved that they are not aware of or are not taking adequately into account.

(Footnote 4 continued)

However, there is another type of externality: The effects that a couple's fertility has on their own lives—for better or worse—may also have implications for others (which they are not likely to take into account in their decision-making). As mentioned, those with no or few children may, for example, be less integrated into the community, which may be acceptable to them (to the extent that it is foreseen), but there may be less positive implications for other people, one reason being the possible positive health effects of social cohesion (Islam et al. 2006). Another individual-level effect of low fertility is that the mothers will be more likely to have paid work. This will probably have important, and perhaps largely positive, societal implications. A related type of spill-over effect would be, for example, that the entire society may be influenced if it is the case that children without siblings tend to be less sociable than other children. Additionally, the distinction between the micro and the macro perspective is blurred because a couple's low fertility may contribute to or be partly a result of others' low fertility through learning and imitation effects (Goldstein et al. 2003; Montgomery and Casterline 1996).

References

Aase, K. B., & Kaldager, R. V. (2014). *Befolkningsframskrivinger 2104–2100: Fruktbarhet.* Economic Analyses 4/2014. Oslo: Statistics Norway.

Aassve, A., & Lappegård, T. (2009). Childcare cash benefits and fertility timing in Norway. *European Journal of Population, 25*(1), 67–88.

Aassve, A., Mazzuco, S., & Mencarini, L. (2006). An empirical investigation into the effect of childbearing on economic well-being in Europe. *Statistical Methods and Applications, 15*(2), 209–227.

Andersson, G. (2004). Childbearing developments in Denmark, Norway, and Sweden from the 1970s to the 1990s: A comparison. *Demographic Research, 3*(7), 153–176.

Andersson, G., Hank, K., Rønsen, M., & Vikat, A. (2006). Gendering family composition: Sex preferences for children and childbearing behavior in the Nordic countries. *Demography, 43*, 255–267.

Andersson, G., Rønsen, M., Knudsen, L. B., Lappegård, T., Neyer, G., Skrede, K., et al. (2009). Cohort fertility patterns in the Nordic countries. *Demographic Research, 20*, 313–352.

Angrist, J. D., Lavy, V., & Schlosser, A. (2010). Multiple experiments for the causal link between the quantity and quality of children. *Journal of Labor Economics, 28*(4), 773–824.

Antonucci, T. C., Arjouch, K. J., & Janevic, M. R. (2003). The effect of social relations with children on the education-health link in men and women aged 40 and over. *Social Science and Medicine, 56*(5), 949–960.

Åslund, O., & Grönqvist, H. (2010). Family size and child outcomes: Is there really no trade-off? *Labour Economics, 17*(1), 130–139.

Bachrach, C. A., & Morgan, S. P. (2013). A cognitive–social model of fertility intentions. *Population and Development Review, 39*, 459–485.

Barefoot, J. C., Grønbæk, M., Jensen, G., Schnohr, P., & Prescott, E. (2005). Social network diversity and risks of ischemic heart disease and total mortality: Findings from the Copenhagen City Heart Study. *American Journal of Epidemiology, 161*, 960–967.

Barne, likestillings, og inkluderingsdepartementet [Ministry of Children, Equality, and Social Inclusion, Norway]. (2012). *Småbarnsforeldres rettigheter.* Oslo: Barne, likestillings, og inkluderingsdepartementet.

Bittman, M., & Wajcman, J. (2000). The rush hour: The character of leisure time and gender equity. *Social Forces, 79*(1), 165–189.

Black, S. E., Devereux, P. J., & Salvanes, K. G. (2005). The more the merrier? The effects of family size and birth order on children's education. *Quarterly Journal of Economics, 120*, 669–700.

Blake, J. (1968). Are babies consumer durables? A critique of the economic theory of reproductive motivation. *Population Studies, 22*(1), 5–25.

Blake, D., & Mayhew, L. (2006). On the sustainability of the UK state pension system in the light of the population aging and declining fertility. *Economic Journal, 116*, F286–F305.

Booth, A. L., & Kee, H. J. (2009). Birth order matters: The effect of family size and birth order on educational attainment. *Journal of Population Economics, 22*, 367–397.

Bradshaw, J., & Finch, N. (2002). *A comparison of child benefit packages in 22 countries.* Research Report 174. York: Department for Work and Pensions, University of York.

Bühler, C. (2008). On the structural value of children and its implication on intended fertility in Bulgaria. *Demographic Research, 18*, 569–610.

Cáceres-Delpiano, J. (2006). The impacts of family size on investment in child quality. *Journal of Human Resources, 41*(4), 738–754.

Caldwell, J. C. (1976). Toward a restatement of demographic transition theory. *Population and Development Review, 2*, 321–366.

Cangiano, A. (2014). Elder care and migrant labor in Europe: A demographic outlook. *Population and Development Review, 40*, 131–154.

Chaix, B., Rosvall, M., Lynch, J., & Merlo, J. (2006). Disentangling contextual effects on cause-specific mortality in a longitudinal 23-year follow-up study: Impact of population density or socioeconomic environment. *International Journal of Epidemiology, 35*, 633–643.
Clark, W. A. V. (2012). Do women delay family formation in expensive housing markets? *Demographic Research, 27*, 1–24.
Cleland, J., Bernstein, S., Ezeh, A., Faundes, A., Glasier, A., & Innis, J. (2006). Family planning: The unfinished agenda. *Lancet, 368*, 1810–1827.
Commission of the European Communities. (2006). *Demographic future of Europe—from challenge to opportunity*. Brussels: Commission of the European Communities.
Conley, D., & Glauber, R. (2006). Parental educational investment and children's academic risk: Estimates of the impact of sibship size and birth order from exogenous variation in fertility. *Journal of Human Resources, 41*(4), 722–737.
Council of Europe. (1996). *Children and work in Europe*. Strasbourg: Council of Europe Publishing.
Crimmins, E. M., Easterlin, R. A., & Sato, Y. (1991). Preference changes among American youth: Family, work and goods aspirations. *Population and Development Review, 17*, 115–133.
De Haan, M. (2010). Birth order, family size and educational attainment. *Economics of Education Review, 29*(4), 576–588.
Demeny, P. (2003). Population policy dilemmas in Europe at the dawn of the twenty-first century. *Population and Development Review, 29*, 1–28.
DiPrete, T. A., Morgan, S. P., Engelhardt, H., & Pacalova, H. (2003). Do cross-national differences in the costs of children generate cross-national differences in fertility rates? *Population Research and Policy Review, 22*, 439–477.
Disney, R. (1996). *Can we afford to grow old?*. Cambridge: MIT Press.
Dørheim, S. K., Bondevik, G. T., Eberhard-Gran, M., & Bjorvatn, B. (2009). Sleep and depression in postpartum women: A population-based study. *Sleep, 32*, 847–855.
Dormont, B., Grignon, M., & Huber, H. (2006). Health expenditure growth: Reassessing the threat of ageing. *Health Economics, 15*, 947–963.
Downey, D. B. (1995). When bigger is not better: Family size, parental resources, and children's educational performance. *American Sociological Review, 60*, 747–761.
Downey, D. B., & Condron, D. J. (2004). Playing well with others in kindergarten: The benefit of siblings at home. *Journal of Marriage and Family, 66*, 333–350.
Easterlin, R., & Crimmins, E. (1985). *The fertility revolution: A supply-demand analysis*. Chicago: University of Chicago Press.
Eibach, R. P., & Mock, S. E. (2011). Idealizing parenthood to rationalize parental investments. *Psychological Science, 22*(2), 203–208.
Esping-Andersen, G. (1999). *Social foundations of postindustrial economics*. Oxford: Oxford University Press.
European Commission (2014). Use of child care in the EU member states and progress towards the Barcelona targets. Short Statistical Report 1. http://ec.europa.eu/justice/gender-equality/files/documents/140502_gender_equality_workforce_ssr1_en.pdf. Accessed March 31, 2015.
Eurostat (2014a). *Marriage and divorce statistics*. http://epp.eurostat.ec.europa.eu/statistics_explained/index.php/Marriage_and_divorce_statistics. Accessed March 9, 2015.
Eurostat (2014b). *Employment statistics*. http://epp.eurostat.ec.europa.eu/statistics_explained/index.php/Employment_statistics. Accessed March 9, 2015.
Eurostat (2014c). *The unadjusted gender wage gap 2012*. http://epp.eurostat.ec.europa.eu/statistics_explained/index.php/gender_pay_gap_statistics#Gender_pay_gap_levels. Accessed March 9, 2015.
Fahey, T., & Spéder, Z. (2004). *Fertility and family issues in an enlarged Europe*. Luxembourg: Office for Official Publications of the European Communities.
Federal Reserve Bank of Dallas (2013). *International house price data base*. http://www.dallasfed.org/institute/houseprice/. Accessed March 9, 2015.
Felmingham, B., Jackson, N., & Zhang, Q. (2002). Indicative impacts of population decline on the operations of local government in Tasmania. *Australasian Journal of Regional Studies, 8*, 95–109.

Ferraretti, A.P., Goossens, V., Kupka, M., Bhattacharya, S., de Mouzon, J., Castilla, J.A., et al., The European IVF-monitoring (EIM), and Consortium, for The European Society of Human Reproduction and Embryology (ESHRE). (2013). Assisted reproductive technology in Europe, 2009: Results generated from European registers by ESHRE. *Human Reproduction, 28*(9), 2318–2331.

Fletcher, B., Gulanick, M., & Lamendola, C. (2002). Risk factors for type 2 diabetes mellitus. *Journal of Cardiovascular Nursing, 16*, 17–23.

Frejka, T. (2008). Overview Chapter 2: Parity distribution and completed fertility size in Europe: Incipient decline of the two-child family model. *Demographic Research, 19*, 47–72.

Galasso, V., & Profeta, P. (2007). How does ageing affect the welfare state? *European Journal of Political Economy, 23*, 554–563.

Gauthier, A. H., & DeGusti, B. (2012). The time allocation to children by parents in Europe. *International Sociology, 27*(6), 827–845.

Gauthier, A. H., & Hatzius, J. (1997). Family benefits and fertility: An econometric analysis. *Population Studies, 51*, 295–306.

Gerdtham, U.-G., Lundin, D., & Sáez-Marti, M. (2005). The ageing of society, health service provision and taxes. *Journal of Population Economics, 18*(3), 519–537.

Goldstein, J., Lutz, W., & Testa, M. R. (2003). The emergence of sub-replacement family size ideals in Europe. *Population Research and Policy Review, 22*, 479–496.

Goux, D., & Maurin, E. (2005). The effect of overcrowded housing on children's performance at school. *Journal of Public Economics, 89*(5–6), 797–819.

Grebenik, E. (1989). Demography, democracy, and demonology. *Population and Development Review, 15*, 1–22.

Grundy, E., & Kravdal, Ø. (2010). Fertility history and cause-specific mortality: A register-based analysis of complete cohorts of Norwegian women and men. *Social Science and Medicine, 70*, 1847–1857.

Haas, L., & Rostgaard, T. (2011). Fathers' rights to paid parental leave in the Nordic countries: Consequences for the gendered division of leave. *Community, Work and Family, 14*(2), 177–195.

Happel, S. K., Hill, J. K., & Low, S. A. (1984). An economic analysis of the timing of childbirth. *Population Studies, 38*(2), 299–311.

Hook, J. L., & Wolfe, C. M. (2012). New fathers? Residential fathers' time with children in four countries. *Journal of Family Issues, 33*, 415.

Islam, M. K., Merlo, J., Kawachi, I., Lindström, M., Gerdtham, U. G. (2006). Social capital and health: Does egalitarianism matter? A literature review. *International Journal of Equity in Health, 5*(3).

Jackson, R., & Howe, N. (2008). *The graying of the great powers: Demography and geopolitics in the 21st century*. Washington: Center for Strategic and International Studies.

Jæger, M. M. (2008). Do large sibships really lead to lower educational attainment? New evidence from quasi-experimental variation in couple's reproductive capacity. *Acta Sociologica, 51*, 217–235.

Jensen, A. M., & Clausen, S. E. (2003). Children and family dissolution in Norway: The impact of consensual unions. *Childhood, 10*, 65–81.

Joutsenniemi, K., Martelin, T., Kestilä, L., Martikainen, P., Pirkola, S., & Koskinen, S. (2007). Living arrangements, heavy drinking and alcohol dependence. *Alcohol and Alcoholism, 42*, 480–491.

Kalleberg, A. L. (2000). Nonstandard employment relations: Part-time, temporary and contract work. *Annual Review of Sociology, 26*, 341–365.

Kalwij, A. (2010). The impact of family policy expenditure on fertility in Western Europe. *Demography, 47*(2), 503–519.

Keister, L. A. (2003). Sharing the wealth: The effect of siblings on adults' wealth ownership. *Demography, 40*, 521–542.

Kendig, H., Dykstra, P. A., van Gaalen, R. I., & Melkas, T. (2007). Health of aging parents and childless individuals. *Journal of Family Issues, 28*, 1457–1486.

Knoester, C., & Eggebeen, D. J. (2006). The effects of the transition to parenthood and subsequent children on men's well-being and social participation. *Journal of Family Issues, 27*, 1532–1560.
Kravdal, Ø. (1994). The importance of economic activity, economic potential and economic resources for the timing of first birth in Norway. *Population Studies, 48*, 249–267.
Kravdal, Ø. (1997). Wanting a child without a firm commitment to the partner: Interpretations and implications of a common behaviour pattern among Norwegian cohabitors. *European Journal of Population, 13*, 269–298.
Kravdal, Ø. (2001). The high fertility of college educated women in Norway: An artefact of the separate modelling of each parity transition. *Demographic Research, 5*, 187–216.
Kravdal, Ø. (2002a). The impact of individual and aggregate unemployment on fertility in Norway. *Demographic Research, 6*, 263–294.
Kravdal, Ø. (2002b). Is the increase in second- and higher-order birth rates in Norway and Sweden from the mid-1970s real or a result of inadequate estimation methods? *Demographic Research, 6*, 241–262.
Kuo, H.-H. D., & Hauser, R. M. (1997). How does size of sibship matter? Family configuration and family effects on educational attainment. *Social Science Research, 26*, 69–94.
Lappegård, T. (2010). Family policies and fertility in Norway. *European Journal of Population, 26*, 99–116.
Lee, R., & Mason, A. (2010). Fertility, human capital, and economic growth over the demographic transition. *European Journal of Population, 26*, 159–182.
Lesthaege, R., & Moors, G. (1995). Is there a new conservatism that will bring back the old family? Ideational trends and the stages of family formation in Germany, France, Belgium and the Netherlands 1981–1990. *Proceedings of the EAPS Conference Milan, 1*, 225–265.
Lesthaeghe, R., & Surkyn, J. (1988). Cultural dynamics and economic theories of fertility change. *Population and Development Review, 14*, 1–45.
Lusyne, P., & Page, H. (2008). The impact of children on a parent's risk of suicide following death of a spouse, Belgium 1991–96. *Population Studies, 62*, 55–67.
Lutz, W. (2007). Adaptation versus mitigation policies on demographic change. *Vienna Yearbook of Population Research,* 19–25.
Lutz, W., & Skirbekk, V. (2005). Policies addressing the tempo effect in low-fertility countries. *Population and Development Review, 31*(4), 699–720.
Manning, W. D., Smock, P. J., & Majumdar, D. (2004). The relative stability of cohabiting and marital unions for children. *Population Research and Policy Review, 23*, 135–159.
Max Planck Institute for Demographic Research (2013). *Cohort fertility rates for 37 developed countries: Graphs by country group.* Data sheet for press release, March 21, 2013. http://www.demogr.mpg.de/mediacms%5C2567_main_MPIDR_lifetime_fertility_on_the_rise_DATASHEET.pdf. Accessed March 9, 2015.
McDonald, P. (2000). Gender equity in theories of fertility transition. *Population and Development Review, 26*, 427–439.
McDonald, G. W., Forgie, V. E., & MacGregor, C. (2006). Treading lightly: The ecofootprints of New Zealand's ageing population. *Ecological Economics, 56*, 424–439.
McNeill, J. R. (2006). Population and the natural environment: Trends and challenges. *Population and Development, 32*(suppl.), 183–201.
Mencarini, L., & Tanturri, M. L. (2004). Time use, family role-set and childbearing among Italian working women. *Genus, 60*, 111–137.
Milligan, K. (2005). Subsidizing the stork: New evidence on tax incentives and fertility. *Review of Economics and Statistics, 83*, 539–555.
Montgomery, M. R., & Casterline, J. B. (1996). Social learning, social influence, and new models of fertility. *Population and Development Review, 22*(suppl.), 151–175.
NAV [Norwegian Labor and Welfare Administration] (2014). *Family related benefits.* https://www.nav.no/en/Home/Benefits+and+services/Family+related+benefits. Accessed March 9, 2015.

Nelson, S. K., Kushlev, K., English, T., Dunn, E. W., & Lyubomirsky, S. (2013). In defense of parenthood: Children are associated with more joy than misery. *Psychological Science, 24*(1), 3–10.
Nomaguchi, K. N., & Milkie, M. A. (2004). Costs and rewards of children: The effects of becoming a parent on adults' lives. *Journal of Marriage and Family, 65*, 356–374.
Norwegian Ministry of Health and Care Services (2013). *Together— against cancer: National cancer strategy 2013–2017.* https://www.regjeringen.no/contentassets/07cd14ff763444a3997de1570b85fad1/i-1158_together-against_cancer_web.pdf. Accessed March 9, 2015.
OECD (Organization for Economic Cooperation and Development) (2013). *Education at a glance 2013: OECD indicators.* http://www.oecd-ilibrary.org/education/education-at-a-glance-2013_eag-2013-en. Accessed April 6, 2015.
Olah, O. S. (2003). Gendering fertility: Second births in Sweden and Hungary. *Population Research and Policy Review, 22*, 171–200.
Olsen, Ø. (2013). *The economic outlook.* Speech by Øystein Olsen, Governor of the Central Bank of Norway, to invited foreign embassy representatives, April 4, 2013. http://www.bis.org/review/r130409e.pdf. Accessed March 9, 2015.
Panayoutou, T. (1994). Population, environment, and development nexus. In R. Cassen (Ed.), *Population and development: Old debates, new conclusions* (pp. 149–180). New Brunswick: Transaction Publishers.
Gauthier A. H., & Philipov, D. (2008). Can policies enhance fertility? *Vienna Yearbook of Demography,* 1–16.
Poortman, A. R., & Van Der Lippe, T. (2009). Attitudes toward housework and child care and the gendered division of labor. *Journal of Marriage and the Family, 71*, 526–541.
Population Reference Bureau. (2014). *World population data sheet.* Washington: Population Reference Bureau.
Puur, A., Olah, L. S., Tazi-Preve, M. I., & Dorbritz, J. (2008). Men's childbearing desires and views of the male role in Europe at the dawn of the 21st century. *Demographic Research, 19*, 1883–1912.
Rand (2004). *Low fertility and population ageing: Causes, consequences and policy options.* Report prepared for the European commission. Santa Monica: Rand.
Rege, M., & Solli, I. F. (2013). The impact of paternity leave on fathers' future earnings. *Demography, 50*(6), 2255–2277.
Rendall, M. S., & Bahchieva, R. A. (1998). An old-age security motive for fertility in the United States. *Population and Development Review, 24*, 293–307.
Rindfuss, R. R., & Brauner-Otto, S. R. (2008). Institutions and the transition to adulthood: Implications for fertility tempo in low-fertility settings. *Vienna Yearbook of Population Research,* 57–87.
Rindfuss, R. R., Guilkey, D. K., Morgan, S. P., & Kravdal, Ø. (2010). Child care availability and fertility in Norway. *Population and Development Review, 36*, 725–748.
Rønsen, M. (2004). Fertility and public policies—evidence from Norway and Finland. *Demographic Research, 10*, 143–170.
Rønsen, M., & Skrede, K. (2008). Fertility trends and differentials in the Nordic countries—footprints of welfare policies and challenges on the road ahead. *Vienna Yearbook of Population Research,* 103–123.
Russo, I. H., & Russo, J. (2007). Primary prevention of breast cancer by hormone-induced differentiation. *Recent Results in Cancer Research, 174*, 111–130.
Salehi, F., Dunfield, L., Philips, K. P., Krewski, D., & Vanderhyden, B. C. (2008). Risk factors for ovarian cancer: An overview with emphasis on hormonal factors. *Journal of Toxicology & Environmental Health Part B: Critical Reviews, 11*, 301–321.
Sardon, J. -P. (2004). Recent demographic trends in the developed countries. *Population: English Selection, 59*, 263–314.
SIFO [National Institute for Consumer Research, Norway] (2013). *Standard budget for consumer expenditures, 2011.* http://sifo.no/files/standardbudsjett2011-eng-print.pdf. Accessed March 9, 2015.

Sigle-Rushton, W., & McLanahan, S. (2002). For richer or poorer? Marriage as an anti-poverty strategy in the United States. *Population: English Edition, 57*(3), 509–526.

Sigle-Rushton, W., & Waldfogel, J. (2007). Motherhood and women's earnings in Anglo-American, Continental European, and Nordic countries. *Feminist Economics, 13*, 55–91.

Skevik, A. (2004). The new family's vulnerable vanguard: Child maintenance reform in Norway. *Social Policy and Society, 3*, 11–19.

Skilton, M. R., Sérusclat, A., Begg, L. M., Moulin, P., & Bonnet, F. (2009). Parity and carotid atherosclerosis in men and women: Insights into the roles of childbearing and child-rearing. *Stroke, 40*, 1152–1157.

Skirbekk, V. (2008). Age and productivity capacity: Descriptions, causes and policy options. *Ageing Horizons, 8*, 4–12.

Sobotka, T., Hansen, M. A., Jensen, T. K., Pedersen, A. T., Lutz, W., & Skakkebæk, N. E. (2008). The contribution of assisted reproduction to completed fertility: An analysis of Danish data. *Population and Development Review, 34*, 79–101.

Solari, D., & Mare, R. D. (2012). Housing crowding effects on children's well-being. *Social Science Research, 41*, 464–476.

Statistics Norway (1991). *Family and Occupation Survey 1988.* NOS B959. Oslo: Kongsvinger.

Statistics Norway (2014). *Births, 2013.* http://www.ssb.no/en/befolkning/statistikker/fodte/aar/2014-04-08. Accessed March 10, 2015.

Tang, J., & MacLeod, C. (2006). Labour force ageing and productivity performance in Canada. *Canadian Journal of Economics, 39*, 582–603.

Texmon, I. (1999). *Samliv i Norge mot slutten av 1900-tallet. En beskrivelse av mangfold og endring* [Cohabitation in Norway towards the end of the 1990 s: A description of variation and change]. NOU 1999:25. Norwegian Public Reports, Appendix 3. Oslo: Statens forvaltningstjeneste/Statens trykning.

Thévenon, O. (2011). Family policies in OECD countries: A comparative analysis. *Population and Development Review, 37*, 57–87.

Tønnessen, M., Syse, A., Aase, K. N. (2014). *Befolkningsframskrivinger 2014–2100: Hovedresultater.* Statistics Norway. http://www.ssb.no/befolkning/artikler-og-publikasjoner/befolkningsframskrivinger-2014-2100-hovedresultater. Accessed March 10, 2015.

Torr, B. M., & Short, S. E. (2004). Second births and the second shift: A research note on gender equity and fertility. *Population and Development Review, 30*(1), 109–130.

Toulemon, L., Pailhé, A., & Rossier, C. (2008). France: High and stable fertility. *Demographic Research, 19*(16), 503–556.

United Nations Nations (2012). World contraceptive use 2011. http://www.un.org/esa/population/publications/contraceptive2011/wallchart_front.pdf. Accessed April 6, 2015.

Van Dalen, H. P., Henkens, K., & Schippers, J. (2010). Productivity of older workers: Perceptions of employers and employees. *Population and Development Review, 36*(2), 309–330.

Vienna Institute of Demography (2014). *European demographic data sheet 2014.* http://www.oeaw.ac.at/vid/datasheet/. Accessed March 10, 2015.

Vikat, A. (2004). Women's labour force attachment and childbearing in Finland. *Demographic Research, 3*(8), 177–212.

Wang, X. T., Kruger, D. J., & Wilke, A. (2009). Life history variables and risk-taking propensity. *Evolution and Human Behavior, 30*(2), 77–84.

White, M. P., & Dolan, P. (2009). Accounting for the richness of daily activities. *Psychological Science, 20*, 1000–1008.

Wiik, K. A., Bernhardt, E., & Noack, T. (2009). A study of commitment and relationship quality in Sweden and Norway. *Journal of Marriage and Family, 71*, 465–477.

World Economic Forum (2014). *The global gender gap report 2014.* http://www3.weforum.org/docs/GGGR14/GGGR_CompleteReport_2014.pdf. Accessed March 10, 2015.

World Values Survey (2014). *Online analysis.* http://www.worldvaluessurvey.org/WVSOnline.jsp. Accessed April 6, 2014.

The Influence of Family Policies on Fertility in France: Lessons from the Past and Prospects for the Future

Olivier Thévenon

Abstract France stands out from most other European countries because of its high and relatively stable fertility rate among the cohorts born since the 1950s. France's broad, long-standing, and consistent family policies contribute to this stability, although the exact contribution is hard to quantify. This chapter presents the main fertility trends in France and the characteristics of French family policies that may influence fertility. It emphasizes the broad spectrum of policy measures that cover a wide range of families, regardless of their civil status, number of children, or the working status of parents. These policies offer continuous support to children throughout childhood. One strength of family policies in France has been their effective adaptation to the increasing diversity of family forms. Population aging, however, requires further adaptations that are also discussed in the chapter.

Keywords Family policy • Fertility • Work-family balance • France • Population aging

France stands out from most other European countries because of its high and relatively stable fertility rate among the cohorts born since the 1950s. Can this be attributed to French family policy? Although hard to demonstrate, there is some evidence that the wide range of policies for families in France matters—even though the effect of each single measure is difficult to evaluate and is likely small.

French family-support policies have evolved over the decades. The priority is now support for a work-family balance, and the number of mechanisms has multiplied. Of these, provision of childcare services is a strongly positive factor in the decision to have children.

This chapter presents the main fertility trends in France and the characteristics of French family policies that may influence fertility. The first section traces the gradual shift in policy design from an objective of direct support for fertility to support for the work-family balance through a variety of mechanisms. It also

O. Thévenon (✉)
Institut National d'Etudes Demographiques (INED), Paris, France
e-mail: Olivier.thevenon@ined.fr

R.R. Rindfuss and M.K. Choe (eds.), *Low Fertility, Institutions, and their Policies*, DOI 10.1007/978-3-319-32997-0_3

outlines the measures introduced since the financial crisis, which began in 2008, initially to cushion the impact on families and then as a component of fiscal austerity policies. Although first and foremost motivated by a concern to reduce social spending, the recent reforms also signal a change of direction in the stated priorities.

The second section flags the difficulties in evaluating the impact of these policies on fertility and then presents the main findings of the evaluations that have been conducted. These findings emphasize the positive but relatively limited impact that changes to financial support or paid leave seem to have had. Comparisons across Europe also highlight the complementarity of support mechanisms and the key role of childcare provision in fertility rate differentials between economically advanced countries. In addition, these comparisons highlight the impact on fertility of measures aimed at facilitating the work-family balance. The decision to have children thus appears increasingly determined by the ability to combine children's care and education with the workforce participation of both parents. The final section discusses the need to adapt family policies to France's aging population, which is raising demand for support for the work-family balance, and to adapt childcare provision to the diverse needs of families and to the variety of their social and demographic backgrounds.

Fertility Trends in France and Policies that Support Families and Fertility

Stable Fertility Near Replacement Level

The period total fertility rate (TFR) decreased drastically in France in the 1960s but then remained almost stable from 1975, at around 1.8 births per woman, before turning up slightly, beginning in 1996 (Fig. 1). The fertility rate rose to 2.02 births per woman in 2010, which was its highest level in about 30 years following a 10-year period of slow growth (Prioux 2007). This placed France in the top position among European and other Organization for Economic Cooperation and Development (OECD) countries. France's fertility rate has remained consistently at around 1.96–2.00 births per women since the mid-2000s, and the 2008 economic crisis has had so far a very weak impact on France's aggregated fertility rate. The long-term trend in completed fertility shows a fairly moderate decline in the average number of births per woman among the cohorts born since the Second World War, stabilizing at two births per woman for all the cohorts born in the late 1960s and the 1970s (Fig. 1).

The timing of fertility is rapidly changing, however. France seems to have evolved from a "model" of early fertility to one of later fertility, concentrated between ages 25 and 35, and with a mean age at childbirth of 30 years and a mean age at first-order childbirth above 28 years (Mazuy et al. 2013). Fertility at ages 34–39 has also continued to rise, with a tendency toward closer average birth spacing for families with two children or more.

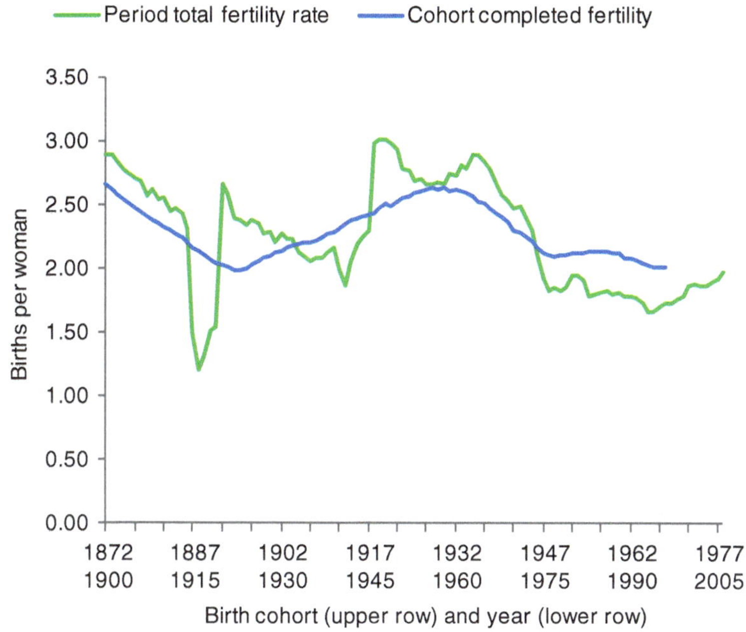

Fig. 1 Trends in period and completed fertility rates in France (Human Fertility Database 2015)

The overall stability of the average fertility rate nevertheless masks significant changes in terms of family size: The number of families with three or more children has fallen significantly in favor of families with two children (Fig. 2). The percentage of women with three or more children remains significantly higher in France (and in other countries where fertility is rather high) than in countries with low fertility, however. In addition, the percentage of women who remain childless throughout their reproductive lives is fairly low in France.[1] Overall, parenthood and families of two or more children are more common in France than in other European countries (Breton and Prioux 2009; Thévenon 2011a).

The circumstances surrounding childbearing have also changed, as shown by the impressive rise in the frequency of non-marital births over the past decades. The proportion was below 9 % in the early twentieth century and changed little in peacetime until the 1960s. It fell to its lowest level in the 1960s, when around 6 % of births occurred outside marriage. Since then, the trend has been upward, with non-marital births accounting for 30 % of total births in 1990 and 57 % in 2012. This rise shows the growing acceptance of new forms of union, as witnessed by the growing popularity of consensual unions, civil partnerships (introduced in 1999 and

[1]The proportion of childless women is quite constant, as is the proportion of men and women wishing to remain childless (Debest and Mazuy 2014). A minority of couples are sterile, and only a small proportion of the couples who have difficulty conceiving and who resort to assisted reproductive technologies (ART) succeed in having children (de La Rochebrochard et al. 2011).

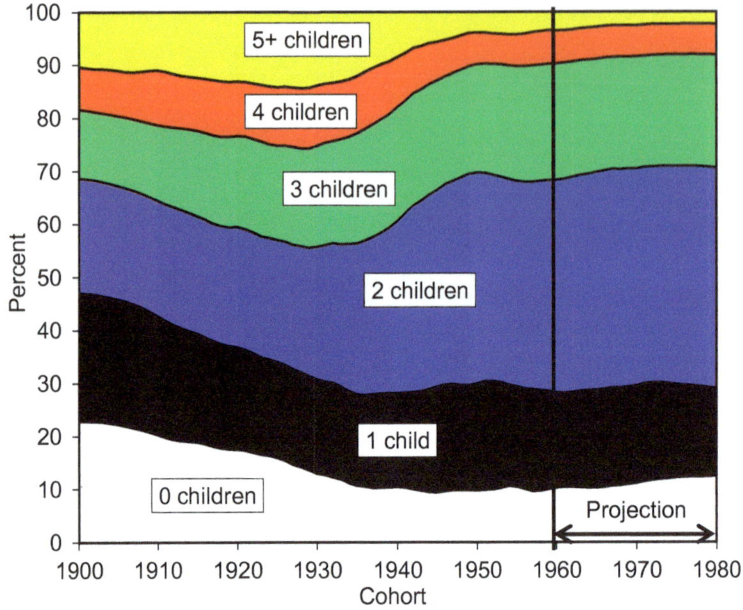

Fig. 2 Percentage of women by total number of children (Toulemon et al. 2008)

called *pacte civil de solidarité* or PACS), and unions where the partners "live apart together" or live together only part of the time.

Another aspect of the French situation is that fertility varies with educational level and migration background, but to a lesser extent than in many other countries. The move to later age at childbearing is observed for all women, and particularly among those with no educational qualifications (Davie and Mazuy 2010). But the process of entry into motherhood differs between social groups: According to the census surveys, mean age at first birth is 25 for the least-educated women compared with 30 for those with a college degree. The latter tend to concentrate their childbearing at around age 31, whereas births among women with no educational qualifications are more spread out over time. Unqualified, non-native-born women have higher fertility than their equivalents in the native-born population, whereas women with college degrees have broadly similar fertility levels whether born in France or not. Finally, fertility of non-native-born women contributes little—less than 0.1 child per woman—to overall fertility.

The trends in France can be attributed to several factors, with links that are extremely difficult to unravel. Children, as a value and a purpose, are essential to a large proportion of French households (Testa 2012). The number of children that people mention as their "personal" ideal is high in France compared with responses in other European countries where people have been surveyed with the same question. The potency of the high "taste" for children in France can also be seen in the weak impact of periods of economic recession on fertility rates. While the household confidence index closely tracks the economic cycle, no significant change can be seen in the behavior of parents-to-be. Fertility has remained at a high level in France despite pessimism and lack of confidence in the future and in institutions, as repeatedly indicated by surveys. Through the ups and downs of economic cycles, the long and consistent existence of family-support and child-protection policies in France indicates an enduring collective attachment to family values.

Encouraging Births: A Historic Objective of Family Policy

Natalism is both a demographic doctrine and a set of policies implemented by governments to promote population growth by stimulating the birth rate. For many decades, it was one of the main motivations for the family policies implemented in France (Rosental 2003). Fears of "depopulation" after the mass loss of life during the Franco-Prussian War of 1870, and then during the two World Wars, have been supplanted by concerns about population aging, the implications of which were set out by Debré and Sauvy as early as 1946 in their book *Des Français pour la France*. The assumption is that a country that encourages large families will be in a better position to cope with population aging. Still today, the advocates of natalism cite the importance of family policies for France's pay-as-you-go pension system, which is easier to balance when fertility is high.

Against this natalist background, over time France has developed a relatively generous system of financial support for families in general and "large" families—with three or more children—in particular. Direct financial support, such as tax breaks through the "family quotient,"[2] increases substantially with third and subsequent children. While the aim of this support is obviously to encourage families to have at least three children, it is also—and now primarily—to reduce inequality in living standards between large families, small families, and childless households (Thévenon 2011a).

By reducing the cost of raising a child, the financial support given to families is intended not only to enable households to have children, but also to provide them with sufficient financial resources to raise their children in favorable conditions. Yet, the financial support paid to families in France is not more generous for low-income households, unlike the situation in countries where financial support for families comes under welfare payments with a redistributive function. On the contrary, the French system is more generous to households at the top of the income

[2]The *quotient familial* ("family quotient") mechanism used to calculate income tax is original to France. Its basic purpose is to compensate for the cost of children by taking the presence of a partner and children into account in the calculation of income tax. The family quotient operates as follows: Total household income is divided by the number of "adult equivalent units" in the household (with the first and second child counting as one-half adult each and the third child counting as one adult), and the relevant tax rate from the progressive scale is applied to this income per unit. The resulting tax rate is then applied to household income.

pyramid, taking into account both the payments via the family allowance and tax breaks through the family quotient. This feature of the French system has been partly "corrected" by the lower income threshold for tax breaks introduced in 2013. At the same time, poor families receive substantial financial support through the combination of means-tested benefits, social assistance, and housing benefits that are significantly upgraded with family size.

Growing concerns about employment, gender equality, housing, and child poverty have progressively reshaped the scope and content of family policy. Based on this perspective, children now have access to childcare services and preschool from a very young age, and this early access is expected to benefit their development and their school achievement as well as helping their parents balance work and family life. Working parents with young children benefit from a continuum of support in cash and services. The increase in housing costs borne especially by large families since the mid-1980s (19 % on average in constant euros) is a growing concern that has so far not been addressed comprehensively, in spite of the introduction of a family-based housing benefit (HCF 2012) (see box).

Housing market in France

Housing markets have an important influence on different stages of family formation—a lack of affordable housing is often a reason to postpone the time at which young adults leave the parental home, form independent partnerships, and have children (Mulder 2006). Couples often prefer to secure housing of a certain quality (including quality of the environment) before having children.

Housing quality is not the only dimension that matters, however; the structure of the housing market is also an important dimension. Countries with the highest quality of housing do not necessarily provide an environment that is conducive to having children if there is a shortage of housing that is appropriate for young people wishing to start a family (Mulder 2006). Another key factor is the affordability of both home ownership and rental housing. A large, affordable rental sector can offer the opportunity for young people to leave their parental home quite early and have a child in a home of their own. Policies making home ownership affordable may also increase the options for young families (Mulder and Billari 2010). In contrast, widespread home ownership combined with a strong norm that favors home ownership and/or low affordability or accessibility of homes to purchase might lead couples to restrict their fertility plans significantly.

Against this background, the proportion of home owners is relatively high in France (20 % of households). Public (social) housing is also quite common (20 % of housing), only higher in the Netherlands (34 %) and the United Kingdom (21 %). Housing costs as a percentage of consumption are lower than average for the OECD, but costs have risen more than in most countries since the mid-1980s. The proportion of households bearing excessive costs is low (less than 10 % of households, including less than 2 % of two-parent families and around 6 % of single-parent families). Moreover, more than 5 million people (including 2.6 million children) live in inadequate housing. Home overcrowding is decreasing, however: 16 % of families lived in overcrowded housing in 2006 compared with 25 % in 1984.

No study has carefully analyzed the relationship between the local housing market in France and fertility behavior. Fertility is consistently lower in urban areas, however, where the relatively high cost of buying or renting a home could compete with the cost of having an(other) child (Courgeau and Lelièvre 1992; Desplanques 2011). Yet, housing markets do not seem to play a significant role in explaining regional disparities in fertility, which have been stable over decades.

Tensions in France's housing market are expected to increase in the coming decades as a result of population aging and changes in family lifestyle. The reduction of family size, combined with the rise of marital separation and widowhood, will increase the demand for small housing units (HCF 2012). A higher demand for small housing units might have an impact on prices that could impede the decision to start a family.

Public Support for Families

France has a very high level of total public spending on families with children as a percentage of national wealth. An important feature of French family policies is that couples in civil partnership have been subject to the same taxation and public spending rules as married couples since 2011. Another feature is the nature of government spending, starting with the relatively large share that takes the form of tax breaks, including tax relief for childcare costs (Fig. 3a).

The high percentage of spending on childcare services is a feature that France shares with the Nordic countries—unlike, for example, Germany where investment in childcare facilities is small compared with financial payments to families (Thévenon 2011b). The share of spending on childcare services allocated to preschool education is strongly dominant, however, with spending on early-childhood facilities (for children under age three) much lower than in the Nordic countries (Fig. 3b). Spending on preschool education accounts for 0.68 % of gross domestic product (GDP) in France, more than the OECD average of 0.38 % but less than 0.7 % in Iceland and Denmark. By contrast, only 0.44 % of French GDP is invested in childcare facilities for children under age three, which, although higher than the OECD average of 0.30 %, is significantly lower than the 0.90 % spent in Denmark.

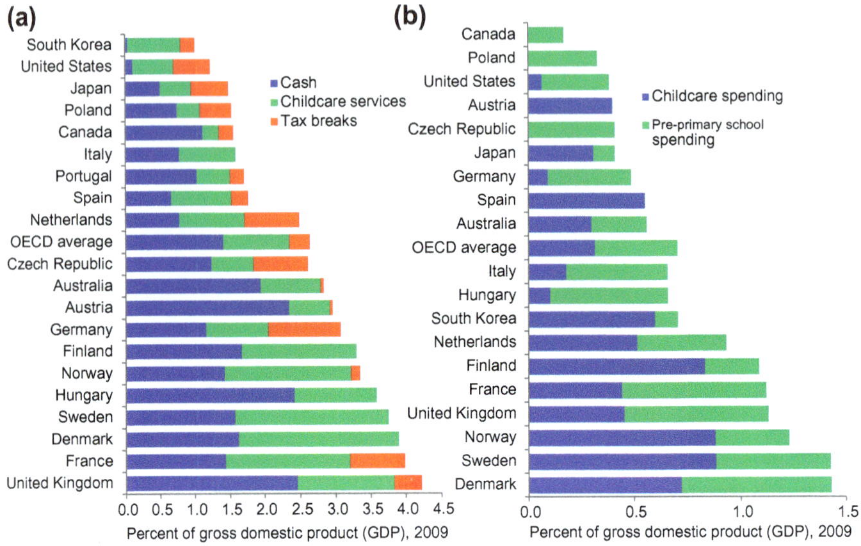

Fig. 3 **a** Public spending on families: breakdown of spending on financial benefits, childcare services, and tax breaks, 2009 (OECD Family Database 2014). **b** Public spending on families: breakdown of spending on services for children under age six, 2009 (OECD Family Database 2014). *Note* Public support only includes support directed exclusively at families (e.g., child payments and allowances, parental leave benefits, and childcare support). Spending in other areas, such as health and housing, although it may also assist families, is not included

In Denmark, more families use childcare services for children under age three and children tend to spend more time in childcare, which helps explain the difference in expenditures.

The Work-Family Balance: A "New" Policy Lever to Support Fertility

Other support mechanisms are of crucial importance in the decision to have children and the timing of births because they help parents, particularly mothers, to balance work and family. A number of support mechanisms mitigate the opportunity cost to a woman's career that results from childbirth and childrearing. Entitlements to parental leave, for example, which guarantee return rights to a job and include replacement income and access to childcare services, can also be an incentive to have a child.[3]

[3]Although not their primary objective, the *Prestation d'accueil du jeune enfant* (PAJE)—replacement income for parents who stop working or work part time in order to care for a child—and childcare services for young children have an influence on fertility by facilitating parents' return to work after the birth of a child.

Parental Leave and Associated Allowances

In France, a parent who is an employee and who meets the eligibility conditions is entitled to take parental leave for up to three years after the birth of a child, after which he/she can return to the same or a similar position with the same employer. This individual leave entitlement can be combined with a stay-at-home allowance paid to the household if one of the parents stops working or works part time in order to care for a young child. The overwhelming majority of beneficiaries of the parental leave and the stay-at-home allowance are women.

The eligibility conditions for the stay-at-home allowance have changed considerably over time. Called *Allocation Parentale d'Education* (APE), this allowance was first introduced in 1985 for parents who chose to stop working or to reduce the number of hours they worked when their third child was born. The allowance was paid for up to 36 months. Eligibility was extended to parents of a second child in 1994.

Policymakers clearly sought to encourage childcare by parents at home, but the stay-at-home allowance was also motivated by employment policy considerations. In this context, it was seen as a way to reduce the pressure on the labor market from the increasing supply of female workers. As a compromise between policy objectives, policymakers decided to exclude parents of a first child from the stay-at-home allowance. Aside from budget considerations, the intention was to avoid hampering women's careers (Thévenon 2006).

A reform in 2004, called the *Prestation d'Accueil du Jeune Enfant* (PAJE) ("young-child package"), extended the stay-at-home allowance to the first child, but for a shorter period and subject to specific eligibility criteria. Within the young-child package, an additional *Complément de Libre Choix d'Activité* (CLCA) is a stay-at-home supplement, available to parents of two or more children and payable for a maximum period of three years to a parent who chooses to stop working or to work less. In 2004, the right to this benefit was extended to parents of one child, but for a limited period of six months only.

In addition, parents of a third child can opt for the *Complément Optionnel de Libre Choix d'Activité* (COLCA) ("optional stay-at-home supplement"). This is a higher benefit (824 euros (US$934 as of 6 May 2015) per month in 2014, compared with 572 euros (US$649) for the CLCA, but it is paid for only 12 months. This benefit has enjoyed only limited success, however, since there were only 2600 recipients of the optional stay-at-home supplement at the full rate in 2008, which is only 1.7 % of the recipients of the CLCA.

Parents of very young children are entitled to take a relatively long period of parental leave compared with parents in other countries—almost 36 months for parents of at least two children. During this period, they may receive a fairly low, fixed stay-at-home allowance, amounting to slightly less than half of the minimum wage. The French leave entitlement thus differs from systems where leave is granted for a much shorter period but compensation is a percentage of the most recent salary (up to a ceiling). Overall, spending on maternity and parental leave is still relatively low in France compared with the Nordic countries and some eastern European countries.

A Variety of Childcare Options

Childcare is another important component of public support for families. There is a wide variety of support in France for different types of childcare. In 2012, 63 % of children under age three were cared for mainly by a parent, 4 % were cared for by a grandparent, 18 % were cared for outside their homes by an individual childminder, 10 % were cared for in a childcare center (*crèche*), 2 % were cared for in their homes by a non-family member (such as an *au pair* or a nanny), and 3 % were cared for through other arrangements (including public preschool).

The type of childcare chosen by parents is heavily dependent on their labor-market status and household income. As income rises, the share of care by parents decreases, and the share of formal childcare increases (especially care by a childminder or at-home care by a non-family member). Thus, 91 % of children from families in the lowest income quintile are mainly cared for by a parent, compared with only 31 % of children from families in the highest income quintile.

The stay-at-home allowance clearly encourages childcare by mothers, particularly given that 98 % of beneficiaries are female. Three-quarters of these mothers have incomes in the lowest or second lowest quintile.

Mothers who claim the stay-at-home allowance at the full rate (conditional on full-time leave from paid employment) are often motivated by low income, poor working conditions, or difficulties in managing the work-family balance because of atypical working hours. In 2008, an estimated 40 % of the (female) recipients of the full-rate allowance would have preferred to continue working, but they were unable to because their working conditions were too restrictive and they did not manage to find satisfactory childcare (HCF 2011). Indeed, the women who opted for parental leave (or to stop working) more frequently held a job with atypical working hours (64 %) than those who returned to work (45 %). The stay-at-home supplement is clearly more of an incentive for low-income households because the amount of the benefit is closer to the wage they are giving up, and it is similar to the childcare allowance provided for other types of childcare (Bechtel et al. 2005; HCF 2011). Most of the recipients of the stay-at-home allowance (70 %) received it for the maximum period (Legendre and Vanovermeir 2011).

Two-thirds of beneficiaries of the stay-at-home allowance eventually return to work, usually to the same job at the same hours. But more than one-fifth (22 %) of women who were working full time before the birth of their child choose to return to work part time. Among former beneficiaries of the stay-at-home allowance who are not working a few months after the allowance finishes, a majority (69 %) say this is due to difficulty finding a job, but another one-fifth say it is because they are receiving another similar allowance because they have had another child.[4] Women who interrupt their careers to take parental leave suffer a drop in salary after they return to work amounting to roughly 10 % for every year of leave they took, and this penalty persists over time (Lequien 2012).

Dual-earner families are more likely to make use of childcare centers. In 2007, 64 % of children under age three who had both parents working were enrolled at a childcare center, compared with 8 % of children for whom at least one parent was not working.

For children whose parents are both working full time, the pattern of childcare is rather different. For this group, 37 % are cared for by a childminder, 27 % by a parent (presumably in situations where the parents are working at different times), 18 % at a childcare center, 9 % by a grandparent, 4 % in their home by a non-family member, and 5 % through other arrangements. Here again, working conditions are key determinants of childcare arrangements in addition to household income, as longer working hours increase the probability of choosing a childminder or a childcare center as the main childcare solution during normal working hours. By contrast, grandparents and/or other family members are the main childcare providers at night or during weekends for parents with non-standard work schedules.

Differences in the "cost" to parents of the different childcare options explain the clear stratification of childcare arrangements by families' socio-economic status. Public childcare centers are clearly the most affordable option for households where both parents work full time and earn the minimum wage. At this income level, this type of childcare costs less than 5 % of household income, versus 10.6 % for a childminder (HCF 2013). By contrast, for households whose income is equivalent to six times the minimum wage, the cost of childcare centers is almost the same as that of a childminder.

For this reason, the "choice" of type of childcare is a decision that remains highly stratified by income level. Only 8 % of children from the least affluent families were cared for outside the family, compared with 68 % of children from the most affluent families.[5]

The diversification of support for different types of early-childhood care theoretically enables parents to choose the solution that best suits their preferences. One positive aspect of this diversity is the complementarity of financial support mechanisms, enabling parents to choose between different types of childcare.

---

[4]Other evaluations have highlighted the impact of the 1994 policy that extended the stay-at-home allowance to the second child. Piketty (2005) has estimated that this reform encouraged an additional 110,000 women to stop working. Over the long run, it seems that this allowance has held back the workforce participation rate of mothers of two children, compared with an increase in workforce participation among mothers of one child or of three children (Thévenon 2009).

[5]Additionally, 13 % of children from households in the lowest income quintile are cared for during the day by a childminder, compared with only 3 % of children from households in the first and second quintiles.

Furthermore, the continuity of support, which is uninterrupted during the first years of a child's life, is an advantage that enables many parents to adapt their childcare solutions to needs that change over time and with the age of the child. Yet while childcare services outside the home are theoretically accessible from a very early age (three months), actual access to different types of childcare remains highly stratified by household income and occupational constraints.

Despite the principle of freedom of choice underpinning the diversification of support, the French system is highly polarized, with support for childcare by parents and support for childcare outside the home benefiting the two ends of the social spectrum differentially. For the most affluent households, access to heavily subsidized childcare outside the home enables both parents to continue working. By contrast, the only choice for women from low-income households is to stop working for a fairly long period, with consequences that may be unanticipated for their ability to return to work and their future careers. In other words, the polarization of the system of childcare support reinforces rather than reduces pre-existing inequalities in workforce participation. Those inequalities are also gender biased: The overwhelming majority (96 %) of the beneficiaries of the stay-at-home allowance in 2008 were women, whereas most men stick to the 11 days of paternity leave to which they are entitled.

The increase in the number of births since the early 2000s and the decline in public preschool places available for children under age three[6] are putting pressure on the supply of childcare. Early-childhood services are expanding, but, while they compensate for the decline in preschool places, they are not "absorbing" the additional births that occur every year. The recent trend is thus an increase in individual at-home childcare by childminders (a 6 % average annual increase between 1995 and 2010) (Fig. 4). Childcare at childcare centers has also increased, but at a much slower pace. At the same time, the number of places in preschools for two-year-old children has contracted by 6 % on average.

The overall result after adding together all forms of childcare provisions is a net increase in the ratio of available places to children under age three (from 41.3 places per 100 children in 1995 to 57.2 in 2010). In other words, it appears that the reduction in preschool places for children under three has been counterbalanced by an expansion of individual and collective childcare options. The expansion of services is not keeping pace with births, however. If provision of early-childhood services is not increased, the number of beneficiaries of the stay-at-home allowance is likely to go up, by default more than by real choice, and the current inequality in access to different types of childcare by income and labor-market status will be reinforced.

[6]Free public preschool is provided for children age three to six in France. There are also a limited number of places in preschools for two-year-old children, but the priority is given to children age three and above, and the number of places available for younger children has shrunk. More than one-third (35 %) of two-year-olds attended preschool in 2000, but only 13.6 % in 2010.

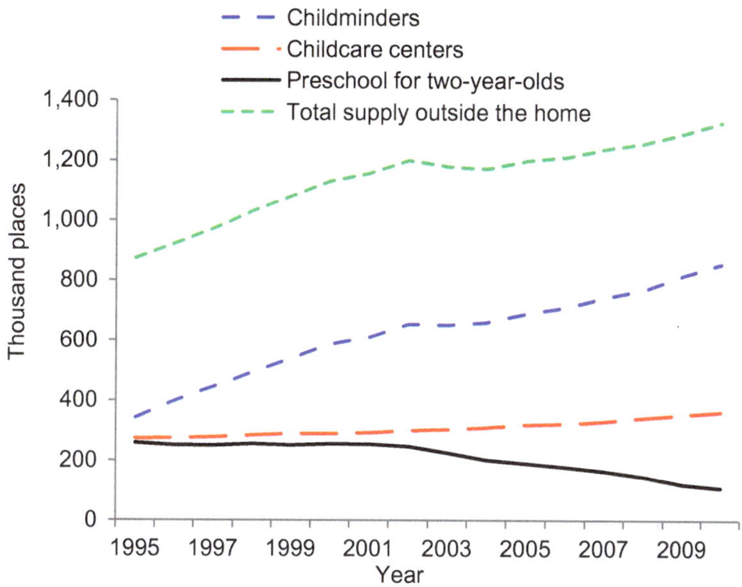

Fig. 4 Childcare provision outside the home, France, 1995–2010 (Vanovermeir (2012) based on DREES, CNAF, Ministry of Education, and IRCEM data). *Note* A childminder is defined as a certified worker who cares for children in his or her own (not the child's) home. Nannies and *au pairs* who care for children at the child's home, whether certified or not, are not included in this definition. For 1995, the number of two-year-olds in preschool is actually for 1994

Apart from childcare, other aspects of the institutional context also ease the work-life balance. In particular, the length of the school day—usually from 8:30 a.m. to 4:30 p.m. with lunch provided for 52 % of students in primary school and 62 % of those in high school—combined with the availability of after-school care (up to 6:00 p.m.) makes it possible for dual-earner families to combine full-time work or long part-time work with responsibility for children.

France is one of the few European countries where the majority of women's jobs are full time and the first child has little impact on the probability of having a full-time job. By contrast, the third child has a significant effect on female labor-market status (Thévenon 2009). As soon as a child enters the preschool system, the mother's work participation rate rises rapidly with the child's age, compared with most other countries where women return to work much later. Part-time work is not as common in France as in some other European countries, even though the proportion of mothers opting for reduced working hours has increased over recent decades. Among those working part time, the hours worked are fairly long compared with those in Germany, the Netherlands, or the United Kingdom, for instance.

The Impact of the Economic Crisis on Family Policies: Between Mitigation and Austerity

The financial crisis of 2008 led to adjustments in family policies that varied in nature and degree in different countries. In terms of social spending in general, these adjustments took place in two phases. Many countries initially increased family and housing benefits or introduced tax measures to cushion the impact of the crisis on household income. Subsequently, family benefits were scaled back in many countries as part of fiscal consolidation. Some governments (Greece, Hungary, the Netherlands, and the United Kingdom) froze family benefits or restricted eligibility, but few countries reduced the amounts allocated to early-childhood services. Overall, the net impact of the crisis was an increase in the percentage of national wealth allocated to family support over the 2007–2010 period.

In France as elsewhere, adjustments to family policies can be divided into two phases. Support measures to mitigate the impact of the crisis initially prevailed, in the form of tax breaks for low-income families as well as a 150-euro (US$170) bonus for low-income families with school-age children. Then, in the first quarter of 2012, the revaluation of family benefits was frozen, marking a change in direction toward reining in expenditure. But the main development in the second phase was the reform of 2013, which, although aimed at fixing the family support deficit by 2017, simultaneously reaffirmed certain priorities.

The lowering of the ceiling for tax breaks through the family quotient and the reduction in the amount of support paid under the young-child package, combined with a simultaneous increase in family supplements paid to low-income families, signaled a decision to refocus support on low-income families and to reaffirm the role of family support as a social policy instrument. The measures introduced in 2013 were rounded out with a reform of family allowance (paid to all families in France from the birth of a second child), which is now on a decreasing scale for households with monthly income above 6000 euros (US$6814). For mothers of at least two children, payment of the stay-at-home allowance during parental leave is now limited to 24 months, instead of 36 months as previously, although it can be extended if the father takes leave. The primary aim of these measures is to cut spending, although some hope that more fathers will be encouraged to take leave.

Most significantly, the reduction in financial support is occurring simultaneously with a major program to expand early-childhood services, with a target of 275,000 new places by 2018. A multi-year poverty-reduction and social-inclusion plan, also introduced in 2013, reinforces these measures by seeking to improve access to childcare places for disadvantaged families through a requirement to reserve 10 % of places for children from families living below the poverty line.

All in all, the package of support received by families from the state is very comprehensive in comparison to the benefits offered in other countries. First, it provides support with a balanced mix of cash, time (through leave entitlements), and services to respond to the diverse needs of families. A large set of benefits also actually provides assistance with income, housing, and social needs. Second, a broad spectrum of families receives support, including traditional and non-traditional families (e.g., married or not, couple families, single parents, poor and rich families, dual-earner and one-earner families, etc.), which encourages the belief that people will be supported when having children whatever their circumstances. Third, this support is continuous, with benefits in-cash and in-kind provided from early to late childhood. This comprehensive system of support is also quite consensual across stakeholders and political parties and has therefore benefited from a high level of stability over time. This stability is key for establishing the trust people need to become parents based on the assumption that they will receive long-term support once they have children.

What Is the Impact of Policies on Fertility?

Evaluating the Impact of Policies on Fertility: A Difficult Exercise

How can we know the precise contribution of France's family policies to fertility? Evaluating the impact of family support is no easy task. For one thing, the available literature on the situation in France requires that we qualify our conclusions because the impacts measured are small. Several factors make the exercise difficult because the evaluation approach is necessarily partial or invalid. Partial, because evaluations often consider only the impact of a specific measure. And they tend to be subject to two important limits. First, estimates of effects may be based on subgroups that are eligible for the intervention, and such groups often have specific characteristics that make their responses difficult to generalize.[7] Second, the effect of one measure may also depend on the existence of another, in which case the evaluation of one measure needs to take into account possible interactions with other measures with which it forms—or does not form—a consistent whole. For this reason, many of the available studies consider a group of measures together, for instance aggregating all financial support paid to some households. Certain aspects of the context may also alter the effects of a policy measure, and it is important to take these into account when doing policy evaluations. Comparative studies can help identify such variations in context that might alter the impact of specific policy measures on fertility.

Another factor that complicates the evaluation of the impact of family policies on fertility is that the decision to have a child is usually planned within a long time

[7]These studies are said to lack external validity, which can be due to the fact that the experience evaluated is limited to a highly specific sub-population with precise characteristics. This might be, for instance, a family policy measure (such as a financial-support mechanism) that targets a specific population group. The measure would not necessarily have a proportional impact if it were extended to the whole population. Similarly, there is no guarantee that the policy result would increase in the proportion measured by the experiment if the financial value of the mechanism were increased.

frame, and policies can influence the planning process at different points in time. Yet the impact of policies can take time to appear all along this decision-making process. Having a child first implies the formation of a more or less firm fertility intention, which various factors may cause to be realized or not. Those factors include the fulfilment of preliminary conditions for having a child, such as being in a stable relationship and having a stable job, some of which may be negotiated over fairly long timeframes between couples. One important parameter in the realization of fertility intentions seems to be the perception about the effects of having a child on a parent's personal life (Ajzen and Klobas 2013). The realization of a fertility intention involves the conception phase, which is itself a process that can take time, prior to the birth of a child, which is the observable datum for the demographer. Policies—and more broadly the institutional context—may influence the various parameters of the decision at various stages in the process between the intention to have a child and its realization. A complete assessment of the influence of policies thus requires a long period of observation, which is lacking in many studies that focus on short-term consequences of a policy reform. By focusing on the short term, a risk lies in identifying only the windfall effects, which are the first to appear, and minimizing the real changes in behavior that show up in the longer term. The period covered by the policy evaluation is therefore a parameter that conditions the size of the impact measured.

Moreover, a policy can take a long time to have an impact, often only after households have had sufficient time to test its effects and its long-term stability. The effectiveness of a policy may be increased if it is perceived to encompass a long period of childhood, rather than being limited to children at very young ages. These factors are particularly important when it comes to fertility, which is a long-term, irreversible decision. The stability of family policies is therefore an essential parameter for household confidence.

Another difficulty is that the mechanisms by which a policy may affect fertility are diverse. Some policies may be aimed explicitly at influencing fertility (through cash subsidies, for instance), while others may have an indirect (and potentially unintended) impact on fertility. In particular, policies that ease the work-family conflict also have an impact on fertility, although this is often not their goal. The effect on fertility is likely to appear after or at the same time as the impact on labor-market behavior. Paradoxically, a comprehensive literature review suggests that the measures introduced with the explicit objective of supporting fertility have had a fairly limited impact, whereas measures designed to support the work-family balance or to raise living standards appear to have a more tangible impact on fertility, even though this was not their primary aim (Thévenon and Gauthier 2011).

These standard precautions voiced, it is nonetheless possible to review the few studies of the impact of family policies on fertility in France. These evaluate different aspects of family policies. We shall begin with those that deal with the combined impact of financial incentives or the impact of a specific measure, such as the family quotient for the third child or the stay-at-home allowance.

Financial Support Has an Impact, but It Is Limited

By estimating the impact on fertility of financial transfers to families unrelated to employment, Ekert (1986) was the first to measure the cumulative impact of the family allowance, family supplement, and housing benefit in the 1970s. While their impact was not negligible, it was limited, pushing up the fertility rate by around 0.2 births per woman. The author believed that full compensation of the cost of raising a child through benefits would have increased the fertility rate by only 0.3 births per woman.

The impact of the tax and social-welfare system on labor-market and fertility behavior was estimated by a micro-simulation model (Laroque and Salanié 2014). This takes account of the interactions between mothers' labor-market and fertility behavior, as well as the possible interactions between different welfare benefits and tax measures. The results are highly dependent on the assumptions used to model the behavior, however, evidenced by the large differences, and even contradictions, in the results obtained by these authors in the three successive versions of their work. The influence of financial transfers on fertility seems to be significant, but the policies are costly. It is estimated that the provision of one additional unconditional child credit of 150 euros (US$170) per month—which would cost 0.3 % of GDP—would potentially only raise fertility by 3.3 % points, equivalent to about 0.06 births per woman, and would reduce female labor force participation by about 0.5 % points. The impact would vary by birth order, with the strongest effect for third-order births.

The reform of the family quotient in 1981 made the third child equivalent to an adult in calculating the tax reduction, instead of a half-adult as used previously. This reform provides an interesting case for assessing the impact of taxation on third-order fertility (Landais 2003). The impact is positive but very small. A 1 % change in tax relief for a third child seems to have boosted the proportion of households with three children by no more than 0.05 %. In addition, the reform was slow to take effect, taking 5–10 years. The impact was more pronounced on higher-income households, for whom the benefit of tax reduction is higher.

Breton and Prioux (2005) take a longer-term perspective by looking at all the reforms that have affected support for a third child since 1970. Very similar cyclical variations from 1970 to 2000 are observed in the probabilities of having a second or a third child. They are fairly congruent with the policy measures aimed at encouraging families to have a third child. This suggests that these measures may have influenced not only the decision to have a third child but also the decision to have a second child, with a view to possibly having a third child later on. In other words, these voluntarist policies may have contagiously influenced a population that is not immediately targeted.

The Impact of Support for the Work-Family Balance

The propensity to have a third child seems much more sensitive to the measures targeting households with three children introduced in the late 1970s and 1980s. These measures had a visible impact on the timing of births and also seem to have contributed to the stability or even to a slight increase in the probability of having a third child until the late 1980s. Among these measures, a home-care allowance was introduced in 1985 for working parents with three or more children having a career interruption for up to three years. This home-care allowance seems to have made a particularly strong contribution to maintaining fertility, even if it is hard to quantify its precise impact. When the home-care allowance was extended to the second child in 1994, the probability of having a second child increased, but the probability of having a third child decreased significantly.

The specific impact of the home-care allowance on second-order fertility is also analyzed by Piketty (2005), who takes into account the fact that the measure can influence the employment status of women even before fertility because that is its primary aim. It is important to be able to estimate what the total number of second- and third-order births would have been without the reform in order to distinguish the causal impact from the windfall effects of births that would have occurred even without the reform. Piketty finds that the reform of the home-care allowance accounted for no more than 20–30 % of the total increase in births observed between 1994 and 2001—at most 10 % of third-order births and 10–20 % of second-order births.

The impact on fertility is preceded by an impact on women's workforce participation. The extension of the home-care allowance to parents of second children appears to have directly caused 100,000–150,000 mothers of two children to interrupt their careers (out of a total of 220,000 withdrawals from the workforce). According to Moschion (2010), a high percentage of women decided to withdraw from the workforce after the birth of a second child, whereas before the extension to second births, this withdrawal would have occurred more frequently after the birth of a third child. The reform seems mainly to have induced temporary withdrawals from the workforce, however, without altering the propensity to return to work. Over the 12 years following the reform, workforce participation (including full time) of women with two children has increased at a comparable rate to that of childless women and women with one child—albeit with a lag corresponding to the years immediately following the introduction of the reform (Thévenon 2009).

These evaluations show that the policies that provide financial support to families or that enable a short interruption of work after the birth of a child have a positive impact on fertility. The identified impacts are nevertheless small and insufficient to explain why France now has the highest fertility rate in Europe, combined with a relatively high female workforce-participation rate. Compared with women in many other European countries, more French women manage to work full time with a child regardless of the age of the child, and more work part time for a relatively long number of hours. The frequency of part-time work increases with a second child and even more with a third child (Thévenon 2009).

The Work-Family Balance: A Key Issue for Fertility

To understand how family policies contribute to the high fertility rate in France, it is useful to compare fertility trends between countries over several decades and attempt to measure the impact of policies on trend differentials. Several studies document the impact of policies on fertility differentials in Europe and other economically advanced countries (see in particular, Gauthier and Hatzius 1997; Kalwij 2010; Harknett et al. 2014; and the literature review by Thévenon and Gauthier 2011). One of the most recent is the study by Luci-Greulich and Thévenon (2013), which estimates the impact of family policies by taking into account their three standard components:

- Leave for the birth of a child, considering differences in the length of leave and the average amount per child paid for leave or as a baby bonus
- Other forms of financial support, measured as an average amount per child under age 18
- The provision of early-childhood services, characterized by the coverage rate and the average expenditure per child under age three

Results suggest that all forms of support have a positive impact on fertility, all other things being equal, and that a combination of these types of support is likely to boost fertility. The impact of the length of leave and associated payments appears, on average, particularly small compared with the impact of coverage of childcare services for children under age three. Furthermore, the impact of the different measures is not uniform across countries and varies according to the overall characteristics of family policies. Thus, financial support has a comparatively larger impact in the Nordic countries, where childcare coverage is relatively high and leave comparatively generous. Conversely, the impact of childcare coverage is larger in "continental" Europe where the coverage rate is lower than in the Nordic countries and where financial support is massive. Overall, these differences suggest that a certain balance between the different measures is likely to have the biggest impact on fertility.

In light of these results, the success of French family policies seems to lie in the diversified system of support that provides parents with supplementary resources in the form of money, time, and services needed to raise children. All of these forms of support and the variety of types of childcare available make the decision to have a child less dependent on the parents', particularly the mother's, employment status. Measuring the respective contribution of each type of support is probably impossible, especially as the total combined impact of all these measures is certainly greater than the sum of the impact of each individual measure, owing to their overall and historic consistency and the confidence that this consistency generates.

Challenges for French Family Policies in an Aging Society

Population aging will necessitate, in the short or medium term, a major adaptation of family policies, particularly measures enabling households to manage the work-family balance. Increasing the supply of childcare services and support for families stands out as a priority, given the positive impact of such measures on the retention of mothers in the workforce and ultimately on fertility. The positive influence of enrolment in childcare services on child development and later accumulation of human capital is an additional motivation to further invest in care and education services.

Population Aging Will Increase Demand for Measures to Support the Work-Family Balance

In France as in other economically advanced countries, population aging is manifested in a sharp increase in the percentage of elderly people. Population projections for France suggest that, by 2060, the number of men and women age 80 and above will have increased sharply, and the number of dependent elderly people will have practically doubled, from 1.15 million in 2010 to 2.3 million in 2060. Given that increases in life expectancy will drive the aging process, changes in fertility will have only a limited impact on the age structure of the population (Fig. 5).

As is already the case now, women will represent a larger percentage of the elderly population than men, despite faster gains in male life expectancy. Compared with the current situation, more women, but fewer men, will live with a spouse. The percentage of women with a surviving spouse will nevertheless still be much lower than for men (Charpin 2011). For both sexes, the presence of at least one surviving child will be much more likely, and these children will be the main potential family caregivers. The evolution of health status at very old ages and the impact of the increase in the number of couples who are separated remain unknowns, however, that create uncertainty about the conditions surrounding aging.

In any case, population aging in France implies an increase in the number of dependent elderly people, whose need for care will be added to the needs of children. Given the increasing age at motherhood, the cohorts born since the 1960s are highly likely to have to care simultaneously for a very young child and a very elderly parent (Mason and Zagheni 2014). This "double burden" should become less frequent for future cohorts, however, as the timing of childbirth stabilizes, fertility rates fall, and life expectancy increases. On the contrary, future cohorts will

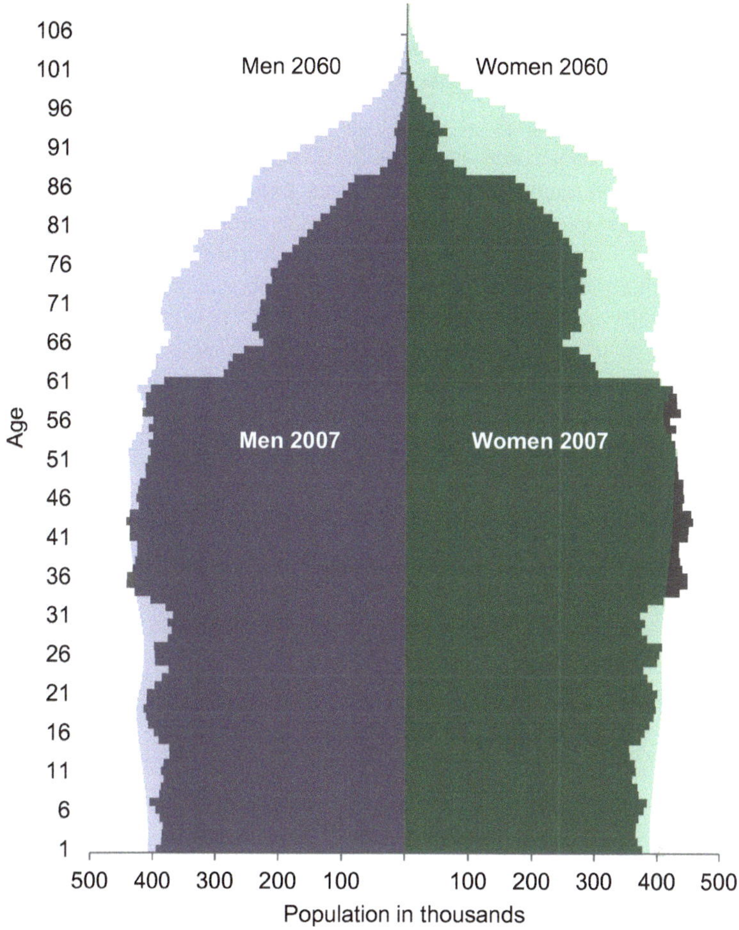

Fig. 5 Aging population in metropolitan France: population age and sex profile in 2007 and projected for 2060 (INSEE 2015)

more frequently become grandparents at an age when they will also have a dependent spouse, and this probability will increase with each subsequent cohort.

In the context of populating aging, the main priorities for family social policies will be to improve the dependency ratio, particularly by extending the workforce participation of seniors (both men and women), and to finance public support for the most vulnerable segments of the population. This also involves facilitating the training of the human capital needed to expand France's system of social protection. Three directions in family policies contribute to these objectives:

- Support for the work-family balance (in a context where the need to balance work and family is occurring at a later age with a double burden of having to care simultaneously for children and elderly parents)

- Gender equality in paid work and care (required to maintain the workforce in employment and provide care at the same time)
- Investment in children's early education and development (key for human-capital formation and to help households bear the cost of raising children)

These policy directions seem desirable for several economic and ethical reasons: favoring retention in employment and avoiding losses of human capital; enabling young adults both to pursue a career and have children; encouraging gender equality; and reducing the social inequality in learning and development that appears early in childhood and is reflected in the inequality in access to childcare outside the family according to household income. These policy directions also seem desirable in terms of fertility, given the result presented by Harknett et al. (2014) that suggest that inter-generational obligations (having to rely on grand-parents to mind children and caring for dependent parents in the absence of alter-natives) have a negative impact on fertility.

Parental Leave Will Have to Be Adapted to Encourage Gender Equality

The relevance of the current mechanisms of support in terms of leave is worth reconsidering in the light of the policy directions evoked above. Leave entitlements enable parents who work to suspend their employment contracts in order to care for dependents, whether children or parents. Caring for young children or for depen-dent elderly parents implies different time constraints, however.

The time that parents need to care for new babies is usually predictable and lasts only a few years. Parental leave enables parents to leave their jobs or reduce their working hours for a period ranging from six months (for the first child) up to several years (for parents of at least two children). As noted earlier, women account for almost all (96 %) of the recipients of parental leave, no doubt partly because the low level of the home-care allowance does not compensate for the generally higher income of men.

In this context, the international literature on the impact of leave suggests that mothers' and fathers' propensity to take parental leave is sensitive to two param-eters: leave entitlements for exclusive use by each parent and the level of com-pensation (OECD 2011). Most countries that encourage fathers to take days off for paternity leave offer compensation proportional to salary (up to a ceiling). Since men very often earn more than their wives, their leave entails a smaller loss of income when the compensation is proportional to their salary than when it is a fixed amount, which tends to be much lower. From this perspective, the current format of parental leave in France—combining a relatively long period with a fixed benefit equal to about half of the minimum wage and no paternal or maternal quotas—does little to encourage fathers to take leave and is thus unfavorable to gender equality. In 2014, the French government decided to reduce to 24 months (from 36 months) the maximum period during which a parent can receive the home-care allowance, with the other 12 months paid only if the other parent takes leave. Even though one of the stated aims of this measure is to encourage fathers to take parental leave, it is unlikely to have a major impact on fathers' behavior without a change in the level of compensation. On the contrary, the measure is more likely to reduce the total number of months the benefit will be paid, and this will cut spending, which is the main objective of the reform.[8]

Employees who have to care for a dependent elderly parent are in a different situation and usually have occasional and unpredictable time needs. To meet those needs, employees with at least two years' service in their company can ask their employer for family-caregiver leave, which is granted for three months renewable, up to one year of interruption, if their parent is severely incapacitated.[9] This leave does not come with any financial compensation. Moreover, it cannot be taken for periods of less than three months or part time and is only granted after a notice period of two months (which may be reduced to two weeks in case of emergency). This type of leave only very partially meets the needs of employees who have to care for a parent on an unpredictable or occasional basis. Family-caregiver leave could be made more flexible by allowing it to be split into shorter periods or taken part time (HCF 2011). Eligibility is also very restrictive, since only an employee whose parent has a severe incapacity that is recognized by social insurance is entitled to apply.

Services to Support Young Children and Their Families

The expansion of care and education services for young children is a particularly relevant policy objective in the context of population aging. The positive impact on several aspects of population aging justifies a special emphasis on supporting the expansion of childcare and education services.

The first benefit identified both in France and in the international literature is the positive impact of collective childcare before age three on children's cognitive, emotional, and social development, as well as on performance when they enter the primary school system and even beyond[10] (for France, see Caillé 2003; Dumas and Lefranc 2012; Goux and Maurin 2010; and the literature review by Ruhm and

[8]Moreover, we can fear that, unless fathers are highly motivated, those most inclined to stop working to take long leave will most likely be employees on low incomes, whose spouses also earns a relatively low income. An increase in the risk of poverty can therefore be expected in families that make this choice.

[9]Employees with a parent whose life is in danger can also apply for family leave. This type of leave, of three months' duration, renewable once, can be taken part time and includes daily compensation that can be received for up to 21 days.

[10]Some studies suggest that access to preschool education is a positive factor in workforce participation and welfare uptake (Havnes and Mogstadt 2011; Algan et al. 2012).

Waldfogel 2011). Moreover, the benefits are clearly identified and higher for children from disadvantaged families, which justifies the expansion of early-childhood services from a perspective of equity as well as efficacy. Eventually, the goal should be to provide children from the earliest age with the resources they need to be successful at school and in the labor market. French society stands to reap collective benefits, in addition to individual gains, if policies aimed at early childhood lead to a lower school-dropout rate, better performance in school, and better workforce integration in the long term.

Expanding access to early-childhood services also has a positive impact on women's employment and the retention of women in the workforce after the birth of children, which is another strong motivation for countries to support it. Human capital and productivity gains can therefore be expected, which help counterbalance the increase in the number of non-workers compared with workers that accompanies the extension of life expectancy. Lastly, the positive impact, mentioned earlier, that increasing coverage of care for children under age three seems to have on fertility is a third lever for mitigating population aging.

As discussed above, France is one of the countries that devotes a high percentage of national wealth to childcare—1.8 % of GDP allocated to all services for children under age six, compared with a European average of 0.95 %. Yet, the estimated shortfall in childcare places for children under three relative to demand could be 400,000 (roughly half of all annual births). The French government has therefore launched a program to expand services with the target of creating 275,000 additional places (100,000 in childcare centers, 100,000 with childminders, and 75,000 in preschools for two-year-olds).

Various factors have led to an in-depth discussion of a unified strategy for children and adolescents. Some of these factors have prompted a review of the structural capacity of the French system to respond to "new" forms of inequality affecting children: the increase in the dropout rate and educational inequality, reflected in part in the OECD's Program for International Student Assessment (PISA) surveys; the impact of the economic crisis on families' standard of living, with almost 440,000 children falling below the poverty line since 2008 (Fanjul 2014); and the difficulties that some parents have with parenting, which suggests the need to strengthen support for parents (Jacquey-Vazquez et al. 2013).

The current discussion aims to establish a consistent framework for action by the different actors that provide services for children and their families around a common core underpinned by the concept of "complete child development" (de Singly and Wisnia-Weill 2015). This concept reflects the need to take into account the possible interactions between children's cognitive, emotional, and social development. It also seeks to encourage actors that provide services for children and their families to better coordinate their actions *in space* (by considering the needs of children and parents together in terms of health, social welfare, and education) and *in time* (by monitoring the actions targeting different segments of the population more effectively over time). Policymakers appear to be seeking a real paradigm shift in action for young children by reviewing the content of the services provided, their complementarity, and the boundaries sometimes created between families and institutions, with a view to adapting support to the different needs of children, families, and other target groups.

Conclusion

The objectives of French family policies have become more diverse over time. They are no longer aimed exclusively at increasing fertility and improving living standards for families, but now seek to support the work-family balance. The range of mechanisms that can influence fertility has thus broadened, although it is not always possible—or even useful—to determine the respective impact of each measure. Most of the studies identified find that the various measures that make up family policy have a positive but small impact on fertility. Financial support, parental leave, and childcare services play complementary roles. In particular, childcare has become crucial to the balance between childrearing and the workforce participation of both parents.

In this regard, France is one of the countries with the most diverse ranges of support. The French system is the result of a historical process characterized by high stability and a strong consensus. This stability gives confidence to families that they will benefit from continuous support from the birth of a child until entry into the school system and beyond and that this support will be adapted to their needs in terms of time, income, and services. Such confidence creates a favorable environment for the decision to have children.

The economic crisis of 2008 triggered a change in family policies, however, by accentuating the redistributive nature of financial-support mechanisms (via a reduction in support for affluent households and a slight increase in support targeting poor households) and by favoring the expansion of early-childhood services. At the same time, the crisis has pushed many families into poverty and made it harder for some households to attain a standard of living favorable to children's care and education. In addition, population aging is creating new needs in terms of the work-family balance. In this context, an issue of vital importance in the years ahead will be to increase the number of places available in childcare facilities and to improve their quality in order to respond to the diversification of families' profiles and needs. Furthermore, population aging makes it even more necessary that men and women share the care of children and elderly dependent parents more equally, and reform of France's family leave policy can encourage this trend. The rising housing costs borne by families and single parents will also require policy adjustments.

One of the primary virtues of French family policy is that it does not force individuals to choose between pursuing a career, starting a family, or fulfilling their duty of care to their parents. A key aspect of policy success is the confidence and trust that French families have in policy effectiveness and consistency. The adjustments suggested here seem essential to maintaining that confidence and trust.

References

Ajzen, I., & Klobas, J. (2013). Fertility intentions: An approach based on the theory of planned behavior. *Demographic Research, 29*(8), 203–232.

Algan, Y., Beasley, E., Tremblay, R. E., & Vitaro, F. (2012). *The long-term impact of social skills training at school entry: A randomized controlled trial*. Paris: Sciences Po.

Bechtel, J., Caussat, L., Courtioux, P., Laib, N., Le Minez, S., & Mirouse, B. (2005). La politique familiale française: Coûts et bénéficiaires. In M. Godet & E. Sullerot (Eds.), *La famille, une affaire publique* (pp. 409–37). CAE Rapport no. 57. Paris: Conseil d'Analyse Economique.

Breton, D., & Prioux, F. (2005). Deux ou trois enfants? Influence de la politique familiale et de quelques facteurs sociodémographs. *Population, 60*(4), 489–522.

Breton, D., & Prioux, F. (2009). The one-child family: France in the European context. *Demographic Research, 20*(27), 657–692.

Caillé, J.-P. (2003). Faut-il développer la scolarisation à deux ans? *Éducation et formations, 66*, 7–11.

Charpin, J. M. (2011). *Perspectives démographiques et financières de la dépendance*. Rapport de groupe de travail. Paris: Ministère de la Cohésion Sociale.

Courgeau, D., & Lelièvre, E. (1992). Interrelations between first home ownership, constitution of the family, and professional occupation in France. In J. Trussel, R. Hankinson, & J. Tilton (Eds.), *Demographic applications of event history analysis* (pp. 120–140). Oxford: Oxford University Press.

Davie, E., & Mazuy, M. (2010). Women's fertility and educational level in France: Evidence from annual census surveys. *Population, 65*(3), 415–450.

de La Rochebrochard, E., Troude, P., Bailly, E., Guibert, J., & Bouyer, J. (2011). Rentrer à la maison avec un bébé après avoir initié un traitement par fécondation in vitro. *Actualité et Dossier en Santé Publique: Revue du Haut Conseil de la Santé Publique, 75*, 20–23.

de Singly, F., & Wisnia-Weill, V. (2015). Pour un développement complet des enfants et des adolescents. Rapport de la Commission Enfance et Adolescence. France Stratégie. http://www.strategie.gouv.fr/sites/strategie.gouv.fr/files/atoms/files/fs_rapport_commission_enfance_29092015_bat.pdf.

Debest, C., & Mazuy, M. (2014). Childlessness: A life choice that goes against the norm. *Population and Societies, 508*.

Debré, R., & Sauvy, A. (1946). *Des français pour la France: Le problème de la population*. Paris: Gallimard.

Desplanques, G. (2011). Les disparités géographiques de fécondité en France. *Espaces, Population, Sociétés, 2011*(3), 459–473.

Dumas, C., & Lefranc, A. (2012). Early schooling and later outcomes: Evidence from pre-school extension in France. In J. Ermisch, M. Jäntti, & T. M. Smeeding (Eds.), *From parents to children: The intergenerational transmission*. New York: Russell Sage Foundation.

Ekert, O. (1986). Effets et limites des aides financière aux familles: Une expérience et un modèle. *Population, 41*(2), 327–348.

Fanjul, G. (2014). *Children of the recession: The impact of the economic crisis on child well-being in rich countries*. Innocenti Report Card 12. Florence: UNICEF Office of Research.

Gauthier, A., & Hatzius, J. (1997). Family benefits and fertility: An econometric analysis. *Population Studies, 51*(3), 295–306.

Goux, D., & Maurin, E. (2010). Public school availability for two-year olds and mothers' labor supply. *Labor Economics, 17*, 951–962.

Harknett, K., Billari, F. C., & Meladia, C. (2014). Do family support environments influence fertility? Evidence from 20 European countries. *European Journal of Population, 30*(1), 1–33.

Havnes, T., & Mogstadt, M. (2011). No child left behind: Universal child care and children's long-run outcomes. *American Economic Journal: Economic Policy, 3*(2), 97–129.

HCF (Haut conseil de la famille). (2011). *Architecture des aides aux familles: Quelles évolutions pour les 15 prochaines années?* Memo. April 28, 2011. Paris: Haut conseil de la famille.

HCF (Haut conseil de la famille). (2012). *Familles et logement.* Memo 14/05. http://www.hcf-famille.fr/IMG/pdf/note_logement_14maiVb.pdf. Accessed November 13, 2015.

HCF (Haut conseil de la famille). (2013). *Point sur l'évolution de l'accueil des enfants des enfants de moins de trois ans.* http://www.hcf-famille.fr/IMG/pdf/point_accueil_jeunes_enfants13_juin_2013.pdf. Accessed November 13, 2015.

Human Fertility Database. (2015). *Max Planck Institute for Demographic Research and Vienna Institute of Demography.* http://www.humanfertility.org/. Accessed November 13, 2015.

INSEE (Institute national de la statistique et des études économiques). (2015). *Indicateurs clés: Population.* http://www.insee.fr/fr/default.asp. Accessed May 14, 2015.

Jacquey-Vazquez, B., Sitruk, P., & Raymond, M. (2013). *Evaluation de la politique de soutien à la parentalité.* Paris: Inspection Générale des Affaires Sociales.

Kalwij, A. (2010). The impact of family policy expenditures on fertility in Western Europe. *Demography, 47*(2), 503–519.

Landais, C. (2003). Le quotient familial a-t-il stimulé la natalité française? *Économie publique, 13* (2), 3–31.

Laroque, G., & Salanié, B. (2014). Identifying the response of fertility to financial incentives. *Journal of Applied Econometrics, 29*, 314–322.

Legendre, E., & Vanovermeir, S. (2011). *Situations professionnelles à l'entrée et à la sortie du complément de libre choix d'activité (CLCA).* Etudes et Résultats No. 750. Paris: Direction de la recherche, des études, de l'évaluation et des statistiques (DREES), l'Administration centrale des ministères sanitaires et sociaux.

Lequien, L. (2012). The impact of parental leave duration on later wages. *Annals of Economics and Statistics, 107*(108), 267–285.

Luci-Greulich, A., & Thévenon, O. (2013). The impact of family policies on fertility trends in developed countries. *European Journal of Population, 29*(4), 387–416.

Mason, C., & Zagheni, E. (2014). *The sandwich generation: Demographic determinants of global trends.* Paper presented at the European Population Conference, Budapest.

Mazuy, M., Barbieri, M., & d'Albis, H. (2013). Recent demographic development in France: Fertility remains stable. *Population-E, 68*(3), 329–374.

Moschion, J. (2010). Reconciling work and family life: The effect of the French paid parental leave. *Annales d'économie et de statistiques, 99*(100), 217–246.

Mulder, C. H. (2006). Population and housing: A two-sided relationship. *Demographic Research, 15*(13), 401–412.

Mulder, C. H., & Billari, F. (2010). Home-ownership regimes and low fertility. *Housing Studies, 5* (4), 527–541.

OECD (Organization for Economic Cooperation and Development). (2011). *Doing better for families.* Paris: OECD Publishing.

OECD (Organization for Economic Cooperation and Development). (2014). *OECD Family Database.* http://www.oecd.org/social/family/database.htm. Accessed May 13, 2015.

Piketty, T. (2005). L'impact de l'allocation parentale d'éducation sur l'activité féminine et la fécondité en France, 1982–2002. In C. Lefèvre (Ed.), *Histoires de familles, histoires familiales: Les Cahiers de l'Ined*, 156 (pp. 79–109).

Prioux, F. (2007). L'évolution démographique récente en France: La fécondité à son plus haut niveau depuis plus de trente ans. *Population, 62*(3), 489–532.

Rosental, P.-A. (2003). *L'intelligence démographique: Sciences et politiques des populations en France (1930–1960).* Paris: Odile Jacob.

Ruhm, C. J., & Waldfogel, J. (2011). *Long-term effects of early childhood care and education.* IZA Discussion Paper No. 6149. Bonn: Institute for the Study of Labor (IZA).

Testa, M. R. (2012). *Family sizes in Europe: Evidence from the 2011 Eurobarometer Survey.* European Demographic Research Papers 2. Vienna: Vienna Institute of Demography, Austrian Academy of Sciences.

Thévenon, O. (2006). Régimes d'Etat Social et convention familiale: Une analyse des régulations emploi-famille. *Economies et Sociétés, série Socio-Economie du Travail, 27*(6), 1137–71. https://halshs.archives-ouvertes.fr/hal-00407181/document. Accessed November 13, 2015.

Thévenon, O. (2009). Increased women's labor force participation in Europe: Progress in the work-life balance or polarization of behaviors? *Population, 64*(2), 235–272.

Thévenon, O. (2011a). Does fertility respond to work and family-life reconciliation policies in France? In N. Takayama & M. Werding (Eds.), *Fertility and public policy: How to reverse the trend of declining birth rates*. Cambridge: MIT Press.

Thévenon, O. (2011b). Family policies in OECD countries: A comparative analysis. *Population and Development Review, 37*(1), 57–87.

Thévenon, O., & Gauthier, A. (2011). Family policies in developed countries: A fertility booster with side-effects. *Community, Work, and Family, 14*(2), 197–216.

Toulemon, L., Pailhé, A., & Rossier, C. (2008). France: High and stable fertility. *Demographic Research, 19*(16), 503–556.

Vanovermeir, S. (2012). *L'accueil des jeunes enfants: Axe majeur de la politique familiale française depuis les années 1970.* Dossiers Solidarité et Santé 31. Paris: Direction de la recherche, des études, de l'évaluation et des statistiques (DREES), l'Administration centrale des ministères sanitaires et sociaux.

Fertility and Population Change in the United Kingdom

Wendy Sigle

Britain is insular, bound up by its trade, its markets...with the most varied and often the most distant countries.... She has, in all her work, very special, very original habits and traditions. In short, the nature, structure, circumstances peculiar to Britain are different from those of the other continentals.... How can Britain, being what she is, come into our system?

—Charles de Gaulle, Paris 1963

Abstract As in most wealthy countries, the United Kingdom (UK) population is aging and is set to continue to age for the next several decades. Recent and projected rates of change in the share of the elderly population are slow, however, compared to most other European Union (EU)-27 countries. Although since 1998 net migration has played some role, the UK's relatively benign demographic profile has much to do with its relatively high fertility rates. Population issues, low fertility in particular, are not considered to be a major policy concern or an appropriate target for government intervention. A combination of moderately high fertility and high female employment has (at least historically) been achieved without implementing the kinds of work-family reconciliation policies that are credited with sustaining fertility elsewhere in Europe. A *laissez-faire* approach to the economy and residual approach to welfare may well have sustained UK fertility levels by facilitating childbearing in more socio-economically disadvantaged families. Recent, path-deviant, work-family reconciliation policies have been adopted, but the wider institutional context has moderated their potential to reduce the costs of childbearing.

Keywords United kingdom · Comparative policy · Welfare regimes · Work-family reconciliation

W. Sigle (✉)
London School of Economics, Gender Institute, London, UK
e-mail: W.Sigle@lse.ac.uk

R.R. Rindfuss and M.K. Choe (eds.), *Low Fertility, Institutions, and their Policies*, DOI 10.1007/978-3-319-32997-0_4

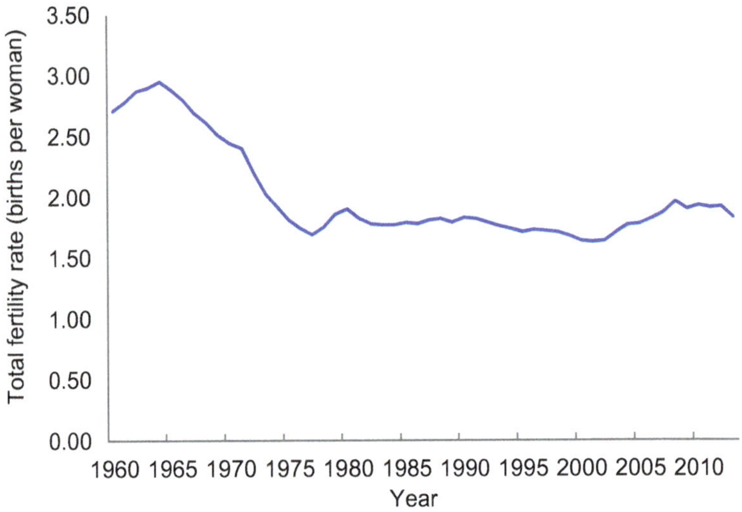

Fig. 1 The UK total fertility rate, 1960–2013 (Office for National Statistics 2012a). *Note* 2010-based national population projections

In 1985, the United Kingdom (UK) had one of the oldest populations in Europe. With 15 % of its population age 65 and older, it ranked second only to Sweden (with 17 %) among the countries that now comprise the European Union (EU)-27 (Office for National Statistics 2012b). A baby boom in the 1960s was followed in the next decade by a substantial fall in the number of births. In 1976, the number of deaths exceeded the number of births for the first time in the 20th century. Numbers of recorded births only started to recover in the early 1980s, in part because the 1960s baby-boom cohorts were entering their reproductive years. Over this same period, the total fertility rate (TFR) fell from nearly 3.0 births per woman to a low of 1.69 (in 1977), eventually stabilizing at around 1.8 in the early 1980s (Fig. 1).

Twenty-five years later, depending on how you look at it, the UK did not appear to be quite so old. The UK population had continued to age, but the pace of change was slow compared with most of the rest of Europe. In 2010, the percentage of the population age 65 and older was slightly below the EU-27 average, and the UK looked relatively well placed to support a larger elderly population. The UK's fall from the top to the middle of the European rankings has much to do with its relatively stable and moderately high fertility rates. Over the entire period from 1985 until 2010, the TFR averaged 1.75. Between 1985 and 1990, the TFR increased slightly from 1.79 to 1.83, after which it fell year on year reaching a low of 1.63 in 2001. From that point, though, it rebounded rapidly, and in 2007, the TFR reached 1.87. In subsequent years (at least until 2013[1]), it has consistently

[1]According to estimates from the Office for National Statistics, the provisional TFR for the United Kingdom in 2013 was 1.83 (Office for National Statistics 2014b).

exceeded 1.9 (Fig. 1). Along with Sweden, France, and Ireland, the UK currently ranks as one of the highest-fertility countries in the European Union.

The UK has recorded positive net immigration since 1994, with marked increases after 2001 and then again after 2004. The new arrivals had a rapid impact on the size and age structure of the UK population.[2] Because young, working-age adults tend to be over-represented in the migrant population, net migration has had a moderating effect on population aging by increasing the relative size of the population below age 65. Moreover, many of the young migrants have gone on to have children after they arrived in the UK. Births to non-UK-born women account for around two-thirds of the increase in the number of births between 2001 and 2007 (Tromans et al. 2009) and more than 69 % of the increase between 2007 and 2011 (Zumpe et al. 2012). In the period from 2004 to 2011, however, the slightly higher period fertility of non-UK-born women elevated the UK TFR by only around 0.1 children (Tromans et al. 2009; Zumpe et al. 2012). This means that trends in TFR since 2004 are largely due to increasing fertility among UK-born women.

While recent demographic trends have reduced the pace of population aging and its potentially negative impact on the British economy and society, they have also brought fairly rapid, and not entirely anticipated, population growth. According to the 2011 census, the UK population was 500,000 higher than suggested in the 2010 population projections (Office for National Statistics 2013). The 7 % increase in the total population recorded in the 2011 census was the largest decennial growth in the UK population since 1961. Put another way, about one-half of the population growth since 1964 took place in the past decade.

Projections indicate that by 2035 the old-age-dependency ratio in the UK will increase to 37.9 (European Commission 2012, p. 299, Tables A.11 and A.12). While an increase in the elderly population to 23 % (European Commission 2012, p. 299, Table A.12) is not insubstantial, it represents a modest pace of change relative to what has been projected for many other EU (European Union) countries. By 2035, only four of the EU-27 countries are projected to have a smaller share of older people in their populations (Office for National Statistics 2012b). If recent projections are accurate, the UK could have, in the course of 50 years, gone from being one of the oldest to one of the youngest countries in Europe.

Whether this demographic future materializes depends, of course, on whether the projections are based on an accurate depiction of future trends. As the largest component of population change, the accuracy of fertility assumptions is particularly important. The 2010-based projections assume that completed family size will fall gradually from 1.98 for the cohort of women born in 1960 and stabilize at around 1.84 for cohorts born from 2005 onwards.[3] Is this realistic or likely?

[2]Between 2001 and 2006, the share of the foreign-born population increased from 8 to 10 %. The increment from 6 to 8 % took place over the previous two decades (Dunnell 2007).

[3]The more recent 2012 projections assume slightly lower short-term rates that stabilize at 1.89 (Office for National Statistics 2013).

As Hobcraft (1996, p. 487) notes, "the grossest errors [in national population projections and forecasts] have resulted from failures (or perhaps just inability?) to anticipate turning points in fertility trends." Even if we put these "grossest errors" to one side, with few exceptions, long-term fertility assumptions have tended to exceed actual fertility rates (Shaw 2007). The 1985-based population projections assumed that the TFR would climb steadily over the next 15 years and stabilize in 2002–2003 at around 2.01. Although these projections were the first to assume long-term fertility at below replacement level, the assumption overestimated actual fertility rates even during recent years when rates were at their highest. It is therefore pertinent to seek to explain and understand the past trends.

From a cross-national policy perspective, the UK provides a potentially instructive case study. Population issues, low fertility in particular, are not considered to be a major policy concern or an appropriate target for government intervention. With its liberal market economy and residual[4] approach to welfare, a combination of high female employment and near-replacement fertility has been achieved without a coherent or generous set of work-family reconciliation policies. For those who want to argue that the "highest-low" fertility achieved in countries such as France and Sweden can be attributed to their generous work-family reconciliation policies, similarly high fertility (almost always based on TFR) in the UK, and indeed in the rest of the Anglosphere, remains to be explained (Sigle-Rushton 2009, 2014). With that goal in mind, the following section provides a brief overview of political and institutional developments that have conditioned the framing and response to population issues and fertility. I then discuss how UK fertility rates have been sustained at moderately high levels following the fertility declines of the 1970s. I first consider the two decades from 1981 to 2000—a period dominated by (center-right) Conservative governments—and then focus on explanations for the increased fertility that was observed in more recent years.

British Population Policy

Although data limitations make it impossible to document precisely, it is clear that British fertility began to fall in the 1870s and reached extremely low levels in the 1930s. This was a rare historical moment. It is worth mentioning because it is one of the few times that the issue of low fertility attracted the attention of British policymakers (Hobcraft 1996). Their response was cautious and restrained, but it left an important intellectual legacy. The 1938 Population (Statistics) Act established a valuable information base, and the Royal Commission on Population was established in 1944 to provide expert advice. These developments, along with the

[4]In contrast to "institutional" models that tend to provide universal welfare benefits and services, the approach of the residual welfare state is more targeted and means tested.

founding of the Population Investigation Committee[5] in 1936, established demography as a scientific and academic discipline in a political context that for most of the 20th century appeared ambivalent, if not entirely unconcerned, about the issue of population growth (Simons 1973).

Population issues next entered the political arena in the early 1970s, this time in response to the rapid population growth of the 1960s. A 1973 report by the government-appointed Population Panel concluded that Britain would do better in the future with a stationary rather than an increasing population (Population Panel 1973, p. 6). The report stopped short of recommending a comprehensive and coherent population policy, although its authors advocated for a program of family planning services to be provided through the National Health Service (NHS) so that unwanted births could be averted. The 1974 NHS Reorganization Act incorporated this recommendation, and from 1 April of that year, family planning advice and supplies were provided free of charge and irrespective of age or marital status. This was the last of a series of reforms extending back to 1967 that liberalized access to family planning information and services and included, from 1968, access to abortion.[6] A number of authors have suggested that a substantial share of the fertility decline that occurred in the early 1970s can be attributed to these legislative changes, which increased access to and use of the contraceptive pill and reduced mistimed or unwanted pregnancies (Murphy 1993; Hobcraft 1996). Pre-marital conceptions, which had increased throughout the 1960s, fell back to 1950s levels by the late 1970s, particularly for women under the age of 20. To the extent that women were averting mistimed rather than unwanted births, some of the period decline recorded in these years would be primarily a tempo effect. This is perhaps why the Population Panel felt confident enough to suggest that completed family size would not fall below replacement "in the foreseeable future" in the same year that the TFR actually fell below that threshold (Fig. 1).

The persistently low fertility rates of the 1970s did not elicit much political debate or response. In the decades that followed, the UK government remained reluctant to intervene directly to influence fertility, save efforts since the 1990s to reduce rates of teenaged motherhood (Department for Education and Skills 2006). The official UK policy, first presented at the 1984 International Conference on Population in Mexico City and reiterated at the 1994 International Conference on Population and Development in Cairo, has been to adapt to low fertility rather than attempt to alter it:

> The United Kingdom government does not pursue a population policy in the sense of actively trying to influence the overall size of the population, its age-structure, or the components of change except in the field of immigration. Nor has it expressed a view about the size of population, or the age-structure, that would be desirable.... The current level of births has not been the cause of general anxiety. The prevailing view is that decisions about fertility and childbearing are for people themselves to make, but that it is proper for

[5]The Population Investigation Committee established the journal *Population Studies* in 1947.

[6]For the first five years, however, abortion services were limited and rates of use were low (Department of Health 2007).

> government to provide individuals with the information and the means necessary to make their decisions effective. To this end, the government provides assistance with family planning as part of the National Health Service. The 'ageing' of the population does raise social and economic issues. However, it is believed that these will prove manageable; and also, to a degree, that society will adapt.... (Office for National Statistics 1993).

As migration rates increased in recent years, accelerated rates of population growth again became a topic of political debate. But politicians have attempted to treat migration and population growth as distinct issues. Speaking to the House Liaison Committee in 2006, then Prime Minister Tony Blair reaffirmed that the UK had a migration policy but no policy on population growth (UK Parliament Select Committee on Liaison 2006). The current Prime Minister, David Cameron, has been more willing to frame immigration as an issue of 'unsustainable' population growth (Cameron 2007; see also Manifesto 2010). But as far as fertility is concerned, the Cameron administration has maintained the long-running non-interventionist stance. Policymakers from both main political parties have shown little enthusiasm for policies that would seek to influence fertility levels or birth rates. Rather, to understand how UK policies and institutions have supported moderately high levels of fertility over the past 35 years requires an exploration of indirect effects and inadvertent consequences.

1981–2000: Relative Stability

When examined in isolation, UK fertility trends in the last two decades of the 20th century might be described as a period of stability followed by a period of substantial decline. Between 1981 and 1990, the TFR fluctuated between 1.77 and 1.83, and it then fell steadily to 1.64 in 2000 (Fig. 1). Compared with the trends of the previous two decades, however, and situated in the context of Europe where nearly all countries reached record lows, some with TFRs below 1.5 (Billari and Kohler 2004), the picture that emerges is one of relative stability. The TFR remained below 1.7 for only a few years at the turn of the century, and by 2002, the UK TFR had more or less recovered, climbing from the middle to the high end of the EU rankings.

Efforts to explain why some European countries have sustained moderately high fertility have tended to look to the Scandinavian countries and France and to focus on policy changes that encouraged (or responded to demands for) modifications to the male-breadwinner model. In the formative years of welfare state development, virtually all capitalist economies negotiated the demand for social reproduction[7] (which would divert resources from capital accumulation) and secured its provision

[7]Social reproduction is a concept used by feminist scholars who study gender divisions of labor. Laslett and Brenner (1989, p. 382) describe it as "...the activities and attitudes, behaviors and emotions, responsibilities and relationships directly involved in the maintenance of life on a daily basis, and intergenerationally."

by providing some form of institutional support for heterosexual marriage and a male-breadwinner/female-caregiver arrangement. Although, the housewife ideal was often unattainable in poorer families and women have always engaged in economic activities to support their families, the assumption that the wife (ideally) would be economically dependent on her husband guided the early development of all modern welfare states (Lewis 1992). As women increasingly wanted to enter and remain in the labor market, they confronted institutions that were incompatible with the responsibilities of social reproduction. When women had the means (with unprecedented access to contraception) and the incentive to postpone (or even forego) childbearing, fertility declined. Whether or not the underlying motivation was a demographic one, those countries that found new ways of supporting social reproduction and, in particular, those that made work and motherhood more compatible, were often countries that averted rapid and deep fertility decline.

This logically coherent and compelling argument, however, fails to account for trends observed in the UK (and the rest of the moderately high-fertility countries of the Anglosphere). While the Scandinavian countries were developing and promoting policies that would provide new sources of social reproduction through the development of publicly subsidized (child) care services or by encouraging a (modest) renegotiation of gendered divisions of paid and unpaid work, the UK remained implacable in its opposition to these kinds of policy interventions. At least until 1997, a strong liberal welfare tradition, giving primacy to the market, set the UK apart from much of the rest of Europe. Successive Conservative governments actively opposed the development of work-family reconciliation policies at both the national and EU level.

Between 1979 and 1992, almost all EU social-policy regulations, save those related to the "working environment," were governed by unanimous consent (Hoskyns 1996; Duncan 2002). Although observers have noted that a predictable UK veto allowed politicians from other countries to pay lip service to policies that they would otherwise not support and provided a politically expedient excuse for restraint (Lange 1992), UK opposition effectively stymied efforts to take forward a social-policy agenda. The UK consistently blocked efforts to develop binding childcare and parental-leave regulations (Duncan 2002). The Pregnant Workers Directive, which entitled working mothers to 14 weeks of maternity leave, was finally put forward as a health and safety measure to obviate the need for British (and Italian) consent. In 1992, the Agreement on Social Policy[8] opened up a wider range of EU social policies to qualified-majority voting.[9] This protocol, and a UK opt-out until 1997,[10] made it possible for the remaining 11 EU member states to overcome the deadlock of previous decades. Parental-leave legislation, first put

[8]Attached as a protocol to the Maastricht Treaty of the European Union.

[9]Under qualified-majority voting, each member state is allotted a number of votes based on its size and population. For more information, see http://www.euro-know.org/europages/dictionary/q.html.

[10]The opt-out meant that the UK was exempt from legislation arising from this protocol.

forward (and vetoed by the UK) in 1983, was finally passed in 1996 (Fusulier 2011).

The transposition of the EU's Pregnant Workers Directive had a limited impact on UK policy in the 1990s, in part because of successful efforts by the UK (Thatcher) government to neutralize its content. Compliance with the EU Directive meant that the strict eligibility conditions[11] in previous legislation were relaxed (McRae 1991). Even so, throughout this period, statutory maternity benefits remained limited in terms of generosity and duration.[12] Some employers offered extended leave or more generous compensation, but this was mostly confined to the public sector (O'Connor et al. 1999). Similarly, when the UK finally introduced a parental-leave policy,[13] it only complied with the minimum requirements set out in the EU Directive (an unpaid individual entitlement of 13 weeks for each parent).

Throughout most of this period, the UK's system of support for families with children remained largely unaltered. A system of universal family allowances, first introduced in 1946, which provided flat-rate cash transfers to families with children, was slightly amended in 1991 to provide a higher benefit for the first child. For most of the period, state involvement in the provision of childcare was restricted to a discretionary role for local authorities in the provision of pre-school education (Butler et al. 2014). There were some minor developments in the 1990s, however, including tax relief for employer-provided daycare in 1990. The Nursery Education and Grant Maintained Schools Act of 1996 laid the groundwork for the expansion of early-childhood education in later years, but it was only in 1998 that a newly elected Labour government published *Meeting the childcare challenge* (Department for Education and Employment 1998), a consultation document that set out a framework for a national childcare strategy.[14]

As numerous scholars have noted, the 1980s and 1990s were a period when families were left to (some would say "trusted to") make their own arrangements for the care of children (OECD 2005), and, given prevailing gender norms, the default option was maternal care. Mothers could enter the labor market *if* they could figure out how to manage *their* care responsibilities. Against this backdrop, it is perhaps not surprising that, for many years, the UK was unusual (along with the

[11]To qualify for maternity benefits, women had to have worked continuously for the same employer at least 16 h per week for two years or eight hours per week for five years. Only about one-half of all working mothers met these eligibility criteria.

[12]Women who met more stringent eligibility requirements relating to their work history (see previous footnote) and to their National Insurance contributions were entitled to a longer period of leave (initially 28 weeks) than the minimum of 14 weeks required by the Pregnant Workers Directive.

[13]When its opt-out from the Agreement on Social Policy ended in 1997, the UK was required to give force to the Parental Leave Directive.

[14]The document set out a proposal that would ensure that all four-year-olds had access to early education by September 1998 and presented a funding plan of £435 million (US$682 million as of 21 May 2015) over five years for the development of childcare services, £310 million (US $486 million) in start-up funds for out-of-school childcare facilities, and a £6 million (US $9 million) investment in the provision of childcare places for younger children.

Netherlands) in Europe for providing low levels of income support to poor lone mothers so that they could remain at home and care for their children full time (Millar 1996). From the early 1970s, a means-tested and work-related benefit was introduced, in part to address poverty in lone-parent households. From 1994, Family Credit[15] claimants could, before the means test was applied, deduct childcare costs of up to £40 (US$63 as of 21 May 2015) a week[16] from their income. This deduction was intended to encourage mothers' employment, but few families in receipt of Family Credit made use of it (Dilnot and Duncan 1992).

To understand how fertility might have been sustained throughout this period, it is important to consider the wider institutional context. Here there is much that distinguishes the UK from its European partners. The Varieties of Capitalism literature[17] has described the UK as conforming more closely to the Liberal Market Economy than to the Coordinated Market Economy that is more typical throughout Europe (Hall and Soskice 2001). Compared to more coordinated economies, labor markets in Liberal Market Economies are more competitive and more fluid. With low levels of regulation, Liberal Market Economies encourage the development of general, transferrable skills and high rates of turnover, but within a highly segmented labor market.

Those who can compete at the top end of the occupational hierarchy can expect great rewards that grow over time, but the competitive work environment can foster a culture of long working hours. Lower-skilled workers participate in a secondary market with few job protections, low wages, and limited firm-specific investments. With few opportunities for progression, their wage trajectories tend to be flat. A marked reluctance to adopt measures that would interfere with labor markets or raise the costs of doing business implies a residual or "liberal" (Esping-Andersen 1990) welfare regime with targeted and minimal social safety nets. When (largely unrestrained) market forces push low wages near minimum living standards, incentives to participate can erode, however. In the context of traditional gender arrangements and low levels of labor-market regulation, the expansion of part-time work opportunities for women at the low end of wage distribution could be used by employers to resist upward pressure on wages (Hurstfield 1978). In more coordinated economies, strong labor-market regulations and a more powerful union presence can restrain these efforts (although sometimes this might mean excluding women/mothers from the labor market altogether).

In earlier work, I have argued that these distinctive aspects of the Liberal Market Economy facilitated the early and moderately high fertility observed in more socio-economically disadvantaged groups in the UK and the rest of the Anglosphere (Sigle-Rushton 2008, 2009). In the absence of adequate childcare

[15]A means-tested benefit for families with an adult working at least 24 (later reduced to 16) hours per week and at least one dependent child. Originally called the Family Income Supplement (FIS), it was renamed Family Credit in 1988 and replaced by the Working Families Tax Credit in 1999.

[16]The deduction was increased to £60 (US$90) per week in the 1995 budget.

[17]A number of authors have criticized this simplistic dichotomy, but for the purposes of the discussion that follows, this stylized framework has some heuristic value.

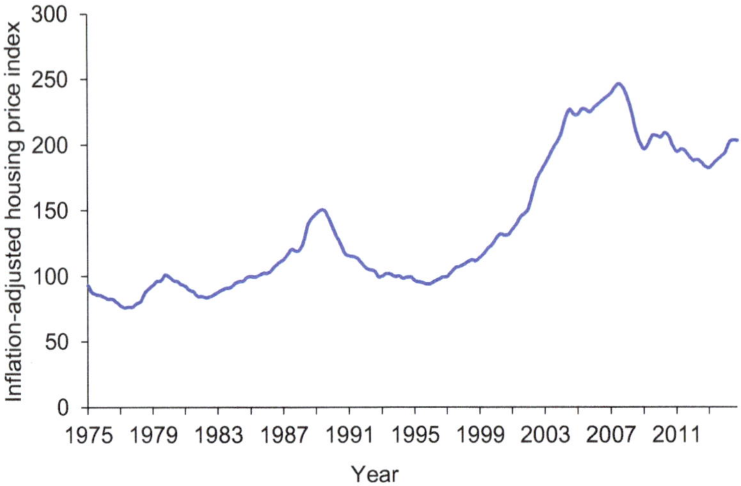

Fig. 2 Inflation-adjusted housing price index for the UK, 1975–2014 (Q1 1985 = 100) (Nationwide Building Society 2015)

support, most mothers would have to withdraw from employment, at least temporarily, when they had a child. If they wanted to return to work, many would struggle to work full time. Although there were part-time job opportunities, these tended to be concentrated where they had always been—at the lower end of the occupational hierarchy and wage distribution, which, prior to April 1999, had no floor in the form of a national minimum wage. As a consequence, for women earning moderate to high incomes, the transition to parenthood could carry substantial costs, particularly over the longer term. A withdrawal from the high end of the labor market and a return to a part-time position would likely require a substantial occupational downgrade, which could be difficult to reverse (Connolly and Gregory 2008; Dex and Bukodi 2012). Faced with the prospect of long-term effects on their occupational attainment and life-time earnings, those women with the most to lose had the strongest incentive to postpone the transition to parenthood.

From the mid-1990s, rapid increases in housing prices (Fig. 2) may well have reinforced incentives to postpone parenthood among middle- and higher-earning couples. For first-time buyers, the ratio of gross earnings to house prices climbed from 2.1 in the fourth quarter of 1995 to around 5.0 at the beginning of 2007. In London, the ratio climbed from just under 3 to over 7 (Fig. 3). As families increasingly required two incomes, first to secure a mortgage and then to meet the payments, childbearing, and the income loss associated with it, might have become unaffordable.

In contrast, lower-skilled, more-disadvantaged women were already at the bottom of the wage distribution, and so a period of inactivity followed by adjustments to their working hours would have little impact on their current or future wages. Incentives to postpone childbearing, even to qualify for maternity benefits, were

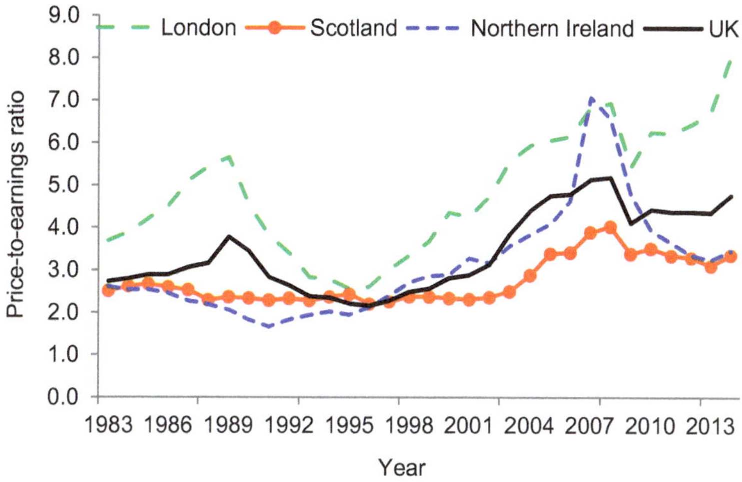

Fig. 3 First-time buyers' gross housing price-to-earnings ratio for the UK and select regions, 1983–2014 (Nationwide Building Society 2015)

weak: The existence of low-level means-tested benefits offered a viable alternative. Over the longer term, their wages were unlikely to grow steeply even if they remained continuously employed.

Rising housing prices also meant that home ownership was increasingly out of reach for those on low incomes. The allocation of the increasingly limited number of public housing units[18] prioritized families with children, however (Lupton et al. 2009), perhaps adding to the disincentive to postpone childbearing. Those who were married to or cohabiting with men at the bottom of the wage distribution could rely on means-tested financial support as insurance against family instability and the loss of their partners' income.

In the UK policy setting, we might therefore expect to see a socially polarized fertility profile, with more postponement, smaller families, and higher levels of childlessness among the most qualified and highest skilled and earlier and larger families among those with lower qualifications and skills. Empirical evidence relevant to this period is largely consistent with these predicted labor-market and demographic patterns. In an analysis using data collected from a number of European countries between 1999 and 2001, Jane Waldfogel and I found that compared to other countries, the UK "motherhood gap" (the gap in earnings between mothers and childless women) is high and does not narrow appreciably as children grow older (Sigle-Rushton and Waldfogel 2007).

---

[18]The "right to buy" program gave tenants in public housing the opportunity to buy their homes at reduced prices and so provided some opportunity for home ownership. The program reduced the stock of public housing, however, and as a consequence, only those families most in need gained access to a public-housing unit (Lupton et al. 2009).

High period and cohort total fertility rates have been achieved with a relatively high variation in completed family size and a relatively high incidence of childlessness (Coleman 1996; Shkolnikov et al. 2007), particularly among the highly educated (Kneale and Joshi 2008; Berrington et al. 2014). The persistence of early childbearing is reflected in a "hump" at young ages in the first-birth fertility schedule, which is typical of the countries of the Anglosphere and suggests a bifurcated fertility regime (Chandola et al. 2002). Similar to what Ellwood and Jencks (2004) found in their analysis of data from the United States (US), lower-educated women appear to have continued to have children at (the same) younger ages, while those who obtained high levels of education started to delay their first birth (Berrington et al. 2014). Conditional on having had a first birth, the transition to the second was more rapid for the highly educated, however (Rendall and Smallwood 2003). Nonetheless, the completed family size of highly educated women, particularly those in highly competitive managerial positions (Ekert-Jaffe et al. 2002), was low relative to that of other women (Berrington et al. 2014).

Cross-national comparisons suggest that the moderately high fertility in the UK during this period was more socio-economically polarized than in France or the Nordic countries (Ekert-Jaffe et al. 2002; Rendall et al. 2005). Importantly, the costs of sustaining moderately high fertility may have fallen disproportionately on those groups with the lowest levels of resources, exacerbating income inequality and contributing to the high child-poverty rates observed in the UK (Sigle-Rushton 2008).

The Period Since 2001

A change of government in 1997 marked the beginning of a period of rapid and extensive policy change in the UK. A new anti-poverty program was implemented with a focus on employment as the best route out of poverty. New policies targeted *worklessness* and the earnings of low-paid workers. High rates of child poverty were a key priority, with ambitious targets to halve child poverty by 2010 and then eradicate it by 2020. In the context of these reforms, childcare issues were successfully reframed as an obstacle to labor-market participation, and work-family reconciliation policies became a new feature of the British welfare state (Daguerre and Taylor-Gooby 2004; O'Connor et al. 1999).

To what extent did these changes modify the fertility regime of previous decades? Work-family reconciliation policies have been credited with sustaining fertility in other moderately high-fertility settings by making it easier for women to combine paid work and childrearing. In earlier decades, the strongest incentives to postpone childbearing were experienced by women who had the most to lose from an occupational downgrade. If a new set of policies redressed these difficulties, there might be less social polarization in the UK fertility profile and possibly even higher fertility, as long as the new policy approach continued to support childbearing at the lower end of the income distribution as well.

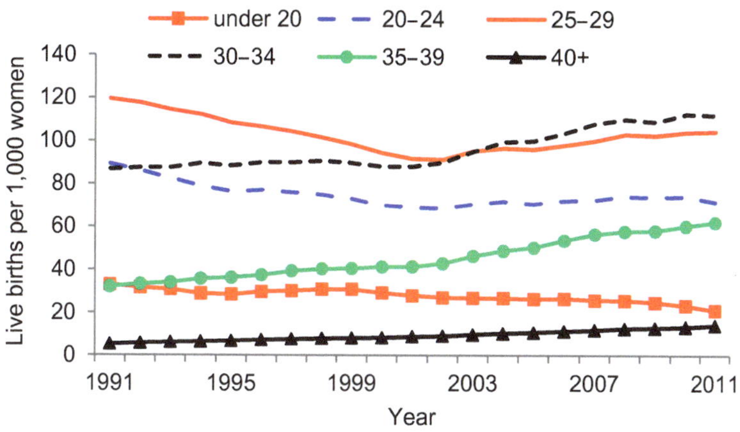

Fig. 4 Age-specific fertility rates (births per 1000 women), England and Wales, 1991–2011 (Jefferies 2008; Zumpe et al. 2012)

In 2001, a few years into the new policy program, fertility in the UK started to rise. Although fertility rates increased for all women over age 20, data for England and Wales (Fig. 4) show that some of the most prominent changes involved women in their thirties and forties. In 2004, the fertility rate at age 30–34 surpassed the fertility rate at age 25–29 for the first time. Since then, 30–34-year-olds have remained the most fertile age group. Between 2001 and 2011, fertility rates for the age groups 35 and older showed the steepest increases, and in 2012, the average age at first birth was over 30 for the first time. Put alongside evidence (also from England and Wales) suggesting that almost all of the initial increase in the TFR (through 2006) can be attributed to first- and second-order births (Jefferies 2008), it appears that recent trends largely reflect childbearing among women who, in the 1980s and 1990s, postponed the transition to motherhood.

It is not clear whether the new policy approach was responsible for these trends. A general upturn in period fertility has been observed across a wide range of countries over the same period (Goldstein et al. 2009). The TFR in other moderately high-fertility European countries (Sweden, in particular) showed a similar trend. This suggests that, in the absence of any policy change, UK fertility may have increased anyway. At issue is whether the new policies delivered the level of work-family reconciliation needed to alter incentives and so alter behavior.

The introduction and expansion of a new set of family-friendly policies marked a significant ideological change in UK politics. The care of children was no longer seen as a "private" matter, but rather as an issue that required government support and involvement. At the same time, the UK government was anxious to avoid interfering in the operation of the labor market or addressing inequality by targeting the high end of the earnings distribution (Sigle-Rushton 2008).[19] These concerns shaped the way the new policies were designed and implemented. The tendency has been to accommodate rather than transform the segmented and gendered labor market.

The approach to childcare policy, for example, appears to be premised on the same expectations that shaped the fertility profile in previous decades—that mothers are secondary workers and should be solely responsible for care. The duration and generosity of childcare leave was significantly extended over this period, with the focus almost exclusively on maternity leave.[20] The rights for fathers to take childcare leave have remained far more limited.[21] The regulated mixed-market approach to childcare services has been criticized for doing more to address access than affordability (Butler et al. 2014). While all three- and four-year-olds[22] have a guaranteed place in early education, the entitlement is part time, covering only 15 h per week (12.5 h per week for 33 weeks per year until 2010). The early-education offer is the only form of childcare assistance that many working parents receive (Butler et al. 2014). The gap between this entitlement and the hours of childcare a working parent requires can be difficult to negotiate, both logistically and financially.[23] It is a policy that appears to facilitate short-hour, part-time employment and so does little to challenge the segmented labor market of previous decades.

---

[19]In a television interview (BBC News 2002), Prime Minister Tony Blair was asked whether he thought "an individual could earn too much money." His response provides a good summary of his Government's view on inequality: "...Do you mean that we should cap someone's income? Not really, no. Why? What is the point? You can spend ages trying to stop the highest paid earners earning the money but in an international market like today, you probably would drive them abroad. What does that matter? Surely the important thing is to level up those people that don't have opportunity in our society."

[20]By 2007, all mothers were entitled to 52 weeks of leave (although the right to return to the same job was only extended to the first 26 weeks). While there has been little change in the likelihood that a mother will return to work within 18 months of birth (in fact, the figure declined slightly between 2002 and 2007), in recent years mothers have been more likely to return to the same employer (Stewart 2013). What is less clear is whether those women returned to the same job or whether they experienced any occupational downgrading subsequent to their return, particularly if they wanted to reduce their working hours.

[21]Since 2003, fathers have been entitled to two weeks of Ordinary Paternity Leave (as it is now called), which is compensated at a flat rate. Throughout the period, parental leave, which included unpaid individual entitlements for men, remained minimal (Lewis and Campbell 2007). From April 2011, qualifying mothers could choose to return to work and transfer up to 26 weeks of their leave entitlement (which was compensated at the same flat rate as additional maternity leave and ordinary paternity leave at £128.15 (US$198) per week when it was first introduced) to their (qualifying) partner (Trades Union Congress 2013). Although the measure provided some opportunity for men to take leave, it clearly reflected and continued to reinforce gendered divisions of labor. From 2015, fathers can take up to 50 weeks of the leave entitlement. Although it has been renamed "shared leave," mothers still must trigger men's entitlement by returning to work.

[22]In 2013, the entitlement was extended to two-year-olds in low-income families.

[23]Estimates from 2008 suggest that the cost of childcare represented an effective tax of about 41 % on the income of a second earner in an average-wage family (OECD 2011).

The nature and quality of part-time work and its impact on mothers have attracted a good deal of attention and research, but only a modest policy response. Since April 2003, parents of young children have had the "Right to Request" more flexible working conditions, including shorter hours.[24] Employers can refuse the request for a number of business reasons, however, and opportunities for legal redress are limited. Although the majority of requests are approved,[25] evidence suggests that the culture of long working hours—something UK policymakers remain unwilling to regulate—still has a negative impact on mothers. Data from the period before and after the Right to Request was implemented show that most mothers still changed their employer when they changed their hours (Smeaton and Marsh 2006). A recent review of the impact of the policy concluded: "…As far as one of the objectives of the Right to Request has been to increase the ability of working mothers to continue at the same level of responsibility, and with the same employer, albeit at reduced hours, the impact of the Right to Request does not appear to have been substantial" (Hegewisch 2009, p. 22).

Although most policy indicators show a substantial improvement in family policy over this period, the potential of new policies to change previous fertility patterns has likely been moderated by the political and institutional legacies of previous decades. It is difficult to imagine that these policy changes would have anything more than a marginal effect on highly qualified and high-earning women. Women in their 30s who had previously postponed childbearing and whose incomes allowed them to purchase sufficient, high-quality childcare might find it easier to negotiate short leaves and to return to the same pre-parenthood working conditions, adopting what Fraser (1994) describes as the universal-breadwinner model. Those who wanted to adapt their working conditions during the first years of parenthood would have the right to request flexible work, but in a culture of long working hours such requests might be refused or difficult to achieve in practice (Lyonette et al. 2010). What is half-time work when all of your colleagues work well in excess of a typical working week?

The simplest explanation for recent trends in first births among older women is a biological one. As they approached the end of their reproductive years, the question became no longer when, but whether, to have a first birth. Data from the British Household Panel Survey (BHPS) collected during the 1990s showed that most childless women—the most highly qualified in particular—still wanted and intended to have children (Tavares 2010, Table 6; see also Kneale and Joshi 2008, Table 4). Younger women with high levels of education and skills would still have incentives to postpone the transition to parenthood related to the labor market and

---

[24]Originally, the Right to Request was available to parents of children under the age of six (18 if the child was disabled), and in 2009 it was extended to parents of non-disabled children age 16 and younger. In 2007, the Right to Request was extended to employees with caring responsibilities for sick or disabled adult household members, and, in 2014, to all workers.

[25]Survey data for the period 2009–2011 indicate that, of those who were not still awaiting the outcome, about 14 % reported that their request was declined, and about 20 % reported that their request was accepted only after "negotiation/compromise/appeal."

reinforced, in this period, by continuous price increases for housing and the introduction and rapid increase of tuition fees[26] for higher education, which meant that many university graduates entered the labor market with substantial debts.

Another potentially important set of policies aimed to reduce child poverty and the number of workless households. Reforms of the income-tax system and increases in both means-tested (Income Support) and universal child benefits supplemented the incomes of the poorest families by as much as 10 %. The Working Families Tax Credit, a refundable tax credit for low-income working families, was one of the largest and most significant of these policy initiatives. As the benefit was calculated at the household level, there were concerns that it might encourage and reinforce a male-breadwinner arrangement in two-parent households (Brewer and Shephard 2004). Evidence suggests that these concerns may have been well founded. A number of analyses of the impact of the policy found a significant increase in the employment activity of lone mothers but little overall effect on the employment activity of women in couples (Brewer et al. 2012). Brewer et al. (2012) argue that the taper rate[27] that created disincentives for the second member of a couple to be employed could also have reduced the opportunity costs of child-bearing. To the extent that women with little education already faced weak incentives to postpone childbearing and had low rates of childlessness (Rendall and Smallwood 2003), it is unlikely that changes in their fertility behavior contributed much to recent trends which, as discussed above, were largely driven by late and low-order births (Jefferies 2008).

These policies take on more relevance when viewed through a transnational lens. When the EU enlarged in 2004, most member states put in place transition measures to temporarily restrict in-migration of workers from the A8 member countries.[28] Only the UK, Ireland, and Sweden provided immediate and open access to their labor markets. As a consequence, annual net migration, which had been increasing since the early 1990s, accelerated substantially.[29] Although recent migrants were coming from countries with low fertility and many were migrating for economic reasons, their period fertility nonetheless exceeded that of the UK-born population and even that of their country of origin (Dorman 2014).

It is not immediately clear why migrants from the A8 countries have had higher fertility than women who remained in those countries. It could be that women who intend to migrate postpone childbearing until after they move (Toulemon 2004),

[26]From £1000 (US$1549) per annum in 1998 to £9000 (US$13,940) per annum since 2012 at most universities in England and Wales.

[27]The rate at which benefits are reduced as household income rises.

[28]The A8 countries are the eight low-income (per capita incomes of about 40 % of the EU average), Eastern European countries (Czech Republic, Estonia, Hungary, Latvia, Lithuania, Poland, Slovakia, and Slovenia) that, along with Malta and Cyprus, joined the EU in 2004.

[29]There was a net migration of 180,000 A8 citizens to the UK between 2004 and 2006, accounting for 13 % of the total long-term immigration. Among the A8 countries, the largest number of immigrants came from Poland, and by 2010 they formed the largest group of non-UK nationals resident in the UK (Office for National Statistics 2011).

and so their higher period fertility represents a tempo effect. It is also possible that the decisions about where to migrate involve more than a comparison of wage differentials. The design of family policy, in particular the gendered family models that the policies presume and most generously support, might be relevant as well. In this regard, membership in the EU community can reduce information costs as well as the costs of movement. A qualitative study that compared the subsequent childbearing intentions of Polish-born parents in London and Krakow found that parents in Krakow often cited the costs of children as an important constraint and compared the Polish context to other, more favorable policy settings as they justified their intentions. Among the migrants living in London, parents who had previously worked in high-status jobs in Poland said they were willing to accept an occupational downgrade in order to raise their families in the UK. They cited better state support for children and greater opportunities for mothers to spend time with children (through part-time work or temporary periods of unemployment) as reasons both to remain in the UK and to have additional children (Marczak 2012). While it is not likely that policy changes brought in to address child poverty since 2001 had much impact on the fertility rates of UK-born women with little education, they may have contributed to higher fertility by making the UK a more attractive place for some international migrants whose family preferences were closely aligned with the (uniquely) gendered incentive structures of those new anti-poverty policies and, at the same time, were not well supported by the family-policy packages offered in their countries of origin.

The financial crisis of 2007 and the first years of coalition government beginning in 2010 brought in a number of austerity measures. Previous developments in work-family reconciliation policies were not reversed, but instead, the generosity of the welfare and benefit system was targeted. While the previous government had made paid employment more attractive by improving its conditions and rewards, for a male breadwinner at least, the current approach has been to substantially reduce decommodification[30] in the benefits system. Previous experience suggests that such measures will probably do more to reverse earlier achievements in the reduction of child poverty than to substantially reduce fertility, at least among UK-born women. The changes might, however, affect fertility by shaping the decisions of the foreign-born either to migrate to the UK in the first place or to remain and build families in the UK. This is an important area for future research.

[30]Decommodification is a concept used to guide the comparative analysis of advanced welfare states. Esping-Andersen (1990, p. 37) defines decommodification as "the degree to which individuals, or families, can uphold a socially acceptable standard of living independent of labour market participation."

Conclusion

As in most wealthy countries, the UK population is aging and will continue to age for the next several decades. Recent and projected rates of change in the share of the elderly population are slow, however, relative to most other EU-27 countries (Office for National Statistics 2012b). Although since 1998 net migration has played some role, the UK's relatively benign demographic profile has much to do with its relatively high fertility rates (Office for National Statistics 2014a; Coleman 2007). From a European policy perspective, its "highest-low" fertility is difficult to explain (Sigle-Rushton 2009). Moderately high fertility rates have been sustained—at least historically—without the work-family reconciliation policies characteristic of many other moderately high-fertility European countries. In earlier work, I have argued that the UK's unique institutional setting created incentives for a moderately high but socially polarized fertility profile (Sigle-Rushton 2008, 2009). In this chapter, I build on previous work and consider how the institutional legacy of previous decades has shaped subsequent fertility trends and perhaps moderated the impact of new policy initiatives that, since the turn of the century, represent deviations from type. The discussion has a wider relevance because it raises a number of theoretical and practical issues that are pertinent to the way we design cross-national studies and make use of the evidence.

Theoretical developments in the study of welfare states (Esping-Andersen 1990) and, more recently, in comparative capitalisms (Hall and Soskice 2001) have represented a significant departure from earlier work that either conceptualized national variations as different stages of the same developmental trajectory or presumed institutional variations would cease to matter as nation states converged toward the same equilibrium model. These contributions stressed the importance of path dependencies and institutional complementarities, which meant that a variety of distinct and stable institutional models was not just possible but likely. Throughout the 1980s and the 1990s, the UK provided a stable and coherent institutional setting that supported a distinct profile of moderately high fertility without making much effort to address issues of work-family reconciliation. Appealing to the UK case, and applying the logic of proof by counter-example,[31] we might be tempted to conclude that the hypothesized relationship between family-friendly policies and fertility can be rejected when, in fact, such policies may well have been effective where they developed as part of a coherent model.

For similar reasons, variations in ideological and institutional legacies can complicate efforts to identify and adopt "best practice." The impact of a single policy intervention or policy reform (as when Germany adopted radical changes to its parental-leave system) can be amplified or muted depending on the extent to which it resonates and interacts with the wider context. This consideration has become increasingly relevant in the UK in the past decade or so. Since the late

[31] A proof structure that allows us to conclude that a property is not true by identifying an example where it does not hold.

1990s, the UK has begun to develop a package of work-family reconciliation policies, sometimes in (a minimalist) response to EU directives that were based on what was seen as best practice in other (usually Scandinavian) institutional contexts. Taken at face value, these innovations should have reduced the costs of childbearing and childrearing. They were inserted into a social and institutional setting that remained largely unmodified, however. When policies are introduced that deviate from previous paths, policy logics, and approaches, the wider context may constrain and shape their impact in potentially complex and unintended ways (Tunberger and Sigle-Rushton 2013). Empirical analyses that do not take these complexities into account may underestimate the importance of the institutions and policies.

References

BBC News. (2002). *Newsnight, 8 February 2002.* http://news.bbc.co.uk/1/hi/events/newsnight/1372220.stm. Accessed September 20, 2014.

Berrington, A., Stone, J., & Beaujouan, E. (2014). *Educational differences in tempo and quantum of childbearing in Britain: A study of cohorts born 1940–1969.* Paper presented at the 2014 Annual Meeting of the British Society for Population Studies, Winchester, UK, September 7–9, 2014.

Billari, F. C., & Kohler, H. P. (2004). Patterns of low and lowest: Low fertility in Europe. *Population Studies, 58*(2), 161–76.

Brewer, M., Ratcliffe, A., & Smith, S. (2012). Does welfare reform affect fertility? Evidence from the UK. *Journal of Population Economics, 25*, 245–66.

Brewer, M., & Shephard, A. (2004). *Has Labour made work pay?* York: Joseph Rowntree Foundation.

Butler, A., Lugton, D., & Rutter, J. (2014). *Where next for childcare? Learning from the last ten years of childcare policy.* London: Family and Childcare Trust.

Cameron, D. (2007). *The challenges of a growing population.* Speech given on 29 October 2007. http://conservativehome.blogs.com/torydiary/files/population.pdf. Accessed May 22, 2015.

Chandola, T., Coleman, D. A., & Hiorns, R. W. (2002). Distinctive features of age-specific fertility profiles in the English speaking world. *Population Studies, 56*(2), 181–200.

Coleman, D. A. (1996). New patterns and trends in European fertility: International and subnational comparisons. In D. A. Coleman (Ed.), *Europe's population in the 1990s* (pp. 1–61). Oxford: Oxford University Press.

Coleman, D. A. (2007). The road to low fertility. *Ageing Horizons, 7*, 7–15.

Connolly, S., & Gregory, M. (2008). Moving down: Women's part time work and occupational change in Britain. *The Economic Journal, 118*, F52–F76.

Daguerre, A., & Taylor-Gooby, P. (2004). Neglecting Europe: Explaining the predominance of American ideas in New Labour's welfare policies since 1997. *Journal of European Social Policy, 14*(1), 25–39.

Department for Education and Employment. (1998). *Meeting the childcare challenge.* Green Paper. London: The Stationery Office.

Department for Education and Skills. (2006). *Teenage pregnancy: Accelerating the strategy to 2010.* Nottingham: Department for Education and Skills.

Department of Health. (2007). *Abortion statistics, England and Wales: 2006.* http://webarchive.nationalarchives.gov.uk/20130123231223/, http://www.dh.gov.uk/prod_consum_dh/groups/dh_digitalassets/documents/digitalasset/dh_075705.pdf. Accessed May 22, 2015.

Dex, S., & Bukodi, E. (2012). The effects of part-time work on women's occupational mobility in Britain: Evidence from the 1958 cohort study. *National Institute Economic Review, 222*, R20–R36.
Dilnot, A., & Duncan, A. (1992). Lone mothers, family credit and paid work. *Fiscal Studies, 13* (1), 1–21.
Dorman, O. (2014). *Childbearing of UK and non-UK born women living in the UK—2011 Census data.* London: Office for National Statistics. http://www.ons.gov.uk/ons/dcp171766_350433.pdf. Accessed May 22, 2015.
Duncan, S. (2002). Policy discourses on reconciling work and life in the EU. *Social Policy and Society, 4*(1), 305–14.
Dunnell, K. (2007). The changing demographic picture of the UK—National Statistician's annual article on the population. *Population Trends, 130*, 9–21.
Ekert-Jaffe, O., Joshi, H., Lynch, K., Mougin, R., & Rendall, M. (2002). Fertility, timing of births and socio-economic status in France and Britain: Social policies and occupational polarization. *Population: English Edition, 57*(3), 475–507.
Ellwood, D., & Jencks, C. (2004). The spread of single-parent families in the United States since 1960. In D. P. Moynihan, T. Smeeding, & L. Rainwater (Eds.), *The future of the family* (pp. 25–65). New York: Russell Sage.
Esping-Andersen, G. (1990). *The three worlds of welfare capitalism.* Princeton: Princeton University Press.
European Commission. (2012). *The 2012 ageing report: Economic and budgetary projections for the 27 EU member states (2010–2060).* http://ec.europa.eu/economy_finance/publications/european_economy/2012/pdf/ee-2012-2_en.pdf. Accessed May 21, 2015.
Fraser, N. (1994). After the family wage: Gender equality and the welfare state. *Political Theory, 22*(4), 591–618.
Fusulier, B. (2011). The European directive: Making supra-national parental leave policy. In S. B. Kamerman & P. Moss (Eds.), *The politics of parental leave policies: Children, parenting, gender and the labour market* (pp. 243–59). Bristol: The Policy Press.
Goldstein, J., Sobotka, T., & Jasilioniene, A. (2009). The end of "lowest-low" fertility? *Population and Development Review, 35*(4), 663–99.
Hall, P., & Soskice, D. (2001). An introduction to varieties of capitalism. In P. Hall & D. Soskice (Eds.), *Varieties of capitalism: The institutional foundations of comparative advantage.* Oxford: Oxford University Press.
Hegewisch, A. (2009). *Flexible working policies: A comparative review.* Manchester: Equality and Human Rights Commission.
Hobcraft, J. (1996). Fertility in England and Wales: A fifty-year perspective. *Population Studies, 50*, 485–524.
Hoskyns, C. (1996). *Integrating gender: Women, law, and politics in the European Union.* London: Verso.
Hurstfield, J. (1978). *The part time trap.* London: Low Pay Unit.
Jefferies, J. (2008). Fertility assumptions for the 2006-based national population projections. *Population Trends, 131*(spring), 19–27.
Kneale, D., & Joshi, H. (2008). Postponement and childlessness: Evidence from two British cohorts. *Demographic Research, 19*, 1935–68.
Lange, P. (1992). The politics of the social dimension. In A. Sbragia (Ed.), *Euro-politics.* Washington: Brookings.
Laslett, B., & Brenner, J. (1989). Gender and social reproduction: Historical perspectives. *Annual Review of Sociology, 15*, 381–404.
Lewis, J. (1992). Gender and the development of welfare regimes. *Journal of European Social Policy, 2*, 159–73.
Lewis, J., & Campbell, M. (2007). UK work/family balance policies and gender equality, 1997–2005. *Social Politics, 14*(1), 4–30.

Lupton, R., Tunstall, R., Sigle-Rushton, W., Obolenskaya, P., Sabates, R., Meschi, E., et al. (2009). *Growing up in social housing in Britain: A profile of four generations, 1946 to the present day.* London: Tenant Services Authority and Joseph Rowntree Foundation.

Lyonette, C., Baldauf, B., & Behle, H. (2010). *Quality part-time work: A review of the evidence.* http://www.researchonline.org.uk/sds/search/download.do?ref=B15834. Accessed June 16, 2015.

Manifesto, C. (2010). *Invitation to join the government of Britain.* London: Pureprint Group.

Marczak, J. (2012). *Transnational groups of reference and intentions for the second offspring among Poles living in Poland and the UK.* Paper presented at the British Society for Population Studies Annual Conference, Nottingham, September 10–12, 2012.

McRae, S. (1991). *Maternity rights in Britain: The experience of women and employers.* London: Policy Studies Institute.

Millar, J. (1996). Mothers, workers, wives: Comparing policy approaches to supporting lone mothers. In E. B. Silva (Ed.), *Good enough mothering?* (pp. 97–113). London: Routledge.

Murphy, M. (1993). The contraceptive pill and women's employment as factors in fertility change in Britain, 1963–1980: A challenge to the conventional view. *Population Studies, 47*, 221–43.

Nationwide Building Society. (2015). *House price index data.* http://www.nationwide.co.uk/about/house-price-index/download-data#tab:Downloaddata. Accessed June 16, 2015.

O'Connor, J. S., Orloff, A. S., & Shaver, S. (1999). *States, markets, families: Gender, liberalism and social policy in Australia, Canada, Great Britain and the United States.* Cambridge: Cambridge University Press.

OECD (Organization for Economic Cooperation and Development). (2005). *Babies and bosses: Reconciling work and family life.* Vol. 4: Canada, Finland, Sweden, and the United Kingdom. Paris: OECD Publications.

OECD (Organization for Economic Cooperation and Development). (2011). *Doing better for families.* Paris: OECD Publications.

Office for National Statistics. (1993). Editorial. *Population Trends, 72.*

Office for National Statistics. (2011). *Polish people in the UK: Half a million Polish-born residents.* London: Home Office.

Office for National Statistics. (2012a). *2010-based national population projections.* London: Office for National Statistics.

Office for National Statistics. (2012b). *Population ageing in the United Kingdom, its constituent countries and the European Union.* London: Office for National Statistics. http://www.ons.gov.uk/ons/dcp171776_258607.pdf. Accessed May 22, 2015.

Office for National Statistics. (2013). *National population projections, 2012-based Statistical Bulletin.* London: Office for National Statistics. http://www.ons.gov.uk/ons/dcp171778_334975.pdf. Accessed May 21, 2015.

Office for National Statistics. (2014a). *Annual mid-year population estimates, 2013.* London: Office for National Statistics.

Office for National Statistics. (2014b). *Provisional UK TFR, 2013.* http://www.ons.gov.uk/ons/about-ons/business-transparency/freedom-of-information/what-can-i-request/published-ad-hoc-data/pop/september-2014/index.html. Accessed May 21, 2015.

Population Panel. (1973). *Population Panel Report (Command 5258).* London: Stationery Office Books.

Rendall, M., Couer, C., Lappegard, T., Robert-Bobe, I., Ronsen, M., & Smallwood, S. (2005). First births by age and education in Britain, France and Norway. *Population Trends, 121*, 27.

Rendall, M., & Smallwood, S. (2003). Higher qualifications, first birth timing, and further childbearing in England and Wales. *Population Trends, 111*, 18–26.

Shaw, C. (2007). Fifty years of United Kingdom national population projections: How accurate have they been? *Population Trends, 128*, 8–23.

Shkolnikov, V. M., Andreev, E. M., Houle, R., & Vaupel, J. W. (2007). The concentration of reproduction in cohorts of women in Europe and the United States. *Population and Development Review, 33*(1), 67–100.

Sigle-Rushton, W. (2008). England and Wales: Stable fertility and pronounced social status differences. *Demographic Research, 19*, 459–502.

Sigle-Rushton, W. (2009). Fertility in England and Wales: A policy puzzle? *Demografie, 51*(4), 258–65.

Sigle-Rushton, W. (2014). *Fertility and family policy: An international perspective.* Paper presented at the meeting of the European Association for Population Studies, Budapest, Hungary.

Sigle-Rushton, W., & Waldfogel, J. (2007). Motherhood and women's earnings in Anglo-American, continental European, and Nordic countries. *Feminist Economics, 13*(2), 55–91.

Simons, J. (1973). The development of population policy in Britain. *International Journal of Health Services, 3*(4), 855–62.

Smeaton, D., & Marsh, A. (2006). *Maternity and paternity rights and benefits: Survey of parents.* Employment Relations Research Series No. 50. London: Department of Trade and Industry.

Stewart, K. (2013). *Labour's record on the under fives: Policy, spending and outcomes 1997–2010.* Social Policy in a Cold Climate Working Paper 4. London: London School of Economics and Political Science, Centre for Analysis of Social Exclusion.

Tavares, L. (2010). *Who delays childbearing? The relationship between fertility, education and personality traits.* ISER Working Paper Series, 2010–17. https://www.iser.essex.ac.uk/files/iser_working_papers/2010-17.pdf. Accessed September 20, 2014.

Toulemon, L. (2004). Fertility among immigrant women: New data, a new approach. *Population and Societies, 400*(April), 1–4.

Trades Union Congress. (2013). *Just one in 172 fathers taking Additional Paternity Leave.* Press release, 16 June 2013. https://www.tuc.org.uk/workplace-issues/just-one-172-fathers-taking-additional-paternity-leave. Accessed September 20, 2014.

Tromans, N., Natamba, E., & Jefferies, J. (2009). Have women born outside the UK driven the rise in UK births since 2001? *Population Trends, 136*, 28–42.

Tunberger, P., & Sigle-Rushton, W. (2013). Public policy and families. In M. Richards, J. Scott, & J. Treas (Eds.), *Blackwell companion to the sociology of families* (2nd ed.). New York: Blackwell.

UK Parliament Select Committee on Liaison. (2006). *Examination of witnesses (questions 400–419): Rt. Hon. Tony Blair, MP.* http://www.publications.parliament.uk/pa/cm200506/cmselect/cmliaisn/709/6070407.htm. Accessed May 21, 2015.

Zumpe, J., Dorman, O., & Jefferies, J. (2012). *Childbearing among UK born and non-UK born women living in the UK.* London: Office for National Statistics. http://www.ons.gov.uk/ons/dcp171766_283876.pdf. Accessed May 22, 2015.

Canadian Fertility Trends and Policies: A Story of Regional Variation

Sarah R. Brauner-Otto

Abstract Fertility in Canada has been declining since the peak of the baby boom in the late 1950s. The period total fertility rate (TFR) was almost 4.00 births per woman in 1959, reached a low of 1.51 in 2000, and currently stands at 1.61. The decline was greatest during the 1960s and then slowed considerably, and Canada's TFR has been fairly stable since the 1970s. The full story of Canadian fertility is not in this dramatic decline, however, but rather in the variation across provinces. Provinces have considerable freedom to implement their own policies and shape their own social institutions. As a result, the varying institutional contexts have supported different fertility trends and levels. Alberta and provinces or territories with relatively large Aboriginal populations have higher fertility, while British Columbia and Ontario have the lowest levels. Québec's fertility was the lowest in the 1980s but has seen a recent increase, likely at least partly a result of pro-natalist policies such as tax incentives, allowances, very low-cost childcare, and expansive parental leave.

Keywords Canada • Sub-regional variation • Childcare • Family benefits • Family policies

Like other wealthy, industrialized countries, Canada experienced a post-World War II baby boom followed by a baby bust. The period total fertility rate (TFR) reached a low of 1.51 births per woman in 2002 and has been between 1.61 and 1.68 since 2006 (Milan 2013). While this overall trend is common among wealthy, industrialized countries, Canada's specific path is actually rather unique. The current TFR is, on the one hand, below what we see in English-speaking and Scandinavian countries but, on the other hand, above that in the other European and low-fertility countries (Rindfuss et al. 2016). According to Esping-Andersen's framework (1990), liberal nations such as the English-speaking countries should have lower fertility than countries with more generous welfare states. The relatively

S.R. Brauner-Otto (✉)
Department of Sociology, McGill University, Montréal, Canada
e-mail: sarah.brauner-otto@mcgill.ca

R.R. Rindfuss and M.K. Choe (eds.), *Low Fertility, Institutions, and their Policies*, DOI 10.1007/978-3-319-32997-0_5

high fertility levels observed in English-speaking countries has perplexed scholars and has not been completely explained. In fact, it is likely that a combination of factors is at work to different degrees in different countries. Higher religiosity, a stronger pro-child value orientation, large immigrant pools with high fertility, and healthier economies are all likely contributors (Hayford and Morgan 2008; McDonald and Moyle 2010). But, as Canada does not have this unexpectedly high fertility, its unique path may be because it follows the Esping-Andersen predictions. Canadians are less religious and face higher youth unemployment rates than their neighbors in the United States (US) (Bélanger and Ouellet 2005). Additionally, Canada is not truly an English-speaking country, so this comparison may be faulty at the outset. Currently, 22 % of Canadians' list French as their mother tongue, and 30 % report being able to have a conversation in French (Statistics Canada 2011d). Québec, where 85 % of francophones live and 80 % of the population reports French as their mother tongue, was originally a French colony (the rest of Canada was British) and has maintained a distinct culture ever since.

This chapter explores recent Canadian fertility behavior and some of the major institutional factors that may be contributing to Canada's unique fertility situation. The first section describes Canadian fertility levels and trends, including details of the country-level fertility changes that have occurred since the early 1900s. For more recent fertility behavior (since the 1980s or 1990s), the chapter describes differences by demographic group (i.e., immigrants, Aboriginals, adolescents, and by relationship status) and by region (province and territory). These within-Canada differences end up being a crucial part of the story, particularly when we compare Québec to the rest of Canada. The second part of the chapter explores macro-level factors related to these observed fertility variations—the economy, education, culture, and social policy.

Fertility Trends

Figure 1 shows the Canadian period and cohort total fertility rates (TFR) from 1926 to 2011 (also shown is the period TFR for Québec, which will be discussed later). Like most wealthy, industrialized countries, fertility in Canada decreased in the 1920s and 1930s, reaching a low during the Great Depression, and then experienced a post-World War II baby boom, peaking with a period TFR of 3.94 births per woman around 1959 and a cohort TFR of 3.40 for the 1930 birth cohort. After this, both the period and cohort TFR began to decline, and by 1976 (for the 1948 birth cohort) both were below 2.00. Since then, the period TFR has fluctuated between 1.72 in 1992 and 1.51 in 2002. The cohort TFR has been steadier, fluctuating between 1.78 and 1.84 and rising to (an estimated) 1.85 in 2005 (for the 1977 birth cohort).

This lengthy, steady drop in TFR, followed by stability at low levels, marks a distinct fertility path for Canada (Rindfuss et al. 2016). Where English-speaking countries experienced a decline in the period TFR and then a leveling off at around

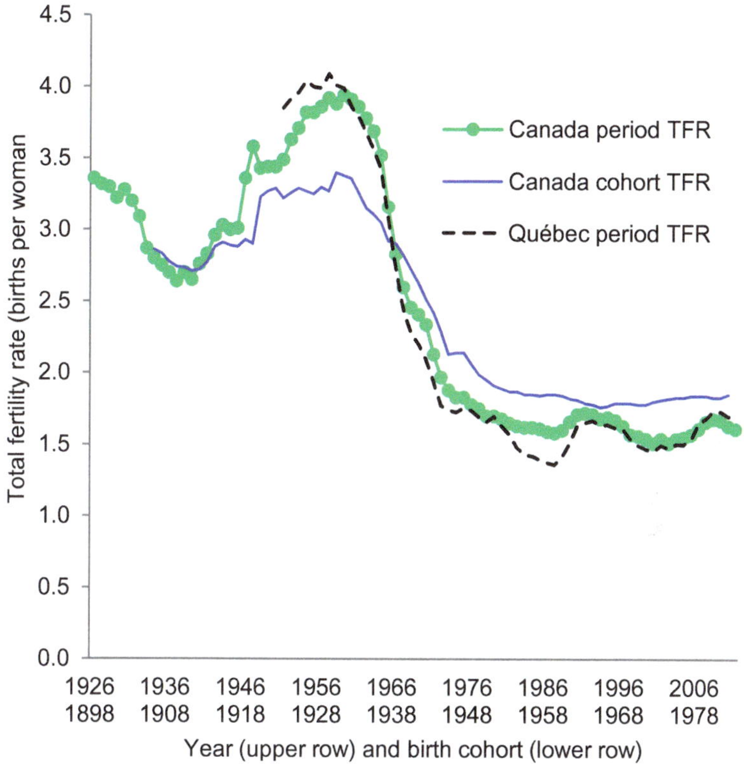

Fig. 1 Period and cohort total fertility rates (TFR), Canada 1926–2010; period TFR, Québec 1950–2010 (Statistics Canada 2015b; Statistics Canada, demography division, unpublished demographic estimates)

the replacement level of 2.1, fertility in Canada dropped more and has leveled off at a much lower rate of around 1.65 since 2008. While English-speaking countries have generally had TFRs above 1.75 since the 1980s, the Canadian TFR was equal to or greater than 1.75 only twice during this period. Scandinavian and Northern European countries had similarly severe decreases in fertility, reaching TFRs at or below 1.6, but they have experienced substantial increases since the mid-1980s and are now clustered with period TFRs between 1.75 and 1.89. German-speaking, Southern European, and Asian countries have continued their fertility declines and currently have TFRs at or below 1.5.

Declines in fertility have occurred across all parities in Canada but have been largest for higher-order births. Figure 2 shows the parity progression ratios (PPR) for birth cohorts from 1929 to 1959. Declines in higher-order parities have driven much of the TFR decrease, as can be seen from the steeper decrease in the PPR for parities three and four for cohorts born in the late 1930s and 1940s (i.e.,

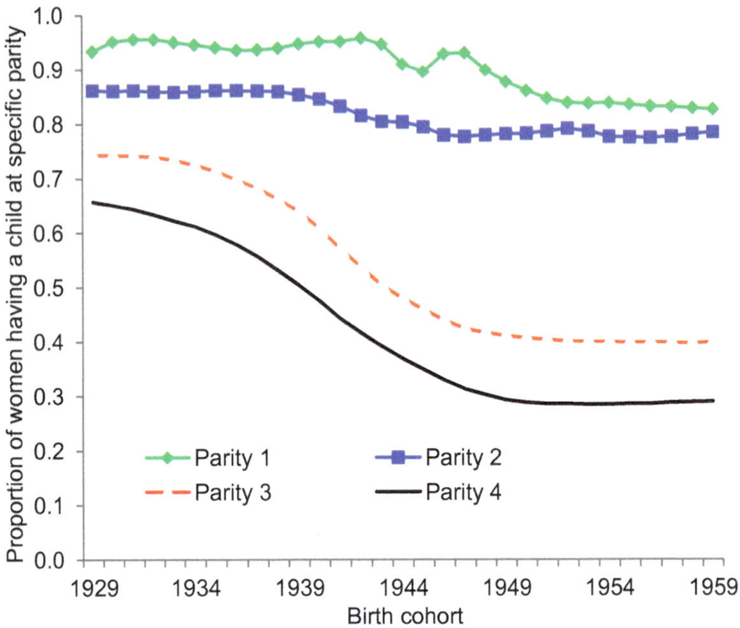

Fig. 2 Parity progression ratios, Canada 1929–1959 birth cohorts (Max Planck Institute for Demographic Research and Vienna Institute of Demography 2014)

those who would have been having their third and fourth births in the 1960s and 1970s). But there have also been sizable decreases in first- and second- parity births over this time period. In fact, the proportion childless rose from about 4 % for the 1942 birth cohort to more than 17 % for the 1958 birth cohort.

Some of the decrease in higher-order births is a result of postponement. Figure 3 shows the mean age of mothers at first and all births in Canada from 1960 to 2011. The mean age has been increasing steadily for first births since 1965, when it was 23.5, and for all births since 1975, when it was 26.7. By 1997, the mean age at first birth was greater than the mean for all births had been in 1975. In 2009, the mean age at first birth was 28.17, similar to that in Norway (27.88) and Finland (28.19) and much higher than in the US (25.6) (Max Planck Institute for Demographic Research and Vienna Institute of Demography 2014). This shift in the timing of childbearing can also be seen from changes in the age-specific fertility rates over time, as shown in Fig. 4. We can see the baby-boom period effect in the peaks across almost all ages in the 1950s. Fertility dropped for all age groups after 1961 but has been increasing for women age 30–34 and 35–39 since then. In fact, fertility for all women over 30 has been slightly greater or about equal to fertility for women age 25–29 since the mid-2000s (Statistics Canada 2008a).

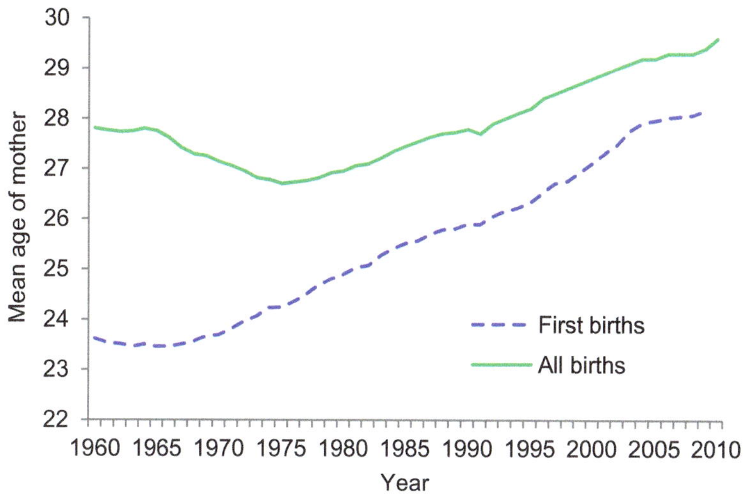

Fig. 3 Mean age of mother at first and all births, Canada, 1960–2011 (for all births: 1944–1990, Statistics Canada, demography division, unpublished demographic estimates; 1991–2010, Statistics Canada 2013b; for first births, Max Planck Institute for Demographic Research and Vienna Institute of Demography 2014)

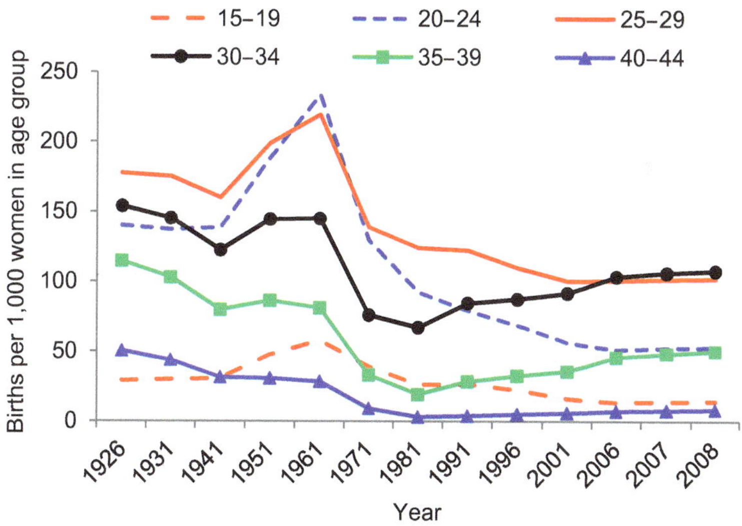

Fig. 4 Age-specific fertility rates, Canada, 1926–2008 (births per 1000 women in age group) (Statistics Canada 2011c)

The decrease and current low level of fertility have contributed to a changing shape of the Canadian population's age distribution (of course, migration and increasing longevity have also contributed). Figure 5 shows population pyramids

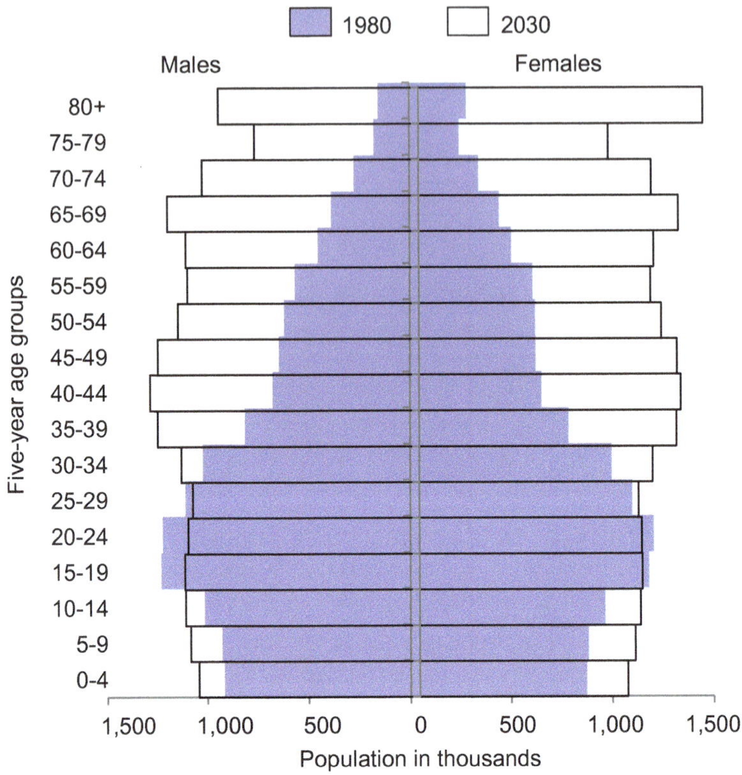

Fig. 5 Age and sex structure of Canada's population, 1980 estimated and 2025 projected (United Nations, Department of Economic and Social Affairs, Population Division 2012)

for 1980 (shaded) and projected for 2030 (outlined). Clearly, with the population distribution becoming increasingly rectangular, these two populations have very different needs. In particular, a larger share of the population will need health services and other care associated with aging, and the educational needs typically associated with young populations will not be as great. Although Canada's old-age dependency ratio is still substantially lower than the youth dependency ratio, they are expected to cross over as soon as 2021 (Denton et al. 2000). The extent to which this shift in the make-up of the Canadian population is problematic depends in part on how well the government addresses the changing healthcare needs and the potential strain on the public pension system (Trovato 2011).

Immigration

Also notable from Fig. 5 is that Canada does not have the inverted pyramid typical of a country with a history of low fertility. The wide base is partly due to immigration. In 2011, 20.6 % of the Canadian population was born outside of Canada (Statistics Canada 2011e). This is the highest proportion of foreign-born populations among the G8[1] countries (Statistics Canada 2011e). In 2001, 68 % of Canada's total population growth was due to immigration (Bélanger 2006). Of course, immigration alters population structures immediately by the influx of young, working-age adults (Statistics Canada 2008a). Additionally, when immigrant fertility is higher than that of the native-born population, immigration can have a longer-term influence on age structure and population growth. Recent immigrants, e.g., those arriving since 1996, do have higher fertility than native-born Canadians (Bélanger and Gilbert 2006; Woldemicael and Beaujot 2012), but this is largely true for women who immigrated when they were 14 years old or older (Adsera and Ferrer 2014). Overall, immigration does not have a compounding effect on Canadian fertility because women who immigrated before age six have essentially the same fertility as native-born women (Adsera and Ferrer 2014), and second-generation immigrant women (i.e., the daughters of immigrants) have lower or similar fertility to native-born women (Bélanger and Gilbert 2006).

The sending country is an important component of immigration with respect to fertility. In the 1981 Canadian census, 62 % of foreign-born women aged 15–54 were from Europe, dropping to 33 % in 2001 (Bélanger and Gilbert 2006; Beaujot and Woldemicael 2010). This contrast is especially important because women immigrating from Europe tend to have lower fertility than native-born Canadians, whereas other immigrant groups tend, at least initially, to have higher fertility. An increasing number of immigrants are coming from Asia (15 % in 1981 vs. 33 % in 2001), and although those from South and Southeast Asia tend to have higher fertility than native-born Canadians, East Asians have lower fertility (Adsera and Ferrer 2013, 2014). In sum, the shift in immigration streams away from Europe and toward higher-fertility countries has bolstered Canadian fertility since the 1990s. The extent to which this immigrant fertility effect will continue is unknown, especially if Asians, and in particular East Asians (who are coming from countries with very low fertility), continue to be the dominant group (Adsera and Ferrer 2014).

Visible Minority and Aboriginal Fertility

The literature on immigrant fertility also touches on the role of other forms of diversity in determining Canada's fertility. Visible-minority status is the key racial/ethnic distinction typically explored in the Canadian context: Visible minorities are "non-Caucasian in race or non-white in colour and who do not report being Aboriginal" (Statistics Canada 2009). There is evidence that much of the

[1]The Group of Eight (G8) consists of eight highly industrialized nations—France, Germany, Italy, the United Kingdom, Japan, the United States, Canada, and Russia.

observed difference in fertility rates for immigrant groups or ethnic groups including native-born Canadians can be accounted for by controlling for socio-demographic characteristics such as education and income (Beaujot and Woldemicael 2010). Even controlling for these characteristics, however, visible minorities still have higher fertility than other groups (Beaujot and Woldemicael 2010; Halli et al. 1996).

Aboriginal women also have higher fertility than non-Aboriginal women (Quinless 2012; Suwal and Trovato 1998).[2] In 1991, the average number of children born to couples in which both the mother and father were Aboriginal was 3.36, whereas it was only 2.12 for non-Aboriginal couples (Suwal and Trovato 1998). In the 2006 census, only 30 % of Aboriginal families had no children in the household, compared with almost 40 % of non-Aboriginal families. Aboriginal families were also more likely to be living with three or more children (17 % vs. 9.9 %) (Quinless 2012). Socio-economic differences likely play a large role in these different fertility behaviors, but there may also be strong cultural norms for larger families and limited access to contraception, particularly as Aboriginal families are more likely to be living in remote areas with poor or non-existent access to healthcare (Quinless 2012). Discussing the fertility of Aboriginal women in Canada helps present as encompassing a picture of Canadian fertility as possible, but it is also important to recognize that the Aboriginal population represented only 4.3 % of the total Canadian population in 2011, so their high fertility rate contributes little to overall fertility trends and levels (Statistics Canada 2011b).

Adolescent Fertility

Although perhaps high by European or Asian standards, adolescent or teen pregnancy rates in Canada are much lower than in the US. The birth rate to women age 15–19 has fallen steadily since the late 1960s and is currently at about 10 births per 1000 women (Statistics Canada 2008a, c, 2013a, 2014a). This is likely due both to more effective use of contraception and better access to abortion than in the US (Nordberg et al. 2014). Not surprisingly given the regional variation in the provision of health services, familial norms, and the distribution of Aboriginal populations [by some estimates, Aboriginal teens are four times more likely to have a pregnancy than other population groups (Murdoch 2009)], the teen pregnancy rate also varies by region (Nordberg et al. 2014).

---

[2] I follow the cited literature when referring to the Aboriginal population, which generally uses the term Aboriginal to include those who identify themselves as Aboriginal and/or as Registered Indians, members of an Indian Band, or First Nation. This includes Inuit and Métis.

Regional Variation

The discussion of immigrant, Aboriginal, and adolescent fertility leads us to a crucial component of the Canadian story—regional variation. The overall level of immigration, dominant migration stream, and relative size of the Aboriginal population vary considerably by province. For example, Asian immigrants are more likely to move to British Columbia and African immigrants to Québec. As of the 2006 census, Aboriginals made up 85 % of the population of Nunavut and 50 % of the population of the Northwest Territories (Statistics Canada 2008b).

Figure 6 shows the TFRs for all Canadian provinces and territories. We see the substantially higher fertility in Nunavut and the Northwest Territories, which is likely due to the large Aboriginal populations in those regions (they are also poor, have very limited access to healthcare, and have low education rates—all factors correlated with high fertility). These two regions only constitute 0.3 % of the total Canadian population, however, making their overall impact on the national-level period TFR small. Other regions with small populations are the Maritime Provinces (New Brunswick, Nova Scotia, and Prince Edward Island), Newfoundland and Labrador, and Yukon. Fertility in these regions has been lower than elsewhere, with recent TFRs between 1.4 and 1.7. Together, these five provinces and territories made up only 5.6 % of the total Canadian population in 2011. The Prairie Provinces —Saskatchewan, Manitoba, and Alberta—have fertility levels close to replacement level and together make up 18 % of the population, although most of that is due to Alberta which accounts for 11 %. Since the four largest provinces of Ontario, Québec, British Columbia, and Alberta account for 86 % of the Canadian population, this chapter will largely focus on those areas. Figure 7 shows the TFRs for these provinces and clearly illustrates the provincial variation.

Fertility in Alberta has been the highest of these four provinces, remaining fairly stable near the replacement level. In fact, the TFR for Alberta is similar to, although somewhat lower than, fertility in other English-speaking countries such as Australia and the United Kingdom (UK). British Columbia (BC) has had lower fertility, with a TFR as low as 1.39 in 2002. The TFR in Ontario, the largest province by population, has been much closer to the level for Canada as a whole, ranging from 1.67 in the late 1990s to 1.47 in 2002. It has also been less variable over time than fertility in BC. Finally, we turn to Québec and see that the TFR was substantially lower than in the other provinces until the early 1990s—it reached a low of 1.37 in 1987. Throughout the 1990s, Québec had a TFR similar to that of BC and Ontario, but around 2000, fertility in Québec started to rise, reaching a high of 1.74 in 2008 and 2009. In fact, fertility in Québec has historically been different from that of the rest of Canada (see Fig. 1). During the first half of the 20th century, Québec experienced a long period of sustained high fertility, higher than in the rest of Canada (Krull 2000; Krull and Trovato 2003; Parent and Wang 2007). Starting in the 1960s it experienced a dramatic decrease in the period TFR—a decrease linked to the major economic and social transformations that occurred during the "Quiet Revolution" discussed below.

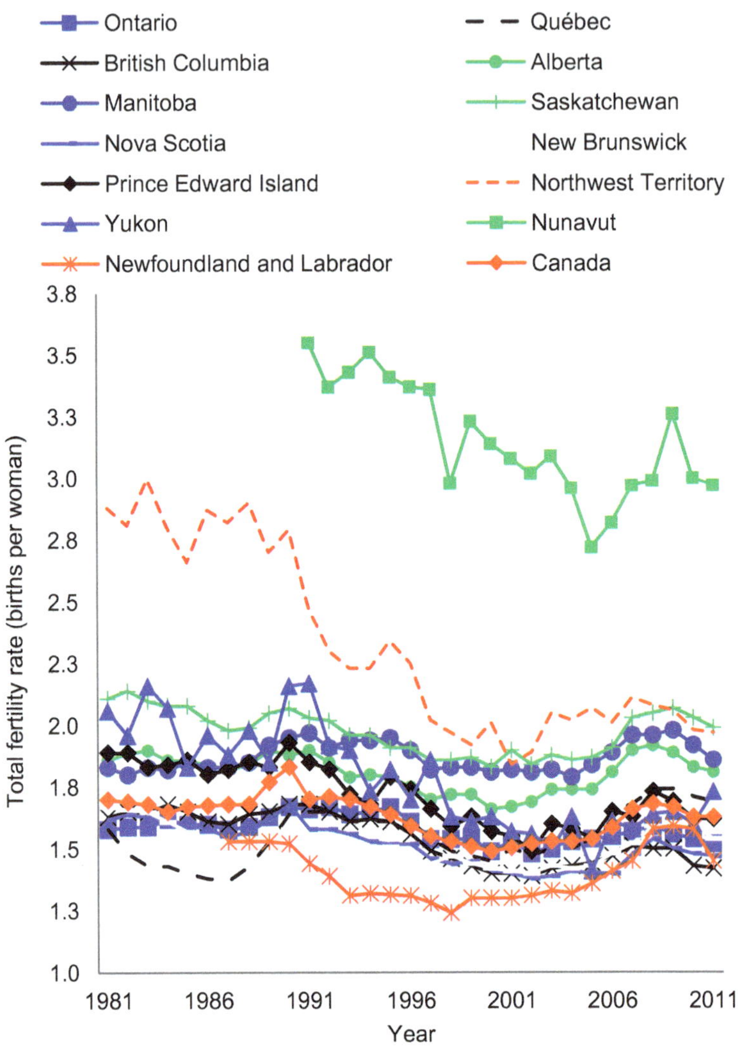

Fig. 6 Total fertility rate (TFR) for Canadian provinces, 1981–2011 (Statistics Canada 2015b; Milan 2013). *Notes* Births to mothers for whom the age is unknown were prorated. Nunavut is included in Northwest Territories before 1991. Data by age of mother are not available for Newfoundland and Labrador before 1991

By way of comparison, the largest difference between the TFR in Alberta and Québec was in 1983, a difference of 0.47 children that was similar to the difference between the Netherlands and Greece at the time. In 2011, the difference of 0.12 children between Alberta and Québec was similar to the difference between Denmark and Australia, while BC and Ontario compared to Alberta as Switzerland and Austria compared to Belgium (Rindfuss et al. 2016).

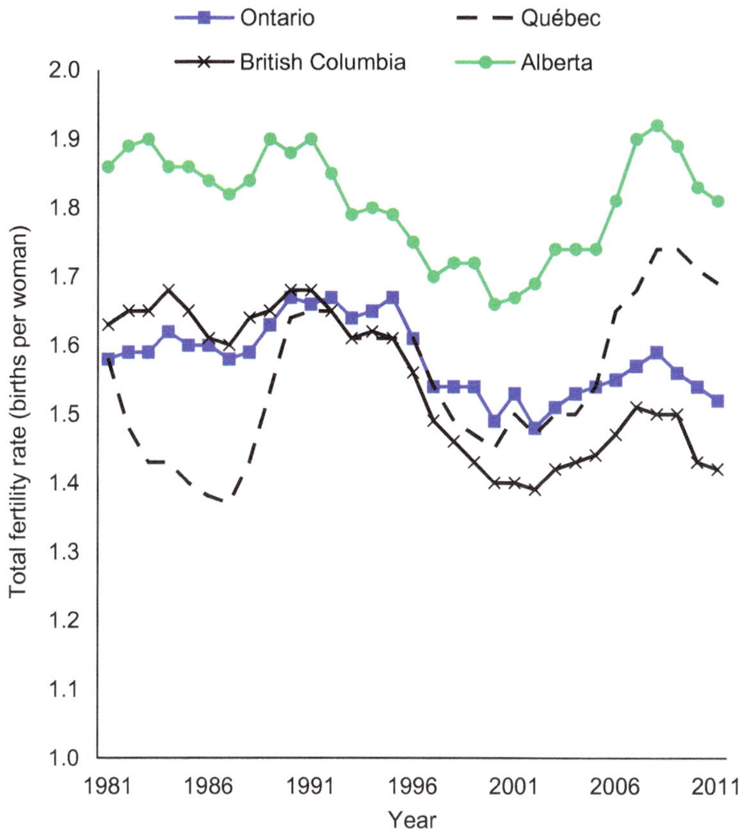

Fig. 7 Total fertility rate (TFR) for major Canadian provinces, 1981–2011 (Statistics Canada 2015b; Milan 2013)

There is also considerable regional variation in the mean age of childbearing. Since at least 1991, the mean age of childbearing has been steadily increasing in all regions except Nunavut and the Northwest Territories where it has remained stable (Statistics Canada 2013b). Of the four major provinces, the largest increase over the 20 years was in BC, where the mean age at childbearing rose 2.4 years to reach 30.4 years in 2011. The smallest increases were in Québec and Alberta where the mean age of childbearing rose 1.9 years to 29.6 and 29.2, respectively. There are also interesting international comparisons. In Ontario and BC, the mean age at childbearing has been similar to that in Norway and Finland, whereas Québec is more similar to Scotland and England and Wales (Max Planck Institute for Demographic Research and Vienna Institute of Demography 2014; Statistics Canada 2013b). Up until the mid-1980s, the mean age at first birth in Québec was higher than that in most Scandinavian countries, but since then it has been lower than in Scandinavia and many other European countries (Roy and Bernier 2007).

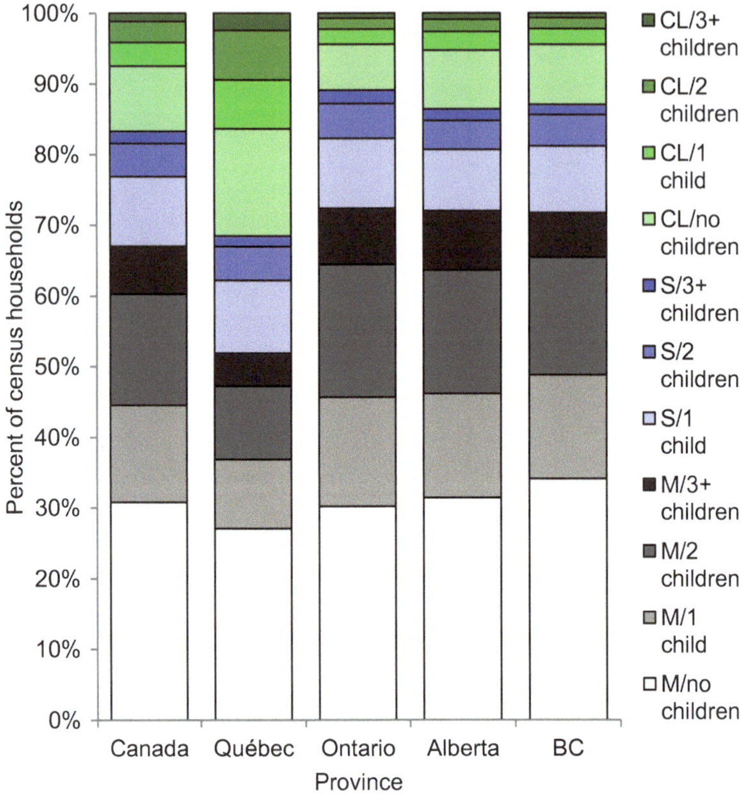

Fig. 8 Structure of Canadian census households by province, 2011 (Statistics Canada 2011a). *Note:* *M* = married, *S* = single, *CL* = common-law; census households exclude households composed of a person living alone

An important way to examine fertility across Canadian regions is by marital status. Common-law unions (as cohabiting unions are referred to in Canada) are more common in Québec than in the rest of Canada. Researchers have described them as a substitute for marriage in Québec but not in the rest of Canada (Le Bourdais and Lapierre-Adamcyk 2004), and in Québec they are not typically associated with lower socio-economic status as they are in other provinces (Kerr et al. 2006; Stalker and Ornstein 2013). Figure 8 shows the distribution of Canadian households by parental and marital status for Canada and the four major provinces. In 2011, 32 % of census families in Québec were common-law unions, compared with 11 % in Ontario, 14 % in Alberta, and 13 % in BC (top four areas of bars in Fig. 8).[3] Additionally, 16 % of census families in Québec are common-law

[3]These percentages exclude single people living alone. In the 2011 census, 32 % of households in Québec had one person, compared with 25 % in Ontario and Alberta and 28 % in BC.

unions with children, compared with 4 or 5 % in the other major provinces. Since the mid-1990s, more than one-half of births in Québec have been to women in common-law unions (Laplante and Fostik 2014). Although age-specific fertility rates remain higher in marriage than in common-law unions, common-law unions contribute 70 % of the overall fertility in Québec because they account for such a large share of the population (Laplante and Fostik 2014). Notably, this difference is driven by the behavior of French-speaking Québécois, because the union-formation and fertility patterns of immigrants and English speakers in Québec tend to be similar to patterns in the rest of Canada (Laplante and Fostik 2014).

Macro-Level Correlates of Regional Variation in Fertility

So why do we see such different fertility behavior in different regions of the same country? The discussions on immigration and Aboriginal populations reveal that some regional differences in fertility likely stem from demographic, compositional differences. There are also macro-level factors that are likely to be particularly salient. Macro-level factors or social institutions such as economic growth or social policy are regularly identified as influential when comparing countries (Castles 2003; Chandola et al. 2002; McNicoll 2009). Canada has a federalist political system with each province having a fair amount of autonomy, meaning that social institutions vary considerably across regions. There are also major regional cultural differences, particularly when comparing Québec to the rest of Canada. Beaujot and Wang (2010) describe the Canadian fertility scheme in terms of risk, pointing out that fertility is highest where the risk is lowest and lowest where the risk is highest. Under this framework, Alberta and Québec have been more successful at reducing risk to young people than BC or Ontario. Alberta has accomplished this through a stronger economy and Québec through a strong system of social-welfare support (Beaujot and Wang 2010). In fact, some have likened Québec to the Nordic countries in terms of its social-welfare institutions and orientation (Beaujot and Wang 2010; Roy and Bernier 2007). Of course, the economy and policies are likely endogenous to these cultural factors. The aim of this chapter is not to definitively identify any one of these as causally related to fertility. Rather, it is to highlight some of the major regional differences that are correlated with the observed fertility differences.

Although all provinces have the same amount of autonomy and same legal relationship at the federal level, Québec, in particular, has had a long history of cultural and institutional differences. As the only former French colony, with stronger cultural ties to France than to England, Québec has an identity and social structure distinct from the rest of Canada. For example, Québec operates under civil law, as in France, while the other provinces and the federal government follow common law. Also, while both English and French are official languages at the federal level, only French is the official language of Québec. In fact, the need to preserve the French language and culture is part of the public discourse surrounding fertility and family policy in Québec. A full discussion of culture in Canada is beyond the scope of this chapter, but here I briefly discuss how language and religion, two major components of cultural identity in Canada, have different social meanings across regions.

Language is one of the many long-held cultural differences between Québec and the rest of Canada and is often seen as the cornerstone of Québec culture. Religion is a social institution tightly connected to fertility that has tremendous provincial variation (Laplante 2006; Wu and Baer 1996). In Québec, the vast majority (roughly 80 %) of residents are Catholic, whereas in the rest of Canada only about 30 % are Catholic and the majority is Protestant (Statistics Canada 2005). These broad statements mask important nuances within language and religious groups, however. Analyses of fertility in Canada in the late 1800s and early 1900s (when fertility was generally higher in Québec than in the rest of Canada) reveals that English-speaking Protestants living in Québec had fertility behavior more similar to English-speaking Protestants living in Ontario than to other Québécois, while in the late 1800s, English-speaking Catholics in Québec (largely of Irish decent) had fertility behavior more similar to French-speaking Catholics (Gauvreau 2006; Gauvreau and Gossage 2001).[4]

These differences may reflect different ideologies but are perhaps more reflective of the relationship between religion and the state. While the Protestant church was never particularly active in state affairs in the rest of Canada, the Catholic Church played a major role in all areas of Québec life. Before the 1960s, the Catholic Church controlled all health and social services, education, labor unions, and credit unions. The pro-natalist effect of this level of control is well illustrated by the fact that in 1901 more-educated women in Québec had larger families than less-educated women in Québec or than all women in Ontario. Québécois women had received their education at Catholic schools, which would have stressed the pro-natalist policies of the Church.

A "Quiet Revolution" started in Québec in the late 1950s and early 1960s with the election of the Lesage Liberal government (Dickinson and Young 2003).[5] This period saw a concerted policy and governmental shift away from the agrarian-focused, cradle-to-grave policies dictated by the Catholic Church toward secular, pro-industrialization policies (Dickinson and Young 2003). The end result of this social upheaval was that virtually all social institutions were controlled by the secular government, essentially ending the control of the Church over the majority of the population. Krull (2007) provides evidence that the big fertility

[4]Irish Catholics in Québec did appear to experience a fertility decline earlier than French-speaking Catholics, so that by 1901 their fertility was between that of the French-speaking Catholics and English-speaking Protestants. The religious-regional variation in fertility is well documented by Gauvreau (2006).

[5]The term "Quiet Revolution" is widely used today, although it is not an official name for this period (Bélanger 2000).

decline in Québec after 1960 is the result of a period effect—the new social climate lowered fertility rates for all ages.

Following the Quiet Revolution, the relationship between religion, region, and fertility essentially reversed, and French-speaking Catholics in Quebec now have lower fertility than English-speaking Protestants (Laplante 2006), while English-speaking Catholics are between English-speaking Protestants and French-speaking Catholics on an array of family-related behaviors and attitudes (Wu and Baer 1996; Laplante and Fostik 2014). One potential explanation for the low fertility among French-speaking Catholics today is that they are less religious than English-speaking Protestants, and research has demonstrated that it is religiosity (practice and/or salience) and not affiliation that is linked to fertility behavior (Frejka and Westoff 2007; Pearce 2002; Thornton et al. 1992; Thornton and Camburn 1987).

Post-"Revolution" Québécois also appear to be more gender egalitarian than people in the rest of Canada (Wu and Baer 1996). We can see these differences in many demographic behaviors. For example, Québec has higher rates of common-law unions (which researchers find to be more gender egalitarian than marriages), lower rates of marriage, higher rates of childbearing within common-law unions, and higher rates of women's laborforce participation than the rest of Canada (Le Bourdais and Marcil-Gratton 1996; Pollard and Wu 1998; Wu and Schimmele 2011). Québécois also typically have less gendered divisions of household labor (Stalker and Ornstein 2013).

A study of attitudes toward family and gender roles using data from the 1984 Canadian Fertility Survey found that French-speaking Catholics were more supportive of egalitarian gender roles (i.e., sharing responsibilities for looking after children, cooking, and housework and accepting the importance for women's happiness of having a job outside the home) than English-speaking Catholics or English-speaking non-Catholics (due to small sample sizes, it was not possible to include French-speaking non-Catholics) (Wu and Baer 1996). The study found a negative correlation between gender egalitarianism and the importance of children among English-speaking Canadians, but a positive correlation among French-speaking Canadians. The authors also saw a negative correlation between the importance of marriage and the importance of children among French-speaking Canadians. This variation in the ways in which attitudes combine for French- and English-speaking Canadians might be connected to the higher fertility observed in cohabiting unions in Quebec than in the rest of Canada. In other analyses, these authors find that English-speaking non-Catholics are more similar to French-speaking Catholics in attitudes about family and gender roles than they are to English-speaking Catholics.

These cultural differences in language, religion, and attitudes toward gender equality and family are generally viewed positively in Québec, which has always been concerned with maintaining a separate identity. In light of this concern and because it saw an even larger decrease in fertility following the baby boom than occurred in the rest of Canada, the Québec government has consistently had more generous family policies than the rest of Canada, generally electing to alter federal policies and implement its own benefits when possible. I discuss these specific policies below in more detail. In the following sections, I go on to discuss other economic and social factors identified as relevant to fertility, paying particular attention to how those factors vary between Québec and the rest of Canada (Rindfuss and Brauner-Otto 2008).

Cash Transfers and Tax Benefits

Although child-related benefits are in place throughout Canada (e.g., the federal child benefit), they have generally been greater in Québec than elsewhere, and in Québec they were initially explicitly designed to encourage childbearing. This section provides highlights of the federal and Québec programs (for a detailed discussion, see Duclos et al. 2001; Ang 2015).

Canadian federal child-related policy has included both a family allowance and tax deductions since 1945. The Family Allowance Act of 1973 extended eligibility to all children under 18 and increased the benefit to CAD240 (US$192 as of 1 June 2015)/child/year (Parent and Wang 2007). Reforms starting in the late 1980s focused on increasing the benefits to working families with children. For example, in 1985 a two-parent, two-child family with an earned income of CAD40,000 (US $31,935) would have received CAD911 per year (US$727). This amount increased by 51 % to CAD1,378 (US$1100) per year in 1995 (Duclos et al. 2001). In addition, the Universal Child Care Benefit was introduced in 2006 and is currently in place. This is a CAD100 (US$ 80)/month taxable payment for each child under the age of six. Increases starting in 2015 were announced at the end of 2014.

Québec has had substantial additional benefits (typically tied to parity) on top of the federal ones. Family allowances were in place from at least the mid-1970s, and for all but the first child the benefits for families in Québec were greater than in the rest of Canada. In 1974, when the Family Allowance program came into effect across Canada, a family in Québec received CAD291.48 (US$233) per year for a second child age 0–11, while a family in the rest of Canada received CAD240 (US $192) for a child at any parity. The differences became more pronounced at higher parities because the amount received in the rest of Canada did not vary by parity, but in Québec it increased to more than CAD500 (US$399) for a fourth or higher-parity child (Parent and Wang 2007).

Another notable policy change occurred in Québec in 1988 with the introduction of the Allowance for Newborn Children (ANC). This "baby bonus" was a non-taxable benefit available to residents of Québec as part of a significant change in policy. Reportedly in response to public demand and concerns about low fertility, the provincial government began in 1981 to place more importance on family, fertility, and family policy (Conseil de la famille et de l'enfance Québec 2008). In the 1988/89 budget, the government addressed these issues, focusing on financial support for families, and for families with many children in particular. The size of the ANC benefit depended on parity and initially paid CAD500 (US$399) at the birth of a first or second child and CAD3,000 (US$2395) at the birth of a third or higher-parity child. The larger payments were made in quarterly installments of CAD500 (US$399). The baby bonuses steadily became more generous for second and higher-parity births, so that by May 1992 families received CAD500 (US$399) for a first child, CAD1,000 (US$798) for a second, and CAD8,000 (US$6387) for a third. This program ended in 1997, as government priorities shifted away from financial support toward service provision. The Québec government announced that it would replace the ANC with an Integrated Child Allowance (an income-tested benefit rather than a universal allowance), expansion and improvement of early-childhood education (i.e., childcare subsidies), and more generous parental leave. In 2005, the previous child tax policy was replaced with a universal refundable tax credit that varies by income and family structure. In 2015, the amount for one child ranges from CAD664 (US$530) to CAD2,366 (US$1889) per year (Regie des rentes Québec 2015).

In sum, families in Québec receive substantially more per-child benefits than families in the rest of Canada. Between 1985 and 1995, benefits at the federal level increased by a factor of 1.5, but they increased by a factor of 5.0 in Québec.

Have these higher benefits translated into higher birth rates for Québec? Analysis of the 1974 Family Allowance Act finds evidence that the benefits influenced the timing of childbearing but not completed fertility (Parent and Wang 2007). Some have said that the ANC was cancelled because it did not effectively increase fertility (see discussion in Milligan 2005), and in fact, the number of births in Québec was lower in 1996 than when the policy was initiated (Statistics Canada 2014b). By contrast, more sophisticated demographic investigations employing a difference-in-difference approach have found that fertility changes in Québec under the ANC were different from those in the rest of Canada. Using vital statistics, Duclos et al. (2001) found a positive effect of the ANC on fertility. The effect was largest for third-parity births, decreased with mother's age, and did have some quantum effect, particularly for third-parity births. Using census data, Milligan (2005) also found a significant positive effect of the policy on fertility—fertility increased by an average of 12 % and by as much as 25 % depending on family composition and income. Furthermore, he found that the effect of the policy was greater for higher-parity births and wealthier families. Most recently, Ang (2015) found that the ANC increased birth rates only slightly (1.72 %), and Kim (2014) found that there was no effect on completed fertility.

These contradictory findings may be because of differences in data (the Ang study used the census master files as opposed to the public microdata files that Milligan used) or because Ang accounted for other financial policies available at the same time. If we acknowledge that childbearing decisions occur over time and are the result of ongoing reassessments, it is possible that all of these findings are correct. That is, it may have been that when the ANC was in place women and couples felt that supporting a larger family was feasible and therefore had another child(ren) with the intention of having a larger completed family size. When the ANC ended, these same people may have reevaluated the situation and now deemed that a smaller family size was ideal. Because the benefit was not in place for a woman's entire reproductive period, we ultimately cannot identify whether a woman's completed fertility was the result of a planned increase in number of children while the benefit was in place minus a recalculated planned number of children once the benefit was withdrawn or whether the benefit only influenced the timing of births.

Childcare

Another area of family policy where Québec has invested more than the rest of Canada is childcare. Canada has no federal childcare policy, although parents can claim childcare deductions on their tax returns. As Québec replaced the "baby bonus" with an income-tested child allowance in 1997, the government also initiated a major expansion of the childcare system. In the first year of the program, full-day, subsidized daycare spaces[6] for four-year-olds were priced at CAD5.00 (US$3.99) per day per child. Each year, the subsidized daycare spaces were made available to children one year younger, so that by 2000, coverage was expanded to all children under five. The number of subsidized places expanded from 74,058 in 1997 to more than 200,000 in 2010, so that reduced-fee daycare is now available to more than one-half of all eligible children age 0–5 (Lefebvre et al. 2011). In 2004, the price of daycare increased to CAD7.00 (US$5.59) per child per day, and in mid-2014 it increased to CAD7.30 (US$5.83). To put this in perspective, the minimum wage in Québec is CAD10.15 (US$8.10)/hour. In November 2014, the government announced a change from the flat-rate fee to a sliding scale based on income. The fee is now CAD7.30 (US$5.83) per child per day for families earning less than CAD50,000 (US$39,919) per year, gradually rising to CAD$8.00 (US $6.39) for families with annual incomes of CAD50,000–CAD75,000 (US$39,919–US$59,878), and CAD20.00 (US$15.97) for families with incomes of CAD155,000 (US$123,749) or more.

As one would expect, a greater proportion of pre-school-aged children are in regulated, center-based daycare in Québec than in the rest of Canada. In 1994–95, 24 % of eligible children were in daycare in Québec compared with 21 % in the rest of Canada. Since then the proportion enrolled has increased much more quickly in Québec, in 2004–05 reaching 72 % of children age 0–5 whose parents were employed or studying, compared with 42 % in the rest of Canada (Cleveland et al. 2008).[7]

[6]Subsidized spaces were created by opening new Centres de la Petite Enfance (CPEs) and by providing subsidy payments to existing centers. Centers are typically open from about 7:00 or 7:30 a.m. to 5:00 or 6:00 p.m. These hours enable most workers to drop off and pick up their children around a typical eight-hour work day.

[7]These data come from the National Longitudinal Survey of Children and Youth (NLSCY) and are only representative of families with both parents employed or studying, not all Canadian families. As Cleveland et al. (2008, p. 6) say "the NLSCY provides an incomplete picture of childcare-use patterns. Still, the data are the best currently available."

At the time the expansion of daycare was announced, the explicit policy goals were to help families balance work and family life and to improve and equalize child development and educational readiness for all Québec children (Conseil de la famille et de l'enfance Québec 2008), not to increase fertility. Accessible childcare should make childrearing easier, however, lowering the costs of having children and therefore increasing fertility. The empirical evaluations of the policy have followed the stated policy expectations, focusing largely on the workforce and on school readiness. For example, existing research has examined the link between daycare expansion and women's laborforce participation and gender equality. Using difference-in-difference approaches comparing Québec with the rest of Canada, this research indicates that the childcare expansion increased mothers' employment in Québec. Estimates reveal that in 2008 an additional 70,000 women have been employed as a result of the daycare expansion than would have been without such an expansion (Fortin et al. 2012) and that laborforce-participation rates of mothers with children age 1–5 increased by 8 % and are now markedly higher in Québec than in the rest of Canada (Beaujot et al. 2013; Lefebvre and Merrigan 2008). These additional laborforce contributions have resulted in a higher gross domestic product (GDP) and a positive tax-transfer balance for the government—meaning the costs of fertility for the economy are less than they would have been otherwise.

In terms of gender equality, daycare expansion has been linked to a decrease in households with a traditional division of household labor. The proportion of families with a breadwinner/homemaker employment model declined in Québec by more than 5 % from 1996 to 2006, compared to a 0.5 % decline in the rest of Canada. One-half of this decrease in Québec was due to an increase in the proportion of couples who both work full time (Stalker and Ornstein 2013). Over the same period, there has also been a small change in the division of childcare between couples, with a slightly greater increase in the number of couples reporting equal sharing of childcare in Québec than in the rest of Canada (Stalker and Ornstein 2013). Improvements in work-family balance and decreases in gendered divisions of household labor are linked to increased fertility in many existing theoretical frameworks.

An additional note on the expansion of subsidized childcare concerns the high take-up rates. Families across income levels are eager to obtain a subsidized place and, even though the system has expanded, demand is still greater than supply. This has led to questions of equity and quality, and some argue for reforms to the program. Given the limited number of subsidized places, parents often exploit their resources and social capital (e.g., personal connections) to obtain a place. Wealthier parents generally have more useful connections, and they have access to more places because they are less constrained by geography. (It is easier to take your child to a Centre de la Petite Enfance (CPE) on the other side of the city if you can drive your car there in 20 min than if you have to spend more than one hour on public transportation.) Regarding quality, research findings suggest that Québec children who have been in daycare are not better prepared for school than other children. Many have voiced concerns that the pressure to increase the number of places has overwhelmed the government's ability to enforce the originally promised high-quality of care.

Parental Leave

Family leave also varies between Québec and the rest of Canada, both in terms of coverage and compensation. Paid maternity leave was first provided at the federal level in 1971 under Unemployment Insurance (UI). The benefit was fairly modest—15 weeks at two-thirds of weekly earnings—and women were only eligible for full benefits if they had worked at least 20 weeks in the previous year (Weise 1972). This policy went largely unchanged until 1996, although many collective-bargaining agreements put in place during this period included benefits more generous than the federal policy (Pulkingham and van der Gaag 2004). In 1996, maternity leave became part of the Employment Insurance Act (EI). Under this plan, women could receive 15 weeks of pregnancy benefits and 10 weeks of parental leave (which technically can be split between parents but is generally taken by mothers) at a salary-replacement rate of 55 % to a maximum of CAD39,000 (US $31,137) per year (Ang 2015). To be eligible for benefits, women had to have worked 700 h in the previous year—self-employed women were not included. There was also a two-week waiting period during which no benefits were paid. In 2000, parental leave was expanded from 10 to 35 weeks, and the eligibility requirement was reduced to 600 h of work in the previous year.

Since January 2006, Québec has offered an alternative, more generous plan, the Québec Parental Insurance Program (QPIP). The Québec government had intended to implement its own plan in 1997 when the province switched from the ANC to childcare subsidies. It was not until 2005, however, that the Québec government was able to reach an agreement with the federal government, and the new plan was introduced in January 2006 (Conseil de la famille et de l'enfance Québec 2008). Table 1 provides the details of how QPIP differs from the federal policy. The Québec plan pays at a substantially higher rate, covers more earnings, has no waiting period, has reserved time for fathers, and makes far more women eligible because it covers the self-employed and has a low earnings threshold. Additionally, parents in Québec have some choice in how they use the benefits—they can elect a special plan that pays at a higher rate but for a shorter time period. Parents who elect the basic QPIP can receive almost twice as much salary replacement as they would if they lived in a different province.

A final note about parental leave policy in Canada: Many employers elect to provide Supplemental Unemployment Benefits (SUB), commonly known as top-ups, to their employees on leave (Marshall 2010). These benefits are regulated at the federal level but are completely voluntary. Most plans limit benefits to full-time regular employees who have a minimum prior work history and are eligible for federal benefits. Typically, employees sign an agreement that they will return to their employer for a specified time after taking parental leave or will repay

Table 1 Parental leave in Canada and Quebec, 2006 (Government of Canada, Justice Laws Website 2015; Éditeur officiel du Québec 2015; Ang 2015)

	Québec (QPIP)		
	Canada (EI)	Basic plan	Special plan
Eligibility	600 h insurable earnings in past year	Insurable earnings of at least CAD2,000 (US $1623) in past year	Insurable earnings of at least CAD2,000 (US $1623) in past year
Birth mothers	15 weeks maternity leave; 55 % of insurable earnings up to CAD39,000 (US $31,656) in 2006; 2-week waiting period	18 weeks maternity leave; 70 % of insurable earnings up to CAD59,000 (US $47,890) in 2006; no waiting period	15 weeks maternity leave; 75 % of insurable earnings up to CAD59,000 (US $47,890) in 2006; no waiting period
Birth fathers	Not covered	5 weeks paternity leave	3 weeks paternity leave
All parents (birth and adoptive)	35 weeks parental leave, taken by one or shared by both parents; benefits same as maternity but no 2nd waiting period	32 (37) weeks parental leave for birth (adoptive) parents, taken by one or shared by both parents; benefits same as maternity except for benefit rate: 7 (12) weeks at 70 % of insurable earnings, 25 weeks at 55 % for birth (adoptive) parents	25 (29) weeks parental leave for birth (adoptive) parents, taken by one or shared by both parents; benefit rate is 75 % of insurable earnings for all weeks
Maximum yearly insurable earnings	CAD21,750 (US $17,654) in 2008 dollars	CAD40,430 (US $32,817) in 2008 dollars	CAD37,522 (US $30,456) in 2008 dollars

the top-up. In 2008, 20 % of women in Canada who received paid leave also received an employer top-up. Mothers in Québec were 2.7 times more likely to report having an employer top-up than in the rest of Canada (Marshall 2010). Some of this may be because women employed in the public sector and those covered by collective-bargaining agreements are more likely to receive top-ups, and both of these employment categories are more common in Quebec (Marshall 2010).

As one might expect, since Québec explicitly reserves some leave for fathers and because the higher maximum benefits make leave more appealing to men, Québec fathers are much more likely to take parental leave than fathers in the rest of Canada. In 2006, take-up rates were 56 % in Québec, compared to 11 % elsewhere (Tremblay 2009). Research outside Canada suggests that higher use of paternity leave is related to more gender equity, which is related to fertility.

There have been a few empirical studies of the relationship between parental leave and fertility in Canada. In a study of Canada as a whole, Phipps (2000) did not find any evidence that parental leave benefits influenced fertility. On the other hand, Ang (2015) used census data in a difference-in-difference approach to assess the effect of Québec's plan on fertility and showed that the QPIP increased the birth rate by 23.5 %. Almost one-half (46 %) of these additional births were second-parity births. Some of this effect is likely due to changes in the timing of childbearing.[8] The QPIP was only implemented in 2006, so we are not able to see its full effect on completed fertility. Given the long period of public debate leading up to its implementation, the additional births may reflect some catching up on intentionally delayed childbearing. Interestingly, Crompton and Keown (2009) found that respondents from Québec in the 2006 General Social Survey were one-half as likely as Canadians in other provinces to report that access to maternity/paternity benefits are a "very important" factor in deciding to have a/nother child.

Empirical research, including some of the work cited above, has also investigated the relationship between parental leave policies and women's labor outcomes in Canada. This research generally finds that more generous policies are associated with higher rates of laborforce participation among women of childbearing age (Ang 2015; McNown and Ridao-Cano 2004).

Economic Conditions

The connection between the economy and fertility is not new, nor is it specific to Canada—fertility tends to be higher under better economic conditions (e.g., higher wages, lower unemployment, more stable economic growth) (Krull and Trovato 2003; Roy and Bernier 2007). The "modernization" of the Québec economy after the Quiet Revolution was a major factor in the dramatic fertility decrease at that time (Krull 2007; Krull and Trovato 2003). The period TFRs for Newfoundland and Labrador and for Alberta also suggest the importance of the overall economic status for fertility (Fig. 5). Newfoundland and Labrador comprise an Atlantic coastal province with a long reliance on fishing. The collapse of the cod fishing industry in the 1990s resulted in massive economic depression for the province and major outmigration. The very low fertility levels seen throughout the 1990s and early 2000s reflect this dire economic situation. In general, the provinces with the highest unemployment rates—Newfoundland and Labrador, Prince Edward Island, and New Brunswick—also have some of the lowest period TFRs (Statistics Canada 2015a). By contrast, Alberta has experienced solid economic growth since the 1980s, and scholars have linked this to its relatively high fertility (Trovato 2010). The province contains one-third of Canada's agricultural land, and farm families tend to have higher fertility. Alberta also has an oil-based economy with no provincial sales tax, low provincial income tax, and higher wages and lower unemployment rates than the other provinces.

---

[8]Ang (2015) does not comment on the size of this effect.

Education System

Several features of an education system may influence fertility. First, the age at which children start school is important because it is related to women's laborforce participation, childcare, and opportunity costs. In Alberta, Newfoundland, Nova Scotia (since the late 1990s), Ontario, and Québec, the maximum age for school entry (i.e., beginning grade one) is six. It is seven in the remaining regions. Kindergarten for children not yet eligible for grade one is not required, and the availability of kindergarten places varies widely by province. In Québec, kindergarten for five-year-olds was expanded to a full-day schedule in 1997, at the same time as the major expansion of daycare.

Second, the degree of openness in the education system in later grades may also influence childbearing (Rindfuss and Brauner-Otto 2008). Open school systems are ones in which it is comparatively easy to return to school, for instance after having a child. The mother-student roles are generally considered to be incompatible, especially when mothering small children, so the ability to move back and forth between the two roles may make childbearing more appealing. In Canada, much as in the United States but in sharp contrast to countries such as Japan, students can apply to any college or university they choose, and they can apply at any time in their lives. Students are also able to return to secondary school or in some cases enroll in postsecondary education without a secondary-school diploma. A recent longitudinal study of Canadians who were 18–20 years old in 1999 found that 17 % had left secondary school at some point, but that by 2007 only 6 % had not obtained a secondary-school diploma or enrolled in postsecondary education (Statistics Canada 2010).

Women generally avoid combining the mother and student roles, so the point at which women finish schooling may also influence their fertility. In other words, when the student role finishes earlier, parenthood may begin earlier (Lutz and Skirbekk 2005; Skirbekk et al. 2004). And indeed, the length of compulsory schooling varies among provinces of Canada. Attendance is compulsory to age 18 in Manitoba, New Brunswick, and Ontario and to age 16 in the other provinces.

Among other differences, the length of secondary schooling varies by province. Until 1984, Ontario had five years of secondary education, whereas the other provinces (except for Québec which is discussed below) had four years. After 1984, students in Ontario could graduate from secondary school after four years, and the fifth year (OAC or Ontario Academic Credit, previously called grade 13) was for those planning on obtaining post-secondary education. In reality, roughly 85 % of all students completed the fifth year of secondary schooling (Casas and Meaghan 1996), however, and it wasn't until 2003 that the fifth year was completely abolished. This means that until 2003 Ontario students were generally a year older (roughly 19 years old) upon secondary-school completion than students in other provinces (except Québec).

In Québec, students complete primary and secondary schooling after 11 years. They can then attend college or CEGEP (Collège d'enseignment général et professionnel) for two years if they are planning on continuing to university or three years if they want a terminal degree (these are typically more trade-oriented degrees). This means that students in Québec are generally a year younger (roughly 17 years old) upon secondary school completion than students in other provinces, who are roughly 18 years old.

The proportion of students who drop out before the end of compulsory schooling also varies among provinces. There have been tremendous changes in high-school dropout rates by province over the past 25 years. For Canada as a whole, the dropout rate decreased from 16.6 % in 1991 to 8.1 % in 2012. The largest reductions in the high-school dropout rate occurred in Newfoundland and Labrador, Prince Edward Island, and Nova Scotia, where there was an almost 60 % reduction. High-school dropouts decreased by about 40 % in Québec over this time, although it still has a relatively high rate (Turcotte 2011b). In 2009–2012, the dropout rate ranged from 5.6 % in BC to 10.6 % in Québec (Statistics Canada 2012).

Do the different educational institutions and structures across regions translate into different education and fertility behaviors? In recent decades, tertiary education has increased tremendously all across Canada, but there are still important differences between Québec and the other provinces. The proportion of women age 25–34 with at least some post-secondary education increased from 43 % in 1990 to 71 % in 2009 (men also experienced a large increase, although only 63 % had some post-secondary education in 2009) (Turcotte 2011b). Much of this increase is due to an increase in women obtaining a university degree, with the proportion more than doubling—from 15 to 34.3 % (Turcotte 2011b). In 2009, a larger percentage of women age 25–54 had some post-secondary education in Québec than in any other region, although the difference between Québec and Ontario was only 0.2 % (Turcotte 2011b). Likely reflecting the role of the CEGEPs in Québec, the proportion of women age 25–54 with a post-secondary certificate or diploma was greater in Québec than in Ontario or BC (41 % vs. 36 and 33 %, respectively), but the proportion with a university degree was lower in Québec (26 % vs. 31 and 27 %) (Turcotte 2011b). Both values were lower in Alberta than in Québec. Some of the high enrollment in Québec may also be because tuition fees are substantially lower than in most other provinces. For the 2010/2011 academic year, average undergraduate tuition fees for full-time Canadian students in Québec were 38 % of those in Ontario—CAD2,411 (US$1925) compared with CAD6,316 (US$5043) (Statistics Canada, Centre for Education Statistics 2014).[9]

To the extent that women delay childbearing until they have completed schooling and that delayed fertility generally translates into foregone fertility, an earlier ending of schooling may be related to earlier and more fertility. For example, the larger percent of women completing a three-year technical certificate in Québec, and therefore completing their education when they are 20 years old, may be contributing to higher fertility than in Ontario or BC, where women are more likely to complete a four-year university degree at age 22. Similarly, the extra year of

[9]Tuition fees are typically higher for out-of-province students.

secondary school may explain some of the very low fertility seen in Ontario. Since the mid-1980s, when the fifth year of secondary schooling was phased out, the TFR in Ontario has slowly become higher than the TFR in British Columbia, the other major province with a similar fertility history.

On the other hand, dropping out of secondary school may lead to substantial economic uncertainty and lower earning potential, which have been linked to lower fertility (Hofmann and Hohmeyer 2013; Philipov et al. 2006). Since dropout rates are higher in Québec where fertility is also higher, this chain of causation seems unlikely, however.[10] While it is true that one-year differences in completion of secondary school may not be enough to contribute greatly to differences in fertility levels, at the very least these differences in education systems are evidence of substantial regional variation in the structure of social institutions. Additionally, the regional differences observed in systems of education may be caused by similar factors that lead to regional variation in observed fertility, or the differences in education may interact with or moderate the effects of other social institutions such as family benefits. For example, the higher dropout rate in Québec may not necessarily lead to lower fertility because the more generous family policies ensure a minimum level of security not available in the rest of Canada (Roy and Bernier 2007).

Housing

Housing is clearly associated with fertility in Canada, although the causal direction is unclear. Families with children are more likely to own their home than to rent (Rajulton 2011). Couples with children are also more likely to be living in single detached homes than others, and they are the most common group living in such homes (Rajulton 2011). No research has investigated the degree to which housing availability and ownership may lead to delayed or foregone fertility, however. The housing market in Canada is similar to that in the US where mortgages are common, down payments are moderate (typically 20 %), the duration of mortgage foreclosure is fairly short, and the judicial system is highly efficient (Chiuri and Jappelli 2003). While urban residents may feel that there is a shortage of desirable housing, the suburbs continue to grow (Turcotte 2011a). There is no real shortage of space for new construction, although there have been zoning changes that make construction of new rental units more difficult (Hulchanski 2006). The down payment percent has decreased since the 1970s, so, if anything, we would expect a positive effect on fertility (Chiuri and Jappelli 2003).

There have been specific housing programs designed to expand the stock of affordable housing and improve access. Federal efforts, overseen by the Canadian

[10]One could also argue that women in Quebec may be dropping out of school in order to have children, but teenage pregnancy is not particularly high.

Mortgage and Housing Corporation (CMHC), consist largely of supports for home ownership. For example, since 1992 the federal government has been insuring mortgages so that buyers can purchase homes with only a 5-% down payment. In addition, families can borrow up to CAD40,000 (US$32,419) from their retirement plans for a down payment on a home (Hulchanski 2006).

Additionally, each province has its own housing authority and, as of 1996, the provinces are solely responsible for public (or social) housing. Provinces receive transfers from the federal government and implement them as they choose. Only 5 % of Canadian households live in public housing, but there are waiting lists, and shortages have been exacerbated due to cuts in federal transfers over time (Hulchanski 2006). As an example of how housing policy varies at the provincial level, only Québec, BC, Manitoba, and Saskatchewan offer housing allowances (Finkle et al. 2006). Another difference, one that highlights the unique place of Québec, concerns how rental contracts are enforced. Recall, Québec operates under civil law, whereas the rest of Canada is under common law. Landlords are not allowed to require a security deposit in Québec—a practice common in the rest of Canada—and housing laws in Québec tend to be more supportive of tenants. These laws have not changed in recent years, however, so it is unlikely that the differences can explain the growing provincial variation in fertility.

Québec did have an explicit family housing policy, the Home Ownership Program, for a few years in the late 1980s (Ang 2015). This was implemented in 1988 as a three-year program with the government backing loans and covering interest charges for seven years for families with two or more dependent children who purchased modestly priced homes (CAD75,000 (US$60,199) maximum in 1988). This program was expanded to include families with only one child and homes valued up to CAD100,000 (US$80,271) in 1989 and CAD110,000 (US $88,306) in 1990. It was not renewed after 1990, and no similar policy was designed to take its place.

Unfortunately, I know of no explicit evaluations of these housing programs or their connection to fertility or even to other family behaviors.

Conclusion

Fertility in Canada has been low for more than 30 years—lower than in other English-speaking countries. Unlike in Scandinavian countries, fertility in Canada has not appeared to rebound in recent years. To understand Canada's unique fertility trend, we need to look at the regional level. Alberta has consistently had higher fertility, at a level similar to that seen in other English-speaking countries. Provinces and territories with high proportions of Aboriginals have had even higher fertility, with TFRs well above replacement, whereas BC and Ontario have had the lowest fertility levels since the mid-1990s. The TFR in all provinces generally decreased throughout the 1960s and has been fairly stable since the early 1970s. The exception is Québec. Initially, fertility in Québec was the lowest of all provinces, but in the 1980s it began increasing, narrowing the gap with other provinces. Fertility in Québec has been higher than BC since the mid-1990s and higher than Ontario since 2005.

The variation we see across provinces points to several macro-level or institutional factors as having an important influence on fertility. Perhaps most obvious is that family policies vary across province, and since the late 1980s, those in Québec have been the most generous. What little empirical evidence exists supports the idea that at least some of these policies are responsible for Québec's unique and rising fertility path. In particular, the generous ANC payments made from 1989–1997 have been credited with raising Québec's fertility from the lowest in the country to a level on a par with or higher than many other regions. The heavily subsidized daycare and more generous parental leave currently in place are likely helping to further boost Québec's fertility over that of other regions. While other institutional components, namely education and housing, may not have such an obvious influence on changes or variations in fertility, they do vary regionally in relevant ways. Again, the institutions in Québec are more supportive of earlier and more childbearing. In sum, the entire institutional context of Québec compared with the rest of Canada (particularly when we exclude Alberta)—shorter, more accessible post-secondary education, the beginning of universally available, full-day kindergarten for five year olds, heavily subsidized daycare for younger children, more generous parental leave, and more renter protections—adds up to greater family supports and a more pro-natalist environment. Indeed, fertility in Québec has increased and has remained stable at higher levels than in the rest of Canada, and some speculate that Québec will experience a fertility rebound similar to that in Scandinavia, only delayed by a decade or so (Roy and Bernier 2007).

As a comparison, Alberta also offers a unique insight into macro-level influences on fertility. Whereas Québec is culturally very different from the rest of Canada, Alberta is similar to Ontario and BC and yet has a dramatically different fertility story. Here the major institutional factor appears to be the economy—Alberta's robust oil and agriculture economy supports childbearing better than the other regions are able to do.

The differences among regions within Canada are not limited to those institutions discussed here, nor does this chapter claim that those institutions are *solely* causing the currently observed fertility behaviors. Rather, the institutions reflect the many differences, some tied to deeply rooted cultural characteristics, that are among the important factors influencing fertility behavior in Canada. While many countries experience regional variation in culture, norms, ideology, and local policies, the degree of provincial independence in Canadian federalism plus Québec's long history of independence add up to unusually large differences in a range of social institutions.

Acknowledgments I would like to thank Jesse Shuster-Leibner for his research assistance, particularly with helping me understand the French documents; Anne Gauthier for her comments and help identifying important resources; Ron Rindfuss and Minja Choe for their comments; and the four reviewers of this chapter for their detailed, thoughtful, and constructive comments.

References

Adsera, A., & Ferrer, A. (2013). *The fertility of recent immigrants to Canada*. Discussion Paper No. 7289. Bonn: Institute for the Study of Labor.

Adsera, A., & Ferrer, A. (2014). Factors influencing the fertility choices of child immigrants in Canada. *Population Studies, 68*(1), 65–79.

Ang, X. L. (2015). The effects of cash transfer fertility incentives and parental leave benefits on fertility and labor supply: Evidence from two natural experiments. *Journal of Family and Economic Issues, 36*(2), 263–288.

Beaujot, R., & Wang, J. (2010). Low fertility in Canada: The Nordic model in Québec and the U. S. model in Alberta. *Canadian Studies in Population, 37*, 375–410.

Beaujot, R., & Woldemicael, G. (2010). *Fertility behavior of immigrants in Canada: Converging trends*. Discussion Paper No. 10-05. London: University of Western Ontario, Population Studies Centre.

Beaujot, R., Du, C. J., & Ravanera, C. R. (2013). Family policies in Québec and the rest of Canada: Implications for fertility, child-care, women's paid work, and child development indicators. *Canadian Public Policy, 39*(2), 221–239.

Bélanger, C. (2000). *The quiet revolution*. http://faculty.marianopolis.edu/c.belanger/QuebecHistory/events/quiet.htm. Accessed June 15, 2015.

Bélanger, A. (Ed.). (2006). *Report on the demographic situation in Canada, 2002. 91-209-XIE*. Ottawa: Statistics Canada.

Bélanger, A., & Gilbert, S. (2006). *The fertility of immigrant women and their Canadian-born daughters: Report on the demographic situation in Canada 2002*. Catalogue number 91-209-XIE. Ottawa: Statistics Canada.

Bélanger, A., & Ouellet, G. (2005). A comparative study of recent trends in Canadian and American Fertility, 1980–1999. In A. Bélanger (Ed.), *Report on the demographic situation in Canada 2001* (pp. 107–136). 91–209-XIE. Ottawa: Statistics Canada.

Casas, F. R., & Meaghan, D. E. (1996). A study of repeated courses among secondary students in Ontario. *The Journal of Educational Research, 90*(2), 116–127.

Castles, F. G. (2003). The world turned upside down: Below-replacement fertility, changing preferences and family-friendly public policy in 21 OECD countries. *Journal of European Social Policy, 13*(3), 209–227.

Chandola, T., Coleman, D. A., & Hiorns, R. W. (2002). Distinctive features of age-specific fertility profiles in the English-speaking world: Common patterns in Australia, Canada, New Zealand and the United States. *Population Studies, 56*, 181–200.

Chiuri, M. C., & Jappelli, T. (2003). Financial market imperfections and home ownership: A comparative study. *European Economic Review, 47*(5), 857–875.

Cleveland, G., Forer, B., Hyatt, D., Japel, C., & Krashinsky, M. (2008). New evidence about child care in Canada: Use patterns, affordability, and quality. *IRPP Choices, 14*(12), 1–42.

Conseil de la famille et de l'enfance Québec. (2008). *La politique familiale au Québec: Visée, portée, durée et rayonnement*. Québec: Conseil de la famille et de l'enfance.

Crompton, S., & Keown, L.-A. (2009). *Do parental benefits influence fertility decisions?* Statistics Canada. http://www.statcan.gc.ca/pub/11-008-x/2009002/article/10919-eng.htm. Accessed June 1, 2015.

Denton, F. T., Feaver, C. H., & Spencer, B. G. (2000). The future population of Canada and its age distribution. In F. T. Denton, D. Fretz, & B. G. Spencer (Eds.), *Independence and economic security in old age* (pp. 27–56). Vancouver: University of British Columbia Press.

Dickinson, J. A., & Young, B. J. (2003). *A short history of Québec*. Montréal: McGill-Queen's University Press.

Duclos, E., Lefebvre, P., & Merrigan, P. (2001). *A "natural experiment" on the economics of storks: Evidence on the impact of differential family policy on fertility rates in Canada*. Working Paper 136. Montréal: Université du Québec à Montréal, Centre De Recherche Sur

l'Emploi Et Les Fluctuations Économiques Cahier De recherche/Center for Research on Economic Fluctuations and Employment.
Éditeur officiel du Québec. (2015). Chapter A-29.011. *An Act Respecting Parental Insurance.* http://www2.publicationsduquebec.gouv.qc.ca/dynamicSearch/telecharge.php?type=2&file=/A_29_011/A29_011_A.html. Accessed June 4, 2015.
Esping-Andersen, G. (1990). *The three worlds of welfare capitalism.* Cambridge: Polity Press.
Finkle, M., Climaco, C., Khadduri, J., & Steele, M. (2006). *Housing allowance options for Canada.* Research Report: Housing Affordability and Finance Series. Ottawa: Canada Mortgage and Housing Corporation.
Fortin, P., Godbout, L., & St-Cerny, S. (2012). *Impact of Québec's universal low-fee childcare program on female labour force participation, domestic income, and government budgets.* Working Paper 02. Sherbrooke: Chaire de recherche en fiscalité et en finances publiques.
Frejka, T., & Westoff, C. F. (2007). Religion, religiousness and fertility in the US and in Europe. *European Journal of Population, 24*(1), 5–31.
Gauvreau, D. (2006). Religious diversity and the onset of the fertility transition: Canada, 1870–1900. In R. Derosas & F. van Poppel (Eds.), *Religion and the decline of fertility in the Western World* (pp. 235–258). New York: Springer.
Gauvreau, D., & Gossage, P. (2001). Canadian fertility transitions: Québec and Ontario at the turn of the twentieth century. *Journal of Family History, 26*(2), 162–188.
Government of Canada, Justice Laws Website. (2015). *Employment Insurance Act S.C. 1996, c. 23.* http://laws-lois.justice.gc.ca/eng/acts/E-5.6/FullText.html. Accessed June 4, 2015.
Halli, S. S., Dai, S. Y., George, M. V., & Verma, R. B. P. (1996). Visible minority fertility in Canada, 1981–1986. *Genus, 52*(1/2), 181–189.
Hayford, S. R., & Morgan, S. P. (2008). Religiosity and fertility in the United States: The role of fertility intentions. *Social Forces, 86*(3), 1163–1188.
Hofmann, B., & Hohmeyer, K. (2013). Perceived economic uncertainty and fertility: Evidence from a labor market reform. *Journal of Marriage and Family, 75*, 503–521.
Hulchanski, J. D. (2006). What factors shape Canadian housing policy? The intergovernmental role in Canada's housing system. In R. Young & C. Leuprecht (Eds.), *Canada: The state of the federation 2004, municipal-federal-provincial relations* (pp. 221–250). Kingston: Queen's University, Institute of Intergovernmental Relations.
Kerr, D., Moyser, M., & Beaujot, R. (2006). Marriage and cohabitation: Demographic and socioeconomic differences in Québec and Canada. *Canadian Studies in Population, 33*(1), 83–117.
Kim, Y.-I. A. (2014). Lifetime impact of cash transfer on fertility. *Canadian Studies in Population, 41*(1–2), 97–110.
Krull, C. (2000). Fertility change in Quebec: 1931–1991. *Canadian Studies in Population (Special Issue on Family Demography), 27*(1), 159–181.
Krull, C. (2007). Perspectives and initiatives: Placing families first: The state of family policies in La Belle Province. *Canadian Review of Social Policy, 59*, 93–99.
Krull, C., & Trovato, F. (2003). Where have all the children gone? Québec's fertility decline: 1941–1991. *Canadian Studies in Population, 30*(1), 193–220.
Laplante, B. (2006). The rise of cohabitation in Québec: Power of religion and power over religion. *Canadian Journal of Sociology, 31*(1), 1–24.
Laplante, B., & Fostik, A. L. (2014). *The recent evolution of fertility within marriage and consensual union in two Canadian provinces: Disentangling the Québec fertility paradox.* Paper presented at the Population Association of America Annual Meeting, Boston, May 1–3, 2014.
Le Bourdais, C., & Lapierre-Adamcyk, E. (2004). Changes in conjugal life in Canada: Is cohabitation progressively replacing marriage? *Journal of Marriage and Family, 66*(4), 929–942.
Le Bourdais, C., & Marcil-Gratton, N. (1996). Family transformations across the Canadian/American Border: When the laggard becomes the leader. *Journal of Comparative Family Studies, 27*(3), 415–436 + iii.

Lefebvre, P., & Merrigan, P. (2008). Child-care policy and the labor supply of mothers with young children: A natural experiment from Canada. *Journal of Labor Economics, 26*(3), 519–548.
Lefebvre, P., Merrigan, P., & Roy-Desrosiers, F. (2011). *Québec's childcare universal low fees policy 10 years after: Effects, costs and benefits*. Working Paper 11–01. Montréal: Université du Québec à Montréal, Centre Interuniversitaire Sur Le Risque, Les Politiques Économiques Et l'Emploi (CIRPÉE).
Lutz, W., & Skirbekk, V. (2005). Policies addressing the tempo effects of low-fertility countries. *Population and Development Review, 31*(4), 699–720.
Marshall, K. (2010). Employer top-ups. *Perspectives on Labour and Income, 11*(2), 5–12.
Max Planck Institute for Demographic Research and Vienna Institute of Demography. (2014). *Human fertility database*. http://www.humanfertility.org. Accessed December 2014.
McDonald, P., & Moyle, H. (2010). Why do English-speaking countries have relatively high fertility? *Journal of Population Research, 27*(4), 247–273.
McNicoll, G. (2009). Legacy, policy and circumstance in fertility transition. *Population and Development Review, 35*(4), 777–795.
McNown, R., & Ridao-Cano, C. (2004). The effect of child benefit policies on fertility and female labor force participation in Canada. *Review of Economics of the Household, 2*, 237–254.
Milan, A. (2013). *Fertility: Overview, 2009 to 2011*. Component of Statistics Canada Catalogue no. 91-209-X: Report on the Demographic Situation in Canada. http://www.statcan.gc.ca/pub/91-209-x/2013001/article/11784-eng.pdf. Accessed June 2, 2015.
Milligan, K. (2005). Subsidizing the stork: New evidence on tax incentives and fertility. *Review of Economics and Statistics, 87*(3), 539–555.
Murdoch, L. (2009). *Young aboriginal mothers in Winnipeg*. http://www.pwhce.ca. Accessed June 15, 2015.
Nordberg, A., Delva, J., & Horner, P. (2014). Adolescent pregnancy in Canada: Multicultural considerations, regional differences, and the legacy of liberalization. In A. L. Cherry & M. E. Dillon (Eds.), *International handbook of adolescent pregnancy*. New York: Springer.
Parent, D., & Wang, L. (2007). Tax incentives and fertility in Canada: Quantum vs. tempo effects. *Canadian Journal of Economics, 40*(2), 371–400.
Pearce, L. D. (2002). The influence of early life course religious exposure on young adults' dispositions toward childbearing. *Journal of the Scientific Study of Religion, 41*(2), 325–340.
Philipov, D., Speder, Z., & Billari, F. C. (2006). Soon, later, or ever? The impact of anomie and social capital on fertility intentions in Bulgaria (2002) and Hungary (2001). *Population Studies, 60*, 289–308.
Phipps, S. A. (2000). Maternity and parental benefits in Canada: are there behavioural implications? *Canadian Public Policy, 26*(4), 415–434.
Pollard, M. S., & Wu, Z. (1998). Divergence of marriage patterns in Québec and elsewhere in Canada. *Population and Development Review, 24*(2), 329–356.
Pulkingham, J., & van der Gaag, T. (2004). Maternity/parental leave provisions in Canada: We've come a long way, but there's further to go. *Canadian Woman Studies/Les Cahiers de la Femme*, 116–125.
Quinless, J. M. (2012). *Aboriginal women in Canada: A statistical profile from the 2006 census*. Aboriginal Affairs and Northern Development Canada. http://www.aadnc-aandc.gc.ca/DAM/DAM-INTER-HQ/STAGING/texte-text/ai_rs_pubs_ex_abwch_pdf_1333374752380_eng.pdf. Accessed June 2, 2015.
Rajulton, F. (2011). Households and housing in Canada. In B. Edmonston & E. Fong (Eds.), *The changing Canadian population* (pp. 60–82). Montréal: McGill-Queen's University Press.
Regie des rentes Québec. (2015). *Amount of the child assistance payment*. http://www.rrq.gouv.qc.ca/en/enfants/naissance/paiement_soutien_enfants/Pages/montant.aspx. Accessed June 2, 2015.
Rindfuss, R. R., & Brauner-Otto, S. R. (2008). Institutions and the transition to adulthood: Implications for fertility tempo in low-fertility settings. *Vienna Yearbook of Population Research, 1*, 57–87.

Rindfuss, R. R., Choe, M. K., & Brauner-Otto, S. R. (2016). The emergence of two distinct fertility regimes in economically advanced countries.*Population Research and Policy Review*, 1–18. doi: 10.1007/s11113-016-9387-z.

Roy, L., & Bernier, J. (2007). *Family policy, social trends and fertility in Québec: Experimenting with the Nordic model?*. Québec: Ministère de la Famille, des Aînés et de la Condition féminine.

Skirbekk, V., Kohler, H.-P., & Prskawetz, A. (2004). Birth month, school graduation, and the timing of births and marriages. *Demography, 41*(3), 547–568.

Stalker, G., & Ornstein, M. (2013). Québec, daycare, and the household strategies of couples with young children. *Canadian Public Policy, 39*(2), 241–262.

Statistics Canada. (2005). *Census of population 2005*. Ottawa: Statistics Canada.

Statistics Canada. (2008a). *Canadian demographics at a glance (91-003-X)*. http://www5.statcan.gc.ca/olc-cel/olc.action?objId=91-003-X&objType=2&lang=en&limit=0. Accessed June 2, 2015.

Statistics Canada. (2008b). *Aboriginal identity population by age groups, median age and sex, 2006 counts for both sexes, for Canada, provinces and territories—20 % sample data*. http://www12.statcan.ca/census-recensement/2006/dp-pd/hlt/97-558/pages/page.cfm?Lang=E&Geo=PR&Code=01&Table=1&Data=Count&Sex=1&Age=1&StartRec=1&Sort=2&Display=Page. Accessed June 2, 2015.

Statistics Canada. (2008c). *Table 106-9002: Pregnancy outcomes, by age group, Canada, provinces and territories, terminated, annual*. http://www5.statcan.gc.ca/cansim/a26?lang=eng&id=1069002. Accessed June 2, 2015.

Statistics Canada. (2009). *Definitions, data sources, and methods*. http://www.statcan.gc.ca/eng/concepts/definitions/minority01. Accessed June 15, 2015.

Statistics Canada. (2010). *Interrupting high school and returning to education*. Education indicators in Canada: Fact sheets, 81-599-X, number 5. http://www.statcan.gc.ca/pub/81-599-x/81-599-x2010005-eng.htm. Accessed June 2, 2015.

Statistics Canada. (2011a). *2011 census profile: 98-316-XWE2011001-101*. http://www12.statcan.gc.ca/census-recensement/2011/dp-pd/prof/details/download-telecharger/comprehensive/comp-csv-tab-dwnld-tlchrgr.cfm?Lang=E#tabs2011. Accessed June 22, 2015.

Statistics Canada. (2011b). *Aboriginal peoples in Canada: First Nations people, Métis and Inuit: National Household Survey, 2011*. Analytic document, number 99-011-X2011001. http://www12.statcan.gc.ca/nhs-enm/2011/as-sa/99-011-x/99-011-x2011001-eng.pdf. Accessed June 2, 2015.

Statistics Canada. (2011c). *Figures for fertility: Overview, 2008: Figure 3. Fertility by age group, Canada, 1926 to 2008*. http://www.statcan.gc.ca/pub/91-209-x/2011001/article/11513/figures/fig-eng.htm#a3. Accessed June 2, 2015.

Statistics Canada. (2011d). *French and the francophonie in Canada: Language, 2011 Census of Population*. Census in Brief, number 98-314-X2011003. http://www12.statcan.gc.ca/census-recensement/2011/as-sa/98-314-x/98-314-x2011003_1-eng.pdf. Accessed June 2, 2015.

Statistics Canada. (2011e). *Immigration and ethnocultural diversity in Canada: National Household Survey, 2011*. Analytic document, number 99-010-X2011001. http://www12.statcan.gc.ca/nhs-enm/2011/as-sa/99-010-x/99-010-x2011001-eng.pdf. Accessed June 2, 2015.

Statistics Canada. (2012). *Learning—School drop-outs*. http://www4.hrsdc.gc.ca/.3ndic.1t.4r@-eng.jsp?iid=32. Accessed June 15, 2015.

Statistics Canada. (2013a). *Table 102-4503: Live births, by age of mother, Canada, provinces and territories, annual*. http://www5.statcan.gc.ca/cansim/a26?lang=eng&id=1024503. Accessed June 2, 2015.

Statistics Canada. (2013b). *Table 102-4504: Mean age of mother at time of delivery (live births), Canada, provinces and territories annual, (years)*. http://www5.statcan.gc.ca/cansim/a26?lang=eng&id=1024504. Accessed June 2, 2015.

Statistics Canada. (2014a). *Table 051-0001: Estimates of population, by age group and sex for July 1, Canada, provinces and territories, annual (persons unless otherwise noted)*.

http://www5.statcan.gc.ca/cansim/a26?lang=eng&retrLang=eng&id=0510001&paSer=&pattern=&stByVal=1&p1=1&p2=37&tabMode=dataTable&csid=. Accessed June 2, 2015.
Statistics Canada. (2014b). *Table 051-0004: Components of population growth, Canada, provinces and territories, annual (persons).* http://www5.statcan.gc.ca/cansim/a26?lang=eng&id=510004. Accessed June 2, 2015.
Statistics Canada. (2015a). *Table 282-0087: Labour force survey estimates (LFS), by sex and age group, seasonally adjusted and unadjusted monthly, (persons unless otherwise noted).* http://www5.statcan.gc.ca/cansim/a26?id=2820087. Accessed June 2, 2015.
Statistics Canada. (2015b). *Vital statistics—Birth database.* Record number 3231. http://www23.statcan.gc.ca/imdb/p2SV.pl?Function=getSurvey&SDDS=3231. Accessed June 15, 2015.
Statistics Canada, Centre for Education Statistics. (2014). *Undergraduate tuition fees for full-time Canadian students, by discipline, by province (Canada).* http://www.statcan.gc.ca/tables-tableaux/sum-som/l01/cst01/educ50a-eng.htm. Accessed June 2, 2015.
Suwal, J., & Trovato, F. (1998). Canadian aboriginal fertility. *Canadian Studies in Population, 25*(1), 69–86.
Thornton, A., & Camburn, D. (1987). The influence of the family on premarital sexual attitudes and behavior. *Demography, 24*(3), 323–340.
Thornton, A., Axinn, W. G., & Hill, D. H. (1992). Reciprocal effects of religiosity, cohabitation, and marriage. *American Journal of Sociology, 98*(3), 627–651.
Tremblay, D.-G. (2009). More time for daddy: Québec leads the way with its new parental leave policy. *Our Schools, Our Selves, 18*(3), 223–228.
Trovato, F. (2010). Fertility in Alberta in a context of rapid economic growth, 1997–2007. *Canadian Studies in Population, 37*(3–4), 497–525.
Trovato, F. (2011). Canada's age and sex composition. In B. Edmonston & E. Fong (Eds.), *The changing Canadian population* (pp. 41–59). Montréal: McGill-Queen's University Press.
Turcotte, M. (2011a). Life in metropolitan areas: The city/suburb contrast: How can we measure it? *Canadian Social Trends—Statistics Canada,* 11-008, 2–19.
Turcotte, M. (2011b). Women and education. In *Women in Canada: A gender-based statistical report* (pp. 89–110). Statistics Canada Catalogue No. 89-503-X. http://www.statcan.gc.ca/pub/89-503-x/89-503-x2010001-eng.pdf. Accessed June 2, 2015.
United Nations, Department of Economic and Social Affairs, Population Division. (2012). *World population prospects: The 2012 revision.* http://esa.un.org/unpd/wpp/unpp/panel_indicators.htm. Accessed June 4, 2015.
Weise, R. W., Jr. (1972). Canada's new unemployment insurance act. *Social Security Bulletin, 35*(2), 31–34, 37.
Woldemicael, G., & Beaujot, R. (2012). Fertility behavior of immigrants in Canada: Converging trends. *International Migration and Integration, 13*, 325–341.
Wu, Z., & Baer, D. E. (1996). Attitudes toward family and gender roles: A comparison of English and French Canadian women. *Journal of Comparative Family Studies, 27*(3), X2-452 + iii–iv.
Wu, Z., & Schimmele, C. M. (2011). Changing Canadian families. In B. Edmonston & E. Fong (Eds.), *The changing Canadian population* (pp. 235–252). Montréal: McGill-Queen's University Press.

The European Middle Way? Low Fertility, Family Change, and Gradual Policy Adjustments in Austria and the Czech Republic

Tomáš Sobotka

Abstract This chapter provides a comparative analysis of fertility and family transformations and policy responses in Austria and the Czech Republic, two neighboring countries in Central Europe that were until 1989 separated by the "Iron Curtain" dividing the two competing political blocs in Europe. The comparison is stimulated by the geographic proximity and shared history and culture of these two countries in the past and their gradual economic and social convergence in the most recent quarter century. During this recent period, both societies became surprisingly similar in their fertility and family patterns and main family policy trends. Fertility in both countries is relatively low, but not extremely low when compared with the countries of Southern Europe or East Asia. The period total fertility rate recently converged to 1.5 births per woman, and cohort fertility rates for the women born in the mid-1970s are projected at 1.65 (Austria) and 1.8 (Czech Republic) births per woman. Austrian fertility rates have been remarkably stable since the 1980s, while in the Czech Republic fertility imploded during the 1990s, following the political regime change, and then partly recovered in the 2000s. In both countries, childbearing has rapidly shifted to later ages and increasingly has taken place outside marriage, with more than one-half of first births now born to cohabiting couples and single mothers. Czech women are much less likely to remain childless, possibly due to the persistently strong normative support to parenthood in the country. Family policies, relatively generous in terms of government expenditures, were until recently dominated by a view that mothers should stay at home for an extended

Research presented in this paper was partly supported by the European Research Council under the European Union's Seventh Framework Programme (FP7/2007–2013)/ERC Grant agreement n° 284238 (EURREP). An earlier, expanded version of this paper has been published as Vienna Institute of Demography (VID) Working Paper 2/2015 and can be accessed at http://www.oeaw.ac.at/vid/download/WP2015_02.pdf. Throughout this chapter, the author refers to this working paper (Sobotka 2015) for additional details.

T. Sobotka (✉)
Wittgenstein Centre for Demography and Global Human Capital,
Vienna Institute of Demography (Austrian Academy of Sciences), Vienna, Austria
e-mail: tomas.sobotka@oeaw.ac.at

R.R. Rindfuss and M.K. Choe (eds.), *Low Fertility, Institutions, and their Policies*, DOI 10.1007/978-3-319-32997-0_6

period with their children, making the return to employment difficult for women. The combination of extensive parental leave, negative attitudes toward working mothers with children below age three, limited availability of public childcare for these children, and in the Czech Republic, limited availability of part-time employment affects childbearing decisions, especially among highly educated women. Recent policy adjustments have made parental leave more flexible in both countries and, in the case of Austria, have supported a gradual expansion of public childcare and a stronger involvement of men in childrearing.

Keywords Fertility · Low fertility · Family · Family policies · Czech Republic · Austria

Austria and the Czech Republic are two neighboring Central European countries with similar population size (8.5 million in Austria vs. 10.5 million in the Czech Republic) and similar surface area (84 vs. 79 thousand square kilometers). They are positioned in the middle of the European Union's country ranking by population size and territory. Both countries were part of the Austro-Hungarian Empire until its implosion in 1918. The paths of these two countries then took different turns, with the Czech Republic forming a joint state with Slovakia—Czechoslovakia. A major long-lasting cleavage emerged after World War II, when Czechoslovakia became incorporated into the "socialist bloc" of countries dominated by the Soviet Union, whereas Austria, while formally neutral, became a parliamentary democracy that leaned politically and economically toward Western Europe. This division cracked with the fall of the Iron Curtain in 1989. Soon thereafter, in 1993, Czechoslovakia split into two independent parts, and the Czech Republic was formed within its current boundaries. Both countries now belong to the European Union.

This chapter provides a comparative analysis of fertility and family transformations and policy responses in Austria and the Czech Republic. The comparison is stimulated by the geographic proximity and shared history and culture of these countries in the past and their gradual economic and social convergence in the past quarter century. An implicit question addressed throughout this chapter is whether family and fertility trends and the associated policy responses have grown increasingly similar in the past 25 years. The analysis focuses mostly on this period, covering changes in fertility, family, living arrangements, family values, and policy trends in these two societies. To give a broader background, the discussion also touches on longer-lasting fertility changes, in particular the historic transformations in cohort fertility, marked by an early emergence of low fertility in both countries. Next, the discussion covers how the combination of prolonged parental leave, limited availability of early childcare, societal norms favoring a long withdrawal of mothers from work after childbirth, and in the Czech Republic, limited availability of part-time employment hinders mothers' employment and may negatively affect fertility. In conclusion, the chapter outlines likely future trends and presents a wish-list of potential policy actions.

Key Social, Economic, and Population Trends in Austria and the Czech Republic Over the Past Century

Austria and the Czech Republic have a similar culture, including the predominant Catholic religious tradition. In the past, both countries were multinational, ethnically diverse societies. This feature became less prominent in Austria after 1918, when once-important migration streams from other parts of the Austro-Hungarian Empire ceased, and even more so during World War II, when the sizeable Jewish population was liquidated or forced to leave. But the new inflow of "guest workers" and migrants from Central and Eastern Europe, Germany, Turkey, and other countries since the 1960s has made Austria more diverse again. In contrast, the Czech Republic became ethnically homogenous after the forced deportation of the Jewish population to concentration camps in the early 1940s and the expulsion of the sizeable German population (around 2.6 million people) after World War II.

In a long-term perspective, the populations of Austria and the Czech Republic have experienced slow growth over the past century. The Austrian population increased from 6 million to 8.5 million between 1900 and 2014, whereas the population of the Czech Republic grew from 9.3 to 10.5 million.

The ties between Austria and the Czech Republic were severed during the lengthy period of state socialism in Czechoslovakia between 1948 and 1989. At that time, the two countries often experienced contrasting demographic trends, also in the domains of fertility and family. Population trends in Austria progressed in tandem with trends in Western and Northern Europe (especially neighboring Germany and Switzerland), including the emergence of a baby boom and a strong endorsement of the traditional family in the 1950s and 1960s. Trends in the Czech Republic converged with those in Eastern European countries, marked by almost universal marriage, early transitions to marriage and first birth, and very low childlessness. Women in the Czech Republic were expected to work and also take almost all the responsibility for childcare and household duties, whereas in Austria the male-breadwinner family ideal was strongly entrenched well into the 1980s. Perhaps the main contrast between the two societies related to the characteristic family changes associated with the "second demographic transition" (Lesthaeghe 2010). These changes, including the postponement of marriage and childbearing, emerged in Austria in the 1970s, but, except for steeply rising divorce rates, they were largely absent in the Czech Republic until the early 1990s (Sobotka et al. 2003). Also, mortality trends diverged from the 1960s to the 1980s as mortality improvements stalled in the Czech Republic. During the same period, the Czech economy was increasingly lagging behind an ever-more-prosperous Austria.

The collapse of the authoritarian state-socialist system in Central and Eastern Europe paved the way for radical changes in fertility and family life in the Czech Republic in the 1990s and 2000s (Sobotka et al. 2008; Kantorová 2004). These changes were mostly an accelerated version of the trends observed earlier in Austria, resembling a fast-paced second demographic transition (Sobotka et al. 2003). The political regime change also led to economic liberalization and reforms in social and family policies, as well as many new life choices for young people. Economic uncertainty became more common, and the new phenomena of unemployment and rising income differences emerged. Housing was privatized, mostly through preferential sale to tenants, but partly also through restitution (return) of buildings confiscated by the socialist state to the original owners or their heirs and through selling housing units to private individuals and firms (Lux and Sunega 2010).

Opportunities for self-realization, travel, leisure, business, and political activities vastly expanded, as did enrollment in university education, transforming the lives of young adults. Post-secondary education became perceived as a prerequisite for future success in life. In the Czech Republic, the share of people age 20–24 enrolled in tertiary education tripled from 12 % in 1994 to 37 % in 2012 (own computations based on Organization for Economic Cooperation and Development (OECD) and Eurostat data). A more gradual expansion of tertiary education occurred in Austria.

In 2004, the Czech Republic joined the European Union and thus completed the transition from its "communist" past. Due to the legacy of long economic stagnation, however, the Czech economy still lags well behind that of Austria, where living standards are among the highest in the European Union (EU). In 2013, Austria had the second highest gross domestic product (GDP, based on purchasing power parity) per capita in the EU after Luxembourg, at 130 % of the EU-wide level, whereas the Czech Republic ranked 12th from the bottom, at 81 % of the EU level. These economic differences play a role in the ability of governments to pursue new family-related policies.

The two countries also differ in the importance of religion in public life. Religion plays a very small role in the Czech Republic, which ranks as one of the most secular countries in Europe (Halman and Draulans 2006). In Austria, the Catholic Church still has a significant, although diminishing, role in public life and education.

Over the past four decades, population trends in both countries have been increasingly shaped by migration. Austria, which has had a natural population increase of around zero since the 1970s, has experienced considerable immigration, which has fueled continuing population growth. The cumulative effect of immigration on the Austrian population is quite sizeable. In 2013, almost one out of six residents (16 %) was born in another country, one of the highest shares in the EU (Eurostat 2014b). In the Czech Republic, immigration has been less intensive, peaking before the onset of the recent economic recession. As of 2013, almost 4 % of the population was born abroad. In contrast with most other post-communist countries of Europe, however, the Czech Republic has not experienced sizeable out-migration. The most distinct minority is the predominantly native-born Roma ethnic group (about 2 % of the total population), which constitutes the most socially disadvantaged and marginalized segment of the population.

The populations of Austria and the Czech Republic are aging quickly, especially due to improvements in life expectancy. Austria has experienced continuous mortality improvements since the 1950s, so that by 2013, life expectancy at birth reached 83.6 years for women and 78.5 years for men. In the Czech Republic, life expectancy at birth is currently about three years lower that in Austria, primarily because of the long period from the 1960s to the 1980s when life expectancy at birth remained particularly low (66–68 years) for men. Since the 1990s, however, rapid improvements in healthcare have quick-started increases in life expectancy.

Fertility Change and Differentials

Long History of Low Fertility

Austria and the Czech Republic have a long history of low fertility. The fertility transition in both countries was practically completed among the late-19th century cohorts: The mean number of children ever born fell below 1.9 for Czech women and below 1.8 for Austrian women born around 1900 (Fig. 1). Such low fertility levels were reached at the same time in England and Wales, Sweden, and in neighboring Germany, while countries in Southern and Eastern Europe had considerably higher fertility (Festy 1979). Period total fertility rates reached a long-term low during the Depression era, falling to 1.66 in the Czech Republic (CSO 2014) and to around 1.5 in Austria in the mid-1930s.[1] These fertility rates are not remarkably low judged by our current standards, but they stand out in being far below the replacement threshold given much higher child and maternal mortality at the time.

After bottoming out, cohort fertility increased in both countries among women born after 1905. Then the trend diverged in the cohorts born after 1920. Czech women born in the period from 1920 to 1960, who had most of their children during the state-socialist period, showed relatively stable fertility at 2.0–2.2 births per woman. Interestingly, this fertility trend resembles that of Swedish women (Fig. 1). In contrast, Austrian cohort fertility exhibited a pronounced baby boom typical of most countries of Western and Northern Europe, peaking at 2.36 births per woman among the 1935 cohort. The Austrian cohort baby boom was followed by a continuous decline, which appears to have persisted until the cohort of women born in 1970. A stable cohort fertility of around 1.65 is projected for the women born in the 1970s (Zeman et al. 2014). In the Czech Republic, cohort fertility has shown a gradual decline among women born after 1955. Czech women born in the mid-1970s still had larger families than their Austrian counterparts, however, with completed fertility falling to just below the 1.8 threshold. Neither Austrian nor Czech fertility levels diverge widely from the European-wide average: Completed fertility in the EU is estimated at 1.70 for women born in 1972 (VID 2014), ranging from 1.4 in Spain to 2.1 in Ireland.

The low cohort fertility for the early 20th century cohorts was marked by high childlessness, which reached close to 30 % in Austria and above 20 % in the Czech Republic (Fig. 2). This pattern was typical of Western European countries, where

[1]Own estimate based on the gross fertility rate published by the League of Nations (1943).

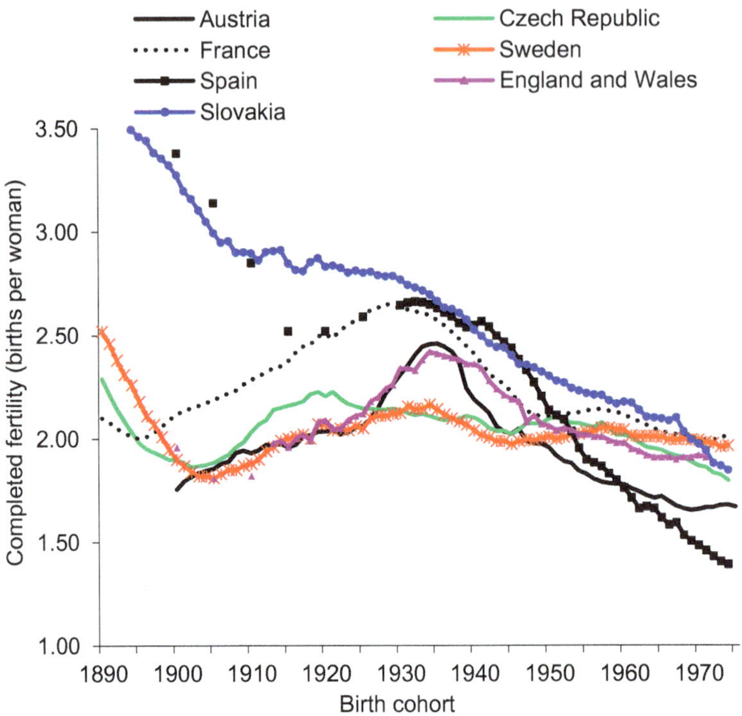

Fig. 1 Completed cohort fertility rate in Austria, the Czech Republic, and selected European countries, women born 1890–1975 (For Austria, Population Censuses 1991 and 2001 combined with vital statistics data for 1984–2012, projected cohort fertility published in Zeman et al. (2014); for Czech Republic and Slovakia, Population Censuses 1950, 1961, and 1980 combined with vital statistics data for 1980–2012; for England and Wales, Festy (1979) and ONS (2013); for France, Festy (1979); for Sweden, Human Fertility Database (2014); for Spain, Festy (1979), Council of Europe (2006)). *Note* Data for the cohorts born between 1968 and 1975 are partly projected (own projection based on combining observed cohort fertility data until 2012 with age-specific trend projection for fertility realized after 2012)

marriage and family formation usually took place only when a couple had sufficient means to form a new household (Hajnal 1965). In both countries, cohorts born up to the 1960s showed a steady increase in the prevalence of two-child families—particularly pronounced in the Czech Republic—and a fall in childlessness followed by its gradual rebound (only recently in the Czech Republic). The Austrian baby boom was driven by a rise of families with three or more children. This was followed by a sharp fall in their share since the late-1930s cohort. The recent differences in family size between the two countries still reflect the fertility contrasts typical of the East-West European divide up until 1989. During the state-socialist era, women in the Czech Republic reached very low levels of childlessness (around 5–6 %) and non-marriage. This pattern changed among women born after 1965,

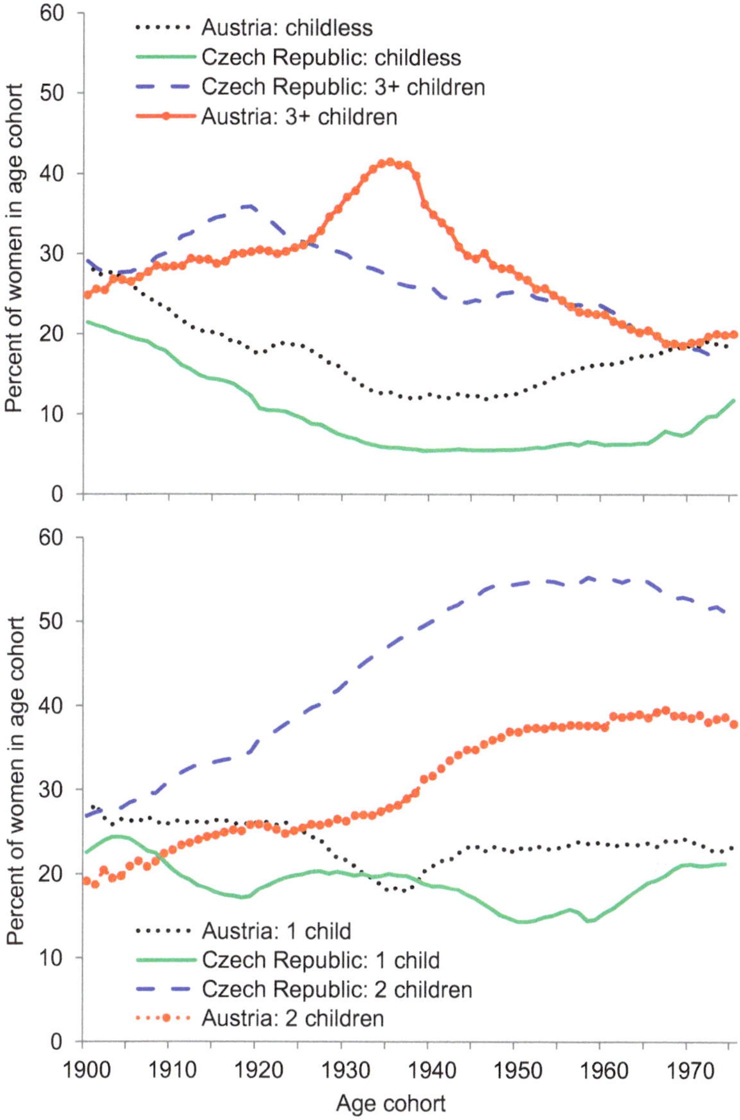

Fig. 2 Cohort parity distribution of women in Austria and the Czech Republic born in 1900–1975 (for Austria, Population Censuses 1991 and 2001 combined with vital statistics data for 1984–2012, projected cohort fertility published in Zeman et al. (2014); for the Czech Republic, Population Censuses 1950, 1961, and 1980 combined with vital statistics data for 1980–2012; data for the cohorts 1965–74 were reconstructed and partly projected from Eurostat (2014a) data). *Note* Data for the cohorts born between 1968 and 1975 are partly projected (own projection based on combining observed cohort fertility data until 2012 with age-specific trend projection for fertility realized after 2012)

with a sharp increase of childlessness and one-child families, thus shifting closer to the fertility patterns of Austrian women.

Period Fertility Developments: The Interplay of Quantum and Timing Changes

Period fertility trends in Austria and the Czech Republic in the post-World War II era differed considerably (Fig. 3). The baby boom of the mid-1950s to mid-1960s in Austria contrasted with falling fertility in the Czech Republic, and much of the post-baby boom fertility decline in Austria took place in the early 1970s, a time of temporary fertility rebound in the Czech Republic. Finally, the massive slump in fertility in the Czech Republic during the 1990s occurred at a time when Austrian fertility rates were broadly stabilizing, albeit at fairly low levels.

These contrasts mirror the prevailing differences in fertility trends between the East and the West of Europe in the 1950s–1990s. In Austria, the post-war baby boom took place during an era of economic recovery and expansion of the welfare

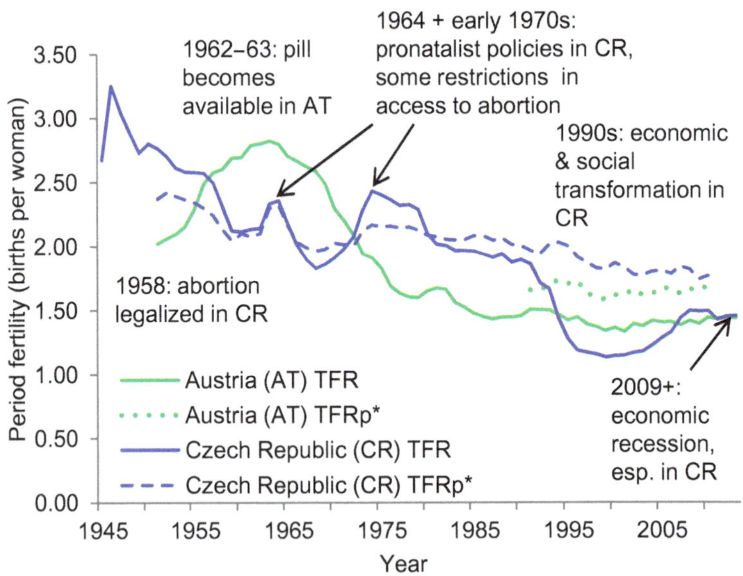

Fig. 3 The period total fertility rate (TFR) and the tempo-adjusted index of period fertility (TFRp*) in Austria (AT, 1951–2013) and the Czech Republic (CR, 1945–2013) (for Austria, own computations from the Eurostat database (2014a) and Zeman et al. (2014); for the Czech Republic, CSO (2014); for TFRp*, Human Fertility Database (2014); the index was computed by Kryštof Zeman, VID). *Note* TFRp* is an index of period fertility controlling for age and parity and adjusted for changes in the timing of childbearing [see Bongaarts and Feeney (2006) and Bongaarts and Sobotka (2012)]

state, but also at the height of the "traditional family" model, characterized by a high prevalence of marriage and a wide adherence to the male-breadwinner model. Many of these trends were reversed in the late 1960s and the 1970s, when the shift toward later and less marriage and family formation began (Fig. 4). This shift also coincided with the gradual increase in the importance of economic activity for women, the spread of the contraceptive pill, and, since 1975, the liberalization of abortion. Since the mid-1980s Austrian fertility has remained remarkably stable, with the period total fertility rate (TFR) oscillating around 1.4, reaching a low of 1.33 in 2001 followed by a very minor recovery.

In the Czech Republic, period TFR fell, with two brief interruptions, from the post-World-War-II peak of more than 3.00 to 1.83 in the late 1960s. At that time, the Czech Republic was one of the few countries in the world with fertility rates below the replacement level. The main reason for this fertility decline was a massive drive to enroll women in the labor force. Gradual expansion of higher education and region-wide liberalization of abortion around 1958 also contributed to declining fertility. The communist governments tried to respond to this

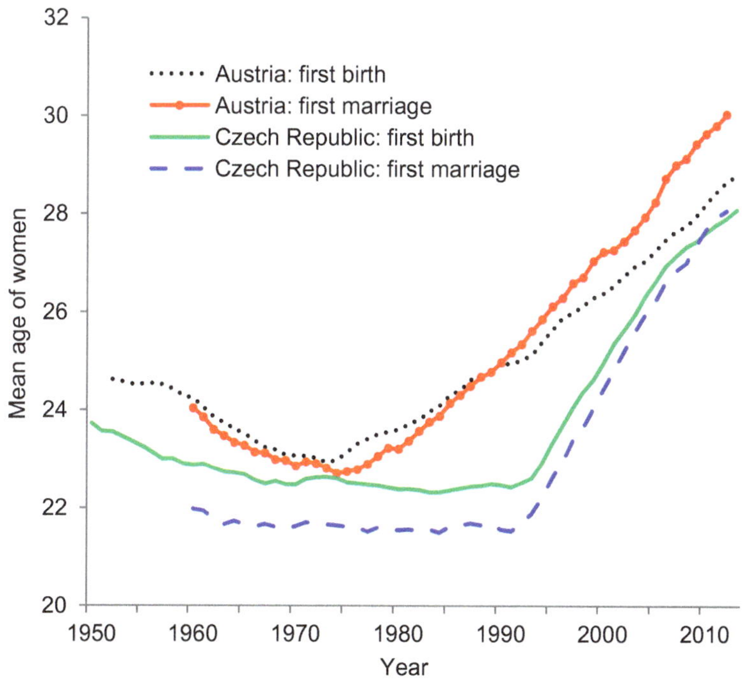

Fig. 4 Women's mean age at first birth and first marriage in Austria and the Czech Republic, 1950–2013 [for mean age at first birth in Austria, Human Fertility Collection (2014) (data computed by T. Sobotka and A. Šťastná), own computations, and Zeman et al. (2014); for mean age at first birth in the Czech Republic, CSO (2014); for mean age at first marriage in Austria, Statistics Austria (2014b); for mean age at first marriage in the Czech Republic, Council of Europe (2006) for data until 2004, and own computations based on Eurostat (2014a)]

unanticipated fertility decline by expanding support for families with children and limiting access to abortion (Wynnyczuk and Uzel 1999; Sobotka 2011). This resulted in a brief upswing in the period TFR in the early 1970s.

The sweeping economic and social changes that occurred in the Czech Republic in the 1990s coincided with a massive fall in period total fertility, which reached an extreme low 1.13 in 1999. This decline was largely fueled by the postponement of family formation. A wide gap emerged between the synthetic indicator of period TFR and the actual family size of the cohorts having children during this period. The mean age at first birth among Czech women shot up from the low level of 22–23 years that had persisted for decades to more than 28 years in 2013, a level typical of Western and Southern Europe today. In Austria, the trend toward delayed childbearing has been much more gradual, starting in the early 1970s (Fig. 4).

The tempo-adjusted index of fertility by age and parity, TFRp* (Bongaarts and Sobotka 2012), tells a very different story of the post-1990 fertility decline in the Czech Republic than the conventional TFR (Fig. 3). Instead of showing a swift fall followed by a partial recovery, it shows a gradual decline from 2.0 in 1990 to below 1.8 in 2009–10, tracing the cohort fertility trajectory. The contrast between the two period fertility indicators can hardly be starker. When the rapid changes in the timing of births are taken into account, fertility in the Czech Republic has consistently remained higher than in Austria over the past two decades. The turbulent times in the Czech Republic during the 1990s were followed by a more stable period, contributing to a gradual recovery of the period TFR, which reached 1.50 in 2008.

The recent economic recession has put a break on the recovery of period fertility rates that took place across Europe in the early 2000s. The observed reversals in fertility trends are linked to economic uncertainty (Sobotka et al. 2011; Goldstein et al. 2013). Austria did not experience a change in the overall fertility trend after 2008, but it witnessed an accelerated decline in teenage fertility. According to the 2013 fertility schedule, only 4 out of 100 women would have a child before reaching age 20, down from 25 in 1970. In contrast, the Czech Republic experienced a temporary reversal of the upward fertility trend in 2009–12, except among teenage women, whose fertility did not change. Fertility fell among women in their 20s, and a strong fertility rebound at ages above 30, which had been underway since the late 1990s, slowed down considerably (Sobotka 2015, Fig. 11). Whereas Austria hardly suffered any symptoms of the economic downturn that began in 2008, the Czech Republic experienced a decline in real wages (falling by more than 5 % from 2008 to 2013 according to Czech National Bank statistics), an increase in youth unemployment, and cuts in family-related benefits. Once the economic recession came to an end, period total fertility in both countries converged in 2014 close to the level of 1.5 (1.46 in Austria and 1.53 in the Czech Republic).

The "postponement transition" is clearly visible in the shifting age pattern of childbearing, especially in the Czech Republic, where most births in the past took place within a narrow age range of 19–25 years (Fig. 5). Between 1990 and 2013, Czech fertility rates plummeted among women at around age 20, while they

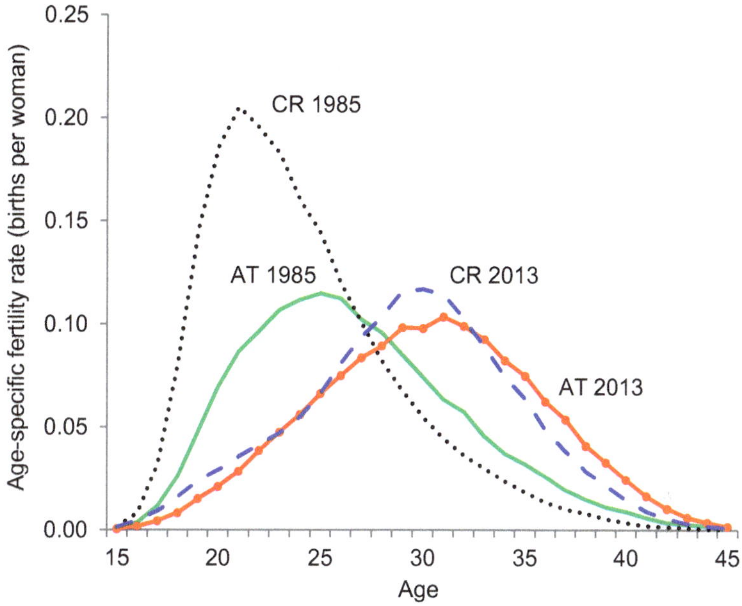

Fig. 5 Age-specific fertility rates in 1985 and 2013 among women age 15–45, Austria (AT) and the Czech Republic (CZ) (for Austria, Zeman et al. (2014); for the Czech Republic, Human Fertility Database (2014) and computations by Kryštof Zeman (Vienna Institute of Demography) from data provided by the Czech Statistical Office)

increased almost fourfold among women above age 35. By 2013, the age pattern of childbearing was similar in both countries, with a symmetric shape and a peak at around age 30.

Negative Fertility Gradient by Education Level

European countries with low fertility often show strong education differentials in family size, characterized by low fertility and high childlessness among women with higher education (e.g., Basten et al. 2014). Austria fits this pattern well: Women born in the late 1950s show a negative education/fertility gradient with respect to their completed fertility and a positive education gradient in childlessness (Table 1). Women with upper-secondary and tertiary education have an average completed fertility of only 1.5, and almost one out of four is childless.

In the Czech Republic, education/fertility differentials among women are slightly narrower than in Austria. Unlike in Austria, these differentials are not linked to differential childlessness, but to the differences in family size among women with children. Czech mothers with elementary or incomplete secondary education have,

Table 1 Completed family size and childlessness by the highest achieved level of education among women in Austria (cohorts 1956–60) and the Czech Republic (cohorts 1956–60 and 1966–70)

	Country and birth cohort		
	Austria 1956–60	Czech Rep. 1956–60	Czech Rep. 1966–70
Completed fertility rate (births per woman)			
Completed primary school or below	2.00	2.24	2.13
Lower-secondary education, including apprenticeship	1.75	2.08	1.95
Upper-secondary education	1.54	1.92	1.81
Tertiary education	1.51	1.76	1.71
Total	1.78	1.98	1.84
Childlessness (percentage of all women in cohort)			
Completed primary school or below	13.4	9.1	14.5
Lower-secondary education, including apprenticeship	14.2	4.4	5.8
Upper-secondary education	23.1	5.3	6.5
Tertiary education	24.6	8.4	10.1
Total	15.7	7.3	8.9

Census 2001, data from the Cohort Fertility and Education (CFE) database (2014); Census 2011 for the Czech Republic, data provided by the Czech Statistical Office; indicators computed by Kryštof Zeman, Vienna Institute of Demography

Note Education categories are based on the International Standard Classification of Education (ISCED), 1997 revision; for definitions see Sobotka (2015), Fig. 12

on average, 2.5 children. Many of these less-educated women belong to the Roma minority, characterized by early childbearing and a high share of large families (Sobotka et al. 2008). Childlessness in the Czech Republic does not follow a clear education gradient, as the highest childlessness is now found among women with the lowest education. Furthermore, all categories of women except the lowest educated share a strong adherence to a two-child family model, with a majority having two children (Sobotka et al. 2008).

Given the observed negative fertility gradient by education level, the expansion of tertiary education in both countries has arguably had a negative compositional effect on aggregate fertility rates.

The Influence of Migration on Fertility in Austria

During the past three decades, Austria has attracted a large number of immigrants, mostly from other European countries and Turkey. Migrants typically arrive as young adults, and they not only boost the labor force, but they also increase the

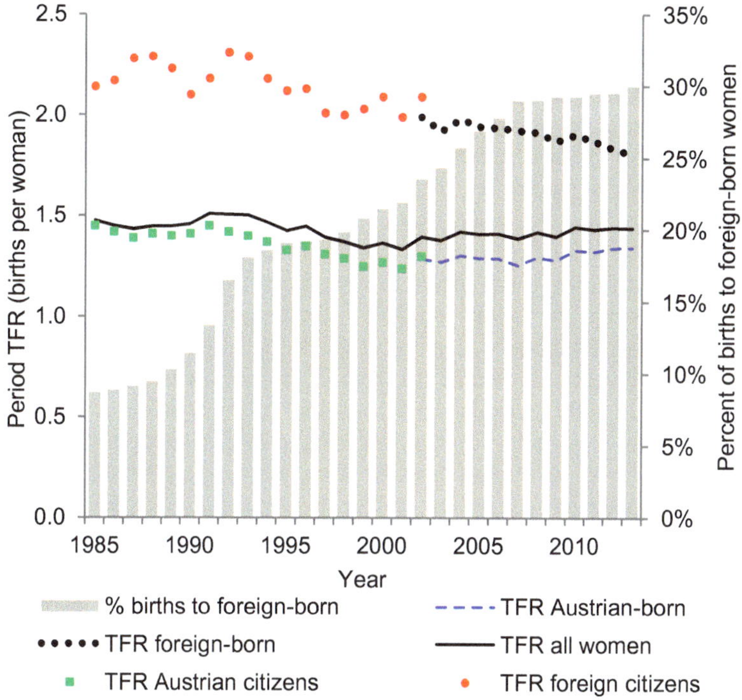

Fig. 6 Period total fertility rate (TFR) by country of birth or citizenship and the share of births to foreign-born women, Austria 1985–2013 (Zeman et al. 2014; Kytir 2005)

population of childbearing age. As in many other countries in Europe, migrants in Austria have higher fertility rates, on average, than native-born Austrians, and they account for a rising share of children born in the country. In 2013, 3 out of 10 newborn children had an immigrant mother, up from 1 out of 10 children in 1989 (Fig. 6). The period TFR of migrant women has gradually declined, however, dropping below 2.0 in the early 2000s and reaching 1.8 in 2013. At the same time, the TFR of native-born women has oscillated around the low level of 1.3 since the mid-1990s. Despite this gradual convergence, migrants in Austria "boost" the period TFR by about 0.10 in absolute terms, and this effect has been stable since the early 2000s (Zeman et al. 2014). Women born in Kosovo, ranking at the top of Europe's fertility rates (VID 2014), have the highest fertility among the major immigrant groups (TFR of 2.9 in 2013), followed by women born in Turkey (TFR of 2.2). The migrants' influence on fertility is strongest in Vienna, which has traditionally served as a magnet for immigration (Zeman et al. 2014). In contrast to Austria, migrant women have only a small influence on fertility in the Czech Republic, owing both to their smaller numbers and to the absence of a distinct group of higher-fertility migrants (Sobotka 2015).

Contraceptive Revolution and Fertility

A quick adoption of modern contraception is an important and often neglected aspect of the post-communist transformation in reproductive behavior in the Czech Republic. Up until the early 1990s, women had limited knowledge of and access to the most effective contraceptive methods, including the pill. Traditional contraceptive methods were widely used, many pregnancies were unplanned, and abortion was frequent. The 1993 Reproductive Health Survey reported that only 66 % of pregnancies in the five years prior to the survey were planned (RHS 1995, Table III.11). During the 1990s and 2000s, the change in contraceptive use and abortion could hardly have been more dramatic. The share of women of reproductive age using the pill rose more than tenfold from a low of 4 % around 1990 to a peak of 48 % in 2007 (Sobotka 2015, Fig. 14). At the same time, abortion rates plummeted: The total induced abortion rate, a hypothetical indicator of the cumulative number of abortions across all reproductive ages, dropped from a high in 1990 of 1.58 abortions per woman (rather close to the level of the period TFR at the time) to 0.31 in 2012, the lowest level observed since abortion was legalized in the late 1950s.

For Austria, data on induced abortion are not collected. Occasional survey data show an earlier expansion of modern contraception but still a fairly high share of partnered women who do not desire to have a child but at the same time do not use contraception (12 % according to the 2008–9 Generations and Gender Survey (GGS 2009)).

Below-Replacement Intended Family Size?

As in other European countries, intended family size in Austria and the Czech Republic consistently exceeds the actual family size women and men achieve by the end of their reproductive lives. The gap is not particularly pronounced, however, as fertility intentions in both countries are close to the low end of the range currently observed in Europe. This is particularly true for Austria, where microcensus surveys (MC) conducted since 1986 have repeatedly found fertility intentions below replacement level (Sobotka 2009). The 2012 MC survey reported a mean intended family size among young women below 1.9 (Table 2). Czech women of the same age reported a slightly higher intended family size of 2.04 in a 2004 GGS. The majority of young women in both countries intend to have two children. This preference is most pronounced in the Czech Republic, where more than 6 out of 10 young women report this family size preference. Although on the rise, intended childlessness remains uncommon in the Czech Republic (Pakosta 2009). Surveys for both countries also show a modest negative education gradient in intended family size (Beaujouan et al. 2013; Šťastná 2007), partly corresponding to actual fertility differentials.

Table 2 Mean intended family size (MIFS) and intended parity distribution among women age 25–29 in Austria and the Czech Republic, 2005–2012

Country, survey, year	MIFS	Share of women by intended family size (percent)				
		0	1	2	3+	N
Austria, GGS 2008	2.12	4.2	13.5	55.8	26.6	530
Austria, MC 2012	1.87	11.9	12.7	56.6	18.7	653
Czech Republic, GGS 2005	2.04	3.8	14.0	62.8	19.5	400

Data computed by Éva Beaujouan, Vienna Institute of Demography/Wittgenstein Centre
Note GGS = Generation and Gender Survey; MC = Austrian Microcensus, special module on fertility intentions. The distribution of intended family size excludes respondents who did not report their intended family size or were uncertain about it

Family Transformations: Increasing Diversity

Since the 1970s, Austria has been a typical case of postponement of key family transitions and a steady erosion of marriage. The Czech Republic has experienced similar shifts but is less typical in that many family changes progressed slowly, if at all, during the state-socialist era but accelerated in the 1990s and the 2000s (Sobotka et al. 2003, 2008).

The Steady Erosion of Marriage

In Austria, the decline and postponement of marriage commenced in the 1970s, hand in hand with fertility decline. In the 1980s, this trend was interrupted by two spikes linked to an anticipated (1983) and the actual (as of 1 January 1988) withdrawal of an allowance granted to couples marrying for the first time (Prioux 1993). In the Czech Republic, marriage rates plummeted in the first half of the 1990s. Since the mid-1990s, both countries have had a similarly low total first marriage rate of about 0.50 for women (Fig. 7), partly reflecting low frequency of marriage and partly the ongoing shift toward delayed marriage. In 2012, the mean age at first marriage for women exceeded 30 in Austria and 28 in the Czech Republic, an increase of six years since the early 1990s (Fig. 4). The Czech Republic saw an unusually quick departure from the previous pattern of early and almost universal marriage. During the state-socialist era, one-half of women were married before age 22, but marriage in this age group has now become rare.

In both countries, mean age at first marriage currently exceeds the mean age at first childbirth, a reordering of key life events, with childbearing now increasingly preceding marriage. The diminishing importance of marriage for fertility is also seen in the steady rise in the share of children born outside marriage, reaching 41 % in Austria in 2012 and 45 % in the Czech Republic in 2013 (Fig. 7). In the latter case this represents a sharp break from the 1970s and 1980s, when only 4–8 % of

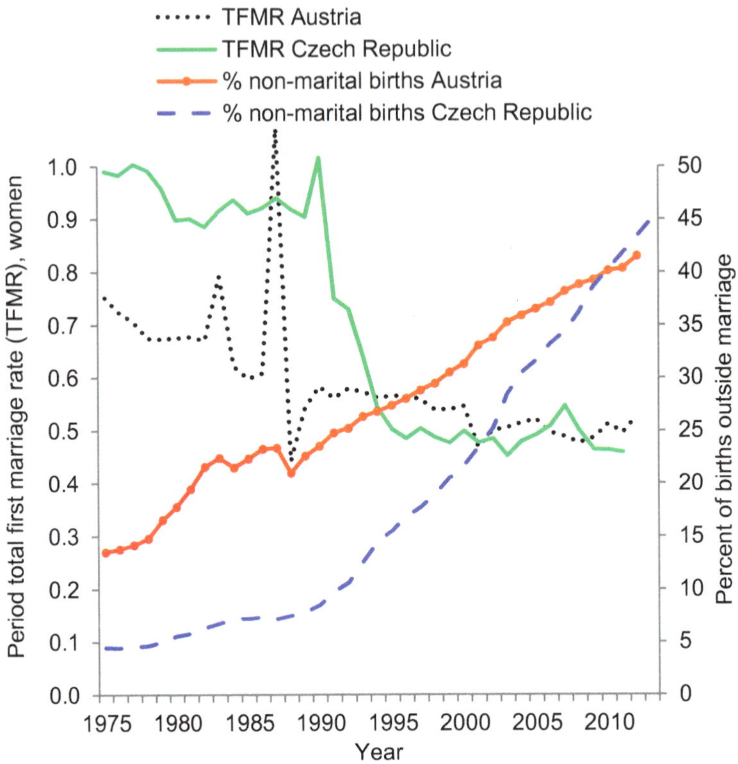

Fig. 7 Period total first marriage rate (TFMR) and the share of non-marital births in Austria and the Czech Republic, 1975–2012 [for Austria, Statistics Austria (2014b); for the Czech Republic, Council of Europe (2006) and Eurostat (2014a)]

births took place outside marriage. In both countries, most first births now take place outside marriage. As a result, "shotgun weddings"—a dominant pattern of first marriage in the Czech Republic until the early 1990s—have become much less frequent. By 2013, their share fell to one quarter in the Czech Republic, and it is even lower in Austria.

For young adults, marriage has been replaced by prolonged periods of living with parents and cohabitation, but also single living and "living-apart-together" partnerships (Kohoutová and Nývlt 2014; Buber-Ennser et al. 2014, Chaps. 6 and 7). Living with parents has become more common especially in the Czech Republic, where many more young people are enrolled in university and cannot afford rental housing. In 2013, 5 out of 10 Czech men and 3 out of 10 Czech women age 25–29 lived with their parents, a sharp increase since the 1990s (Kohoutová and Nývlt 2014). Living with parents is less common in Austria (Buber-Ennser et al. 2014, Chap. 4), where fewer young people study at university and regulated rental housing is widely available.

Cohabitation has become a dominant form of partnership among people in their twenties (Kohoutová and Nývlt 2014); in fact, marriage without previous experience of cohabitation has become unusual. Paloncyová and Šťastná (2012) showed that 90 % of first partnerships among Czechs born in the 1980s started with cohabitation, up from 23 % among those born in the second half of the 1950s. The rise of less traditional living arrangements has also affected families with children. Most problematic from the policy perspective is the high share of single mothers in both countries, fueled by a mix of unintended pregnancies, voluntary single motherhood, and instability of marital and cohabiting unions. At present, 15 % of all families with children in the Czech Republic and 14 % in Austria are single-parent families (Nývlt and Šustová 2014; OIF 2014). Both countries also show strong variation in family transitions by social status. As in other rich countries, women and men with little education experience complex family transitions, with a frequent experience of single parenthood, a large share of children born outside marriage, a high rate of union dissolution, and a strong likelihood of living in a blended family (Sobotka 2015, Sect. 6.2).

Marriage has been further eroded by high divorce rates. The total divorce rate—an indicator of the cumulative share of marriages ending in divorce assuming a continuation of divorce rates observed in a given year—reached high levels of 40–50 % in both countries, although in Austria it has recently shown a trend reversal, peaking in 2007 at 50 % and declining to 40 % in 2013 (Statistics Austria 2014b). In the Czech Republic, high divorce rates had signaled the rising fragility of marriage well before the end of the state-socialist era.

On balance, partnership instability appears to have a slight negative effect on fertility, especially for women, which is in line with the evidence for most European countries (Van Bavel et al. 2012). The 2011 Census data for the Czech Republic show small differences in completed family size by marital status. Among women born in 1966–1971, the mean number of children was 2.00 for those currently married, 1.87 for the divorced, and 1.86 for those who were cohabiting (including the divorced).

Shifting Family Values and Attitudes

Trends in family-related attitudes in Austria and the Czech Republic illustrate the ideational background of contemporary fertility and family patterns. Three main conclusions can be drawn.

First, populations of both countries have widely accepted non-traditional living arrangements, in particular unmarried cohabitation, including for raising children. In the Czech Republic, the strongest shift since 2003 has been observed in the approval of parenthood outside marriage: The share of respondents stating that people intending to have children should marry has declined from 50 to 60 % in 2003 to around 30 % in 2011 (CVVM 2014). This may have a positive effect on fertility, as it broadens the choice of living arrangements considered suitable for childbearing.

Second, the attitude toward having children remains more pronatalist and less accepting of childlessness in the Czech Republic, whereas voluntary childlessness is generally accepted as a lifestyle option in Austria, partly owing to its widespread occurrence. Almost 9 out of 10 Czech women and men consider having children as a natural part of women's lives (Pakosta 2009). In 2008, a slight majority of Czech respondents at reproductive age agreed that a woman should have children in order to be fulfilled (Rabušic and Chromková-Manea 2012, Fig. 9).

Third, both societies show a preference for parents (preferably mothers) to stay at home during a child's first three years of life. This is paradoxical in the Czech Republic, where the official ideology during the state-socialist period strongly promoted women's full employment. As in Germany, working mothers in Austria have often been seen as "bad mothers," whose children suffer as a result of their (selfish) career orientation. Between 1990 and 2008, Austrians shifted toward a more positive view of working mothers, but almost two-thirds of respondents in 2008 still thought small children are likely to suffer if their mothers work (Hamachers-Zuba et al. 2009, Table 11). In Czech society, a conflicting view persists, considering that small children suffer when their mothers work but at the same time that women's employment is important as the source of a second income in the family and a means to promote women's independence (Chaloupková and Šalamounová 2004, p. 35).

Family-Related Policies: Key Trends

Although many policy differences persist between Austria and the Czech Republic, both countries have displayed similar family policy trends during the past two decades. This is in contrast with the situation prevailing until the late 1980s, when Austria, but not the Czech Republic, embraced "conservative policies" characterized by generous cash support for families with children, extended parental leave, and limited public childcare, especially for children below age three (Prskawetz et al. 2008). During the same period, government policies in the Czech Republic encouraged women's employment,[2] typically on a full-time basis, and supported

[2]Women's employment during the state-socialist period was strongly encouraged for two reasons—economic, in order to cope with the shortage of labor in an inefficient state-directed economy and ideological, whereby everyone had a duty to contribute to society by his or her work. The "right and duty to work" was explicitly stated in the constitutions of 1948 and 1960. In addition, "avoidance of work" and "parasitism" (i.e., living without working or making a living from illegal activities) were punishable by law (Havelková 2009). In practice, this law was not always strictly enforced, and some women could stay at home after completing their maternity leave. However, women's employment was also considered a financial necessity for most families.

early childbearing and universal marriage through preferential housing for families with small children, special loans for newlyweds, and other policies (Sobotka et al. 2008).

Soon after the political regime change in 1989, Czech social and family policies underwent substantial changes. Unlike the situation in many other countries of Central and Eastern Europe, cash benefits were not radically cut, and social policy kept a strong focus on reducing poverty and income inequalities. At the same time, pronatalist incentives were eliminated, including the birth-order-specific provision of parental leave. Administrative allocation of housing was abandoned and gradually replaced by a private housing market, with only a small portion of rental apartments retained by municipalities (Lux and Sunega 2010). The dismantling of the previous pronatalist policy orientation marked a shift toward a more *laissez-faire* approach (Kocourková 2002) combined with a more conservative family policy model ("refamilization") that preferred mothers to stay at home for prolonged periods with young children. This policy model was also characterized by an extension of paid parental leave and a collapse of public childcare for children below age three (Kocourková 2002; Saxonberg and Szelewa 2007). Only in the early 2000s, following the fall in fertility to very low levels, did family policies emerge as an important topic for public discussion.

In both countries, spending on family policies tends to be high, amounting to 2.6 % of GDP in the Czech Republic (which is average for OECD countries) and 3.0 % in Austria. Both countries spend below the OECD average on public childcare (0.6 % of GDP compared with the OECD average of more than 0.9 %) and above the average on cash benefits for families (Austria) and tax breaks (Czech Republic) (OECD 2014a, Table PF1.1).

The development of family policies has been driven by the perceived needs of families with children as well as the ideological orientation of the governing political parties and the policy recommendations and directives of the European Union. These include, in particular, policies stipulating equal treatment of women and men as well as an expansion of childcare for children below age three. This description will cover the main policy areas—especially parental leave policies, childcare provision, and mothers' labor market participation—and will summarize other policy trends, including changes during the recent recession.

Toward Ever More Flexible Parental Leave

Parental leave policies in Austria and the Czech Republic were developed early on and have expanded over time. Both countries now have among the longest paid leaves in the OECD. In 1961, employed mothers in Austria became entitled to paid, job-protected leave until the child's first birthday (Prskawetz et al. 2008). Since then, the leave period has been repeatedly expanded and revised. In both countries, parental leave is preceded by paid maternity leave, lasting 16 weeks in Austria (with full income replacement) and 28 weeks in the Czech Republic (with 69 % of income replaced).

In the Czech Republic, the expansion of parental leave culminated in 1995, when the leave benefit was extended up to the child's fourth birthday, although employment protection remained set at three years (Kocourková 2002). By coincidence, a major move toward more leave flexibility occurred in both countries in January 2008, when a "multispeed" leave was established. Parents could choose between three options, combining different leave durations and corresponding monthly allowances. Subsequent amendments have made parental leave even more flexible. At present, Austrian parents can chose from five leave options, lasting from 12 to 30 months (or from 15 to 36 months if both parents participate). Four of these options are not dependent on previous employment and provide a flat-rate leave allowance. The fifth option is income-dependent, amounting to 80 % of the pre-leave income for a period of 12 (or 15) months (see Table 3). The Czech Republic has gone even further in expanding leave flexibility. The total parental allowance is fixed at 220,000 Czech Koruna (CZK) (US$8,553 as of 9 April 2015),[3] distributed in monthly instalments over 19–48 months. This is quite generous: The Czech Republic now spends more on parental leave than any other OECD country (OECD 2014a, Chart PF2.1.B). Parents are allowed to be economically active during their leave, and mothers and fathers are allowed to alternate working and staying at home. On average, Czech parents obtained 46.4 % of the full-time equivalent wage when on leave in 2013 (OECD 2014a, Table PF2.1.A), which is comparable to some leave options in Austria (Table 3).

In both countries, most parents chose to take an extended leave, implying a long interruption of employment. In Austria, one-half of the parents on leave in 2011 chose the longest option (30 + 6 months), followed by 26 % choosing the second-longest option (20 + 4) and 14 % choosing the short, income-dependent option (Rille-Pfeiffer and Kapella 2012, Table 1). In the Czech Republic, most parents opt for a three-year leave, the maximum period for which their employment is protected by law.

Frequent changes in parental leave regulations in Austria have stimulated shifts in the spacing of births. Some parents have tried to space their second and later births so that they could qualify for an uninterrupted continuation of their parental leave and the related allowance. This effect was most evident when paid leave was extended in 1990. It is unclear whether these changes had any lasting effect on fertility. Lalive and Zweimüller (2009, pp. 1384–1385) showed a permanent effect on second birth rates on the order of 3.0–3.5 % among women first entitled to the extended leave, whereas individual birth data analyzed by Šťastná and Sobotka (2009) indicated no lasting effect of the leave extension on second and third birth rates.

[3]This sum almost equals the average annual net income of a childless employed person in 2012, which amounted to CZK 233,602 (US$9083) (OECD 2015a).

Table 3 Parental leave variants and associated leave allowance, Austria, 2014

Variant	Flat rate payment				Income-dependent
	12 + 2 months	15 + 3 months	20 + 4 months	30 + 6 months	12 + 2 months
Maximum duration for one parent (months)	12	15	20	30	12
Pre-leave employment required?	No	No	No	No	Yes
Daily payment in EUR (2014)	33	26.6	20.8	14.53	80 % of previous income (max. EUR66)
Income replacement: Leave payment as a share of median annual net income in 2012 (percent)					
Women	79.1	63.8	49.9	34.8	(80)
Men	53.8	43.4	33.9	23.7	(80)

For leave variants, Arbeiterkammer (2014); for income replacement, own computations based on the median annual net income in 2012 for women (EUR15,221, equivalent to US$16,916 as of 5 Jun 2015) and men (EUR22,371 (US$24,862), published by Statistics Austria)

Expanding Childcare Provision in Austria and Parents' Labor Market Participation

In the 1970s and 1980s, Austria and the Czech Republic had quite different policies on the provision of childcare. Public childcare was more extensive in the Czech Republic, especially for children below age three. The situation reversed in the 1990s, when the system of childcare centers collapsed in the Czech Republic due to three interrelated factors: mothers staying at home on prolonged parental leave, tough regulations that made the childcare centers costly to operate, and closures of the centers following the transfer of responsibility for funding from the central government to municipalities. In Austria, a gradual expansion of early childcare accelerated after 2005, with enrollment for children age 0–2 reaching 23 % in 2013 (still below the EU average of 32 %). Also the provision of childcare to children age 3–5 expanded in Austria, but remained flat in the Czech Republic. At present, 9 out of 10 Austrian and 8 out of 10 Czech children in this age group are in publicly funded childcare (Table 4).

In the Czech Republic, almost all childcare facilities are open all day. In Austria, where childcare is largely financed by federal regions, a large variation in care availability, fees, open hours, and closing days persists. The city of Vienna shows the strongest commitment toward providing accessible and free full-day childcare for all children aged 0–5, providing massive subsidies for this purpose. This results in particularly high rates of early childcare enrollment (Table 4).

Maternal employment differs considerably between the two countries. In the Czech Republic, a sharp contrast exists between mothers of children age 0–3, who typically stay at home, and mothers of older children, who are typically in full-time employment. In 2011–13, only 9 % of working mothers with children below age 15 worked part-time (Nývlt 2014b). In Austria, there is more part-time employment, and the contrast by children's age is less sharp. As their youngest children become

Table 4 Childcare enrollment (percent) of children age 0–2 and 3–5 in Austria and the Czech Republic, 1989–2013

	Children age 0–2			Children age 3–5	
	Czech Republic	Austria	Vienna	Czech Republic	Austria
1989	16.8	–	–	81.9	–
1995	–	4.6	16.9	–	70.6
2000	4.4	7.7	24.3	81.6	77.6
2005	7.0	10.2	22.1	79.4	82.7
2010	7.3	17.1	28.1	78.1	90.7
2013	–	23.0	40.3	–	90.8

For Austria, Statistics Austria (2014a); for the Czech Republic, Saxonberg and Szelewa (2007, Table 1) for 1989, UNICEF (2013) for other years

Note The OECD Family Database suggests lower enrollment rates at age 0–2, amounting to 3–5 % in the Czech Republic in 2003–11 and 14 % in Austria in 2010 (OECD 2014a, online Table PF3.2)

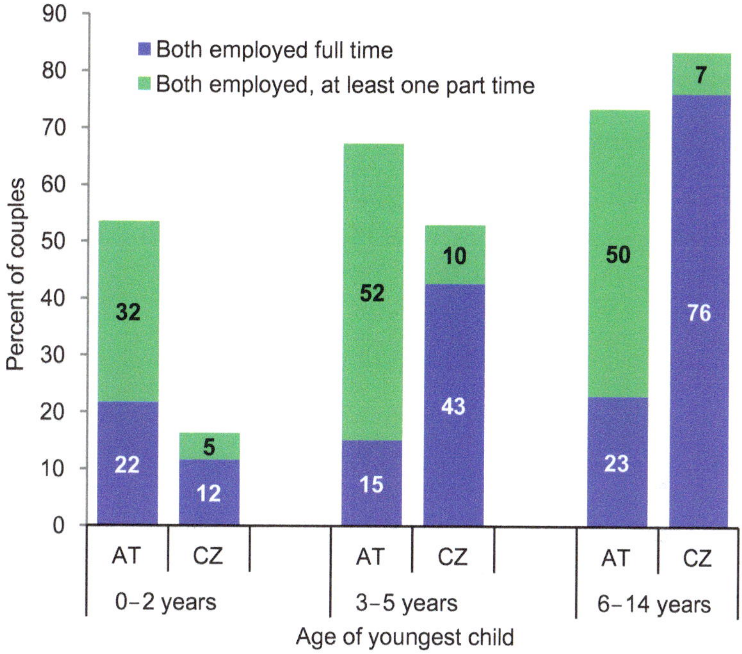

Fig. 8 Employment among couples by age of the youngest child, Austria (AT) and the Czech Republic (CZ), 2011 (OECD 2014a, online Table LMF2.2.A). *Note* The remaining combinations (making a total of 100 %) include couples where only one is working (full or part-time) and those where neither is working. In a vast majority of cases, the combination of "both employed, at least one part time" actually means that the mother is working part time and the father is employed full time

older, women gradually return to employment, usually on a part-time basis (Fig. 8). Berghammer (2014) describes this as a "modernized male-breadwinner pattern" and shows that it has now become common across all educational categories.

Other Important Policies and Policy Trends

Cash Benefits

Cash benefits constitute a prominent component of family policy packages in both Austria and the Czech Republic (OECD 2011; Thévenon 2011). In Austria, child allowances are most important. Parents with dependent children up to age 24 receive monthly payments that vary with the age of the child and the number of children in the family, increasing for larger families. In 2014, they ranged from EUR109.70 (US$116.95) for families with one child age 0–2 up to EUR158.90

(US$169.40) for each dependent child over age 19; the latter amount represents roughly 10 % of the net median income per person. In the Czech Republic, child allowances are very low (CZK 500–700 (US$19–27) per month) and are paid only to low-income families. There is also a system of birth grants, but these have declined in importance following recent spending cuts. In both countries, tax deductions and means-tested social benefits keep poverty rates for couples and for children below the average for OECD countries. These transfers are less successful in alleviating poverty in single-parent families with children, however, especially in the Czech Republic (Thévenon 2011, Appendix Table A5). In 2011, more than one-third of these families in the Czech Republic were poor, in particular because a high share of their income was spent on housing (Nývlt 2014a).

Housing Availability and Cost

Austria has a long tradition of providing housing, mostly owned and maintained by municipalities, to lower-income residents. Around one-fifth of the population lives in low-rent public housing. Moreover, rents in most private rental apartments are regulated (Reinprecht 2007), making rental housing affordable for most people and giving young adults the opportunity to establish their own households. Around 70 % of people live in rental apartments, and the average expenditure on housing is 21 % of disposable income, at the OECD average (OECD 2015b). In contrast, very limited public housing exists at present in the Czech Republic. Most housing is owner occupied, following massive privatization in the 1990s and 2000s, and housing costs are among the highest in OECD countries, averaging 25 % of disposable income (OECD 2015b). Young adults moving away from their parents and those planning to have a child often face difficulties in acquiring a suitable apartment. Mortgages have become widely available over time, but are relatively costly given that incomes are typically still well below the EU average. Low-income households qualify for a housing allowance, which is often used to pay an overcharged price for a substandard apartment.

Fathers' Involvement in Childcare

At present, neither Austria nor the Czech Republic provides statutory paternity leave after childbirth. Austria was one of the first countries in Europe to provide an incentive for fathers to participate actively in parental leave, applying a "take it or lose it" criterion for an additional leave period in 1996. Austrian fathers still show very low participation, however. In 2012, their share in total parental leave was only 4.7 %, with only 17 % of all fathers taking at least some leave, typically for several months only (Herrnböck 2012). Even fewer fathers take parental leave in the Czech Republic.

Cuts in Family Policies During the Economic Recession

There were no significant cuts in government spending for families in Austria, which was little affected by the recent economic downturn. In the Czech Republic, by contrast, several rounds of fiscal consolidation led to reductions of monetary benefits to families (OECD 2014b, Table 1.2). Birth allowances, initially provided to parents of each newly born child, were reduced in 2008. They became means-tested and available only for the parents of first children in 2011 (in 2015 they were partly reinstated for second children). Also, maternity leave allowance was reduced in 2009 (OECD 2014b).

Policy Evolution: Future Plans and Discussions

Family policies are now relatively high on the government agenda in Austria, where a dedicated ministry focuses on families and youth. In 2014, the Minister, Sophie Karmasin, launched an ambitious policy agenda, with a stated goal of Austria "becoming the most family-friendly country of Europe" by the year 2025.[4] Achievement of this goal will be measured by continuous monitoring of progress in 10 selected indicators of family-friendliness, which include the gap between intended family size and fertility, government expenditures on families, childcare availability, and fathers' participation in parental leave, as well as the evaluation of family friendliness in public opinion polls. Specific policy goals for the near future include dedicated funding for childcare expansion in 2015–2018, especially for children below age three. A radical revamp of the parental leave system is being considered, to be introduced in 2016, similar to the changes introduced earlier in the Czech Republic. The current options for parental leave would be replaced with a fixed-sum "childcare account" plus flexibility in choosing the duration of leave, the corresponding monthly payment, and the way the leave is shared between mothers and fathers.

In the Czech Republic, the family policy agenda is more modest. The present government has partly reversed the previous cutbacks in birth allowances, reinstating in 2015 an allowance for second births, although with a lower payment and on a means-tested basis. Expanding childcare availability for children below age three is among the priorities, also using cheaper and less conventional solutions, such as new, company-based childcare centers and so-called "children's groups." The latter aim to provide care for smaller groups of children (up to 24) and are less strictly regulated and therefore more flexible and cheaper to set up than institutional childcare centers. The law allowing and regulating their establishment was passed

[4]Press release and additional information available at http://www.bmfj.gv.at/ministerin/Aktuelles/Themen/Familienfreundlichkeitsmonitor.html.

by the upper chamber of Parliament in November 2014. It remains to be seen whether children's groups will become widespread enough to make a difference in the meager provision of care for young children.

Institutional Influences on Fertility: The Intersection of Education, the Labor Market, Family Policies, and Social Norms

As in other parts of Europe, attaining a good education and participating in employment have become key features of women's life plans in both Austria and the Czech Republic. Women now clearly outnumber men in completing tertiary education. According to OECD data for 2012, a majority of Czech women (54 %) and 42 % of Austrian women are expected to obtain a tertiary degree, compared with only 3 out of 10 men in both countries (OECD 2015c: Table A3.1.a). Family policies, labor markets, and persistent social norms pertaining to gender roles and childcare have not yet caught up with this development, however. Highly educated women, in particular, are trapped in this "incomplete gender revolution" (Esping-Andersen 2009), and find it difficult to reconcile family and career plans. It is not by coincidence that university-educated women in both countries have the lowest fertility rates. In Austria, many of these women remain involuntarily childless.

How do the education system, labor market, family policies, and gender norms interact to make the combination of work and career difficult for many women and even for men?

Education systems in both countries present two kinds of obstacles for couples planning a family. The first obstacle is the low availability of childcare for children below age three. In many parts of Austria, facilities for young children have short open hours and are closed on many days. There is also limited after-school care for older children. Second is the rather rigid pattern of progressing to higher education, so that pursuing education later in life remains quite uncommon. Most young adults are expected to complete their education before having a family and starting a career.[5] Consequently, the expansion of tertiary education has been the key driving force in the shift toward delayed parenthood in recent decades.

The employment of mothers is closely tied to the availability of extended parental leave and the limited supply of public childcare. Although leave allowance is paid by the government, employers are obliged to provide employment-protected leave for up to two years in Austria and up to three years in the Czech Republic. There is a mismatch between the job-protection period and the maximum length of

[5]Despite the ongoing expansion of university education, Austrian data show that having children while studying remains rare. In 2002–2012, around 1400 children were born annually to mothers who were students, which is less than 2 % of all births.

maternity and parental leave in both countries (30 months in Austria, four years in the Czech Republic), however, so that parents opting for the maximum leave period may lose their jobs. The labor market in the Czech Republic is rather rigid in terms of worktime flexibility, especially regarding opportunities for part-time work. This is partly explained by the unwillingness of employers to offer part-time contracts, although many women would prefer to work part time, especially before their children reach school age (Sirovátka and Bartáková 2008; Nývlt 2014b). The lack of part-time work opportunities delays the return of mothers to employment and makes it more difficult for them to cope with their multiple duties once they start working again. In contrast, part-time jobs are widely available in Austria.

Long parental leave also hinders subsequent career advancement. A Czech woman with two children typically interrupts her career for a total of six years. Even if she then returns to her earlier job position (unless the company or the position has ceased to exist in the meantime), such a long break in employment implies considerable depreciation of skills, stalled career advancement, and reduced lifetime income (Boeckmann et al. 2014). Yet another sign that a long leave may be detrimental to career comes from statistics on unemployment—the proportion of people who are not currently employed but are actively seeking employment. In the Czech Republic, mothers of children age 3–6 have high unemployment rates (15.6 % in 2011)—more than twice as high as unemployment among mothers with children age 7–14 (7.4 %) or among childless women (6.8 %) (Nývlt 2014b). No such effect is visible for fathers of preschool children, whose unemployment rate is actually well below that of childless men.

The prolonged parental leave is also intertwined with the prevailing normative view in both societies that small children may suffer if their mothers work. Mothers may face disapproval from their friends and relatives if they return to work "too early" after childbirth. Combining work and family is further hindered by large disparities in the gender division of household labor. Geist's and Cohen's (2011) analysis of data on preparing dinner, doing laundry, and shopping in 13 developed countries put Austria and the Czech Republic among the most gender unequal, together with Bulgaria, Poland, and Hungary. Miranda's (2011) study of time-use data on unpaid work by people age 15–64 showed Austria close to the OECD average, with women spending about twice as much time as men (270 vs. 140 min per day) on house work, care, shopping, and volunteering.

Concluding Discussion

A quarter of a century after the implosion of state socialism, Austria and the Czech Republic, once positioned on opposite sides on the Iron Curtain dividing Europe, have come to resemble each other in terms of fertility, family patterns, and family policy. Total fertility rates in the two countries converged at 1.5 in 2014, which is low, but not extremely low when compared with Southern Europe or East Asia. Czech women have somewhat larger families and are much less likely to remain childless than Austrian women, possibly due to a continuing strong normative value placed on parenthood in the Czech Republic. Both countries have experienced sweeping family changes typical of the second demographic transition, and general attitudes have turned positive or at least tolerant toward most of these changes.

Family policies in both countries have attempted to respond and gradually adapt to the challenges of the ongoing family and fertility shifts through a mixture of flexible parental leave, tax rebates, and expanded childcare coverage. The policy debates have been relatively pragmatic and generally free of the explicit pronatalism and nationalism typical of many Eastern European countries today. Especially Austria has made good progress toward becoming a more family-friendly country, where parents have a range of options on how to combine their family and work obligations. Both countries are becoming neither family heavens nor feminist paradises, but their policies reflect a mixture of different measures aiming to address the needs of families, children, and parents. Austria can no longer be seen as a "conservative" welfare state promoting the traditional division of domestic tasks and the male-breadwinner family model. Within Austria, the city of Vienna has adapted particularly well to the transformation in gender relations and family patterns. It offers the widest availability of subsidized housing and has by far the best early childcare availability in Austria. Not by coincidence, fertility in Vienna, extremely low in the past, has converged to match levels in the rest of the country (Sobotka 2015, Sect. 4.4; Zeman et al. 2011). Vienna has also acted as a magnet for immigrants, which partly explains the city's rise in fertility.

Is the current low fertility a potential threat for these societies? Arguably, the current period TFRs are below the level that can be considered "optimal," but different tempo-adjusted fertility indicators and completed cohort fertility are in the range of 1.6–1.8. This is a moderate sub-replacement level that should not be a matter of concern and can actually be supportive of higher standards of living in the long run (Lee et al. 2014). Moreover, both Austria and the Czech Republic have attracted considerable migration flows. When migration is taken into account, the Austrian population has been more than "replacing" itself during the past decades (Wilson et al. 2013).

Period total fertility is likely to increase modestly in both countries once the shift toward delayed childbearing comes to an end. The period TFR may then rebound to around 1.6–1.7. This expectation is broadly in agreement with the views of population experts (Basten et al. 2014), but it is higher than the medium-projection scenarios of the national statistical offices.

It is more difficult to predict longer-term trends in family size. Fertility intentions in both countries are at the lower end of the range typical for Europe today. Family size is likely to increase slightly in Austria, where the long-term decline in cohort fertility has come to an end among women born in the 1970s. The combination of a stable economic and policy environment, expanding childcare availability, and continuing immigration from higher-fertility countries may contribute to this rebound. The prospects are different in the Czech Republic, where women and couples still face considerable challenges when planning their families. It is likely that one-child families will become more common, eroding the prevailing strong orientation toward a two-child family model (Rabušic and Chromková-Manea 2007; Šťastná 2007). As a result, family size in the Czech Republic is likely to decline moderately.

What policies would make it easier for prospective parents to realize their fertility plans? Institutional adjustments are needed more than additional monetary support. An expansion of childcare provision for children below age three should be the priority. Austria has made considerable progress, but in the Czech Republic the share of young children in childcare centers remains marginal. In addition, Czech women have only a slim chance of finding part-time work. Creating opportunities for more flexible work conditions should be high on the government agenda. Addressing the lack of affordable housing for young people and single parents should be another priority for Czech policymakers. In this area, they can actually receive plenty of inspiration from Austria. Finally, in both countries, governments should pursue policies that are tailored to the changing character of the family. For instance, a wider legal recognition of cohabiting couples, including partnership registration as is currently common in France, might help such couples obtain more rights (and some duties) with respect to the management of their shared property and children.

References

Arbeiterkammer [Austrian Chamber of Labor]. (2014). *Parental leave schemes.* http://media.arbeiterkammer.at/ooe/berufundfamilie/2014_Infoblatt_Kinderbetreuungsgeld_Varianten.pdf. Accessed October 22, 2014.

Basten, S., Sobotka, T., & Zeman, K. (2014). Future fertility in low-fertility countries. In W. Lutz, W. P. Butz, & K. C. Samir (Eds.), *World population and human capital in the 21st century* (pp. 39–146). Oxfiord: Oxford University Press.

Beaujouan, É., Sobotka, T., Brzozowska, Z., & Neels, K. (2013). *Education and sex differences in intended family size in Europe, 1990s and 2000s.* Paper presented at the Conference on Changing Families and Fertility Choices, Oslo, June 6–7, 2013.

Berghammer, C. (2014). The return of the male breadwinner model? Educational effects on parents' work arrangements in Austria, 1980–2009. *Work, Employment & Society, 28*(4), 611–632.

Boeckmann, I., Misra, J., & Budig, M. J. (2014). Cultural and institutional factors shaping mothers' employment and working hours in postindustrial countries. *Social Forces, advanced online access,*. doi:10.1093/sf/sou119.

Bongaarts, J., & Feeney, G. (2006). The quantum and tempo of life cycle events. *Vienna Yearbook of Population Research, 2006*, 115–151.

Bongaarts, J., & Sobotka, T. (2012). A demographic explanation for the recent rise in European fertility. *Population and Development Review, 38*(1), 83–120.

Buber-Ennser, I., Neuwirth, N., & Testa, N. R. (Eds.). (2014). *Families in Austria 2009–13: Descriptive findings on partnerships, fertility intentions, childbearing, and childrearing.* Vienna: Vienna Institute for Demography/Wittgenstein Centre and Austrian Institute for Family Studies.

CFE (Cohort Fertility and Education) Database. (2014). Data on completed fertility of women in Austria and the Czech Republic by level of education in the Cohort Fertility and Education Database. http://www.cfe-database.org. Accessed October 8, 2014.

Chaloupková, J., & Šalamounová, P. (2004). *Postoje k manželství, rodičovství a k rolím v rodině v České republice a v Evropě*. [Attitudes to marriage, parenthood, and family roles in the Czech Republic and in Europe]. *Sociologické Studie*, 2004/7.

Council of Europe. (2006). *Recent demographic developments in Europe, 2005*. Strasbourg: Council of Europe Publishing.

CSO (Czech Statistical Office). (2014). *Annual time series of the key indicators of population and vital statistics in the Czech Republic, 1785–2013*. http://www.czso.cz/csu/redakce.nsf/i/obyvatelstvo_hu. Accessed April 10, 2015.

CVVM (Centrum pro Výzkum Veřejného Mínění). (2014). *Postoje českých občanů k manželství a rodině—prosinec 2013*. [Attitudes of Czech citizens to marriage and family—December 2013]. Press release ov140120. Prague: The Public Opinion Research Centre. http://cvvm.soc.cas.cz/en/relations-attitudes/attitudes-of-czech-citizens-to-marriage-and-family-December-2013. Accessed April 10, 2015.

Esping-Andersen, G. (2009). *The incomplete revolution: Adapting to women's new roles*. Cambridge: Polity Press.

Eurostat. (2014a). *Data on live births by age of mother, first marriages by age of bride, population by age and marital status, fertility rates by age, net migration, and population balance*. Eurostat online statistics database. http://epp.eurostat.ec.europa.eu. Accessed June, August, and October 2014.

Eurostat. (2014b). *Eurostat population statistics: Foreign-born and non-national population*. http://epp.eurostat.ec.europa.eu/. Accessed October 24, 2014.

Festy, P. (1979). *La fécondité des pays occidentaux de 1870 à 1970*. Travaux et Documents No. 85. Paris: INED, PUF.

Geist, C., & Cohen, P. N. (2011). Headed toward equality? Housework change in comparative perspective. *Journal of Marriage and Family, 73*(4), 832–844.

GGS (Generations and Gender Survey). (2009). *Familienentwicklung in Österreich. Erste Ergebnisse des Generations and Gender Survey (GGS) 2008/09*. [Family developments in Austria. First results of the Generations and Gender Survey (GGS) 2008/09]. Vienna: Vienna Institute for Demography and Austrian Institute for Family Studies.

Goldstein, J. R., Kreyenfeld, M., Jasilioniene, A., & Örsal, D. D. K. (2013). Fertility reactions to the 'Great Recession' in Europe. *Demographic Research, 29*(4), 85–104.

Hajnal, J. (1965). European marriage patterns in perspective. In D. V. Glass & D. E. C. Eversley (Eds.), *Population in history: Essays in historical demography* (pp. 101–143). Chicago: Aldine.

Halman, L., & Draulans, V. (2006). How secular is Europe? *The British Journal of Sociology, 57* (2), 263–288.

Hamachers-Zuba, U., Lehner, E., & Tschipan, C. (2009). Partnerschaft, Familie, und Geschlechterverhältnisse in Österreich [Partnership, family, and gender relations in Austria]. In C. Friesl, R. Polak, & U. Hamachers-Zuba (Eds.), *Die Österreicher-innen. Wertewandel 1990–2008* (pp. 87–141). Vienna: Czernin.

Havelková, B. (2009). Pracovní právo [Labor law]. In M. Bobek, P. Molek, & V. Šimíček (Eds.), *Komunistické právo v Československu. Kapitoly z dějin bezpráví. Mezinárodní politologický ústav* (pp. 478–512). Brno: Masarykova univerzita. Available at www.komunistickepravo.cz

Herrnböck, J. (2012). Väterkarenz: Streit über Zahlen [Peternal leave: A fight over the numbers]. *Der Standard*, 20, November 2012. http://derstandard.at/1353206775448/Papamonat-Streit-ueber-Zahlen. Accessed October 21, 2014.

Human Fertility Collection. (2014). *Period fertility rates by age and birth order for Austria, 1952–1983*. Estimated by T. Sobotka and A. Šťastná. http://www.fertilitydata.org. Accessed April 29, 2015.

Human Fertility Database. (2014). *Period fertility data for Austria and the Czech Republic and cohort fertility data for Sweden*. http://www.humanfertility.org. Accessed August 2014.

Kantorová, V. (2004). Education and entry into motherhood: The Czech Republic during the state socialism and the transition period (1970–1997). *Demographic Research, 3*(10, Special Collection), 245–274.

Kocourková, J. (2002). Leave arrangements and childcare services in Central Europe: Policies and practices before and after transition. *Community, Work, and Family, 5*(3), 301–318.

Kohoutová, I., & Nývlt, O. (2014). *Rodina a statistika* [Family and statistics]. Press conference, 9 April 2014, Prague: Czech Statistical Office. http://www.czso.cz/csu/tz.nsf/i/prezentace_z_tk_rodina_a_statistika/$File/csu_tk_rodina_prezentace.pdf. Accessed October 6, 2014.

Kytir, J. (2005). Demographische Strukturen und trends 2001–2004 [Demographic structure and trends 2001–2004]. *Statistische Nachrichten, 2005*(9), 776–789.

Lalive, R., & Zweimüller, J. (2009). How does parental leave affect fertility and return to work? Evidence from two natural experiments. *The Quarterly Journal of Economics, 124*, 1363–1402.

League of Nations. (1943). *Statistical year-book of the League of Nations, 1941–42*. Geneva: League of Nations, Economic Intelligence Service. http://digital.library.northwestern.edu/league/stat.html#1941. Accessed April 29, 2015.

Lee, R., Mason, A., et al. (2014). Is low fertility really a problem? Population aging, dependency, and consumption. *Science, 346*(6206), 229–234.

Lesthaeghe, R. (2010). The unfolding story of the second demographic transition. *Population and Development Review, 36*(2), 211–251.

Lux, M., & Sunega, P. (2010). Private rental housing in the Czech Republic: Growth and…? *Sociologický časopis/Czech Sociological Review, 46*(3), 349–373.

Miranda, V. (2011). *Cooking, caring, and volunteering: Unpaid work around the world*. OECD Social, Employment, and Migration Working Papers No. 116. Paris: OECD Publishing.

Nývlt, O. (2014a). *Perspektivy mladé generace při zakládání rodiny* [Perspectives of young adults for family formation]. Press conference, 7 May 2014, Prague: Czech Statistical Office. http://www.czso.cz/csu/tz.nsf/i/prezentace_z_tk_perspektivy_mlade_generace_pri_zakladani_rodiny/$File/csu_tk_mladi_prezentace.pdf. Accessed October 6, 2014.

Nývlt, O. (2014b). *Sladění rodinného a pracovního života* [Reconciliation of family and work life]. Presentation to the Czech Demographic Society, 19 Feb 2014. https://www.natur.cuni.cz/geografie/demografie-a-geodemografie/ceska-demograficka-spolecnost/diskusni-vecery-1/prezentace-ke-stazeni/2014-02-19-sladeni-rodinneho-a-pracovniho-zivota/view. Accessed October 8, 2014.

Nývlt, O., & Šustová, Š. (2014). Rodinná soužití s dětmi v České republice z pohledu výběrových šetření v domácnostech. [Family arrangements with children in the Czech Republic from the perspective of household surveys]. *Demografie, 56*(3), 203–218.

OECD (Organization for Economic Cooperation and Development). (2011). *Doing better for families*. OECD Publishing. http://dx.doi.org/10.1787/9789264098732-en. Accessed April 20, 2015

OECD (Organization for Economic Cooperation and Development). (2014a). *OECD family database*. http://www.oecd.org/social/soc/oecdfamilydatabase.htm. Accessed October 2014.

OECD (Organization for Economic Cooperation and Development). (2014b). *Society at a glance 2014: The crisis and its aftermath*. OECD Publishing. http://www.oecd.org/els/societyataglance.htm. Accessed April 29, 2015.

OECD (Organization for Economic Cooperation and Development). (2015a). *Statistics on social protection and wellbeing: Benefits, taxes, and wages–net incomes*. http://stats.oecd.org/Index.aspx?DataSetCode=FIXINCLSA. Accessed February 5, 2015.

OECD (Organization for Economic Cooperation and Development). (2015b). *OECD better life index: Housing indicators*. http://www.oecdbetterlifeindex.org/topics/housing/. Accessed February 6, 2015.

OECD (Organization for Economic Cooperation and Development). (2015c). *Education at a glance 2014*. http://www.oecd.org/edu/education-at-a-glance-2014-indicators-by-chapter.htm. Accessed February 7, 2015.

OIF (Austrian Institute for Family Studies). (2014). *Familien in Zahlen (FiZ)*. Vienna: Austrian Institute for Family Studies.

ONS (Office for National Statistics). (2013). *Cohort fertility, England and Wales, 2012.* Data released 5 Dec 2013. London: Office for National Statistics. http://www.ons.gov.uk/ons/rel/fertility-analysis/cohort-fertility-england-and-wales/2012/index.html. Accessed August 20, 2014.

Pakosta, P. (2009). Proč chceme děti: hodnota dítěte a preferovaný počet dětí v České republice [Why we want children: The value of children and the preferred number of children in the Czech Republic]. *Sociologický časopis/Czech Sociological Review, 45*(5), 899–934.

Paloncyová, J., & Šťastná, A. (2012). Sňatek a rozchod jako dva možné způsoby ukončení nesezdaného soužití [Marriage and breakup as two possible paths away from cohabitation]. *Demografie, 54*(3), 214–232.

Prioux, F. (1993). The ups and downs of marriage in Austria. *Population: An English Selection, 5*, 153–182.

Prskawetz, A., Sobotka, T., Buber, I., Gisser, R., & Engelhardt, H. (2008). Austria: Persistent low fertility since the mid-1980s. *Demographic Research, 7*(19–12), 293–360.

Rabušic, L., & Chromková-Manea, B. E. (2007). Jednodětnost v českých rodinách. Kdo jsou ti, kdo mají nebo plánují pouze jedno dítě [One-child families in the Czech Republic. Who are the people who have or plan to have just one child?]. *Sociologický časopis/Czech Sociological Review, 43*(4), 699–719.

Rabušic, L., & Chromková-Manea, B. E. (2012). Postoje, hodnoty a demografické chování v České a Slovenské republice v období transformace (1991–2008) [Attitudes, values, and demographic behavior in the Czech and Slovak Republics in the period of transformation (1991–2008)]. *Data a výzkum—SDA Info, 6*(1), 27–49.

Reinprecht, C. (2007). Social housing in Austria. In C. Whitehead & K.J. Scanlon (Eds.), *Social housing in Europe* (pp. 35–43). London: London School of Economics and Political Sciences. http://vbn.aau.dk/files/13671493/SocialHousingInEurope.pdf. Accessed April 29, 2015.

RHS (Reproductive Health Survey). (1995). *1993 Czech Republic reproductive health survey: Final report.* Czech Statistical Office, Factum, WHO, and Centers for Disease Control and Prevention. http://ghdx.healthdata.org/record/czech-republic-reproductive-health-survey-1993. Accessed April 29, 2015.

Rille-Pfeiffer, C., & Kapella, O. (2012). *Evaluierungsstudie Kinderbetreuungsgeld: Einkommensabhängige und pauschale Bezugsvariante 12+2 Monate* [Evaluation study of leave allowances: Income-dependent and flat rate variant of 12+2 months]. Forschungsbericht No. 9–2012. Vienna: Austrian Institute for Family Studies.

Saxonberg, S., & Szelewa, D. (2007). The continuing legacy of the Communist legacy? The development of family policies in Poland and the Czech Republic. *Social Politics: International Studies in Gender, State, and Society, 14*(3), 351–379.

Sirovátka, T., & Bartáková, H. (2008). Harmonizace rodiny a zaměstnání v České republice a role sociální politiky [Harmonizing work and family in the Czech Republic and the role of social policy]. In T. Sirovátka & O. Hora (Eds.), *Rodina, děti a zaměstnání v české společnosti.* Brno: Masaryk University, Faculty of Social Science.

Sobotka, T. (2009). Sub-replacement fertility intentions in Austria. *European Journal of Population, 25*(4), 387–412.

Sobotka, T. (2011). Fertility in Central and Eastern Europe after 1989: Collapse and gradual recovery. *Historical Social Research, 36*(2), 246–296.

Sobotka, T. (2015). *Low fertility in Austria and the Czech Republic: Gradual policy adjustments.* VID Working Papers 2/2015. Vienna: Vienna Institute of Demography.

Sobotka, T., Zeman, K., & Kantorová, V. (2003). Demographic shifts in the Czech Republic after 1989: A second demographic transition view. *European Journal of Population, 19*(3), 249–277.

Sobotka, T., Šťastná, A., Zeman, K., Hamplová, D., & Kantorová, V. (2008). Czech Republic: A rapid transformation of fertility and family behaviour. *Demographic Research, 19*(14–Special Collection), 403–454.

Sobotka, T., Skirbekk, V., & Philipov, D. (2011). Economic recession and fertility in the developed world. *Population and Development Review, 37*(2), 267–306.

Šťastná, A. (2007). Druhé dítě v rodině–preference a hodnotové orientace českých žen. [Second child in the family: The preferences and values of Czech Women]. *Sociologický časopis/Czech Sociological Review, 43*(4), 721–746.

Šťastná, A., & Sobotka, T. (2009). *Changing parental leave and shifts in second- and third-birth rates in Austria.* VID Working Papers 7/2009. Vienna: Vienna Institute of Demography.

Statistics Austria. (2014a). *Childcare statistics.* http://www.statistik.at/web_de/statistiken/bildung_und_kultur/formales_bildungswesen/kindertagesheime_kinderbetreuung/index.html. Accessed October 22, 2014.

Statistics Austria. (2014b). *Demographische Indikatoren—erweiterte Zeitreihen ab 1961 für Österreich.* [Demographic indicators—expanded time series for Austria from 1961]. Vienna: Statistics Austria. http://www.statistik.at/web_de/statistiken/bevoelkerung/demographische_indikatoren/index.html. Accessed August 6, 2014.

Thévenon, O. (2011). Family policies in OECD Countries: A comparative analysis. *Population and Development Review, 37*(1), 57–87.

UNICEF (United Nations Children's Fund). (2013). *TransMonEE 2013 Database.* UNICEF Regional Office for CEE/CIS. Released June 2013. http://www.transmonee.org/. Accessed August 2013.

Van Bavel, J., Jansen, M., & Wijckmans, B. (2012). Has divorce become a pro-natal force in Europe at the turn of the 21st century? *Population Research and Policy Review, 31*(5), 751–775.

VID (Vienna Institute of Demography). (2014). *European demographic data sheet.* Vienna: Vienna Institute of Demography and IIASA/Wittgenstein Centre for Demography and Global Human Capital. http://www.oeaw.ac.at/vid/datasheet/DS2014/DS2014_index.shtml. Accessed April 29, 2015.

Wilson, C., Sobotka, T., Williamson, L., & Boyle, P. (2013). Migration and intergenerational replacement in Europe. *Population and Development Review, 39*(1), 131–157.

Wynnyczuk, V., & Uzel, R. (1999). Czech and Slovak Republic. In H. P. David (Ed.), *From abortion to contraception: A resource to public policies and reproductive behavior in Central and Eastern Europe from 1917 to the present* (pp. 91–119). Westport: Greenwood Press.

Zeman, K., Sobotka, T., Gisser, R., Winkler-Dworak, M., & Lutz, W. (2011). *Geburtenbarometer Vienna: Analysing fertility convergence between Vienna and Austria.* VID Working Paper 07/2011. Vienna: Vienna Institute of Demography.

Zeman, K., Sobotka, T., Gisser, R., & Winkler-Dworak, M. (2014). *Geburtenbarometer 2013.* Vienna: Wittengenstein Centre for Demography and Global Human Capital and Vienna Institute of Demography/Austrian Academy of Sciences. http://www.oeaw.ac.at/vid/barometer/downloads/Geburtenbarometer_Ergebnis_2013.pdf. Accessed April 10, 2015.

Fertility Decline and the Persistence of Low Fertility in a Changing Policy Environment—A Hungarian Case Study

Zsolt Spéder

Abstract In the period following the Second World War, Hungary was the first country in Europe in which the total fertility rate (TFR) fell below the replacement level of 2.1 children per woman (in 1962), and as of 2013, Hungary's TFR was still among the lowest in Europe. The period in between these two dates was characterized by considerable fertility fluctuation combined with long-term decline. These fertility trends were clearly influenced by the profound structural changes that took place in Hungary, while the effects of various social-policy interventions are less obvious. The lowest points in Hungary's fertility were clearly connected to two fundamental changes of regime—the transition from capitalism to communism and back to modern capitalism. In terms of social-policy interventions, the past 60 years can be divided into two periods: a time of continuously expanding programs that supported fertility under the communist regime followed by a period of changing policies accompanied by fertility fluctuations and decline. There is clear evidence that Hungarian fertility was able to recover from the first low due to active social-policy interventions under communism, but we know less about the role and effect of social policy in the more recent period of fertility fluctuation and decline.

Keywords Fertility · Population policy · Social change · Transitions · Political transformations · Hungary

The long-term evolution of fertility in Hungary followed a classic transition pattern from high to low levels, but with some special characteristics (Demény 1997). Hungary's fertility decline began early, despite the country's relative economic backwardness, and was simultaneous with a similar decline in Western Europe. A level of conscious marital birth control could be observed as early as the 18th and 19th centuries (Andorka 1987), long before the emergence of modern birth-control methods. This early reduction in the number of children was based on the parents' wishes, without any state intervention. The last stage of the demographic transition,

Zs. Spéder (✉)
Hungarian Demographic Research Institute, Budapest, Hungary
e-mail: speder@demografia.hu

R.R. Rindfuss and M.K. Choe (eds.), *Low Fertility, Institutions, and their Policies*, DOI 10.1007/978-3-319-32997-0_7

however, marked by the achievement and stabilization of modern fertility behavior, was not entirely free from government influence. A brief period of state intervention took place between 1952 and 1954, marked by signs of coercion. Then by the mid-60s, when the demographic transition should have been completed, a new set of population policy measures was in the making.

Two vitally important changes of regime have taken place in Hungary in the past 60 years. One was the socio-economic and political transformation following the Second World War, which established and reinforced the communist social system. The development of the communist (Soviet) system was full of social tensions, however, which led to the uprising of 1956. The immediate demographic consequence of the 1956 revolution was that about 200,000 people emigrated from Hungary within a few weeks (Tóth 1996). The long-term political consequence was the creation of a redistributive economic system, including market mechanisms, with an eye on consumption goals. The existence of "the happiest barrack," as Hungary was described in the communist system, was made possible by the revolution of 1956 and the subsequent market- and consumption-friendly economic policy. Small-scale agricultural production based on private ownership was allowed beginning in the 1960s, and market-stimulating measures were introduced in the industrial production system in 1968.

The second profound transition was the change of regime—"retransition"—to modern capitalism, starting in 1989/1990. The effects, still lasting today, include the restoration of parliamentary democracy and the "re-creation" of a market economy. Thus over a short period, in a historical perspective, Hungary's socio-economic and political system changed twice, radically transforming the lives and living conditions of families and individuals in the lifetime of one generation.

Awareness of low fertility, and especially of the one-child phenomenon, had appeared as early as the 1930s in Hungarian public life (Andorka 1975). The worried intelligentsia (priests, writers, local politicians) considered modernization, individualization, and selfishness as causes of this phenomenon. A generation later, at the time of the first fertility low in the 1960s, public discourse focused on the dilemma of "car or baby," and consumption and selfishness were again considered responsible for the drop in childbearing. After this, the fertility level has been a consistent topic of public debate. The specific reasoning is less important than the general level of concern. Indeed, public awareness of population issues and worries about the survival of the Hungarian population have exerted a constant pressure on policymakers to take a stance.

For families, the cultural climate provides an important context for fertility decisions (Reher 1998). Religiosity and religious denomination are the crucial and most widely available indicators of the cultural system. The majority of the Hungarian population (60 %) is Roman Catholic, but there is a significant share of Calvinists (15 %) and Evangelicals (5 %). The proportion that is non-religious or does not practice a religion has increased steadily. In terms of religiosity in former communist countries, Hungary stands between the strongly secularized Czech Republic and the religious Poland. International value surveys, such as the World Value Survey and the International Social Survey Programme (ISSP), indicate that the Hungarian population's attitudes and beliefs about family relations are very similar to those of other communist societies (with the exception of East Germany and perhaps the Czech Republic) but are more traditional or conservative than the attitudes of populations in Western Europe (Arts et al. 2004; Inglehart and Baker 2000; Spéder and Kapitány 2014).

This chapter will present fertility trends and the characteristics of fertility behavior in Hungary since the Second World War by describing different fertility indicators. Then, divided into two periods—the period of communism and the period of transition to capitalism—the analysis will cover the socio-structural factors underlying fertility trends and how government policymakers have reacted to low fertility. Finally, we interpret the role of policy interventions in the evolution of fertility levels in Hungary.

Fertility Change Since the Second World War

Trends

The decades following the Second World War were characterized by a declining total fertility rate (TFR) along with permanent, intensive fluctuation (Fig. 1). This fundamental duality, combining significant long-term changes in fertility with swings between highs and lows, was connected to profound transformations of institutions and social structures, which twice created a radically new context for individual and family decision making, including decisions on childbearing. This

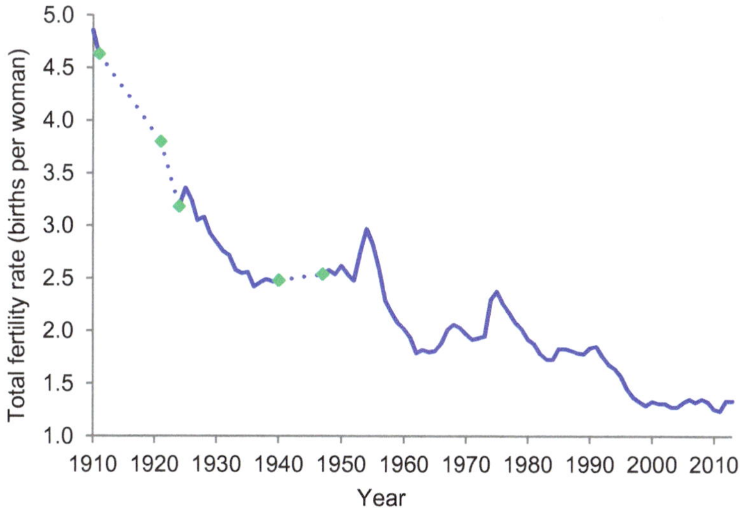

Fig. 1 Total fertility rate (TFR) in Hungary, 1910–2013 (KSH 1992; own calculations based on Hungarian Central Statistical Office (HCSO) vital statistics)

duality was also the consequence of deliberate social-policy measures that attempted to change the declining fertility trend by "external" means, mostly by encouraging families to have more children but sometimes by prohibitive measures, such as a ban on abortions.

The "baby boom" in Hungary after World War II was negligible, compared to the pattern in other European countries. Coercive measures, however, "produced" a peak in fertility at the beginning of the 1950s. The fertility rise between 1952 and 1954 was partly the consequence of an abortion ban and other coercive policies introduced by the government, following a Soviet pattern. Public intolerance of coercive measures soon became manifest, and these policies were cancelled, followed by a fertility decline. In the early 1960s, Hungary became the first country in Europe in which the TFR declined below the replacement level of 2.1 children per woman (Table 1). The TFR hit bottom in 1962, at 1.79. In the same period, neighboring socialist countries were also characterized by low fertility—2.11 in Czechoslovakia, 2.34 in Romania, and 2.32 in Bulgaria. Fertility was significantly higher in Poland, at 2.98, and in Western European countries—2.70 in neighboring Austria, 2.20 in Sweden, and 3.14 in Portugal. So at this time, and before reaching below-replacement fertility in the West, low TFRs were typical of socialist countries, and the level was lowest in Hungary.

As a result of continuous social-policy interventions using an increasing variety of means, a fertility regime evolved between 1967 and 1994 that had a certain degree of stability. The TFR began to rise following the first general population policy intervention in 1967. Marriage was nearly universal, and childbearing typically began in the early 20s. The share of large families (four or more children) declined, but childlessness and one-child families also declined with the spread of the two-child family model (Table 2). As a result, completed fertility did not decrease, and it even increased to some extent among those born at the end of the 1950s. As of 2010, the completed fertility of the cohort born in 1960 was 1.96. In

Table 1 Total fertility rate (TFR) in selected communist and Western European countries, 1960, 1985, 2010

Countries	Year		
	1960	1985	2010
Communist countries			
Bulgaria	2.32	1.98	1.57
Czech Republic	2.11	1.96	1.51
Hungary	2.02	1.85	1.25
Poland	2.98	2.32	1.41
Romania	2.34	2.31	1.59
Western countries			
Austria	2.70	1.47	1.44
France	2.73	1.81	2.03
Portugal	3.16	1.72	1.39
Sweden	2.20	1.74	1.98

Council of Europe (2004, p. 76), Eurostat (2015)

Table 2 Distribution of women age 40–44 by number of children, 1970, 1980, 1990, 2000, 2005, and 2011 (percent)

Number of children	Percentage of women age 40–44					
	1970	1980	1990	2000	2005	2011
0	12.8	10.2	8.5	7.8	8.5	12.0
1	24.2	28.2	22.0	20.0	21.3	25.5
2	34.9	41.9	50.5	51.1	47.5	41.1
3	15.6	12.2	13.7	15.0	16.2	15.3
4	6.4	3.8	3.1	3.6	4.0	3.8
5+	6.0	3.7	2.1	2.3	2.6	2.3
Total	100	100	100	100	100	100
(Average number of children)	(2.034)	(1.873)	(1.897)	(1.959)	(1.959)	(1.824)

KSH (2006b), own calculations

order to achieve this level of fertility, a continuously expanding "active population policy" was necessary (Andorka 1987), which led to the evolution of a reproductive regime called the "socialist greenhouse" (Sobotka 2004).

Fertility and the Timing of Childbearing

Throughout the 20th century, most Hungarians became parents. Although the proportion of higher-order children was constantly decreasing, around four-fifths of Hungarians became parents before turning 25, followed by the birth of a second child in 2–3 years. Women's mean age at first birth was under 23 in 1960 and 1975, and by 1990 it had increased by less than one year (Fig. 2).

Then starting in the early 1990s, the mean age of first birth began to rise steadily, from 23.4 in 1995 to 28.2 in 2010. Since then, it has remained fairly constant. Similarly, mother's mean age at all births rose less than one year in the 20 years between 1970 and 1990, and then increased by almost three years between 1995 and 2010. Thus the increase in mother's age for all births is somewhat lower than the increase for first births, which is basically the consequence of shrinking birth intervals, especially for higher-order births.[1]

A comparison of age-specific fertility rates helps shed light on the age characteristics of fertility behavior (Fig. 3). Despite wide variation in period fertility during the communist era from 1949 to 1989, the age-specific profile of fertility barely changed. This means that when fertility suddenly rose or dropped, the change occurred across nearly all childbearing ages. The shape of the curve exhibits

[1]In the past 15 years, the average interval between the births of first and second children dropped from 3.4 to 2.2 years. The interval between the births of first and third children dropped from 6.5 to 3.6 years, and the interval between the births of first and fourth children dropped from 8.0 to 4.3 years.

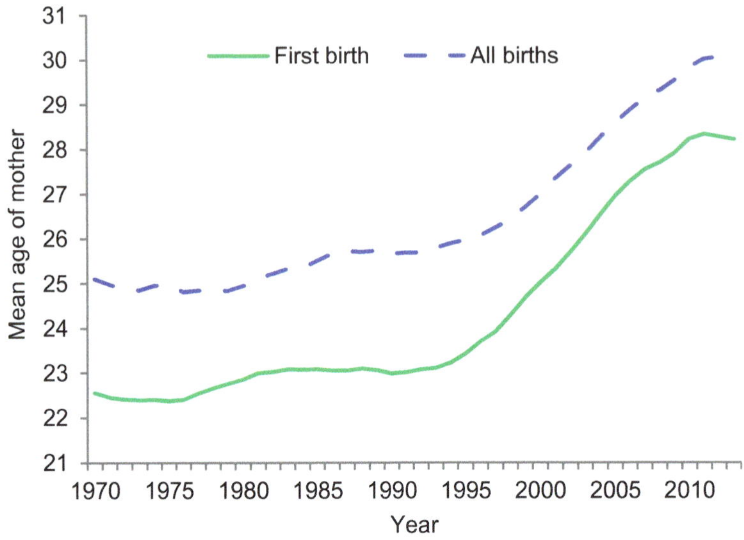

Fig. 2 Mean age of mother at first birth and at all births, Hungary, 1970–2013 (own calculations based on HCSO vital statistics)

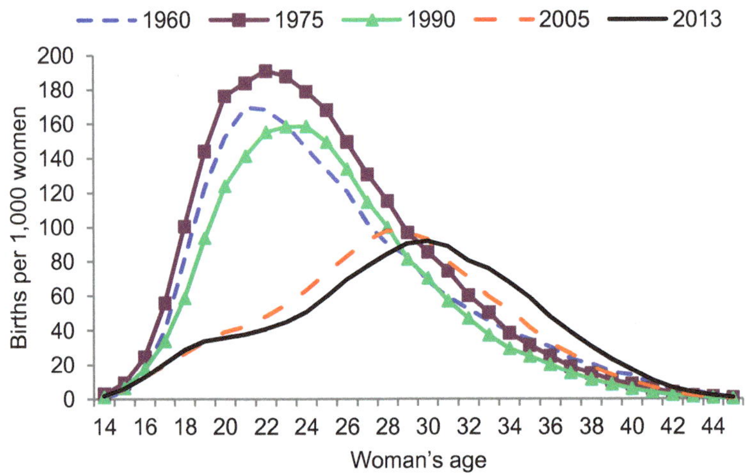

Fig. 3 Age-specific fertility rate, Hungary, 1960, 1975, 1990, 2005, and 2013 (own calculations based on HCSO vital statistics)

a left-sided asymmetry because for decades women tended to bear a child most frequently in their early 20s. The important rise in fertility in the mid-1970s did not change this pattern.

The first signs of change in the age-specific fertility rate appeared around 1990, and later the shape of the curve changed radically, increasingly resembling a normal

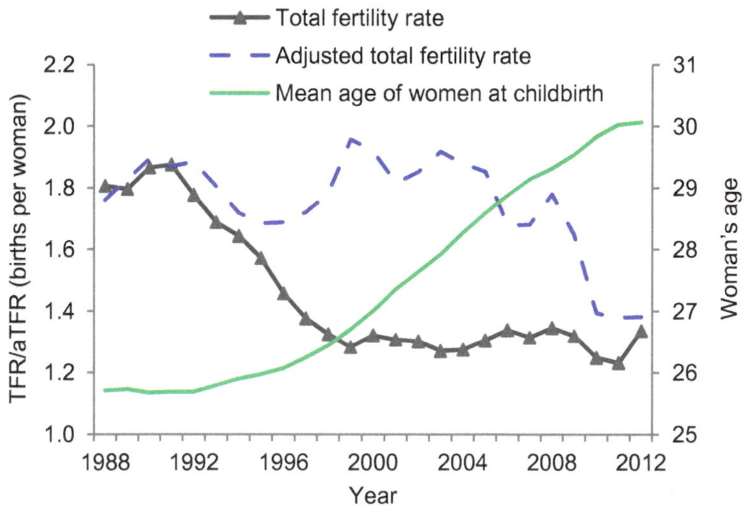

Fig. 4 Total fertility rate (TFR), adjusted total fertility rate, and mean age of women at childbirth, Hungary, 1989–2012 (own calculations based on HCSO vital statistics)

distribution. Another characteristic of fertility change in the past decades is clearly visible: The standard deviation of childbearing age increased, and the curve became flatter. This was the result of increasing variation in total number of children and, to a lesser extent, increasing variation in the timing of first births.

Demographers are well aware that the TFR is distorted during a period when women are postponing childbearing. The adjusted TFR (aTFR) developed by Bongaarts and Feeney (1998)[2] makes it possible to assess whether a quantum effect played a part in Hungary's fertility decline and stagnation or whether postponement (a tempo effect) was solely responsible for this trend.[3]

Based on adjusted TFR, three periods can be distinguished (Fig. 4). Between 1992 and 1996, the aTFR decreased slightly from 1.89 to 1.69, indicating that fertility decline during this period was due to a quantum effect. It may be possible that this fertility decline occurred due to a shock and/or euphoria after the change of regime (Zapf and Mau 1993), so overall fertility decreased before women began postponing births. Then between 1997 and 2004, childbearing was characterized by large-scale postponement. During the same period, however, the aTFR actually rose slightly, suggesting that postponement was not having an effect on the quantum on fertility. In the third period, between 2005 and 2010, there was a significant drop in

[2]After Bongaarts and Feeney's article was published, a debate started about their formula's validity and possible distortions. The authors modified their method in a later study, and the new adjusted TFR generated for Hungary shows less fluctuation. The original Bongaarts-Feeney formula is still accepted, however.

[3]The adjusted total fertility rate (aTFR) gives information about how the average number of children (TFR) would have evolved if postponement had not occurred.

the aTFR (from 1.85 to 1.39). Since by this time the increase in the mean age of birth was levelling off, fertility should have increased if Hungary's low TFR had been simply the result of postponement. In summary, postponement (tempo) appears to be almost exclusively responsible for the overall fertility decline in Hungary until 2004, whereas quantum change is the main cause of low fertility thereafter. A parity-specific analysis reveals that the decline of aTFR after the millennium is primarily due to a decline of first births (not shown).

Family Size, Completed Fertility, and Birth Rates by Parity

In contrast to the high fluctuation in period TFR, fertility behavior in the communist era approached from a cohort perspective was characterized by a high degree of stability. The total completed fertility rate (TCFR) stopped declining among those born during the Second World War, remaining at around 1.87, and then began to increase, if only slightly, among those born after the war (Fig. 5). It rose to 1.98 among those born in 1961–62 and then declined slightly.

We can draw a more specific picture of this process if we examine the distribution by family size of cohorts (age groups) with nearly completed fertility at different times. During the second half of the 20th century, the period of communism, the two-child family pattern was clearly prevalent. Nearly completed fertility, the fertility of those aged 40–44, oscillated at around 2.0 over a 30-year period (between 1970 and 2000). The proportion of women bearing two children rose from 34.9 % in 1970 to 52.1 % in 1995 across the female population age

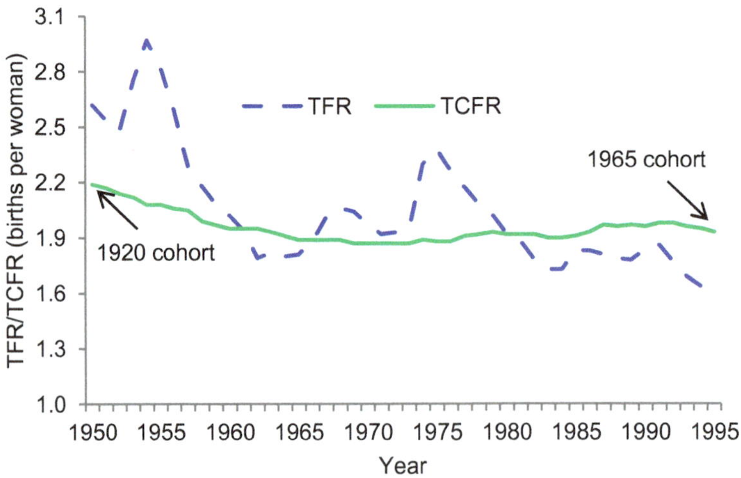

Fig. 5 Total fertility rate (TFR) and total completed fertility rate (TCFR), Hungary, 1950–1995 (Kamarás 2012)

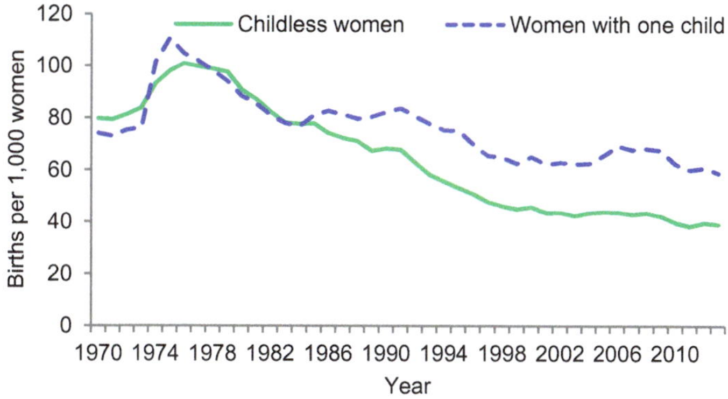

Fig. 6 Births per 1000 childless women and per 1000 women with one child, Hungary, 1970–2013 (own calculations based on HCSO vital statistics)

40–44 (Table 2). After 2000, the proportion with two children declined slightly, but in 2005 it still stood at 47.5 %. The proportion of every other family size decreased. It is well known that the proportion of large families (3+ children) decreased steadily over the 20th century; far less known, however, is that substantially fewer people remained childless or had only one child. It is therefore reasonable to refer to a universalization of the two-child family model. In fact, there is hardly any difference in close-to-completed fertility among those cohorts that were largely responsible for the fluctuations in TFR (see Fig. 1). The fertility behavior of these cohorts fits into a basic trend toward homogenization and standardization. The evolution of the completed total fertility rate and the trend toward homogenization of family size allow us to consider the period between 1967 and 1995 as a stable fertility regime.

The general trend appears to have faltered at the time of the millennium, since in 2005 the proportion of women age 40–44 with two children decreased, while the proportion with three children or one child increased. Considering these changes in fertility behavior, what expectations can we have for future family size in Hungary? To answer this question, we can examine birth rates for women at parity 0 and parity 1 from 1970 to 2013.

It meets our expectations, and fits in with the process of postponement, that the probability of first births clearly declined after the change of regime in 1989/1990 (Fig. 6). The decline was particularly steep between 1992 and 1998. In later years, the live birth rate remained at around 40 per 1,000 women. As the increase in age at first birth slowed down and then came to a halt in 2011 (Fig. 2), we would expect that the live birth rate would rise. So far, this has not been observed. Rather, by comparing census data and vital statistics, our estimation is that childlessness stood at 19.1 % in 2013 among those born in 1975, i.e., at age 38.[4] Since childbearing

[4]Our thanks to Dávid Kelemen for providing the data.

after age 38 is rare, we assume that the rate of childlessness in the cohort born in 1975 will be around 17–18 %. This rate, compared with the 8.5 % rate of childlessness among those born in 1963, makes it obvious that we can anticipate significant changes in the number of children born in Hungary above and beyond any changes due to postponement of births.

If postponement of first births had been the major contributor to fertility change in Hungary after 1989, the childbearing probability (live birth rate) of those with one child (parity 1) should not change. However this rate decreased slightly up to 1995 and then more steeply up to 1999 before leveling off, increasing, and then declining again (Fig. 6). While there were 80.8 childbirths per 1000 women with one child in 1992, there were 63.0 in 2002 and 60.9 in 2012. By contrast, the propensity of women with two and three children to have another child did not change significantly.

All in all, not only has the timing of first births become more variable since the beginning of the millennium, but the distribution of the population by family size is also predicted to change. This should give rise to increasing heterogeneity.

Non-marital Childbearing

Non-marital childbearing had long been insignificant in Hungarian fertility. Lying on the edge of the Hajnal line, early childbearing was generally accompanied by even earlier marriage. The proportion of non-marital births remained at about 5 % in the 1960s and 1970s and never exceeded 10 % until the 1980s. In case of an unexpected pregnancy, couples tended to prefer marriage rather than non-marital childbearing.[5] Since the regime change in 1989/1990, the proportion of births occurring outside marriage has increased at an accelerated pace, rising first above 10 % at the end of 1980s, reaching 20 % in the mid-1990s, then more than 30 % after 2000, and 45 % in 2013 (Fig. 7).

The age profile of non-marital births has also changed. Up to 1990, childbearing outside marriage was more typical of older people. These births predominantly occurred in cohabiting relationships after the breakup of a marriage (Carlson and Klinger 1987). By contrast, younger mothers who had children outside marriage were more likely to be single parents. Today non-marital childbearing is common among every age group, but as a proportion of all childbearing, it is concentrated much more among younger women (Fig. 8a, b). Most young mothers who have children out of wedlock are in cohabitating relationships, and these partnerships often turn into marriage. Nevertheless, we can still find young single mothers. Among women in their 30s who have a second child while living in a cohabitating relationship, the rate of subsequent marriage is lower. These women appear to consider cohabitation as an alternative to marriage. Finally, breaking up of

[5]As of the mid-1970s, 22–25 % of brides were already pregnant at the time of their marriage.

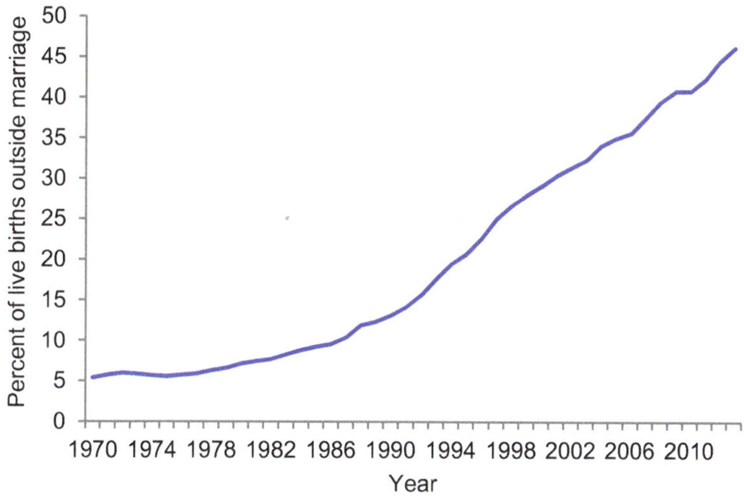

Fig. 7 Proportion of all live births that occurred outside marriage, Hungary, 1970–2013 (own calculations based on HCSO vital statistics)

marriages, forming new partnerships, and childbearing with new partners is not uncommon. This pattern is the main source of the new and growing trend toward mosaic families.

In an in-depth analysis elsewhere, we showed which factors contribute to a person's decision to have a child outside marriage (Spéder 2005). With the more widespread occurrence of non-marital births, their connection to specific social groups weakens, although the likelihood of non-marital births can still be associated with certain characteristics. Based on our multivariate analysis, non-marital childbearing tends to occur among those with low education, the non-religious, and members of the Roma ethnicity. We arrive at the same outcome when comparing childbearing within cohabitation with marital fertility. Thus the increasing occurrence of non-marital births in Hungary does not follow "fashion"—spreading from top to bottom—rather, it is "leaking upward."

Fertility Trends in Summary

In this section, we gave an overview of the main features of fertility change in Hungary following the Second World War. We argued that fertility levels fluctuated periodically within a long-term trend of fertility decline. We highlighted that fertility declined quite early after World War II in every communist country and was much lower than in Western Europe, but Hungary was the first country in which fertility declined to below-replacement level. Regarding the entire communist era, typical features were standardization of the timing of childbearing (universal and

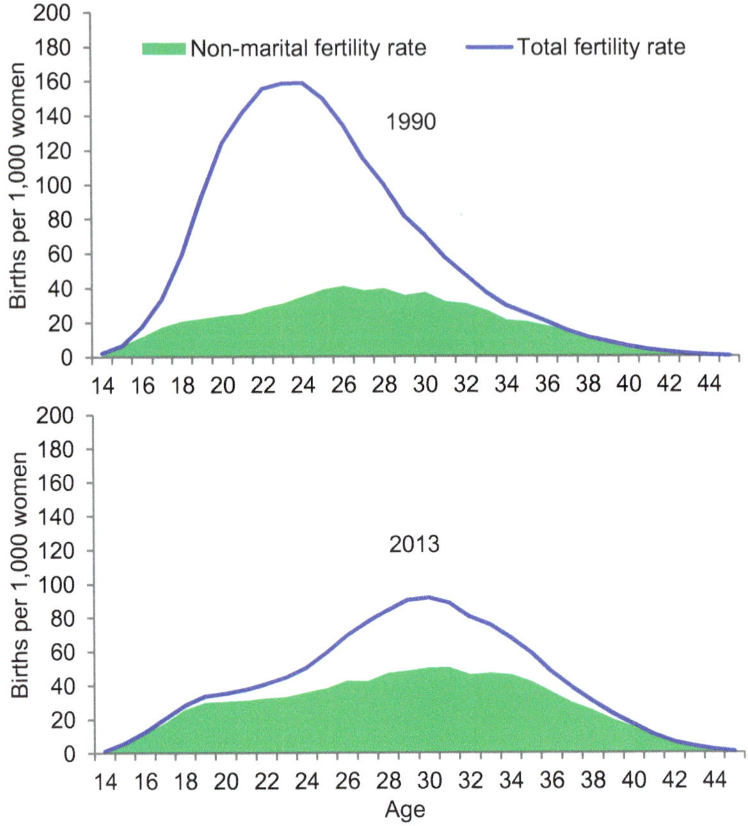

Fig. 8 Non-marital, age-specific fertility rate, Hungary, 1990 (*top*) and 2013 (*bottom*) (own calculations based on HCSO vital statistics)

early marriage and childbearing) and homogenization around the two-child family model. Following the change of regime after 1989/1990, profound changes took effect. Childbearing was postponed to a later age, non-marital childbearing (within cohabitation) became common, and there were signs that the distribution of population by number of children would become more heterogeneous. Looking ahead, childlessness will certainly rise, and the proportion of those with one child will very likely rise also, while the probability of bearing three or more children will barely change. As a result of this transformation, the dominant "two-child" family model will become less common.

We already indicated that major regime change has undoubtedly played a role in shaping fertility trends in Hungary. Government family policies and related measures may have also played a role. Now we will describe the social processes that led to Hungary's low fertility levels and the government interventions that were enacted in response. Next we will discuss whether the effectiveness of any of these interventions can be determined.

The Context for Fertility Decisions: Profound Societal Change and Continuous Policy Amendments

It appears reasonable to divide the period following the Second World War into two separate periods: a communist reproductive period (until 1989/1990) and a transition period thereafter. Within these two very different social systems, institutional programs relevant to fertility were introduced and modified continuously, but the basic differences between the two systems have had profound effects on the decision making of ordinary people, including the decision on whether and when to have children.[6]

Under communism between 1948 and 1990, Hungary's economy was integrated through a state-owned bureaucratic and totalitarian system, which determined the life circumstances of individuals and families, including the circumstances relevant to fertility. For example, childbearing costs were profoundly affected by wages and prices, which were both prescribed by the central government. In addition to wages, government policies determined such factors as the price of consumer goods, the quality of education, the availability of childcare, and the provision of free early-childhood education. In a capitalist economy, by contrast, wages and consumer prices are shaped by demand and supply, and measures by the government essentially influence childbearing conditions through secondary income redistribution.

The well-known discontinuity in Hungarian society in the years since World War II has to be emphasized because the two different social systems, communism and capitalism, entail fundamentally different social conflicts and demographic challenges. The two periods are connected by a certain level of institutional continuity, however, which somewhat disguises the fact that childbearing behavior after the transition to capitalism faced fundamentally different conditions, opportunities, and constraints. Although there was no interruption of family policies and programs, and some were even expanded, the same programs fulfilled a different role in a capitalist market economy.

The Key Challenge of the Communist Reproductive System

During the communist era, the completion of the state socialist economy was realized through the nationalization of private property, the reorganization of agricultural production, and the centralization of industrial production. Economic expansion was facilitated by extensive industrialization, which was based on the rapid expansion of industrial employment. The human resources for this expansion

---

[6]There are a number of excellent comparisons of the differences between communist and capitalist societies and economies. This discussion is based primarily on the work of Kornai (1980, 1992).

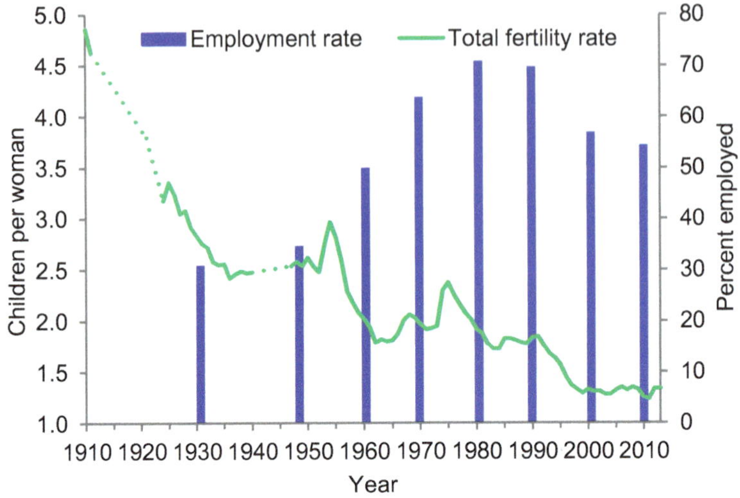

Fig. 9 Total fertility rate (TFR) and employment rate of women age 15–54, Hungary, 1910–2013 (KSH 1992; own calculations based on census data)

were the men and women who had been working in agriculture and the women who had been working in households. During the 10 years between 1949 and 1960, the number of employees grew by 18 % points, from 4.08 to 4.76 million. Growth in the number of female employees was even larger, from 1.19 to 1.69 million, i.e., an increase of 41.7 % points. In 1949, the 35 % employment rate of women aged 15–54 hardly exceeded the 1930 level (34.6 %). Ten years later, in 1960, 49.9 % of women in this age group were full-time employees, and by 1970, 63.7 % of such women were employed full time (Fig. 9).

The rapid expansion of female employment during this period was not confined to Hungary—it was typical of every communist country. Although female employment also grew to some extent in certain Western European countries, the expansion of employment in communist countries was different not only in its pace but also in its nature. What drove women to enter the labor market was not the opportunity of high wages, but rather the pressure from low wages. The basic strategy of the communist economic system was to keep wages low so that a single (male) wage was insufficient to provide for family subsistence. Thus women had no other option than to enter the labor market. The related literature has stressed the forced nature of the expansion of female labor force participation. The real wage grew by only 5 % points over the period of economic expansion between 1950 and 1955, while later, between 1955 and 1960, the real wage expanded by about 5 % a year, reaching 154 % of the 1950 value in 1960. Another feature of female employment in the former communist countries is that it was and still is generally full-time employment (8 h per day).

As we know, there was a strong negative relationship between the macro indicators of female employment and fertility over this period (Andorka 1987). So it is by no accident that the forced expansion of female employment was associated with a steep decline in fertility. This may particularly be the case because the very rapid expansion of full-time female employment was accompanied by a much slower development of childcare facilities, inevitably leading to a conflict between childrearing and work responsibilities.

How did women feel about this dramatic expansion of female employment and the issues involved in balancing family roles with expectations at the workplace? In a 1973 public-opinion poll, the majority of women (63.2 %) agreed that "if an employed woman has children under 10, she should stay at home" (Table 3). A significant minority (36.8 %), however, said "an employed woman, if possible, should carry on working even if she has small children" (Pongrácz and Molnár 1976). Further questions revealed that women justified staying at home by

Table 3 Preferences regarding the roles of women with children under age 10, different groups of female respondents, 1973

A woman with a child under age 10 should…	Respondents			
	All women age 18–55	Women with children under 10	Managers, professional women	Subordinate female white-collar/office workers
Stay at home				
To establish a good family atmosphere	26.7	24.9	22.4	24.7
A man's job is to support the family, a woman's job is to raise children, keep the family together	33.7	33.6	10.4	26.1
Other reason	2.8	3.7	3.0	1.3
Total who think women with young children should stay at home	63.2	62.2	35.8	55.1
Work for pay				
The country needs women's work	2.0	1.5	4.5	2.1
The family needs the woman's earnings	19.2	23.4	22.4	14.0
Managing the household cannot satisfy a woman	11.9	10.7	31.3	23.9
It is the only way to ensure equal rights for women	3.3	1.9	4.5	4.5
Other reason	0.4	0.3	1.5	0.4
Total who think women with young children should work for pay	36.8	37.8	64.2	44.9
Total all women	100.0	100.0	100.0	100.0

Pongrácz and Molnár (1976, pp. 186–189)

supporting traditional roles (33.7 %) and acknowledging the importance of managing a family (26.7 %). Women who favored continuing to work mentioned the contribution of women's earning to subsistence (19.2 %) and the higher prestige of employed work over household work (11.9 %).

Of course women's opinions were not homogenous. The majority of women in managerial and professional occupations favored woman's employment (64.2 %). Most of these women (31.3 %) mentioned the higher prestige of paid employment, but another significant portion (22.4 %) mentioned financial reasons. The opinions of women with small children were not different from the opinions of the total female population, which suggests that the views surrounding childbearing and work were a widespread feature of Hungarian public opinion.

Population Policy Measures in the Communist Era

Population policies were adopted in 1967, 1973, and again in 1985 in an attempt to reconcile the conflict between women's work and family responsibilities. Figure 10 provides an overview of the timing and content of major policy changes since the

	Year	Family allowance	Maternal/ parental leave	Housing support, price subsidies	Daycare centers, crèches, kindergarten	Tax relief
	1938	Introduction, limited access				
Communist regime	1946	Extended				
	1950s				Expansion of daycare centers (for 0–2-year-olds) provided by employer and kindergartens (for 3–5-year-olds) provided by the government	
	1967		2.5-year, flat-rate paid leave		No further expansion of employer-provided daycare	
	1973	Increased real value		Housing support, price subsidies of consumer goods for children introduced		
	1985		2-year, wage-related paid leave			
	1988	Increased real value				Introduced
Market economy	1993	Inflation reduced real value	Flat rate to mother with 3+ children until 8th birthday of youngest child	Price subsidies removed	Employer-provided daycare eliminated	
	1995	Limited access, means tested	Flat rate, limited access, means tested			
	1999	Universal access	Flat-rate paid leave	Housing support extended		Extended/ generous tax relief
	2002			Housing support reduced		
	2006	Increased				
	2009		Shortened to 2 years paid leave			
	2010		Paid leave extended			Extended/ generous tax relief

Legend: Slight support; Medium/ general support; Major/ generous support; Major reduction/ change

Fig. 10 Changes in the institutional settings and family support system, Hungary, 1938–2010 (own tabulation)

late 1930s. Low fertility, fertility decline, and opinions about the reasons for fertility decline all played a role in the development of policies and programs for family support. Other considerations also played a part, such as economic conditions and labor-market regulations.[7]

Policies and programs designed explicitly to influence fertility included the development of a system of paid maternity and parental leave, a complex system of housing benefits, and a price subsidy scheme to facilitate children's consumption. In addition, a number of measures were adopted that were not designed specifically to affect fertility, but that nevertheless very likely had fertility effects. These included housing programs and the creation and expansion of childcare centers.

Starting in 1938, a family allowance was introduced with the intention of lowering childrearing costs. This family allowance has been Hungary's most significant cash-based family benefit program in terms of both magnitude and longevity. Recipients are entitled to a lump-sum allowance per child on a monthly basis until a predefined age of the child (currently 18 years). As of 1946, family allowances were granted to employees in the public sector for every child until the age of six. Among cooperative farmers, those with three children became entitled from 1953, and those with two children from 1966. Between 1953 and 1959, however, the program for government employees was cut back to cover only families with two or more children. Rules for entitlement changed frequently, with the changes generally tending toward expansion[8] (Jarvis and Micklewright 1992). The rate of the family allowance was related to wages, so that its real value changed continuously. The average value per child in 1960 was 5.2 % of average earnings. It went up to 10.4 % in 1975, 21.2 % in 1990, and then went down to 7.8 % in 2003 (Gábos 2005, p. 173). As of the early 1960s, the family allowance comprised nearly all cash-based family benefits provided by the state. At the time of the change of regime (1990), it made up three-fifths of all family-related state expenditures.

In February 1953, the healthcare department adopted coercive pronatalist measures that were particularly restrictive and prohibitive. Reporting and registering pregnancies was made obligatory, accessibility to induced abortions became stringent, and sales of and access to contraceptives were controlled. Violations of the new rules were strictly punished—hundreds of people were prosecuted within weeks, using expedited procedures that resulted in severe verdicts. The rigorous regulations controlling induced abortion lasted only three years and were cancelled in 1956.[9]

Given the massive expansion of female employment, combined with the erosion of traditional kinship and neighborhood networks including access to support by

[7]For example, whether a particular industry needed female labor.

[8]While the family allowance was granted to just over one-half of children in 1950, starting from the 1980s, the overwhelming majority (more than nine-tenths) of children received it.

[9]Such measures were adopted in other socialist countries as well. Coercive pronatalist measures lasted longest in Romania, where they were in effect from 1967 until 1990.

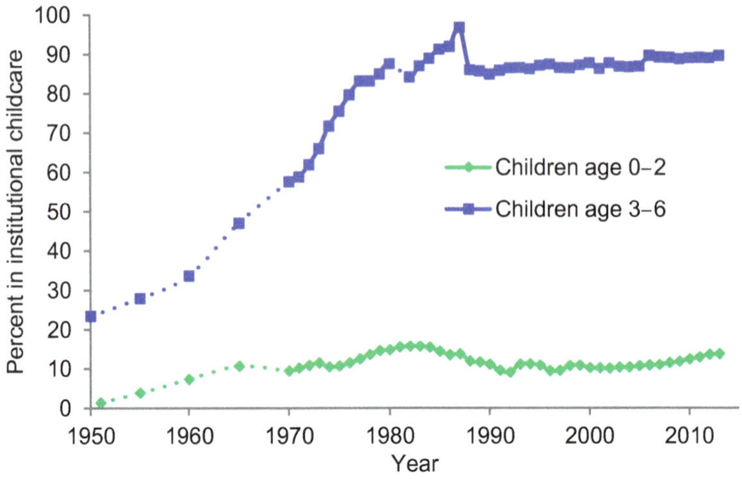

Fig. 11 Percentage of children age 0–2 and 3–6 in childcare centers, nursery schools, and kindergartens, Hungary, 1950–2015 (own calculations based on HCSO Statistical Yearbooks)

grandparents, the need for formal childcare institutions became acute. Recognizing this problem, the government set out to increase childcare capacity for children age 3–5 (Léderer 1992). At the time, every employed woman was entitled to free childcare for children in this age group.

The expansion of women's employment also triggered an expansion of childcare centers for children age 0–2. The central government was not strongly committed to providing care for this age group, however, so responsibility was largely passed on to employers. As a consequence, enrollment rates grew slowly, stabilizing at around 10 % (Fig. 11). As with other public services, center-based childcare was offered free of charge. Although capacity was increasing, the availability of institutional childcare could hardly catch up with the expansion of female employment. The contradiction between the rapid increase of employment among women age 20–24 and the much slower increase of available places in childcare centers suggested an intensifying conflict between childbearing and employment, which potentially exerted a downward pressure on fertility.[10] Then in 1967, the introduction of a long, paid maternity leave allowed women to take care of their young children at home, making the expansion of childcare centers less urgent.

Beginning in 1967, the government began offering a generous provision of maternity leave with financial support. The goal was to facilitate the reconciliation of family and work and to make childbearing possible for employed women. This provision, although frequently adjusted over the years, still exists. It initially

[10]Between 1949 and 1960, the rate of female employment increased from 20.2 to 59.5 % among childless married women and from 14.8 to 41.5 % among married women with one child.

provided employed women 2.5 years (later 3 years) of maternity leave following childbirth, including financial support at a flat rate. On its adoption, the maternity leave payment was equivalent to almost 40 % of mean female net earnings. In 2006, it was 26 %. Once maternity leave expired, the employer was obliged to reemploy the mother.

In addition, a complex population program was adopted in 1973. The goal was to ensure lasting fertility at the replacement level and to counter the trend toward population aging. The program comprised a number of supportive measures for families with children. One feature was an increase in the real value of existing programs (family allowance, maternity leave payment). A new element was assistance with family formation through special housing benefits. Families with three or more children were provided low-rent public housing[11] with a relatively short waiting period, and newly married couples were granted interest-free housing loans. Additionally, the government provided couples with housing grants in return for a promised number of children, to be reimbursed only if the couple did not have the number of children they had promised. Certain restrictive measures affecting the permission for induced abortions were also adopted.[12]

In the early 1980s, fertility again declined to below replacement level (Fig. 1), and unfavorable mortality conditions caused life expectancy to decrease, resulting in population decline for the first time in Europe (still ongoing). In response, population policies were adopted in late 1984, aimed at slowing down population decline, halting it in the long run, and then achieving population increase with a favorable age structure. The most significant measure at this time was the adoption of a new type of benefit, a wage-adjusted parental leave. Mothers who were employed full time for two years before childbirth received 75 % of their average earnings prior to the birth until the child turned two, reduced to 65 % if they had worked for a shorter time before the birth. This measure, if only latently, recognized the opportunity cost of childbearing.

Other measures included tax relief for large families. Hungary adopted a personal income tax in 1988 but provided tax relief to families with more than three children. One of the last acts of the communist government, in 1990, was to make the family allowance universal, rather than tied to employment, so that unemployed parents would also be eligible.

Controlling prices of goods and services was also an important method of resource allocation during the communist era (Kornai 1992). The government used its system of price controls to subsidize the cost of consumer goods for children, such as children's clothing, shoes, and baby food (Fig. 10). These items were available at prices lower than their production costs.

---

[11]A significant government-backed housing program was in effect from the early 1970s until the mid-1980s.

[12]The new rules on abortion were rather liberal, however. Only 1 % of applications were rejected.

Fertility Effects of Population Policy Measures in the Communist Era

Hungarian population policy from the mid-1960s up to the social transformation of 1989/1990 (and even up to 1994) was characterized by the introduction and expansion of programs explicitly designed to create more favorable circumstances for childrearing, including the reduction of childrearing costs. In addition, measures were introduced that indirectly influenced childbearing behavior. The continuous expansion of such measures was an important part of the reproductive regime of communist Hungary (Andorka 1987). Some claim that these measures only had a temporary effect, that they were not able to counterbalance the long-term decline of fertility, and therefore that they basically proved unsuccessful. It is quite a complex task, however, to assess if and how much the government's policy measures influenced fertility behavior and trends. Three investigations offer some insight into this issue.

Andorka analyzed the evolution of fertility by processing census data, using the traditional differential demographic approach, by cohort and education level (Andorka 1987, pp. 287ff; Andorka 1996). This approach enabled him to filter out compositional effects and thus detect fertility changes by education level. He noticed that the negative educational gradient of fertility changed during the 1970s, and the fertility of women with different levels of completed education converged (Table 4). Completed (cohort) fertility stabilized, and the fertility of more highly educated women increased.

Gábos clearly demonstrated the effect of cash-based family benefits on fertility in his econometric analysis. His dependent variable was the annual change in TFR,

Table 4 Mean total lifetime number of births per 100 married women by age and education level, 1960–1990

Age and completed level of education	Number of live births			
	1960	1970	1980	1990
25–29 years				
Did not complete primary (6–7 years)	171	183	238	256
Completed primary (8 years)	148	147	178	188
Completed secondary	111	108	137	141
Completed college or university	94	93	112	115
Total	161	145	158	157
30–34 years				
Did not complete primary (6–7 years)	211	205	258	294
Completed primary (8 years)	174	174	200	208
Completed secondary	150	139	165	174
Completed college or university	135	133	159	166
Total	200	184	188	191

Andorka (1987, p. 326), KSH (2006a, pp. 65–67)

which is correlated with the change in per capita cash-based family benefits from the previous period (Gábos 2005; Gál and Gábos 2004).

Kapitány (2008) used a simulation approach to estimate the effect of measures adopted in 1985 (earnings-related parental support) on childbearing of fertile cohorts. He estimated that these measures increased the number of children per 100 women by about 9 %, and the total number of children born by 5 %.

In summary, we agree with those who depict these various policy measures as an integrated part of the communist reproductive regime (Andorka 1987; Sobotka 2004). We tend to assume that without these measures the period of declining fertility would not have been followed by increases in TFR, and cohort fertility would have declined to a far lower level than it actually did. It is difficult, however, to assess the exact extent of effects due to policy measures.

The Change of Regime from Communism "Back" to Capitalism

A multitude of analyses[13] discuss the fertility changes associated with the rapid and profound social transformation that accompanied the transition from communism to capitalism ("retransition"), beginning abruptly in 1989/1990. These changes, Hungary's so-called "societal transition," covered all areas of life. A detailed overview of social changes relevant to fertility would reach beyond this chapter. It is essential to take into account some general circumstances, however, because they are important for understanding Hungary's family policies and how the old and new programs have functioned in a changed environment.

Although some market mechanisms were retained in Hungary during the communist era, there is a qualitative difference between a redistributive economy based on state ownership and an economy based on private ownership (Kornai 1992). Hungary's economic transition, in reality, meant that the operation, organization, and allocation of resources within the economy and the behavior of each actor underwent a fundamental change.[14] People were thrown into totally new circumstances in a very short period of time, including the circumstances that surround childbearing. With the emergence of free-market pricing, rising energy prices, and the elimination of price subsidies for children's consumer goods, the direct costs of childbearing increased rapidly. Costs also rose because nursery schools, childcare centers, vacations for children, and other social services provided by employers were eliminated. Even more significant was the emergence of economic and

[13]To select but a few, we have to mention two books on this subject and some key studies. These are Józwick and Kotowska (2003), Frejka et al. (2008), Frejka (2008), Sobotka (2008), Billingsley (2010), Spéder and Kapitány (2014).

[14]Of course not everything changed at once, and our current argument is that the dividing line in family policy emerged during a second stage of regime change.

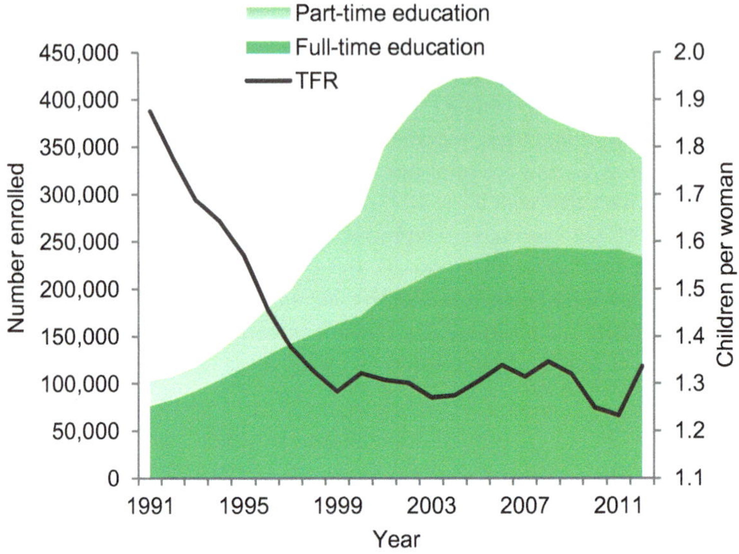

Fig. 12 Participants in full- and part-time higher education and total fertility rate (TFR), Hungary, 1991–2012 (own calculations based on various sources and HCSO education statistics)

labor-market uncertainty. This uncertainty had two origins. On the one hand, it resulted from uncertainty related to Hungary's economic transition, since under free-market conditions every previous activity was reevaluated and repriced. On the other hand, uncertainty arose from Hungary's increasing exposure to global markets. Opening up a closed market involves far more unpredictability than simply increasing the exposure to globalization in a market that is already relatively open.

Labor-market conditions are particularly significant because they transmit the dynamics of the economy to every individual.[15] In 1992, within a year, unemployment rose from zero to 10 %. Taking early retirement into account, the number of available jobs decreased by 20 % from one year to the next. Given the shrinking labor market, it was increasingly difficult for employees to defend and hold their current positions and almost impossible to get a new job. At the same time, the power relations controlling labor conditions changed, and employees became more defenseless at their workplaces. So after the change of regime it became much more difficult to reconcile family and work responsibilities than it had been in the economy of the 1980s based on state ownership.

In response to the shrinking labor market as well as modern economic and social challenges, the government started an intense expansion of higher education (Fig. 12). With the introduction of the market system, the value of a higher degree increased. The expansion of higher education and the incompatibility between

[15]Spéder (2002) provides a detailed discussion of the related theoretical approaches. This discussion is based on that research.

student and parent roles (Blossfeld and Huinink 1990) made a strong contribution to the postponement of childbearing.

Family formation also underwent radical change. Cohabitation became widespread, the popularity of marriage declined, the timing of partnerships and marriage in the life course changed, and the stability of partnerships underwent a change as well (Bukodi 2004; Carlson and Klinger 1987; Csernák 1992; Spéder 2005). Cohabitation as first partnership had already appeared in Hungary in the 1980s, but it became widespread following the change of regime (Spéder 2005; Home et al. 2009). Today it is common for young people to start their first partnership in cohabitation. The majority of couples living in cohabitation eventually marry, although the transition to marriage has decreased slightly over time. This has implications for fertility because couples in cohabitation are less likely to have children than couples who are married. To put it simply, the changing fertility status of the total population and the decline in the number of children were heavily influenced by the fact that many more people were starting a partnership in cohabitation than was the case under communism.

The change of regime fundamentally transformed the social conditions and challenges that surround fertility. For one thing, the cost of raising a child increased. Secondly, decisions about work and careers were made in a context of growing uncertainty, unpredictability, and risk. Thirdly, the work-family conflict reappeared, although in a slightly different form. Fourthly, changes in partnership behavior and the increase in cohabiting relationships were incompatible with the need for long-term commitment to become a parent. Finally, the expansion of higher-level schooling inevitably added to the postponement of childbearing. A key question is how much have changes in family policy been able to respond to these new challenges.

Population Policy Measures in the Capitalist Era: A Continuous Political Battle Around Family-Support Programs

After the change of regime, family policy became a major battlefield within Hungarian politics. In slightly more than two decades, the basic principles of family policy have changed several times along with changes in the government (Ignits and Kapitány 2006). To summarize, conservative, right-wing parties and governments have considered stabilizing the population and preventing fertility decline a strategic issue. Left-wing liberal parties and governments, on the other hand, have viewed social policies relevant to fertility from the perspective of alleviating inequalities and poverty.

The first freely elected government (1990–1994), which was committedly conservative, considered population a strategic goal. Policymakers not only preserved but also expanded the system of benefits that preceded the change of regime. They made substantial efforts, in the face of high inflation, to maintain the real value of cash-based family benefits, and they also launched a number of new programs. Among their first measures were to increase the amount of the family allowance significantly and to make paid maternity leave, which was previously tied to employment status, universal. The entitlement to tax relief, previously limited to large families, was extended in 1992 to families with one or two children. As part of the conservative family model, family childcare support was introduced in 1993. Parents, step-parents, and guardians who were rearing three or more minor children in their own household were entitled to this benefit, which extended from the youngest child's third to eighth completed year.

The second democratically elected government (1994–1998) was socialist oriented but at the same time committed to cutting social expenditures in order to balance the budget. The decision on which social groups should be disadvantaged by cuts was a matter of political orientation.[16] The "Bokros austerity package," adopted in 1995, radically changed Hungary's family policies. It converted a system of benefits based on contributions and employment to one based on means testing. Under the new system, only families whose per capita income was below a certain level were eligible for the family allowance or the flat-rate maternity leave payment granted until the child's third birthday. The wage-related, contribution-based maternity leave granted until the child's second birthday was cancelled, and a one-year, wage-related but means-tested maternity leave was introduced, thus in effect shortening maternity leave. Finally, tax relief related to childrearing expenses was also canceled.

The second conservative government (1998–2002) restored the family benefit system of the first conservative government almost entirely. The 1999 Family Support Act canceled income testing and even made the previous employment-based, flat-rate parental benefit universal. The earning-related "compensating" parental benefit was reintroduced, with eligibility linked to the previous employment of the mother. In addition, a tax-relief scheme based on number of children was introduced, which was far more generous than previous ones.

The next socialist government (2002–2010) continuously debated the issue of family benefits, but fundamental changes were confined to limiting the availability of tax relief in 2005. Only families with three or more children and earning less than a specific income were entitled to tax relief, and the amount was reduced. It is clear that this change was motivated by political considerations rather than fiscal austerity because the government adopted, at the beginning of the legislative period, an extremely expensive pension increase, which was the equivalent of providing an additional one-month payment to pensioners every year from 2002.[17] Although debated, the universal family allowance was finally restored and was doubled in

[16]Of course, the impetus to curtail social expenditures was not surprising since experts considered the state's welfare expenses excessive compared to the gross domestic product (GDP) and labeled the former communist countries, including Hungary, as "premature welfare states".

[17]The extra 13th month gratuity, awarded yearly to all pensioners, was cancelled in 2009.

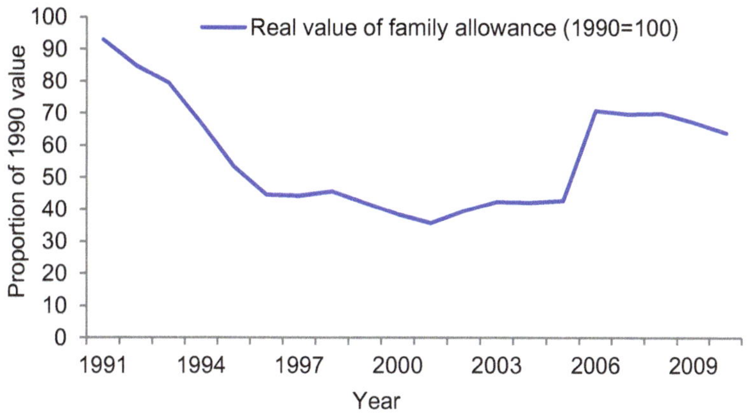

Fig. 13 Change in the real value of the family allowance per child in a two-child family, Hungary, 1991–2010 (1990 = 100) (own calculations based on HCSO Statistical Yearbooks)

2006 (Fig. 13). In 2009, due to the global economic crisis, the socialist government reduced the term of the universal, flat-rate parental leave from three to two years.

As expected, the new conservative government (2010–2014) has restored and enlarged tax relief for families. The sum deductible from income tax now increases with the number of children up to parity three. The parental leave was also restored to three years.

Fertility Effects of Policy Measures During the Post-communist Era

It is difficult to evaluate the role of family policies in Hungary during the societal transition around 1989/1990 and during the shift from early to late fertility. Hungarian family policy is relatively generous if we examine the rate of family expenditures related to the gross domestic product (GDP). According to OECD (Organization for Economic Cooperation and Development) data, Hungary is one of the more generous countries in Europe if we also consider in-kind public expenditures on children (OECD 2014). A study on Central and Eastern European family policy also concluded that Hungarian family benefits were the broadest and most consistent between 1990 and 2000, compared to the post-communist countries joining the European Union in 2004[18] (Szelewa and Polakowski 2008). How can it be explained, then, that in the second decade of the new millennium fertility in Hungary is among the lowest in Europe? (Although, admittedly, fertility in other post-communist countries is not much higher.)

[18]These are Estonia, Latvia, Lithuania, Poland, Czech Republic, Slovakia, and Slovenia.

A possible explanation is that family policy had only a delaying role or no role at all during the period of rapid fertility postponement that has characterized the post-communist fertility transition. The social transition that has been taking place has been so profound and sweeping, pervading all aspects of life, that perhaps changes in government policies and programs might not have had a significant effect on the targeted population.

We have strong evidence, however, that changes in family policy, or at least the cancellation of programs, had a clear impact on fertility behavior in Hungary. Earlier studies showed that measures between 1995 and 1998 (cancellation of earnings-based benefits, introduction of income testing for family benefits) had two types of consequence for fertility (Aassve et al. 2006). On the one hand, this time period was characterized by an increase or acceleration of fertility postponement. Withdrawing benefits intensified the ongoing postponement transition, while their reintroduction had only distributional effects, making fertility more similar among different education groups. On the other hand, childbearing among those with higher-secondary and tertiary education decreased substantially—by one-half—over the 1995–1998 period, compared with childbearing levels among those with primary and lower-secondary education (differentiating effect). In the subsequent period when earnings-based benefits were restored, the difference between child-bearing levels of the two education groups disappeared. This would fit expectations, since cancellation of the earnings-based benefits and applying income testing to the remaining flat-rate benefits adversely affected those with secondary and higher education but benefitted the less educated.

A second explanation is that the changes in family policy did not respond adequately to the challenges raised by the newly emerging capitalist society and economy. This could be because policymakers did not recognize the fundamental challenges of the new economic order or because their responses were limited by other constraints (resources) or because their approach to family policy was motivated by other considerations (poverty alleviation). The first hypothesis is supported by the fact that few genuine measures were adopted to resolve the problem of reconciling family and work. As to the second hypothesis, Hungary's economic decline and shrinking government revenues did not allow family benefits to preserve their real value. Finally, the introduction of redistributive principles into family policies, for example the implementation of means testing for benefits, cannot be considered an adequate response to the challenges faced by families in different economic strata.

A third explanation is that the frequent changes in family policy created a sense of mistrust in the stability of family benefits in the long term. This may have been important because predictability is particularly valuable in times of market fluctuations and economic instability. This explanation would be supported by the argument of Neyer and Andersson (2008) that the effects of family policies largely depend on how those affected perceive them.

It is probable that all three of these processes played a role in limiting the fertility effects of Hungary's relatively high level of family support. The first hypothesis may well be the most compelling—that even generous policy measures have a limited effect in times of profound social and economic change. A definitive answer, however, would require further research.

In Conclusion

This chapter describes the changes and trends in Hungarian fertility since the Second World War. To understand changes in fertility levels, we describe the most important social and economic changes that took place in Hungary over this period as well as changes in population policies and programs.

The TFR in Hungary has fluctuated over the past 60 years but has declined in the long term. A more detailed analysis shows that completed fertility did not decrease in the communist period and slightly increased in the 1980s. Following the change of regime in 1989/1990, the decisive role in fertility decline was clearly related to a transition from early to late fertility. Although it is too soon to draw conclusions, there are signs that this transition to late childbearing entails a lowering of fertility overall.

We showed that the low fertility level in Hungary and other communist countries in the 1950s was the result of forced industrialization and the rapid expansion of full-time employment of women, which created unfavorable conditions for those wishing to have a child. The government adopted a number of supportive, and some coercive, measures in an attempt to raise fertility. Population policies included a generous family allowance, a long parental leave with an allowance compensating for earnings, free childcare for young children, housing benefits, and price subsidies for items consumed by children.

The change of regime in 1989/1990 radically transformed Hungary's economic system and created essentially new conditions for childbearing. In such times of profound social and economic change, it is not surprising that people would wish to avoid risk and postpone decisions with long-term consequences, such as the decision to have a child (Rodin 2011). Fertility postponement was also encouraged by a large-scale expansion of education shortly after the change of regime. In the meantime, family policy showed signs of both continuity and discontinuity.

Hungary's experience raises a question of whether family policy can have a significant influence on fertility during a transition to late childbearing under a new economic system. To be successful, family policy needs continuity and predictability, which was not the case in the 1990s. Although we can see numerous signs of continuity up to 1995, since then the basic principles of family policy (universal vs. income tested, universal vs. contributions related) have become a political battleground. This unpredictability may have largely contributed to the fact that fertility in Hungary is very low in spite of generous family benefits relative to GDP.

Childbearing decisions are deeply embedded in personal circumstances, economic conditions, and institutional systems. The fertility behavior of Hungarian and other post-communist societies has been shaped by profound social and economic change (communism vs. capitalism, bureaucratic economic coordination vs. free markets, state ownership vs. private ownership) as well as government policies and programs (family allowance, parental leave, childcare). These factors together shape the objective conditions of childbearing, but they are not always synchronized. In addition, it is difficult to assess how those people who are making childbearing decisions actually perceive the institutional and policy environment and what factors they consider in their decision-making process. These questions, and with them the explanation of how the institutional environment in Hungary and other former communist countries affects fertility, require further analysis.

References

Aassve, A., Billari, F. C., & Spéder, Zs. (2006). Societal transition, policy changes and family formation: Evidences from Hungary. *Journal of European Population, 2*, 127–152.

Andorka, R. (1975). Az ormánsági születéskorlátozás története. [The history of contraceptive use in Ormánság]. *Valóság, 18*(6), 45–61.

Andorka, R. (1987). *Gyermekszám a fejlett országokban.* [Fertility in advanced societies]. Budapest: Gondolat.

Andorka, R. (1996). Demographic changes and their main characteristics from 1960 to our days. In P. P. Tóth & E. Valkovics (Eds.), *Demography of contemporary Hungarian society.* Highland Lakes: Atlantic Research and Publication.

Arts, W., Geliessen, J., & Luijkx, R. (2004). Shall the twain ever meet? Differences and changes in socio-economic justice norms and beliefs in Eastern and Western Europe at the turn of the Millennium. In J. Hagenaars & L. Halman (Eds.), *The cultural diversity of European unity* (pp. 185–216). Leiden: Brill.

Billingsley, S. (2010). The post-communist fertility puzzle. *Population Research and Policy Review, 29*(2), 193–231.

Blossfeld, H. -P., & Huinink, J. (1990). Human capital investment or norms of role transition? How women's schooling and career affect the process of family formation. *American Journal of Sociology, 97*, 143–168.

Bongaarts, J., & Feeney, G. (1998). On the quantum and tempo of fertility. *Population and Development Review, 24*(2), 707–726.

Bukodi, E. (2004). *Ki, mikor, kivel (nem) házasodik?* [Who, when, whom do (not) marry?] Budapest: Andorka Rudolf Társadalomtudományi Társaság –Századvég Kiadó.

Carlson, E., & Klinger, A. (1987). Partners in life: Unmarried couples in Hungary. *European Journal of Population, 3*, 85–99.

Council of Europe. (2004). *Recent demographic developments in Europe.* Strasbourg: Council of Europe Publishing.

Csernák, J. (1992). Élettársi kapcsolatban élő nők néhány társadalmi, demográfiai jellemzője Magyarországon [Selected social and demographic characteristics of women living in cohabitation]. In J. Csernák, T. Pongrácz, & S. Molnár (Eds.), *Élettársi kapcsolatok Magyarországon* (pp. 15–58). Budapest: KSH, NKI Kutatási Jelentések.

Demény, P. (1997). A huszadik század Magyarországának népesedése a nemzetközi összehasonlítások tükrében [The 20th century population development of Hungary in international comparison]. In J. Kovacsics (Ed.), *Magyarország történeti demográfiája [The demographic history of Hungary]* (pp. 379–390). Budapest: KSH and MTA.

Eurostat. (2015). *Dataset details: Total fertility rate.* http://ec.europa.eu/eurostat/en/web/products-datasets/-/TSDDE220. Accessed May 20, 2015.

Frejka, T. (2008). Determinants of family formation and childbearing during the societal transition in Central and Eastern Europe. *Demographic Research, 19*(7), 139–170.

Frejka, T., Sobotka, T., Hoem, J. M., & Toulemon, L. (Eds.). (2008). Childbearing trends and policies in Europe. *Demographic Research, 19*(Special Collection 7).

Gábos, A. (2005). *A magyar családtámogatási rendszer termékenységi hatásai [Fertility consequences of the Hungarian family support system].* Budapest: Corvinus Egyetem, PHD értekezés.

Gál, R. I., & Gábos, A. (2004). Az intergenerációs közjavak termékenységi hatásai: magyarországi eredmények [Fertility output of the intergenerational public goods: Hungarian results]. In T. Kolosi, I. G. Tóth, & G. Vukovich (Eds.), *Társadalmi riport 2004* (pp. 165–175). Budapest: TÁRKI.

Home, J., Kostova, D., Jasilioniene, A., & Mureşan, C. (2009). Traces of the second demographic transition in four selected countries in Central and Eastern Europe: Union formation as a demographic manifestation. *European Journal of Population, 25*(3), 239–255.

Ignits, G., & Kapitány, B. (2006). A családtámogatások alakulása: célok és eszközök [Trends of family support schemes: aims and means]. *Demográfia, 49*(4), 383–401.

Inglehart, R., & Baker, W. E. (2000). Modernization, cultural change, and the persistence of traditional values. *American Sociological Review, 65*(1), 19–51.

Jarvis, S. J., & Micklewright, J. (1992). *The targeting of family allowance in Hungary.* Florence: European University Institute.

Józwick, J., & Kotowska, I. E. (2003). *Population of Central and Eastern Europe: Challenges and opportunities.* Warsaw: Statistical Publishing Establishment.

Kamarás, F. (2012). A születések és a termékenység hazai irányzatai [Hungarian fertility trends]. *Demográfia, 55*(4), 243–267.

Kapitány, B. (2008). A "gyed-hatás": Az 1985 és 1996 közötti családtámogatási rendszer termékenységre gyakorolt hatása [The "gyed-effect": The fertility effect of the family support system between 1985–1996]. *Demográfia, 5*(11), 51–78.

Kornai, J. (1980). *Economics of shortage.* Amsterdam: North-Holland.

Kornai, J. (1992). *The socialist system: The political economy of Communism.* Oxford: Oxford University Press.

KSH (Központi Statisztikai Hivatal). (1992). *Történeti statisztikai idősorok 1867-1992: Népesség-népmozgalom* [Historical statistical trends 1867–1992: Population]. Budapest: Központi Statisztikai Hivatal.

KSH (Központi Statisztikai Hivatal). (2006a). *Mikrocenzus 2005. 4. Termékenységi adatok* [Microcensus 2005, Band 4. Fertility data]. Budapest: Központi Statisztikai Hivatal.

KSH (Központi Statisztikai Hivatal). (2006b). *Termékenységi adattár 1990–2005* [Fertility data 1990–2005]. Budapest: Központi Statisztikai Hivatal.

Léderer, P. (1992). Nyomás az óvodákon [Pressures on kindergartens]. *Esély*, 92–104.

Neyer, G., & Andersson, G. (2008). Consequences of family policies on childbearing behaviour: Effects or artifacts? *Population and Development Review, 34*(4), 699–724.

OECD (Organization for Economic Cooperation and Development). (2014). Public spending on family benefits. In *OECD family database.* www.oecd.org/social/family/database. Accessed January 3, 2015.

Pongrácz, T., & Molnár, S. E. (1976). *Népesedési kérdésekkel kapcsolatos közvéleménykutatás* [Public opinion research on population issues]. KSH Népességtudományi Kutató Intézet Közleményei 43. Budapest: KSH (Központi Statisztikai Hivatal).

Reher, D. S. (1998). Family ties in Western Europe: Persistent contrasts. *Population and Development Review, 24*(2), 203–234.

Rodin, J. (2011). Fertility intentions and risk management: Exploring the fertility decline in Eastern Europe during transition. *Ambio, 40*, 221–230.

Sobotka, T. (2004). *Postponement of childbearing and low fertility in Europe.* Dissertation. Groningen: Rijksuniversiteit Groningen.

Sobotka, T. (2008). The diverse faces of the second demographic transition in Europe. *Demographic Research, 19*(7), 171–224.

Spéder, Zs. (2002). *Fertility and structural change in Hungary*. Working Papers on Population, Family, and Welfare No. 04. Budapest: Demographic Research Institute, Budapest.

Spéder, Zs. (2005). The rise of cohabitation as first union and some neglected factors of recent demographic developments in Hungary. *Demografia [English edition], 49*(5), 77–103.

Spéder, Zs, & Kapitány, B. (2014). How are time-dependent childbearing intentions realized? Realization, postponement, abandonment, bringing forward. *European Journal of Population, 25*(4), 503–523.

Szelewa, D., & Polakowski, M. P. (2008). Who cares? Changing patterns of childcare in Central and Eastern Europe. *Journal of European Social Policy, 18*, 115–131.

Tóth, P. P. (1996). International migration and Hungary. In P. P. Tóth & E. Valkovics (Eds.), *Demography of contemporary Hungarian society* (pp. 139–169). Highland Lakes: Atlantic Research and Publication.

Zapf, W., & Mau, S. (1993). Eine demographische Revolution in Ostdeutschland? Dramatischer Rückgang der Geburten, Eheschließungen und Scheidungen. *Informationsdienst Soziale Indikatoren (ISI), 10*, 1–5.

The Policy Context of Fertility in Spain: Toward a Gender-Egalitarian Model?

Pau Baizan

Abstract Fertility levels have remained very low in Spain since the mid-1980s, implying a future rapid aging of the population. The stagnation of fertility levels is closely linked to the substantial changes in the welfare regime experienced during this period, involving shifts in the share of the cost of children between social institutions. While exchanges of care and financial support across generations are still high, including a prolonged coresidence of young adults with their parents, the role of households as providers of care and other services has substantially declined. The rapid increase in women's labor-market participation has led the dual-full-time-earner family model to become the norm, although this trend has not been matched by a similar increase in men's unpaid work. These processes have weakened the ability of households to provide care and have created a demand for both state intervention and market solutions. The resulting care gap has been partially filled by the expansion of non-family childcare, in which the state has had an important role both as provider and regulator of the market. At the same time, childcare within the family has been undermined by policies in the domains of parental leave, part-time opportunities, and child benefits/tax allowances that provide little support to parenthood. Moreover, labor-market deregulation, focused on the young, has brought with it an increase in uncertainty about income, leading to the postponement of family transitions and depressing fertility.

Keywords Fertility · Social policy · Family policy · Spain · Aging

When fertility in Spain dropped to "lowest-low" levels in the early 1990s, it surprised many demographers. So did the massive immigration rates and the high divorce rates recorded in the mid-2000s, which both reached the highest levels in Europe at that time. These changes illustrate the profound and rapid transformations experienced by Spanish society that, although shared to some extent with other

P. Baizan (✉)
Catalan Institution for Research and Advanced Studies (ICREA) and Pompeu Fabra University, Barcelona, Spain
e-mail: pau.baizan@upf.edu

R.R. Rindfuss and M.K. Choe (eds.), *Low Fertility, Institutions, and their Policies*, DOI 10.1007/978-3-319-32997-0_8

advanced societies, also show several special features. This chapter will sketch the main trends in fertility and aging during the past few decades, followed by an overview of some of Spain's family and gender policies. Support for childrearing from a variety of institutions is examined, including the labor market and the state, as well as from extended families and male partners. Based on existing theories of fertility, it is assumed that contextual conditions that lessen the costs of childrearing for parents and reduce gender inequalities will be associated with higher levels of fertility (McDonald 2000; Diprete et al. 2003; Rindfuss et al. 2003). Existing evidence for this assumption is summarized.

In order to evaluate the role of particular policies, it is useful to adopt a welfare-regime framework, including contributions from the gender perspective[1] (Orloff 1993; Esping-Andersen 1999; Mayer 2001; Lewis 1998, 2002). Together with other Southern European countries, the Spanish welfare model is often depicted as a particular version of the "conservative" regime, in which families retain a maximum of welfare responsibilities. In this model, active family policies are underdeveloped compared with the situation in other conservative welfare states, such as Germany or France. The low levels of state provision and the conspicuous gaps go hand in hand with the major role of kinship relationships (Ferrera 1996; Moreno 2006; Naldini 2003). These characteristics are rooted in long-standing cultural ideas prevalent in Spanish society, in particular the wide prevalence of strong family ties (Reher 1998; Dalla Zuanna 2001). Exchanges of care and financial support across generations are generally high, including an increasingly prolonged coresidence of young adults with their parents and a declining, but still important, role of grandparents in the care of children.

The Spanish welfare and gender regime has also been characterized by an unusually high prevalence of the male-breadwinner/female-housewife family model. Indeed, up to the 1970s, this family model was explicitly supported by the state and by the Catholic Church, which remained a central influence in policy-making (Nash 1991). Yet, the prevalence of this family model has progressively diminished. Crucial in this respect has been the rapid expansion of the education system, which has especially benefited women. Cohorts of women born since the 1970s clearly surpass men in educational attainment. The labor-market participation of women has also increased steadily since the 1980s, leading to a situation in which dual-full-time-earner households have become the norm. As a result, the caring capacity of families has been seriously weakened, undermining the foundations of familism. At the same time, men's roles have changed only marginally, and adaptation of the welfare state to these new gender roles has been slow and partial.

[1]"A welfare regime can be defined as the combined, interdependent way in which welfare is produced and allocated between state, market, and family" (Esping-Andersen 1999, p. 35).

Parallel changes in family values and behavior, in line with "reflexive modernization"[2] (Giddens 1991), have pushed toward modification of many of the laws affecting the family. A decisive milestone was the democratic constitution of 1978, which introduced the principles of gender equality and the expansion of social rights. These principles and rights were developed in several laws issued subsequently. Some examples include the introduction of individual taxation (1979), a new divorce law (1981), as well as laws liberalizing abortion (1985) and the use of contraceptives (1978). Social policies aimed to consolidate and universalize the welfare state in the areas of education, health, and pensions (Guillén 2010).

A second wave of rapid and extensive policy change took place during the period 2004–2011, when the Social-Democratic Party was in government. Laws introduced during this period reflected changes in the values and norms of the Spanish population, for example facilitating divorce and shared custody of children by divorced parents, recognizing same-sex marriages, and introducing a new law on abortion, which received wide popular support. Another set of policies aimed to promote gender equality, primarily through enhancing women's integration into the labor market, and to a lesser extent to increase young people's autonomy. These policies included the introduction of a new universal scheme to assist dependent people in need of care (basically the elderly), provisions for the expansion of formal childcare, affirmative-action measures favoring gender equality in the labor market and in politics, and a cash benefit for housing directed to young people.[3]

Although the actual substantive impact of these policies has been uneven, they mark a path deviation in the principles and aims of the Spanish government (Naldini and Jurado 2013). The care of children and frail elderly is no longer seen as a family matter only, but as an issue requiring government financial support and involvement. Similarly, assistance to young adults is no longer seen exclusively as a family responsibility. Labor-market and economic-growth policies have been at the center of public debates, triggered by high rates of female and youth unemployment and stimulated by European Union (EU) directives and recommendations.[4] By contrast, despite the persistence of very low fertility for more than two decades, support for raising children has been largely absent from public discussions, and fertility increase has not been a prominent issue in government policy.

This chapter will review fertility trends in Spain, policies changes, and the effects that policies might have on fertility. I will argue that the expansion of the dual-earner household norm and the weakening of familism since the 1980s,

---

[2]"Reflexive modernization" refers to a change in the principles of industrial society involving an increased capacity for individuals to pursue personal autonomy and to construct their own identities rather than having those identities defined for them by societal norms and institutions (Giddens 1991).

[3]This means-tested cash benefit was introduced in 2008 and discontinued in 2010. It consisted of a subsidy for rented housing paid to young people (age 22–29). The amount paid was €210 (US $240 as of 15 May 2015) per month in 2010 (Ministerio de Vivienda 2010).

[4]Pension-system reform has also triggered a recurring political debate, again stimulated by EU policies.

together with more recent policy reorientation, amount to a significant departure from the previous welfare regime. According to this interpretation, Spain is shifting toward a model that borrows several traits from both the liberal and the social-democratic regimes. The stagnation of fertility levels is closely linked to these changes in the welfare and gender regime.

Fertility Trends

The Spanish total fertility rate (TFR) has fluctuated at very low levels since 1988, remaining below 1.5 children per woman (Fig. 1). Just as the post-World War II baby boom took place almost two decades later in Spain than in most other European countries, the subsequent fertility decline also arrived relatively late. Between 1958 and 1975, fertility hovered slightly above 2.8 but shortly after started a fast decline, reaching its lowest level, at 1.15, in 1998. As in many other developed countries, the first years after 2000 brought a modest recovery, with the TFR reaching 1.46 children per women in 2008 (Myrskylä et al. 2009). This trend was truncated by the "great recession," leading fertility to drop to 1.27 in 2013

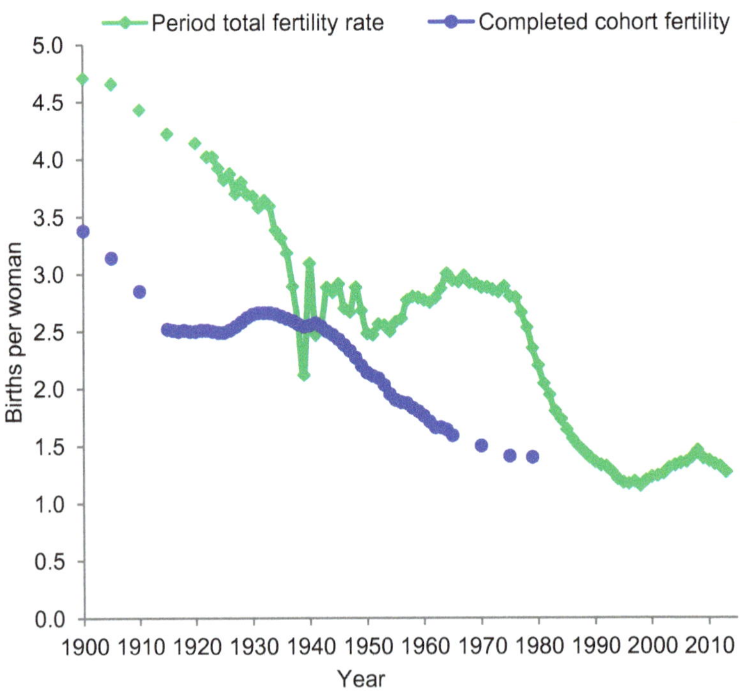

Fig. 1 Period total fertility rate (TFR) and birth-cohort completed fertility, Spain 1900–2013 (Institut National d'Etudes Démographiques 2014; Myrskylä et al. 2012)

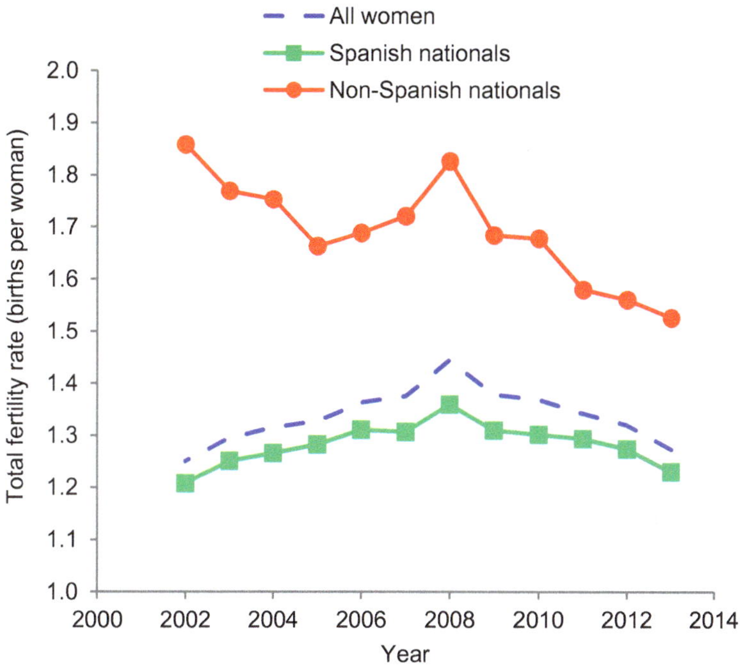

Fig. 2 Total fertility rate (TFR) in Spain by nationality (INE 2014b)

which, considering the depth of the economic crisis in Spain, may be viewed as a fairly modest decline.

These changes in fertility levels, measured in terms of TFR, have been greatly influenced by a significant postponement of births in the life course. In 1980, women's mean age at first birth reached a low of 25.0 years in parallel with declining ages at marriage.[5] By 2000, the mean age at first birth had jumped to 29 years, depressing cross-sectional fertility. The subsequent slowdown in the pace of fertility postponement contributed to the partial recovery of TFR, although this process has not disappeared, with the mean age at first birth reaching 30.3 years in 2013.

The large immigration wave experienced in 2000–2007, no doubt, helps explain both the slowdown in the postponement of births and the partial recovery of fertility levels. As can be seen in Fig. 2, immigrants show higher levels of fertility than the native-born, albeit fertility among immigrants is also low and seems to rapidly converge with the native-born level. The processes of migration and family formation appear to be closely interrelated, resulting in fertility peaks around migration time or shortly after (González-Ferrer 2011; Bledsoe et al. 2007). Given the fairly small proportion of immigrants in the population, however, rising from 1.6 % in

[5]Both the lowest age at marriage (23.3) and at first birth for the whole 20th century were recorded around 1980 (Cabré 1989).

1998 to 12.2 % in 2010, their overall contribution to the TFR is only about 0.082 children per woman (Castro-Martín and Rosero-Bixby 2011). Birth statistics for 2011, however, indicate that nearly one out of four newborns in Spain (23.1 %) had at least one foreign-born parent. The timing of fertility is substantially younger among immigrants than among the native-born, particularly among immigrants from Latin America and Africa who made up more than one-half of all immigrants during this period. More recently, the increasing importance of immigration from Eastern Europe (mainly Romania and Bulgaria) seems to be related to a trend toward lower and later immigrant fertility.

Figure 1 depicts the trends in completed birth-cohort fertility, providing a complementary perspective to the one given by the period TFR. Lifetime family size has been declining almost continuously since the cohorts born at the beginning of the 20th century, from 3.4 children for women born in 1900 to 1.6 for women born in 1965. Projections for the 1975 birth cohort foresee a continuation of this trend, reaching 1.4 children per women (Myrskylä et al. 2012). An almost monotonic reduction of parity three or higher-order births across birth cohorts is the main factor behind the family size reduction (INE 2014b; Castro-Martín and Martin-García 2013). Only 12.5 % of women born in 1965 had three or more children, compared with 60.7 % of women born in 1940. Births have been increasingly concentrated in parities one and two: About 28 % women born in 1965 had one child and 46 % had two. Childlessness has risen among recent birth cohorts (13 % for the 1965 birth cohort), although the rate is still low compared with most other West European countries.[6]

The family context of childbearing has been substantially altered in the past few decades. In 2012, 39 % of births were to non-married women, a sharp increase from 1980 (4 %) and 1995 (11 %). Most of this increase is attributable to childbearing in cohabiting families, which accounted for 23 % of all births in 2011. By the age of 35, 39 % of women born in the 1970s had entered their first conjugal union through cohabitation, compared with 17 % of women born in the 1960s and 6 % of women born in the 1950s (Domínguez-Folgueras and Castro-Martín 2013).

Population Aging

In Spain, as in other European countries, fertility and mortality rates have been falling for more than a century. In 1900, 5.2 % of the population was age 65 and above, compared with 17.4 % in 2012, while the population under 15 was 33.2 % and 15.2 %, respectively. The suddenness and magnitude of the fertility decline

[6]Figures of definitive childlessness are likely to be underestimated, possibly by as much as 5 % of total births. According to Devolder et al. (2008), official registry data misclassify multiple births and unknown-order births, resulting in a wrong attribution of births by order. Demographic data used in this chapter come from the website of the National Institute of Statistics (INE 2014b) unless stated otherwise.

experienced since the end of the 1970s has led to an age structure with relatively few children and young people, but also relatively few elderly individuals.[7] The members of the baby-boom birth cohorts, born in the 1960s and the 1970s, will reach retirement age starting in 2025, at a time when the younger age groups will be relatively small because of the past 30 years of low fertility. This situation creates the potential for an important future increase in the proportion of the elderly population, which is likely to be a short-term phenomenon, as subsequent birth cohorts have much lower numbers.

The process of aging is fueled by a combination of very low fertility since the mid-1980s and one of the highest life expectancies in the world (80.0 years for men and 85.6 for women in 2013). A third factor added to the picture between the late 1990s and 2007—a net immigration of more than six million individuals. By 2012, the proportion of Spain's foreign-born population reached 14.2 %. This increase in migration is directly related to the fast increase in the number of employed individuals, from 13 million in 1997 to more than 20 million in 2007, which could only be partially supplied by the native-born population (Oliver 2008). Among immigrants, family reunification and family formation have proceeded quite quickly (González-Ferrer 2011), and immigration has significantly rejuvenated the age structure of the country, as most immigrants are young adults and their children. The bulk of the immigrants have added to the already large number of Spanish baby boomers, however, potentially aggravating the aging momentum expected in the years 2025–2050. Since the economic recession, net migration has become negative, reaching about 250,000 net out-migrants in 2013.

The most recent projections of the National Institute of Statistics extrapolate current demographic trends into the future (INE 2012b). Consistent with previous trends, these projections assume that life expectancy will increase to 87 years for men and 91 years for women in 2051. Fertility is assumed to slowly increase to 1.56 births per woman in 2051. Net migration is assumed to be negative until 2031 (a yearly average of −130,000 in 2012–2021 and −50,000 in 2022–2031) and positive afterwards. Given these assumptions, Spain's total population will decline from 46.8 million in 2012 to 41.6 in 2051. The number of deaths will become higher than the number of births in 2018, and the proportion of individuals age 65 and above will reach 37 % in 2051.

Of course, these assumptions may be unrealistic. In particular, several arguments can be provided questioning the assumption that a negative net migration rate will persist in the future. For one thing, current trends are based on a period of deep economic crises. Given the existing age structure, future entrants into the labor market are unlikely to meet labor demand if economic growth is positive and sustained, while the existence of a large community of recent immigrants, with network links to their countries of origin, should stimulate the persistence of positive net migration flows.

---

[7]Cohorts born in the 1930s and 1940s are relatively small in size due to low fertility and high infant mortality at that time.

Among several existing projections, the Wittgenstein Center for Demography and Global Human Capital (2012) assumes that life expectancy at birth will increase to 87.0 years for men and to 93.2 for women in 2050. Based on expert views, it is assumed that the total fertility rate will increase to 1.7 children per woman in 2050. Following previous projections from Eurostat, net migration is assumed to be moderately positive, reaching 209,000 immigrants in 2050. According to this projection, total population will increase to 56 million in 2050 (43.5 million with zero net migration during the period of projection), and 30.7 % of the population will be 65 and above. This projection suggests that immigration can make an important contribution toward boosting population numbers and slowing down population aging.

Delayed Transition to Adulthood

Spain's historic gap in educational attainment compared with other economically advanced European countries has been reduced, albeit not completely eliminated. This can be illustrated by the increase across birth cohorts in the median age at school leaving—which went from 14 years for women and 15 years for men among the cohorts born during the 1950s to 20 years for women and 19 years for men among the cohorts born two decades later (Baizan et al. 2002). The educational attainment of the population shows an important polarization, however, which largely reflects parental education and social class differentials (Salido 2007). In 2010, among individuals age 25–34, 45 % of women and 34 % of men had completed tertiary education, while 30 % of women and 41 % of men had completed lower-secondary education or less (OECD 2013a). These figures show a substantial gender gap, which is likely to be the result of increasing returns to education for women relative to men and the removal of barriers to women's careers.[8] The fact that women have overtaken men in educational attainment is likely to have important implications for labor-market outcomes, marriage patterns, and gender relations (van Bavel 2012).

The expansion of the education system has been one of the main achievements of the Spanish welfare state, together with expansion of the public-health system. Both provide universal access and are mostly supported through general taxation. In 2009, education expenditures were 5.6 % of GDP, of which 88 % was public spending, including subsidies[9] (OECD 2013a). This implies a substantial public

[8]Gender educational differentials are complex phenomena, in which education systems, families, and non-cognitive abilities of children interact (Eurydice, European Commission 2010; Pekkarinen 2012).

[9]The OECD average spending on education was 6.3 % of GDP, of which public spending accounted for 86 %, with important variations by country. Figures for France are 6.3 % (92 % public), Italy 4.5 % (92 % public), United Kingdom 6.0 % (88 % public), and Sweden 6.7 % (99 % public) (OECD 2013a).

contribution to the cost of children. The expansion of the education system has been politically motivated, in order to increase economic productivity,[10] but it also has been driven by the population's social-mobility aspirations in a highly competitive labor market. Since tuition fees are relatively low or nonexistent, the main cost of secondary and higher education for households is children have foregone labor-market earnings (which in any case are low due to low wages and chronic high unemployment among the young). A peculiarity of the system is that educational institutions are located close to residential areas, so that most students live with their parents, limiting the cost of access to education. Thus while general investments in children have increased, the related costs have only partially fallen on parents, reducing possible quantity-quality trade-offs that might limit fertility.

The Spanish education system has been characterized as highly standardized (with little ranking among institutions) and weakly stratified into different tracks (Iannelli and Soro-Bonmatí 2000). The general nature of educational content and credentials means that schooling is only weakly tied to the labor market, lengthening the school-to-work transition. Although barriers to entry are low, in practice few individuals re-enter the education system, especially after starting a family (Martin-García and Baizan 2006).

Increasing educational enrollment and attainment has been one of the main drivers of the postponement of family formation (Castro-Martín 1992; Baizan 2001; González and Jurado-Guerrero 2006). More years spent in education directly delay such transitions as entering the labor force, leaving the parental home, and forming a partnership. For women, the effects of higher educational attainment on labor-market participation also lead to a postponement and reduction of marriage and fertility. The link between educational attainment and postponement of marriage and fertility has weakened across birth cohorts, however, and today postponement is pretty much across-the-board. In 2010, the mean age at first birth among college-educated women was 32.9, among those with upper-secondary education it was 30.8, and among those with lower-secondary education it was 28.2 (Castro-Martín and Martín-García 2013). Moreover, it has been shown that the field of education is more important for fertility timing than the level of education: Educational fields related to the care of individuals or involving social skills (such as teaching, medicine, and humanities) are associated with relatively early and high fertility compared with other fields of study (Martin-García and Baizan 2006).

The age at entering the labor market has been hugely delayed across birth cohorts. Thus, among those born in the 1950s, the median age for starting a first job was 16 for men and 17 for women, while for the cohorts born in the 1970s, it increased by five years (Baizan et al. 2002). But these figures do not convey the

[10]The expansion has particularly focused on general secondary education and university education, rather than on vocational training. This has resulted in a mismatch between qualifications and labor-market demand.

tremendous deterioration of the labor-market situation experienced by young adults in the past few decades. In the 1980s, intensified international competition and the Spanish economy's lack of competitiveness led the government to partially deregulate the labor market in 1984.[11] This labor-market liberalization included the promotion of short-term contracts, generally lasting a few months, which characteristically focused on new entrants into the labor market, i.e., young people and women (and later, immigrants), keeping untouched the job guarantees enjoyed by middle-aged "male breadwinners" (Polavieja 2003; European Commission 2006). In this model, workers who have "regular" jobs enjoy better wages, and firing them is more difficult and more costly for employers. As a result, companies are slow to hire additional "protected" workers.

Within a few years after the introduction of the new policy to deregulate the labor market, the proportion of temporary contracts had jumped to one-third of total employment. Unemployment rates have remained among the highest in Europe, however, as the typical integration of individuals into the labor market has come to involve a long sequence of unemployment and temporary-employment periods. Both relative real wages of young people and the overall proportion of wages in the economy have shown a declining long-term trend (Consejo Económico y Social 2013). Subsequent reforms have added more flexibility to the labor market but have not fundamentally changed the model (Guillén 2010). In recent years, the increase in job precariousness has been significantly extended to middle-aged individuals, in a pattern related more to socio-economic status than to life-course stage.

A number of studies have analyzed the effects of uncertainty in employment and income on family and household formation (Ahn and Mira 2001; De la Rica and Iza 2005; Baizan 2001, 2007; Adsera 2011). For instance, one study (Baizan 2007) found that during the 1990s and early 2000s, women unemployed or with a temporary contract showed a 40 % reduction in the probability of having a first birth compared with women in stable employment, accounting for the endogeneity of employment and fertility. The depressing effect was not as strong for second and higher-order births, especially among the unemployed. All birth orders were strongly affected, however, when the job status of both members of a couple was unstable. All these effects were particularly pronounced for those with low education.

The economic restructuring that started in the 1980s also included a deregulation of the housing market. Public subsidies focused on home owners through the tax system, while public rental housing became less than 2 % of total housing. As rental

[11]Between the late 1970s and the mid-1990s, the last stage of the sectoral shift between employment in agriculture and in industry overlapped with a deep industrial crisis, resulting in high unemployment (Marimon and Zilibotti 1998). Furthermore, the timing of the opening to international markets in connection with accession to the European Community in 1986 unfortunately coincided with the arrival in the labor market of the baby-boom cohorts.

housing became economically unattractive, its share declined progressively to less than 10 % of the total housing stock (Inurrieta 2007). Even with public subsidies, however, purchasing a house is a large investment relative to the wages of young people, and in addition, would-be homeowners are generally required by banks to hold a stable labor contract in order to access credit. Not surprisingly, the result has been delayed household formation (Holdsworth and Irazoqui-Solda 2002).

The response of families to changes in the economic status of young adults has been as would be expected from a familistic system. Extended parental support in the form of room and board and also social and economic capital to support continuing education, finding a job, and purchasing a dwelling—all this provides the basis for young-adult life, including family formation. This extended support also leads to a delay in all life transitions. For instance, young unemployed people can wait to find the "right" job, avoiding low-status jobs and keeping unemployment rates high.[12] Family formation is delayed, with the departure from the parental home generally occurring at the time of marriage or entering cohabitation[13] (Baizan 2001). Of course, parental ability to provide support is socially differentiated, maintaining intergenerational social and economic inequalities.

This path to household formation makes both young-adult poverty (unless the parents are also poor) and family formation at young ages unlikely (teenage births are virtually nonexistent except in some immigrant groups). Until recently, it also meant little unmarried cohabitation, but this has changed (Domínguez-Folgueras and Castro-Martín 2013). Parents are still involved in helping new couples, for example, by helping with housing costs or with finding a job, but these days parents seem to be highly tolerant of unmarried cohabitation. Both the young-adult and the parental generation tend to view cohabitation as equivalent to marriage.[14] This living arrangement is generally quite stable, has been increasingly associated with fairly high fertility, and is no longer limited to highly educated couples (Creighton et al. 2013). In recent years, the diffusion of cohabitation has led to a rapid increase in births to unmarried women.

---

[12]Substantial shortages of workers in particular sectors appeared in the late 1990s in spite of unemployment rates above 15 %. Many new job vacancies were filled by immigrants, which favored wage moderation and the expansion of care-related jobs and domestic service.

[13]For instance, for the cohorts born in the 1960s, 75 % of women and 61 % of men left their parental home for the first time and stared their first married or unmarried cohabitation simultaneously (i.e., in the same month).

[14]Unmarried cohabitation usually takes place at a fairly late age and often starts simultaneously with departure from the parental home. In these respects, it is quite similar to marriage (Creighton et al. 2013). Living alone or independently from parents during young adulthood is much less common in Spain than in most European countries, a situation that does not facilitate entering cohabitation. For instance, in the mid-1990s, 16 % of men age 23–27 had left their parents' home and 14 % were living with a partner. The corresponding figures for Italy were 13 and 9 %, for France 53 and 34 %, and for Sweden 100 and 23 % (Berthoud and Iacovou 2002).

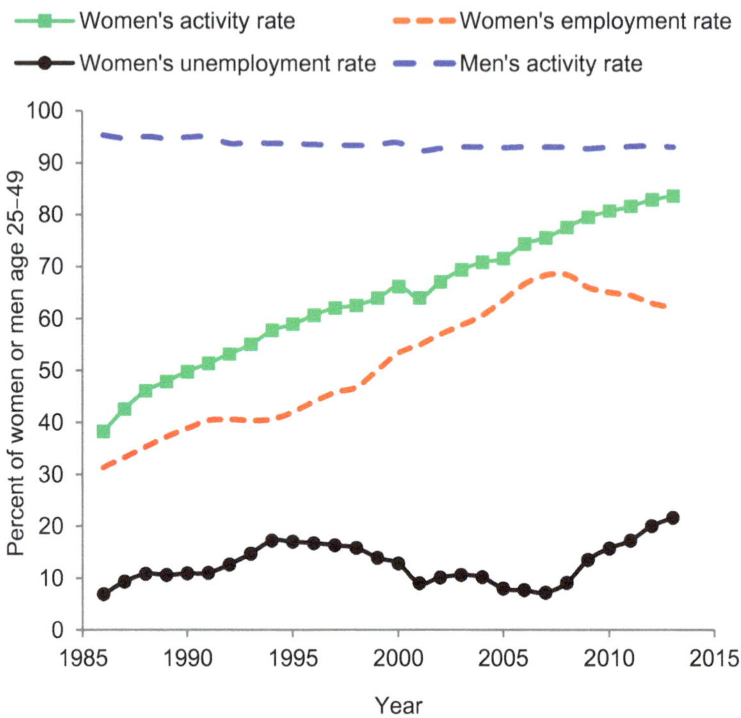

Fig. 3 Activity, employment, and unemployment rates at age 25–49, Spain, 1986–2013 (Eurostat 2014). *Note* Activity rates are the sum of employment and unemployment rates

The Transition to a Dual-Earner Model

Despite unfavorable policies and the cyclical economic crises of the past three decades, the increase in women's labor-market participation has been constant, reaching 69 % in 2013 for the age group 15–64 (Eurostat 2014). Most women under age 25 are students, however, and cohorts born before the 1960s have a much weaker attachment to the labor market. When we focus on the main childbearing and childrearing ages, i.e., 25–49, women's activity rate was nearly universal, at 84 % in 2013 (Fig. 3).[15] Recent data, however, show that the current economic crisis has had a devastating effect on female employment in Spain, characterized by a move from employment under fixed-term contracts to unemployment.

The increase in women's laborforce participation rates in Spain is associated with the sharp increase in women's education levels, although educational differentials in labor-market participation are quickly disappearing (León and Migliavacca 2013).

[15]For comparison, in 2013 the activity rate for women age 25–49 was 67 % in Italy, 84 % in France, 83 % in Germany, 79 % in the United Kingdom, and 88 % in Sweden (Eurostat 2014).

The entrance of women into the labor market is likely to have been indirectly stimulated by the erosion of the "family wage" and by the introduction of mechanisms that make labor-market participation more flexible. The relatively high levels of horizontal and vertical segregation by gender in Spain's labor market, compared with the EU average, shows that high participation rates involve trade-offs with equality (Bettio and Verashchagina 2009).[16]

The increase in women's laborforce participation implies an extension to women of the traditional male model of work and welfare (Gershuny 2000; Lewis 2002). This has meant an extension to women of employment-based welfare entitlements, including rights to unemployment benefits, retirement pension, child benefits, and maternity leave. Employment is crucial for getting access to individually based social rights (as opposed to family based), given the absence of universal income-support measures and the extreme weakness of means-tested benefits (including child benefits).

Women have joined the labor market under the same conditions as men, including a lack of accommodation for childcare needs. The standard work week is fairly long for both men and women: As of 2013, men employed full time worked on average 42.7 h per week, and women worked 40.4 h[17] (Eurostat 2014). Such long work weeks have been shown to be a barrier to the involvement of fathers in childcare and housework (Hook 2010; Baizan et al. 2014), and they do not facilitate women's laborforce participation on a full-time basis (Rubery et al. 1998). As noted above, women's overall laborforce participation rates are similar to those found in Germany or in Britain, but much less part-time employment is available than in those countries. In 2013, about 25 % of employed women had a part-time job,[18] although this figure has increased in recent years due to the economic crises and labor-market reforms. Limited opportunities for part-time work mean that women often have to choose between working full time or not working at all (Del Boca 2003). Even when part-time work is available, it is associated with precarious labor-market conditions and low-status jobs, with timetables set by the needs of employers rather than to facilitate work-family reconciliation (Ibáñez 2011).

The difficulties in making work and family-care needs compatible are exacerbated by the chronic high unemployment rate that strongly reduces the probability of re-entry after a period out of the labor market (Salido 2011, Fig. 3). Moreover, interruptions are heavily penalized in a system in which family and personal

---

[16]"Horizontal segregation is understood as under-(over-) representation of a given group in occupations or sectors, not ordered by any criterion and is often referred to as segregation *tout court*. Vertical segregation denotes the under-(over-) representation of the group in occupations or sectors at the top of an ordering based on 'desirable' attributes—income, prestige, job stability, etc." (Bettio and Verashchagina 2009, p. 7).

[17]The 40-h work week limit was legally introduced in the early 1980s, but this limit is frequently not respected, as employers often require longer working hours from their employees. On the other hand, many sector agreements stipulate a 37.5-h week, most notably for public-sector employees.

[18]By comparison, the share of part-time work out of total women's employment in 2013 was 32 % in Italy, 25 % in France, 47 % in Germany, 42 % in the United Kingdom, and 38 % in Sweden.

relationships are often crucial for obtaining a job and where seniority mechanisms are important, reducing the probability of getting a job with a similar status or pay after re-entry. As a result, women postpone having children until they are in a stable job situation, and they avoid quitting their jobs when they become mothers (González and Jurado-Guerrero 2006). Incentives to postpone childbearing are thus not restricted to individuals with high-status jobs or the highly educated, although such women may have additional incentives to postpone births (Gustafsson 2001).

The increase in gender equality in employment has not been matched by an equivalent increase in gender equality at home, although some changes in that direction have occurred. The results of time-use surveys in 2002 and 2009 are illustrative (Domínguez-Folgueras 2015). They show that for couples under the age of 50 there is some gender convergence in the number of average daily minutes devoted to employment: Women worked an average of 132 min a day in 2002 and 136 min in 2009, while men worked an average of 281 min a day in 2002 and 229 min in 2009. The equivalent figures for domestic work (excluding care) were 197 and 168 min for women and 37 and 54 min for men. Men seem to be slowly increasing their contribution to childcare: Women devoted 64 min a day to childcare in 2002 and 81 min in 2009, while men devoted 27 min a day to childcare in 2002 and 51 min in 2009. Detailed regression results that control for several variables, including time spent in different activities and the age of children, show significant differences between 2002 and 2009. There are some signs that a greater father involvement in childcare may exert a positive effect on fertility in Spain as in other countries (Brodmann et al. 2007; Cooke 2009).

The Expansion of Formal Childcare

Spain's formal childcare system has expanded with the increase in women's laborforce participation, but with a significant time lag. By the late 1990s, nearly all children age three to five were enrolled in school, and enrollment had increased substantially for children under three. By 2012–2013, 44 % of children under three were enrolled in some kind of center-based care,[19] including 32 % in officially recognized educational centers[20] (Fig. 4). Another 16 % of children under three

[19]Data on participation of children under three in preschool education or center-based care from the EU Survey on Income and Living Conditions provide a similar figure for 2011, at 39 % (European Commission 2014). Comparable figures from the same source are 44 % for France, 26 % for Italy, 24 % for Germany, and 51 % for Sweden.

[20]There are two types of childcare centers for young children: officially recognized schools (*escuelas infantiles*) and care centers (*guarderias*). The Spanish Education Law contains general principles and objectives that apply to schools for children from birth to age six. Regional governments are responsible for establishing more detailed educational programs and setting teacher's qualifications and assessment methods for these schools (Ministerio de Educación, Cultura y Deporte 2014; European Commission 2014).

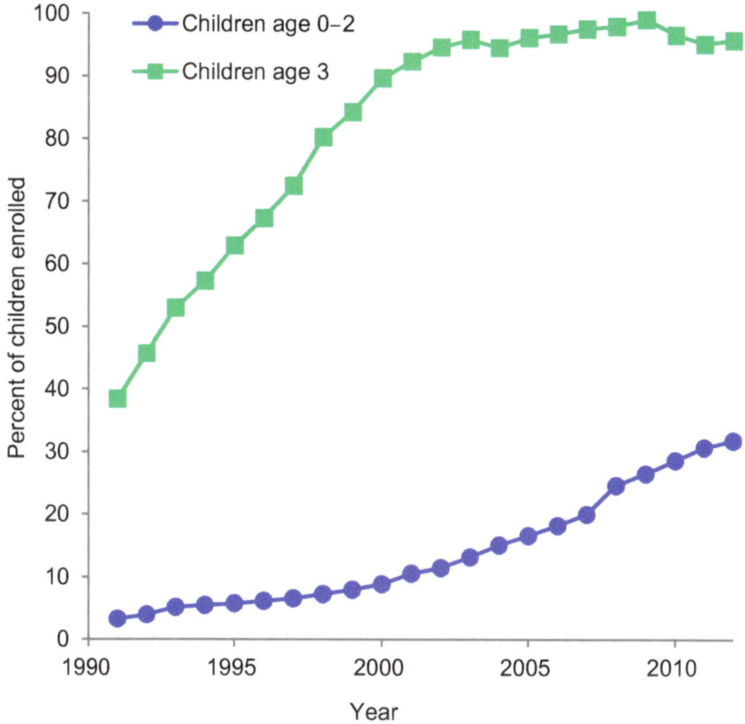

Fig. 4 Percentage of children enrolled in school by age, Spain, 1991–2012 (Ministerio de Educación, Cultura y Deporte 2015)

received regular (paid or unpaid) childcare that was not center based (Ministerio de Educación, Cultura y Deporte 2012, 2015; INE 2012a). This last figure may include some of the children enrolled in educational or care centers, so the percentages should not be added. Children enrolled in an educational or care center spent an average of 26 h per week in this type of childcare, while children who were cared for by childminders received an average of 24 h per week of care.[21]

The Ministry of Education provides detailed data on enrolment rates by age: 10 % of children under one, 33 % of one-year-olds, 52 % of two-year-olds, and 96 % of three-years-olds attended educational centers in 2014. Among those enrolled, about one-half of children under three were enrolled in public institutions. Prices in the public sector are moderate in comparison with average wages: about €200–€350 (US $230–US $400 as of 15 May 2015) per month for each child,

[21]The Ministry of Education does not specify how these averages are computed (Ministerio de Educación, Cultura y Deporte 2015). In particular, it does not specify whether weekly hours include lunch time and time spent by the children in childcare centers before and after school hours, but it is unlikely that these "extra" hours are included in the figures provided.

including lunch.[22] Usually, public centers stipulate preferential access and lower prices for some categories of families, such as low-income and single-parent families. The range of prices in the private sector is much wider, although private centers may receive public subsidies, depending on regional policies (Ministerio de Educación, Cultura y Deporte 2014). From age three, children are legally entitled to free preprimary education.

Substantial geographic differentials exist in the availability of early education and care for children under three, stemming from the diversity of policies adopted by regional and local governments. Educational facilities have expanded rapidly all over the country, however, since the Ministry of Education adopted a new law in 2008 called Educa3. This program expanded the number of slots available in some of the regions that previously had lagged behind (Andalucia and Castilla la Mancha[23]), but not in others (Canary Islands, Extremadura).

All these data suggest that formal care availability has increased substantially, albeit the demand is far from being fully met, and waiting lists in public centers are long.[24] Formal childcare has become a crucial means to allow compatibility of childrearing with paid work for an increasing proportion of couples. In particular, the increase in formal childcare availability since the mid-1990s has stimulated the laborforce participation of women (Baizan and González 2007). The consistent increase of female laborforce participation suggests that without childcare expansion fertility rates would have dropped to much lower levels. Indeed, the availability of childcare is likely to explain part of the increase in fertility experienced in the early 2000s. A study using regional fixed-effects methods shows a significant and positive effect of daycare availability on both first and higher-order births (Baizan 2009).

Important gaps in care for children under three persist, however. These are especially serious in the case of children under one, since maternity/paternity leave from employment is very short. Children of mothers with little education are also less likely to be enrolled in formal childcare than children of more-educated mothers (Sarasa 2011). Although full-time care is usually available in childcare centers (about 8 h per day, including lunch time[25]), it may not suffice to match parental working times, especially in the public childcare sector, where timetables

[22]According to the national Structure of Earning Survey of 2011, women's median gross wage was €1400 (US $1603) per month and men's was €1790 (US $2050) (INE 2014a). The minimum monthly wage set by national legislation for a full-time job was €645 (US $739) in 2013.

[23]According to the Ministry of Education, the region of Andalucia increased the enrollment rate of children under three from 6 to 24 % between 2007 and 2008 (Ministerio de Educación, Cultura y Deporte 2015).

[24]In the past few years, the waiting lists have shortened in many cities, most likely due to the economic crisis, price increases, and lower women's employment (Aunión 2014).

[25]As of 2011, school hours were usually from 8:30 a.m. or 9:00 a.m. to 5:00 p.m., with a break for lunch. Most schools provided lunch services (83 % of pre-primary schools and 73 % of primary schools) as well as childcare services outside school hours (Ministerio de Educación, Cultura y Deporte 2014).

tend to be less flexible. As a result, grandmothers still have an important role in childcare (Fernández Cordón and Tobío Soler 2005). The fact that the demand for formal childcare is much higher than the supply means that parents must enroll children well in advance (just after the birth of the child) to secure a place, with little flexibility to adapt to changes in the parents' employment situation or geographic mobility.

The importance of educational content in the care of children under age six should also be emphasized. As a number of studies have shown, early-childhood education is key to the acquisition of cognitive and non-cognitive skills, to later educational attainment, to leveling social-class inequalities (European Commission 2014; Heckman 2006), and to producing new cohorts with a high potential for economic productivity. This is critical because Spain's adaptation to an aging society not only involves a sustainable fertility level but also an increase in the economic performance of the future population.

Short Maternity/Paternity Leave

Mothers have been entitled to a maternity leave from employment of 16 weeks since 1989, with 100 % compensation of the previous wage up to a fairly high ceiling.[26] In addition, a parental leave of up to three years was established in 1980. Since parental leave is unpaid, however, only about 3 % of eligible mothers and 0.1 % of eligible fathers make use of it, making parental leave of little practical relevance (Lapuerta et al. 2011). In order to claim leave rights, a worker must have made a minimum amount of contributions into social security, which is normally set at 180 days during the seven years immediately before beginning leave or 360 days during the mother's or father's entire working career (Ministerio de Empleo y Seguridad Social 2014). As a consequence, the leave system excludes some groups of women with an insufficient record of contributions, most notably many unemployed women and women working in the underground economy. Women with fixed-term contracts may avoid having a child because if they take maternity leave their contract may not be renewed, even in the public sector. Benefit levels are closely related to an individual's previous earnings history, creating additional incentives to postpone childbearing until a stable, well-paying position is attained.

A paternity leave of two weeks was introduced in 2007, in addition to the two days previously existing. This fully paid time off from work can be taken simultaneously or after the end of the mother's leave. Take-up rates have fluctuated at around 80 % since its introduction. The government planned to extend paternity leave to four weeks in 2013, but due to budgetary restrictions this extension has

---

[26]Self-employed mothers have had the right to some compensation since 2006 but did not achieve full equality with employees until 2014.

been delayed. This very short leave is an exception in a policy context that otherwise does not provide explicit support for childcare by men.

Overall, there is relatively little economic or normative support for childcare by parents in the form of maternity or parental leave compared with the situation in most "conservative" or social-democratic countries.[27] Although leave provisions are gendered, their short duration implies few negative consequences for women's labor-market trajectory and income, given that most women return to their jobs after just 16 weeks of leave. At the same time, the short duration of paid leave in Spain is likely to present an obstacle to combining parenthood with laborforce participation as it does not provide sufficient time to care for children. Moreover, there seems to be no coordination with formal childcare policies, resulting in a care gap during most of the child's first year of life. This may be because leave legislation is established by the Ministry of Labor, while childcare provision mostly depends on regional education ministries and municipalities.

Child Allowances and Tax Deductions

During the past few decades, the Spanish government has allocated fairly low levels of public expenditure to benefits and tax breaks for families. In 2009, after several increases, family benefits amounted to 0.67 % of GDP, and tax breaks for families amounted to 0.25 % (OECD 2013b). During the dictatorship period (1939–1977), the government provided a substantial package of "traditional" family support, alongside a pronatalist rhetoric (Iglesias de Ussel and Meil 2001). These policies included monthly payments for workers' dependents, birth grants, and special benefits for dependent women, granted through the social-security system.[28] Lack of political support for these measures and financial constraints led to their practical disappearance during the 1970s, as the benefits were not updated with inflation (Bianculli et al. 2013).

Apart from small tax deductions for families, the most relevant policy initiated in the late 1970s was the introduction of individual taxation for married couples,

[27]This weak provision of leave entitlements, together with other social and fiscal policies providing little explicit support for the unpaid work of women, fits the "unsupported familism" described by Saraceno (1994) and the "implicit familialism" of Leitner (2003). These concepts no longer describe the situation in Spain, however, which has evolved since the late 1990s away from familism, both in terms of policies and in social behavior and ideologies. This can be seen, in particular, in the trends in women's labor-market participation, the development of non-family childcare, the practical disappearance of the "family wage" linked to the increasing flexibility of the labor market, and the universalization of several key programs, including the pension and healthcare systems.

[28]The package provided to (formal-sector) employees included other entitlements for family members, such as healthcare and survivors' pension. This policy stems from a "family wage" ideal (in which the male breadwinner earns enough to support the family) and legal gender discrimination in the labor market.

which effectively eliminated incentives for gender role specialization. This tax system implies that two-earner households find it advantageous to file separately, while one-earner households benefit from joint filing.

More recently, there have been several attempts to increase direct economic support for parents. The amounts involved have generally been modest, however, implying fairly small effects in terms of fertility or female employment disincentives. In 1999, the government introduced some tax deductions for households with children, and these were substantially increased (from €300 (US $344) to €1200 (US $1374) per year) in 2003 for children under the age of three. In addition, a new tax credit of €1200 (US $1374) per year was introduced for mothers with children under age three, conditional on employment.[29] A careful study of the effects of the 2003 reforms found that they significantly increased both fertility (by almost 5 %) and the employment rate of mothers with children under age three (by 2 %). These effects were most pronounced among less-educated women (Azmat and González 2010).

In 2007, the government introduced a "baby bonus" of €2500 (US $2863), paid at the birth of each child. Using regression discontinuity-type analysis, González (2013, Fig. 2) showed that this benefit caused a small increase in births in 2008. This study also found that families who received the benefit did not increase their overall expenditures or their consumption of directly child-related goods and services. Instead, eligible mothers stayed out of the laborforce significantly longer after giving birth, which in turn led to their children spending less time in formal childcare and more time with their mothers during their first year of life. This benefit was eliminated in 2010, both for budgetary reasons and because it had little political support.

Conclusions

Fertility levels in Spain have remained very low since the mid-1980s, implying a rapid aging of the population in the future. This low level of fertility has persisted within a continuously changing social and policy context. These changes concern the welfare regime in particular, involving shifts in the share of the cost of children between social institutions, coupled with a clear departure from the previous familistic and gender-inegalitarian model. This chapter has identified the main characteristics of Spain's emerging model of welfare, several of which are unique compared with the situation in most European counties. At the same time, some aspects of Spain's new welfare system are not well settled, as the processes that make up the new model are still unfolding and several policy measures are

[29]The fiscal reform scheduled to be applied in 2015 foresees further increases in family deductions.

very recent.[30] This may account for some of the important welfare gaps identified here. The path deviation in the model of welfare has not yet removed Spain from the list of countries with very low fertility, but the new model may well lead to changes in the future level and social profile of fertility.

Perhaps the most consistent structural trend has been the rapid increase in women's laborforce participation, which has extended the dual-full-time-worker family model. One of the consequences of this process has been that labor-market conditions have become increasingly relevant for fertility, as most women of childbearing ages are in the labor market. Deregulation of the labor market and persistent high unemployment create incentives to postpone and reduce fertility. The still limited availability of part-time work and difficulties in accessing (and re-entering) the labor market create additional disincentives for fertility. Since long-lasting job precariousness affects most strongly those with little education, family formation patterns are increasingly linked to educational and occupational status. Today the highest rates of divorce and cohabitation occur among the least educated, reversing the previous pattern of positive correlation with education. Similarly, the pattern of fertility may well reverse in the future, leading to a positive correlation with education.

Increased gender equality in labor-market participation has not been matched by a similar increase in men's unpaid work, although time-use data seem to point to some movement in this direction. This fits the "lagged adaptation" scenario postulated by Gershuny (2000), common to many advanced countries. These processes have been fueled by women's remarkable overtaking of men with respect to education. But up to now there has been very little support for the caring role of men, either in terms of labor-market policies or family policies related to parental leave. In this context, policies favoring early-childhood education and care (via public or market provision) have been key in providing a modicum of conciliation between employment and parenthood, albeit availability has clearly lagged behind the fast-growing demand. Although grandmothers still play a role in filling some of the gaps in early childhood care, especially during the first year of life, their role is likely to decline as they also join the labor market. Overall, the role of households and women as providers of unpaid care and other services has sharply declined, creating a demand for both state intervention and market solutions.

Given the familistic roots of the Spanish welfare state, it may seem surprising that policies have systematically failed to provide the support for the familization of care. Leave policies have remained ungenerous, as has the system of family benefits and tax allowances. In addition, the limited availability and the characteristics of part-time jobs have contributed to the growing number of couples who both work full time, seriously jeopardizing the ability of families to provide care for their children. One unintended effect of these policies, given the weakness of the income-support system and the concentration of precarious work conditions among

[30]The economic crisis that started in 2008, which hit Spain particularly hard, has created additional uncertainty with respect to future policy orientation.

the less educated, has being rates of child poverty that consistently rank among the highest in Europe. Another likely effect of the policy environment for families has been to depress fertility levels.

References

Adsera, A. (2011). The interplay of employment uncertainty and education in explaining second births in Europe. *Demographic Research, 25*(16), 513–544.

Ahn, N., & Mira, P. (2001). Job bust, baby bust? Evidence from Spain. *Journal of Population Economics, 14*(3), 505–521.

Aunión, J.A. (2014). Desiguales desde la guarderia, *El Pais.* 12 July, Madrid. Accessed on February 14, 2015 http://www.elpais.es.

Azmat, G., & González, L. (2010). Targeting fertility and female participation through the income tax. *Labour Economics, 17*(2010), 487–502.

Baizan, P. (2001). Transitions to adulthood in Spain. In M. Corijn & E. Klijzing (Eds.), *Transitions to adulthood in Europe* (pp. 279–312). European Studies of Population 10. Dordrecht: Kluwer Academic Publishers.

Baizan, P. (2007). The impact of labour market status on second and higher-order births: A comparative analysis based on the European Community Household Panel. In G. Esping-Andersen (Ed.), *Family formation and family dilemmas in contemporary Europe* (pp. 93–127). Madrid: Fundación BBVA.

Baizan, P. (2009). Regional childcare availability and fertility decisions in Spain. *Demographic Research, 21*(27), 803–842.

Baizan, P., Domínguez, M., & González, M. J. (2014). Couple bargaining or socio-economic status? Why some parents devote more time to their children than others. *European Societies, 16*(1), 3–27.

Baizan, P., & González, M. J. (2007). ¿Las escuelas infantiles son la solución? El efecto de la disponibilidad de escuelas infantiles (0–3 años) en el comportamiento laboral femenino. In V. Navarro (Ed.), *La Situación Social en España* (Vol. 2, pp. 411–444). Madrid: Biblioteca Nueva.

Baizan, P., Michielin, F., & Billari, F. C. (2002). Political economy and life course patterns: The heterogeneity of the occupational, family and household trajectories of young Spaniards. *Demographic Research, 6*(8), 191–240.

Berthoud, R., & Iacovou, M. (2002). *Diverse Europe: Mapping patterns of social change across the EU.* Swindon: Economic and Social Research Council.

Bettio, F., & Verashchagina, A. (2009). *Gender segregation in the labour market: Root causes, implications and policy responses in the EU.* Luxembourg: European Commission, Publications Office of the European Union.

Bianculli, A., Jenne, N., & Jordana, J. (2013). From dismantling by default to arena shifting? Child benefits policy in Spain. In M. W. Bauer, A. Jordan, C. Green-Pedersen & A. Héritier (Eds.), *Dismantling public policy: Preferences, strategies, and effects.* Oxford: Oxford University Press (Oxford Scholarship Online).

Bledsoe, C., Houle, R., & Sow, P. (2007). High fertility Gambians in low-fertility Spain: The dynamics of child accumulation across transnational space. *Demographic Research, 16*(12), 375–412.

Brodmann, S., Esping-Andersen, G., & Guell, M. (2007). When fertility is bargained: Second births in Denmark and Spain. *European Sociological Review, 23*(5), 599–613.

Cabré, A. (1989). *La reproducció de les generacions catalanes, 1856–1960.* Ph.D. thesis. Barcelona: Universitat Autònoma de Barcelona.

Castro-Martín, T. (1992). Delayed childbearing in contemporary Spain: Trends and differentials. *European Journal of Population, 1992*(8), 217–246.
Castro-Martín, T., & Martin-García, T. (2013). The fertility gap in Spain: Late parenthood, few children and unfulfilled reproductive desires. In G. Esping-Andersen (Ed.), *The fertility gap in Europe: Singularities of the Spanish case* (pp. 45–81). Social Studies Collection 36. Barcelona: La Caixa.
Castro-Martín, T., & Rosero-Bixby, L. (2011). Maternidades y fronteras. La fecundidad de las mujeres inmigrantes en España. *Revista Internacional de Sociología, 69*(1), 105–37.
Consejo Económico y Social. (2013). *Distribución de la Renta en España: Desigualdad, cambios estructurales y ciclos*. Informe 3/2013. Madrid: Consejo Económico y Social.
Cooke, L. P. (2009). Gender equity and fertility in Italy and Spain. *Journal of Social Policy, 38*(1), 123–140.
Creighton, M., Esping-Andersen, G., Rutigliano, R., & van Damme, M. (2013). Is fertility influenced by couple instability? In G. Esping-Andersen (Ed.), *The fertility gap in Europe: Singularities of the Spanish case* (pp. 102–120). Social Studies Collection 36. Barcelona: La Caixa.
Dalla Zuanna, G. (2001). The banquet of Aeolus: A familistic interpretation of Italy's lowest low fertility. *Demographic Research, 4*(5), 133–162.
De la Rica, S., & Iza, A. (2005). Career planning in Spain: Do fixed-term contracts delay marriage and parenthood? *Review of Economics of the Household, 3*, 49–73.
Del Boca, D. (2003). The effect of childcare and part-time opportunities on participation and fertility. *Journal of Population Economics, 15*, 549–573.
Devolder, D., Merino, M., & Treviño, R. (2008). *The use of population censuses to correct the distribution of births by order of the vital registration system: Application to Spanish data in the 1975–2005 period.* Papers de Demografia 335. Barcelona: Centre d'Estudis Demogràfics, Universitat Autònoma de Barcelona.
DiPrete, T. A., Morgan, S. P., Engelhardt, H., & Pacalova, H. (2003). Do cross-national differences in the costs of children generate cross-national differences in fertility rates? *Population Research and Policy Review, 22*, 439–477.
Domínguez-Folgueras, M. (2015). Parentalidad y división del trabajo doméstico en España, 2002–2010. *Revista Española de Investigaciones Sociológicas, 149*, 45–64.
Domínguez-Folgueras, M., & Castro-Martín, T. (2013). Cohabitation in Spain: No longer a marginal path to family formation. *Journal of Marriage and Family, 75*(2), 422–437.
Esping-Andersen, G. (1999). *Social foundations of postindustrial economies*. Oxford: Oxford University Press.
European Commission. (2006). Flexibility and security in the EU labour markets. In European Commission, *Employment in Europe.* Luxembourg: European Commission.
European Commission. (2014). *Key data on early childhood education and care in Europe*. Eurydice and Eurostat Report. Luxembourg: Publications Office of the European Union.
Eurostat. (2014). *Statistics: Labor market.* Luxembourg: European Commission, Eurostat. Accessed on February 27, 2015 http://epp.eurostat.ec.europa.eu/portal/page/portal/labour_market/.
Eurydice, European Commission. (2010). *Gender differences in educational outcomes: Study on the measures taken and the current situation in Europe.* Brussels: Education, Audiovisual and Culture Executive Agency. Accessed on August 8, 2014 http://www.eurydice.org.
Fernández Cordón, J. A., & Tobío Soler, C. (2005). *Conciliar las responsabilidades familiares y laborales: Políticas y prácticas sociales*. Documento de trabajo 79/2005. Madrid: Fundación Alternativas.
Ferrera, M. (1996). The southern model of welfare in social Europe. *Journal of European Social Policy, 6*(1), 17–37.
Gershuny, J. (2000). *Changing times: Work and leisure in postindustrial society*. Oxford: Oxford University Press.
Giddens, A. (1991). *Modernity and self-identity*. Cambridge: Polity Press.

González, L. (2013). The effects of a universal child benefit on conceptions, abortions, and early maternal labor supply. *American Economic Journal: Economic Policy, 5*(3), 160–188.

González-Ferrer, A. (2011). Spousal reunification among recent immigrants in Spain: Links with undocumented migration and the labour market. In A. Kraler, E. Kofman, M. Kohli, & C. Schmoll (Eds.), *Gender, generations and the family in international migration* (pp. 193–218). Amsterdam: Amsterdam University Press.

González, M. J., & Jurado-Guerrero, T. (2006). Remaining childless in affluent economies: A comparison of France, West Germany, Italy and Spain, 1994–2001. *European Journal of Population, 22*(4), 317–352.

Guillén, A. (2010). Defrosting the Spanish welfare state: The weight of conservative components. In B. Palier (Ed.), *A long goodbye to Bismarck? The politics of welfare reforms in continental Europe* (pp. 183–206). Amsterdam: Amsterdam University Press.

Gustafsson, S. (2001). Optimal age at motherhood: Theoretical and empirical considerations on postponement of maternity in Europe. *Journal of Population Economics, 14*(2), 225–247.

Heckman, J. J. (2006). Skill formation and the economics of investing in disadvantaged children. *Science, 312*, 1900–1902.

Holdsworth, C., & Irazoqui-Solda, M. (2002). First housing moves in Spain: An analysis of leaving home and first housing acquisition. *European Journal of Population, 18*(1), 1–19.

Hook, J. L. (2010). Gender inequality in the welfare state: Sex segregation in housework, 1965–2003. *American Journal of Sociology, 115*(5), 1480–1523.

Iannelli, C., & Soro-Bonmatí, A. (2000). The transition from school-to-work in Southern Europe: The cases of Italy and Spain. In *Comparative Analysis of Transitions from Education to Work in Europe (CATEWE) Project, CATEWE Final Report to the European Commission.* Dublin: Economic and Social Research Institute.

Ibáñez, Z. (2011). Part-time employment in Spain: A victim of the "temporality culture" and a lagging implementation. In A. M. Guillén & M. León (Eds.), *The Spanish welfare state in European context* (pp. 165–186). Farnham: Ashgate.

Iglesias de Ussel, J., & Meil, G. (2001). *La política familiar en España.* Barcelona: Ariel.

INE (Instituto Nacional de Estadística). (2012a). *Encuesta de Condiciones de Vida, Año 2012.* Tabla D1.5. Madrid: INE. Accessed on July 17, 2014 http://www.ine.es.

INE (Instituto Nacional de Estadística). (2012b). *Proyecciones de población 2012.* Madrid: Instituto Nacional de Estadística. Accessed on November 1, 2014 www.ine.es.

INE (Instituto Nacional de Estadística). (2014a). *Encuesta Anual de Estructura Salarial 2011.* Madrid: INE. Accessed on January 20, 2015 http://www.ine.es.

INE (Instituto Nacional de Estadística). (2014b). *Inebase.* Madrid: Instituto Nacional de Estadística. Accessed on July 28, 2014 www.ine.es.

Institut National d'Etudes Démographiques. (2014). *Database on developed countries.* Accessed on July 20, 2014 http://www.ined.fr.

Inurrieta, A. (2007). *Mercado de vivienda en alquiler en España: Más vivienda social y más mercado profesional.* Laboratorio de Alternativas Documento de Trabajo 113/2007. Madrid: Fundación Alternativas.

Lapuerta, I., Baizan, P., & González, M. J. (2011). Individual and institutional constraints: An analysis of parental leave use and duration in Spain. *Population Research and Policy Review, 30*, 185–210.

Leitner, S. (2003). Varieties of familialism: The caring function of the family in comparative perspective. *European Societies, 5*(4), 353–375.

León, M., & Migliavacca, M. (2013). Italy and Spain: Still the case of familistic welfare models? *Population Review, 52*(1). doi:10.1353/prv.2013.0001.

Lewis, J. (1998). *Gender, social care and welfare state restructuring in Europe*. Aldershot: Ashgate.

Lewis, J. (2002). Gender and welfare state change. *European Societies, 4*(4), 331–357.

Marimon, R., & Zilibotti, F. (1998). 'Actual' versus 'virtual' employment in Europe. Is Spain different? *European Economic Review, 42*(1), 123–153.

Martín-García, T., & Baizan, P. (2006). The impact of the type of education and educational enrolment on first birth. *European Sociological Review, 22*(3), 259–275.

Mayer, K. U. (2001). The paradox of global social change and national path dependencies: Life course patterns in advanced societies. In A. Woodward & M. Kohli (Eds.), *Inclusions and exclusions in European societies* (pp. 89–110). New York: Routledge.

McDonald, P. (2000). Gender equity, social institutions and the future of fertility. *Journal of Population Research, 17*(1), 1–15.

Ministerio de Educación, Cultura y Deporte. (2012). *Estadística de las Enseñanzas no universitarias, curso 2011–2012*. Estadística y Estudios. Madrid: Ministerio de Educación, Cultura y Deporte. Accessed on July17, 2014.

Ministerio de Educación, Cultura y Deporte. (2014). *Datos y cifras. Curso escolar 2014–2015*. Madrid: Ministerio de Educación, Cultura y Deporte. Accessed February 14, 2015.

Ministerio de Educación, Cultura y Deporte. (2015). *Estadísticas de Educación*. Madrid: Ministerio de Educación, Cultura y Deporte. Accessed on February 14, 2015 http://www.educacion.gob.es/educabase.

Ministerio de Empleo y Seguridad Social. (2014). *Normas sobre paternidad y maternidad*. Madrid: Ministerio de Empleo y Seguridad Social. Accessed on July 20, 2014 http://www.seg-social.es/.

Ministerio de Vivienda. (2010). *La Renta Básica de Emancipación ha llegado ya a más de 252,000 jóvenes*. Nota de prensa. Madrid: Ministerio de Vivienda.

Moreno, L. (2006). The model of social protection in Southern Europe: Enduring characteristics. *Revue Française des Affaires Sociales, 5*, 73–95.

Myrskylä, M., Goldstein, J. R., & Cheng, Y. A. (2012). *New cohort fertility forecasts for the developed world*. MPIDR Working Paper WP-2012-014. Rostock: Max Planck Institute for Demographic Research.

Myrskylä, M., Kohler, H. -P., & Billari, F. C. (2009). Advances in development reverse fertility declines. *Nature, 460*(7256), 741–743.

Naldini, M. (2003). *The family in the Mediterranean welfare states*. London: Frank Cass.

Naldini, M., & Jurado, T. (2013). Family and welfare reorientation in Spain and inertia in Italy from a European perspective. *Population Review, 52*(1), 43–61.

Nash, M. (1991). Pronatalism and motherhood in Franco's Spain. In G. Bock & P. Thane (Eds.), *Maternity and gender policies: Women and the rise of the European welfare state, 1880s–1950s* (pp. 160–177). London: Routledge.

OECD (Organization for Economic Cooperation and Development). (2013a). *Education at a Glance 2013*. Paris: OECD.

OECD (Organization for Economic Cooperation and Development). (2013b). *Families and children*. Paris: OECD.

Oliver, J. (2008). Inmigración y mercado de trabajo en 2007: El último impulso de la década prodigiosa. In E. Aja, J. Arango, & J. Oliver (Eds.), *La inmigración en la encrucijada* (pp. 16–35). Barcelona: Edicions Bellaterra.

Orloff, A. S. (1993). Gender and social rights of citizenship: The comparative analysis of gender relations and welfare states. *American Sociological Review, 58*, 303–328.

Pekkarinen, T. (2012). *Gender differences in education*. Discussion Paper 6390. Bonn: Institute for the Study of Labor (IZA).

Polavieja, J. G. (2003). *Estables y precarious: Desregulación laboral y estratificación social en España*. Madrid: Centro de Investigaciones Sociológicas.

Reher, D. (1998). Family ties in Western Europe: Persistent contrasts. *Population and Development Review, 24*(2), 203–234.

Rindfuss, R., Guzzo, K., & Morgan, S. P. (2003). The changing institutional context of low fertility. *Population Research and Policy Review, 22*(5–6), 411–438.

Rubery, J., Smith, M., & Fagan, C. (1998). National working-time regimes and equal opportunities. *Feminist Economics, 4*, 71–101.

Salido, O. (2007). *El Informe PISA y los retos de la educación en España*. Documento de Trabajo 192. Madrid: Fundación Alternativas.

Salido, O. (2011). Female employment and policies for balancing work and family in Spain. In A. M. Guillén & M. León (Eds.), *The Spanish welfare state in European context* (pp. 187–208). Farnham: Ashgate.

Saraceno, C. (1994). The ambivalent familism of the Italian welfare state. *Social Politics, 1*(1), 60–82.

Sarasa, S. (2011). *Deferred effects of nursery school on adolescents' school performance in Spain.* DemoSoc Working Paper 2011-40. Barcelona: Universitat Pompeu Fabra, Department of Political and Social Sciences.

Van Bavel, J. (2012). The reversal of gender inequality in education, union formation and fertility in Europe. *Vienna Yearbook of Population Research, 10*, 127–154.

Wittgenstein Center for Demography and Global Human Capital. (2012). *European demographic data sheet 2012: Population projections, data, methods and assumptions.* Accessed on January 14, 2015 http://www.iiasa.ac.at.

Aging Italy: Low Fertility and Societal Rigidities

Maria Letizia Tanturri

Abstract For many decades, the Italian population has been characterized by increasing longevity, persistent low fertility, and fertility postponement. Italy is a country of many contradictions, as low fertility interplays—to a certain extent paradoxically—with strong family ties and values, high parental investment in child quality, and low female labor-market participation. This chapter offers reflections on the main institutional factors leading to Italy's low and late fertility. I point out the features of the Italian context—in general not easily quantifiable or measurable—that plausibly represent elements of viscosity impeding a rapid and smooth process of family formation and transition to parenthood. The identification of social rigidities that make changes in reproductive behavior particularly difficult suggests possible policies to raise fertility in order to abate an unprecedented aging process.

Keywords Low fertility · Delayed childbearing · Transition to adulthood · Childlessness · Institutional factors · Work-family reconciliation · Gender roles · Family policies · Childcare · Italy

Italians are living longer than ever before. The extraordinary longevity revolution has raised life expectancy at birth to 84.4 years for women and 79.6 for men (ISTAT 2015b). This spectacular gain in life expectancy—especially at older ages—and decades of very low fertility have shaped the Italian population structure as one of the oldest in the world. About one person out of five was over 65 in 2013, and by 2030—when the baby boomers will cross the aging threshold—one-third of Italians will be older than 65 (ISTAT 2015b). Most people in today's age cohorts are likely to survive to age 65, and life expectancy at 65 is a further 22 years for women and 18.5 years for men.

M.L. Tanturri (✉)
Department of Statistical Sciences, University of Padova, Padova, Italy
e-mail: tanturri@stat.unipd.it

R.R. Rindfuss and M.K. Choe (eds.), *Low Fertility, Institutions, and their Policies*, DOI 10.1007/978-3-319-32997-0_9

At the same time, the younger cohorts have been shrinking dramatically. At the end of the 1990s, there was one individual over 65 for every young person under 16, but now the ratio is remarkably unbalanced in favor of the older generation, with more than 1.5 over 65 for every 1.0 under 16. For each pre-school child, there are likely to be four surviving grandparents over 65. The kinship networks have become "tall and lean," meaning that each child has fewer siblings and cousins but has two, and in many cases three, generations of surviving ancestors.

If the increased lifespan is great news for individuals, it raises many issues for families and the social welfare state. The consequences of the aging process are enormous in terms of a rapidly increasing old-age dependency ratio, with three individuals at working age supporting one individual at retirement age. In addition, the number of older workers who are about to retire will be more than the number of young people who are about to enter the labor market (without further migration flows). As a result, the working-age population is expected to shrink in the future. Of course the consequences are even wider. For instance, the aging process is mirrored by the progressive aging of the electorate, which has an average age of around 51 and 53, given the different voting rules for the two chambers of the Parliament.[1] The old age of the average voter could plausibly favor policies that guarantee transfers and protection to the older generations rather than to the younger ones. Finally, a major concern is the sustainability of the pension and healthcare systems, as well as of the welfare state as a whole, in a context characterized by a high level of public debt (around 128 % of gross domestic product (GDP) in 2013).

One possible solution to alleviate the aging process would be to increase fertility levels that have been low—or lowest low—for at least three decades. Italy is a country of many contradictions, and low fertility interplays—to a certain extent paradoxically—with strong family ties and values (Reher 1998; Livi Bacci 2001), high parental investment in child quality (Dalla Zuanna 2001; Dalla Zuanna and Micheli 2004), and low labor-market participation of women (Del Boca 2003). The increase in both direct and indirect costs of children (De Santis and Livi Bacci 2001; De Santis 2004), the difficulties in combining motherhood and labor-market participation (Del Boca et al. 2005; Del Boca 1997; ISTAT 2014a), and the lack of gender equity in the division of domestic tasks and childcare (McDonald 2000a, b; Mencarini and Tanturri 2004; Mills et al. 2008; Anxo et al. 2011) all help explain the reluctance of couples to have more children.

This chapter offers a view of the main factors leading to Italy's low and late fertility rate and identifies the social rigidities that make a change in Italian reproductive behavior particularly difficult. An understanding of the main factors behind Italy's fertility decline and stagnation may help to suggest policies to raise fertility in the face of an unprecedented aging process. In the first section, I describe the main trends and changes in reproductive behavior that have occurred in Italy.

[1]To vote for the Chamber of Deputies, citizens must be at least 18 years old, while to vote for the Senate they must be at least 25 years old.

In the second section, I try to identify the societal rigidities that make the transition to parenthood and the choice to have a second or a third child particularly problematic. The third section describes the main policy measures that have been adopted until now. In the conclusion, I suggest the policies that, in my opinion, will be necessary to face the challenge of low fertility in the coming years.

Persistent Low and Delayed Fertility

The Italian case has been amply studied in the demographic literature as a combination of very low and late fertility. After the Second World War, fueled by the Italian "economic miracle" in the 1950s and early 1960s, the country experienced a baby boom related to the so-called "golden age of marriage," with marriage becoming almost universal and occurring at younger ages. After 1964, fertility started to decline, and since the mid-1970s, period total fertility rates (TFR) have fallen below the replacement level (Fig. 1). Italy was one of the first countries in the world to reach "lowest-low" fertility levels (with a TFR of 1.19 births per women) in the mid-1990s (Kohler et al. 2002). Since 2000, a slight recovery has brought the Italian TFR close to 1.46. Scholars described this as a "new spring" for the Italian population (Billari and Dalla Zuanna 2008). The economic recession after 2009 called a halt to this positive trend, however, and fertility has stalled at around 1.4 births per woman in recent years, with a marked decrease in the number of births (ISTAT 2014d). In the past five years, 62,000 fewer births were registered than in the previous period, and this trend has been pervasive across regions, partly as a

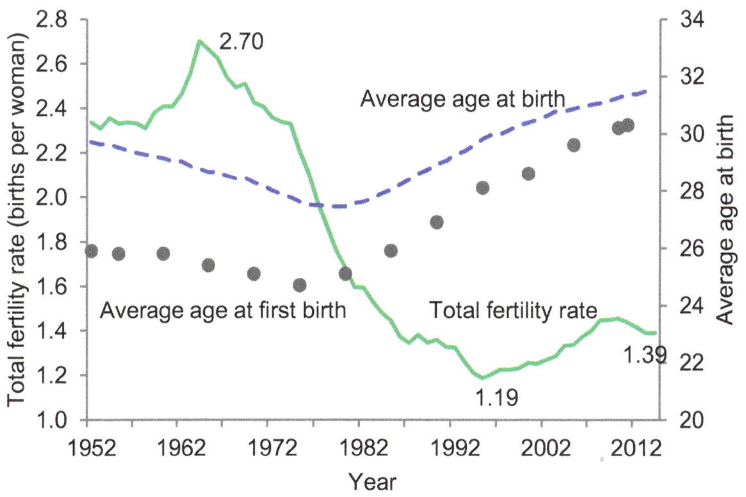

Fig. 1 Total fertility rate (TFR), average mother's age at birth, and average mother's age at first birth, Italy, 1962–2014 (ISTAT 2015a)

result of the economic crisis and partly due to a reduction in the number of women at reproductive age (ISTAT 2014c). Even if the economic downturn comes to an end, the structural constraints associated with low birth rates will persist over the next few decades, as the new cohorts of women entering reproductive age are smaller than the baby boomers who are leaving this age group. Therefore, even with a constant fertility rate, the number of births is expected to decrease.

National trends actually hide remarkable differences between the southern and northern regions (Fig. 2). Over the past 50 years, fertility in northern and southern Italy has followed two distinct patterns (Caltabiano et al. 2009). In the past, the southern regions had higher fertility than the northern regions, with the gap particularly wide (1.5 children) in the 1950s. After the baby boom in the 1960s, fertility started to decrease rapidly in both regions, but the fertility gap persisted. The gap only started to shrink in the 1990s, when fertility levels stabilized in the north but continued to decline in the south. Since the mid-1990s, fertility has unexpectedly started to increase in the north, while remaining almost stable in the south. The increase in TFR in the north stems basically from a slowing down of fertility postponement, a catch-up in fertility at later ages among the cohorts that were mainly responsible for delayed fertility in the previous decade, the growing

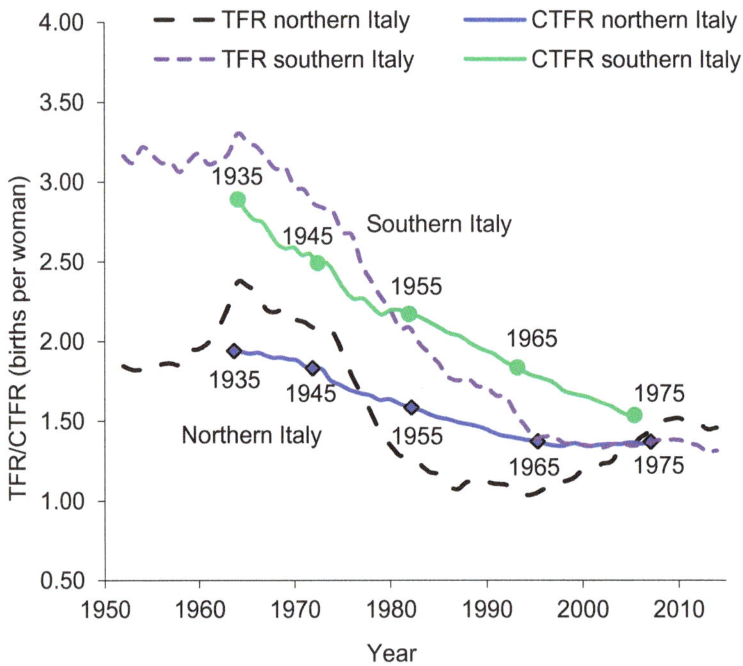

Fig. 2 Total fertility rate (TFR) and cohort completed total fertility rate (CTFR), north and south Italy, 1950–2015 (Caltabiano et al. 2009; for 1952–1993, Santini 1995; for 1994–2001 and 2013–2014, ISTAT 2015a; for 2002–2011, Eurostat 2015a). *Note* Numbers on lines for CTFR are mother's year of birth

contribution to fertility of the immigrant population, and finally the increase in out-of-wedlock births (Billari and Dalla Zuanna 2008; AISP 2007). Since 2004, the southern regions—the most traditional in terms of family values and gender roles—have had lower total fertility rates than in the north. This is only one of the paradoxes of Italian reproductive behavior.

The transition toward later births seems to be unstoppable and has spread all over the country. Women's average age at first birth in Italy is the oldest in Europe—30.6, compared with an average of 28.7 for European Union (EU) member states (Eurostat 2015b)—and it has increased by two years in the past decade (Fig. 1). If we exclude foreigners living in Italy, the average age at first birth is 31. More than 60 % of births are to women over 30 (close to 70 % among women who are Italian citizens), and among these 6.1 % are births to women over 40 (8.7 % for Italian citizens). These last percentages have doubled in one decade. Among European countries, only Spain has a higher proportion of first births after age 30 (Eurostat 2015b).

Over more than a decade, scholars have attempted to understand the factors associated with postponement of parenthood in Italy (Livi Bacci 2006; Ongaro 2001; Aassve et al. 2002). All in all, a delay in all the steps of transition to adulthood—in a sort of "delay syndrome" as Livi Bacci (2008) defines it—seems to be the main cause of delayed childbearing. This situation calls for "tempo policies" in order to remove some of the obstacles to the process of autonomy and family formation.

Childlessness: A Growing Component of Italian Population Dynamics

The process of delayed childbearing is associated with a change in fertility pathways across generations. The proportion of high-parity women in the cohorts born since the 1940s has fallen considerably, and the norm has gradually shifted from having "at least two children" to having "no more than two" (Santini 1995). The higher parities have declined considerably since the cohorts born in the 1930s, while the two-child model—although still prevailing—has been decreasing in importance since the cohorts born in the 1960s. Among women born since 1950, around one in four has only one child, and the prevalence of permanent childlessness has increased steeply—from 13.4 % among women born in 1960 to 21 % among women born in 1970 (ISTAT 2014b) (Fig. 3).

The dramatic increase in the prevalence of childlessness, both temporary and permanent, has become a peculiar facet of the Italian low-fertility regime, in contrast with other Mediterranean countries such as Spain where the prevalence of childlessness is almost stable across cohorts (Miettinen et al. 2015). In an exploratory survey carried out in selected urban areas, as many as one-third of Italian women in their 40s who lived with a partner and did not suffer from any

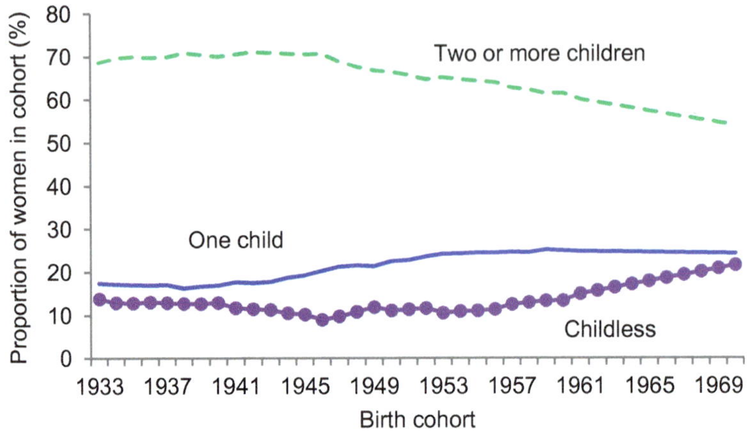

Fig. 3 Parity distribution among women born from 1933 to 1970, Italy (ISTAT 2015d). *Note* Data for cohorts born from 1962 to 1970 are estimated

physical impediment to fertility were voluntarily childless (Tanturri and Mencarini 2008). The same research showed that in several other cases, childlessness was the unintended outcome of delaying the decision to have a child or the result of adverse external circumstances, particularly the fragility of the partnership. If one assumes that the proportion of childless women in Italy as a whole is the same as observed in the five cities examined in this study, then it is conceivable that 12 % of the cohorts born around 1965 are involuntarily childless, and around 8 % have deliberately rejected motherhood. This is in stark contrast to the 1.5 % childless among the cohorts born just one or two decades earlier (Bonarini et al. 1999).

Recent studies show a pervasive increase in childlessness among both sexes and across social classes (Fig. 4). Although the prevalence of childlessness at age 40–44 is still much higher among the most educated women, and is still increasing in this group (up to about 30 % for highly educated women born in 1965–1969), a remarkable spread of the phenomenon has been observed among women with only primary education or less (18 % for less educated women born in 1965–1969) (Fig. 4). We can therefore argue that childlessness in Italy is not only a matter of prolonged education or women's career aspirations, but other factors seem to be associated with childlessness among all women.

A very large proportion remains childless in their 30s, increasing remarkably among cohorts regardless of education level (Fig. 4). Among women born in 1975–1979, the proportion childless is close to 30 % for women with little education, 50 % for women with secondary education, and 70 % for the most-educated women. One can reasonably doubt that all of these women will catch-up on childbearing at later ages. If a decade ago scholars were concerned that policies should remove the obstacles that impede couples from having a second child, today the main issue is how to allow Italian people to have at least one child before it is too late.

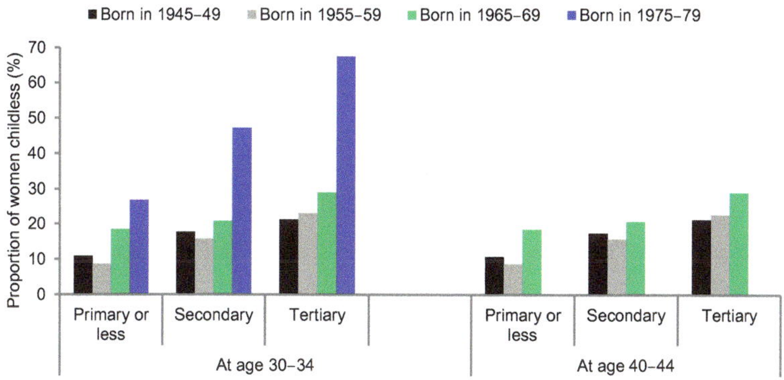

Fig. 4 Prevalence of childlessness at ages 30–34 and 40–44 by education level and birth cohort (author's calculations based on data from 2009 ISTAT survey *Famiglia e Soggetti Sociali*)

Changing Context of Childbearing

In Italy, the family as an institution seems to be holding steady on the whole, in contrast to the situation in many other Western countries. Divorce rates—despite their increase in the past decade—are still among the lowest in Europe. Husband-wife constellations remain the predominant family form, and most children under age five (more than 94 %) are living with both parents. While 5.3 % of children live with their mothers only or with their mothers and other family members, families headed by single fathers are still very rare (less than 0.5 %) (Ruspini and Tanturri 2015).

Family structures have not changed significantly in the past decade, but marriage rates have decreased sharply and are now in line with those observed in France and Spain. This is in part a side effect of the population-aging process, but also a consequence of the growing preference for less institutionalized forms of union (essentially cohabitation and "living apart together").[2] Italy ranks among the first countries in Europe—together with Austria—for the prevalence of couples who are living apart together, at about 20 % of adults age 18–45 (Mortmelans et al. 2015). According to the 2011 census, about 9 % of couples were cohabiting ("*more uxorio*," living together without being married), while a decade before the proportion was only 3.6 %. The number of cohabiting couples more than doubled in one decade, reaching 1.2 million. At the same time, the proportion of couples comprising an Italian citizen and a non-citizen is increasing—a sign of the gradual integration of immigrants. As an example, in 2013, 9.4 % of all weddings were between an Italian citizen and a non-citizen (most often—7.4 %—between an Italian groom and a foreign bride) (ISTAT 2014c).

[2]Living apart together refers to couples that have an intimate relationship but live at separate addresses.

In the past decade, these new family structures have been mirrored in the pattern of births. New phenomena include the growth of out-of-wedlock births, most within "*more uxorio*" cohabitation, an increasing contribution of foreign people to Italian fertility, and a rising demand for assisted-reproduction technology. In 1995, less than one birth in ten (8 %) was from unmarried parents. Since then, the proportion has tripled to one birth in four (26 %). In the north, the proportion is close to one birth in three, and it is even higher in big cities (ISTAT 2014c).

The proportion of births born to at least one foreign[3] parent increased from 6 % in 1999 to 20 % in 2012. Among these, 15 % were born to two foreign parents. As in many other countries, the young age structure of Italy's migrant population makes their contribution to the birth rate more important than their proportion in the total population (less than 7 %) would suggest. In some northern provinces, non-citizens account for more than 30 % of all births.

Increasing Demand for Assisted-Reproduction Technologies (ART)

Despite restrictive legislation in Italy,[4] assisted-reproduction technologies (ART) have allowed new opportunities for many Italian couples previously considered sterile or desiring to have children at a later age. Data collected by the Italian Assisted Reproductive Technologies Register (IARTR) show that—although the use of ART is still relatively rare compared to the potential demand—its use has increased by 56 % over six years, from 46,000 couples in 2005 to more than 72,000 in 2011. These data include only those couples who received ART treatment in one of the authorized centers in Italy. There is no official information on those travelling abroad for fertility treatment (Zanini 2011), but the Osservatorio per il Turismo Procreativo (Observatory for Procreative Tourism)—managed by the Italian Association CECOS (Center for the Study and Preservation of Eggs and Sperm)—estimates that around 4000 Italian couples sought reproductive care in another country in 2011.

[3]The definition of resident "foreign people" in Italy is linked to citizenship and not to place of birth. In the most recent census (2011), the foreign community accounted for about 7 % of the total population.

[4]The first Italian law on medically assisted procreation, known as Law 40 and issued in 2004, has radically transformed Italy from what was perceived as an unregulated "wild west" of assisted-reproductive practice to a country with one of the most restrictive laws in Europe. In its original version, the law restricted ART to heterosexual infertile couples, established that no more than three embryos could be produced during any cycle, required that all embryos be implanted immediately, limited research on embryos, and banned cryopreservation of embryos, embryo donation, and surrogacy (Zanini 2011, 565–66). A series of court judgments abrogated some of these restrictions, as they are unconstitutional or in contrast with other norms, but the law on the whole is still in force.

In line with trends in other European countries, the success rate for ART treatments in Italy is increasing (de Mouzon et al. 2012). One woman in five succeeds in getting pregnant after ART treatment, and 75 % of this group go on to have a live birth. In 2012, about 12,000 births in Italy were associated with ART treatment. This was about 2.2 % of total births for the year, twice as high as in the United States, but lower than in Scandinavian countries where ART-assisted births account for 4–6 % of the total.

A policy debate has emerged about subsidizing the cost of ART treatments, totally or in part, in selected cases (for instance, according to characteristics of the parents, such as age, that affect the probability of success), and from what government budget (health or family policies). At the moment, only a few regions provide subsidies for medically assisted procreation. "Heterologous fecundation"[5]—originally forbidden—has only recently been allowed by a ruling of the Constitutional Court.

Social and Cultural Context

In spite of a strong traditional pro-family ideology, the context in which Italian couples make the decision to have children is not as family friendly as it might appear at first glance. There are features of the Italian context that are not easy to quantify and measure but that plausibly are taken into account by couples when they decide whether to have a child. I defined these as "societal rigidities" because they represent elements of viscosity that impede a rapid and smooth process of family formation and transition to parenthood.

Italian Culture: Pros and Cons of Familist Values

Italian culture may be defined as "familist," referring to a set of normative beliefs that describes a strong attachment and loyalty to one's family, emphasizes the centrality of the family unit, and stresses the obligations and support that family members owe to both nuclear and extended kin (Saraceno 2003; Rossi 2009). This includes a strong reliance on family members (especially women) for material and emotional support. In Italy, the family acts as an informal support network (a social-security buffer), offering good-quality care services for children, the elderly, and sick people—services often provided by the welfare state in other countries (Alesina and Ichino 2009). I would define it as a "hypertrophic family,"[6] that is equipped to offer services that in general are beyond the usual family competences.

---

[5]The use of egg or sperm from an external donor.

[6]In the sense that it has too many obligations and duties.

For example, in Italy young adults of both sexes usually live with their parents until they marry or begin cohabiting with a partner, and they are financially supported by their parents as long as they stay in the family home (Facchini 2002). In general, they do not provide their parental family with either a financial contribution or substantial domestic help, especially if they are boys (Mencarini et al. 2010). Even after they leave home to establish a new family, they usually live in close proximity to their parents. More than one adult out of two lives within five kilometers of his or her parents, and about one adult out of three lives less than one kilometer from his or her parents (Bordone 2009). Adult children maintain strong relationships with their parents and in-laws and visit and contact them regularly in a continuous flow of mutual exchange (Barbagli et al. 2003; Bordone 2009). Moreover, the most common way to find a job is through a family network, and in case of divorce or unemployment, it is not uncommon for children to re-enter the parental home.

The survival of the familist cultural system largely relies on "traditional" gender relations. This is reflected in a large investment of women's personal resources in family life, a suspicious attitude toward formal care arrangements for children or the elderly, and a reluctance to adopt an egalitarian division of household labor. Even among young couples—most of whom are dual income—the traditional division of labor predominates, and wives/mothers/daughters generally have the primary responsibility for care of children (and also for older or disabled family members) (Ruspini and Tanturri 2015). At the same time, the rest of society is often organized on the assumption that mothers are housewives. For instance, the school day is generally much shorter than the typical work day.

The familist culture has contributed to creating a model of "few but high-quality children" (Dalla Zuanna and Micheli 2004; Dalla Zuanna 2001; Livi Bacci 2001) as a strategy to protect and transmit the well-being of the family and to allow social mobility for descendants. A family's expectations and investment in financial resources and time are concentrated in their few children—often only one—not only in childhood, but throughout life. Empirical studies that try to estimate the cost of Italian children, both in terms of monetary resources (De Santis 2004) and parental time (Tanturri 2012; Mencarini et al. 2010), confirm a high parental investment throughout the life course.

The Long and Problematic Transition to Adulthood and the Dualistic Labor Market

The general trend toward postponing family formation that has been observed in most advanced economies is extreme in Italy. Indeed, the "transition to adulthood" of Italian young people has been defined as "problematic" (Sironi and Rosina 2012).

Leaving the family of origin is a critical step. In Italy, young people leave the parental home at a very late age—in most cases to form their own family—in comparison with other Western countries. More than 44 % of Italians age 25–35 still live with their parents. This peculiar phenomenon can be explained by both cultural and structural factors. On the one hand, the presence of strong intergenerational ties, the investment by parents in increasing their children's human capital, the high level of domestic comfort in parental homes, and the democratization of relationships between parents and children encourage young people to continue living in their family of origin. On the other hand, individual autonomy is often hampered by structural constraints: the lack of opportunities in the labor market, the paucity of rental housing, and the low level of public welfare available to young people.

In the past two decades, labor-market reforms in Italy have substantially deregulated the use of temporary "atypical" contracts, while maintaining stringent firing rules for permanent contracts,[7] resulting in a labor market with an extreme dual structure. The associated social risks particularly affect young Italians in terms of "precarious employment, unstable and carousel careers, and… exclusion from welfare entitlements" (Barbieri 2011). The over-protected market for older workers (mainly male breadwinners) is usually not accessible to the young, who frequently work on temporary or atypical contracts,[8] with no protection in case of job loss and reduced health benefits and maternity leave. No minimum wage is guaranteed for those "atypical" workers who experience spells of unemployment. Moreover, the difference between the entry-level salary for the young and the national average salary is much greater than in any other EU country (Aassve et al. 2007). Young people in Italy also face a high degree of discrepancy between level of education and job responsibilities: Among women and men born after 1979, around 40 % are more educated than required for their first job, while among those born in the 1940s the proportion was less than 10 % (ISTAT 2014b).

With the start of the great recession in 2007, the largest employment losses took place in the part of the economy most exposed to temporary contracts—the youth (Garibaldi and Taddei 2013; Aassve et al. 2013). Among Italians age 15–24, 43 % work on temporary contracts. While the Italian unemployment rate was aligned with the EU27 average from 1992 to 2012, youth unemployment was always almost 10 % higher (Garibaldi and Taddei 2013). This difference narrowed between 1998 and 2007, but the economic recession has amplified the discrepancies once again. The Organization for Economic Cooperation and Development (OECD) Employment Outlook (2012) observed that in Italy "job losses have been

[7]Typical permanent contracts guarantee the employee against firing and provide social protection, health and maternity leave, social-security contributions, and unemployment benefits in case of termination.

[8]In 1997, the Treu Bill deregulated the labor market allowing "atypical contracts" (e.g., *contratto a progetto*), which were not only open ended but had lower social-security contributions, did not envisage any parental or sick leave compensation, and did not entitle workers to unemployment benefits (Garibaldi and Taddei 2013).

concentrated among youth and the low skilled: the rate of long-term unemployment, an indicator of severe labor market distress, has risen very sharply for youth and, to a much lesser extent, for the low skilled and prime age men. Compared to the OECD average, the increase in the long-term unemployment rate was more marked in Italy and less evenly distributed across socio-demographic groups." Among Italians age 19–29, the unemployment rate in 2013 was close to 30 % in 2013, the highest level recorded since 1977.

New concerns have also arisen about the emerging phenomenon of young people who are not in education, employment, or training (NEET). In Italy, the number of NEETs has increased dramatically in the past few years, up to 2.5 million. Among young people age 15–29, one out of four is a NEET, one of the highest rates in the EU, and the proportion is one out of three in the south (ISTAT 2014d). This situation amplifies young people's feelings of insecurity and uncertainty about the future, with a consequent tendency to postpone choices that entail the assumption of responsibilities (Blossfeld et al. 2005).

The Housing Market and the Controversial Role of Intergenerational Transfers

Young Italians face severe difficulties in the process of achieving financial and residential autonomy. Italy is more and more characterized by widespread home ownership, with a shrinking rental market and an increase in the cost of rental housing (Billari and Dalla Zuanna 2008; D'Alessio and Gambacorta 2007). Home ownership is not only the norm, but also almost the only way of obtaining housing for a family, as Mulder and Billari (2010) observe. At the end of the 1970s, most Italian couples rented a home after marriage, but today less than one-third become renters. Indeed, owning a good home has become a prerequisite for family formation (Vignoli et al. 2013; Mencarini and Tanturri 2006), making the process much more demanding in terms of financial resources. Vignoli et al. (2013) show a positive association between a couple's fertility intentions and the degree to which they feel secure about their housing conditions, other things being equal.

In Italy—as in other southern European countries—homeownership has become almost universal (three-quarters of the population). This trend has been driven by non-policies, as the government has failed to regulate the rental market and has not invested in social (public) housing. In addition, the government has failed to regulate the credit market to allow young people access to mortgages (Bernardi and Poggio 2004). In Italy, there are no companies that track an individual's credit worthiness, so bankers have little information about a person or a couple who apply for a mortgage. In addition, bankers usually refuse to lend money to people working on temporary or atypical contracts, regardless of their future earning potential. Rather, bankers require a large down payment or, alternatively, another house (commonly the parental home) as a guarantee for a mortgage loan, making it very difficult for young people to purchase a home without the help of their families. In general, young people can only become homeowners through the pooling of family resources (money and labor) and intra-vivo transfers, imbedded in a pattern of providing care to the older generation in exchange for the intergenerational transmission of housing wealth (e.g., Poggio 2011). Parental assistance with home-ownership might take the form of gifts (money, land, labor), loans, or mortgage guarantees, and it is more and more necessary.

The necessity for parental help to acquire a home reinforces both the temporary intergenerational co-residence of young adults as well as close geographic proximity when young people do leave the parental home[9] (Tommasini et al. 2003). This situation has pros and cons: On the one hand, it reinforces the mechanism of mutual help between generations, but on the other hand, it is associated with difficult entry into the housing market (Dalla Zuanna 2001). Moreover, it may discourage residential mobility among young people wishing to find better employment opportunities. Last but not least, it may reinforce social inequalities (Bernardi and Poggio 2004) since only those whose parents have the means can obtain the financial support necessary to buy a house.

This home-ownership regime has a role in postponing the exit from the parental home and family formation (Mencarini and Tanturri 2006), and it seems also to have negative consequences for fertility (Mulder and Billari 2010; Vignoli et al. 2013). Young Italians need to live with their parents even after they become financially independent in order to accumulate enough money to buy a house. The timing of their forming an independent household depends on personal savings, family help, and inheritance (Dalla Zuanna 2001). Mulder and Billari's study (2010) confirms that fertility is very low in countries where a high share of homes are owned rather than rented and it is difficult to obtain a mortgage.

The Unresolved Work-Life Balance and Rigidities in the Labor Market

Similar to other countries in southern Europe, Italy is a classic example of a situation where it is difficult to combine family life and paid work (Matysiak and Vignoli 2013). Paradoxically, in Italy, relatively low female employment goes hand in hand with very low fertility: Low fertility among working women is not compensated by high fertility among housewives. Women participating in the labor market—subject to workplace rigidities[10] and facing the double burden of work and

[9]It was common in the past for young couples to reside with parental families, but this has now largely been replaced by residential proximity.

[10]In Italy, flexibility is rare in the scheduling of work hours, the amount of hours worked, or the place of work. For instance, badge control is more common than control by results, and teleworking is very rare. The small average size of enterprises and the lack of diversity in management culture slow down the implementation of such measures.

family responsibilities—may be deterred from having (more) children for fear that children might compromise their job opportunities or damage their personal lives (Del Boca et al. 2005). Apart from the obstacles they face in reconciling family and professional career, women also often face a highly unstable work situation, which has a negative impact on their decision to have children. Italian couples in which the woman is unemployed or in a precarious work situation are less likely to plan childbearing than other couples in the short run (Modena et al. 2014). Lack of career-advancement opportunities for young mothers also tends to limit their preferences about number of children or their desire to have children at all. At the same time, Italian women out of the labor market do not have much higher fertility because of budget constraints and lack of policies to support large one-income families. It is well known that the risk of falling under the poverty threshold is five time higher for children with only one working parent than for those in dual-income households (OECD 2014).

Social norms seem to reinforce the idea of low compatibility between motherhood and work outside the home, as the representation of working mother is still negative. European Social Survey data (2008) show that three-quarters of Italians think that a pre-school child suffers to some extent if his/her mother works (compared with 41 % of the French).

The difficulties in reconciling family and work are aggravated by characteristics of the Italian labor market, with high rates of self-employment,[11] high shares of people employed in small firms,[12] a high degree of employment protection for the male breadwinner, and a high degree of informal flexibility, mainly through the underground economy (Tanturri 2010). Self-employed people usually work longer hours, pay higher costs if they are on leave, and have less welfare protection than those in the formal labor market. Those working in small enterprises are less likely to benefit from company childcare centers, childcare benefits, or flexible working hours. Moreover, a small company is likely to pay a high cost when an employee is on leave, as they must pay the employee and also pay a substitute. Finally, many women still work in the black market, especially in domestic service or agriculture, and they are therefore "invisible" to the social-protection system—they do not pay taxes, but they do not receive benefits such as maternity or sick leave.

Women's employment levels in Italy are among the lowest among OECD countries (58.9 % among women age 20–54; see Table 1), and they are rising very slowly compared with the rest of Europe. This is despite the fact that women have overtaken men in levels of education: Among Italians age 30–34, 27 % of women have a university degree compared with 18 % of men (ISTAT 2015c). Most working women (67 %), have a full-time contract, but on average women work fewer hours than men (33 h per week) because part-time is rare among men. At

[11]As of 2012, Italy had the highest proportion of self-employed workers in the total workforce in Europe, at 30 %.

[12]In Italy, there are 64 enterprises for every 1000 inhabitants, one of the highest proportions in Europe. These enterprises tend to be small—on average 3.9 workers per firm in the country as a whole and 2.8 in the south.

Table 1 Female employment (age 25–54) and maternal employment rates by number of children under 15 and by age of the youngest child, 2011 (%)

	Female employment rate (all women age 25–54)	Maternal employment rate (women with at least one child under age 15)	Maternal employment rate by:					
			Age of youngest child			Number of children		
			<3 years	3–5 years	6–14 years	1	2	3+
Italy	58.91	55.27	53.40	50.56	56.60	58.39	52.69	38.56
OECD average	70.67	65.23	52.16	65.65	72.58	69.16	65.63	50.52

OECD (2014)

55.3 %, maternal employment is slightly lower than the rate for women as a whole and significantly lower than the OECD average. Mother's employment does not vary appreciably according to the age of the youngest child (Table 1): 53.4 % of Italian mothers whose youngest child is under three are employed compared with 50.6 % of mothers whose youngest child is age 3–5, even though educational services are almost universal for this older age group. This might be due to a cohort effect because mothers of younger children belong to cohorts in which women in general have higher workforce participation rates. The employment rate rises a little among mothers of children age 6–14 (56.6 %). Mother's employment decreases steeply, however, according to number of children (Table 1). Among mothers with three children, the employment rate is 38.6 %, about 20 % points lower than among mothers of one child and well below the average for OECD countries (OECD 2014).

The labor-market penalties for Italian working mothers are considerable. Despite gains in recent decades in participation rates among younger women, Italy still faces higher exit rates from employment among new mothers than in other countries. Optional parental leave is poorly paid, part-time job opportunities are limited, and most Italian regions (especially in the south) lack adequate childcare provision (Del Boca et al. 2005, 2009). It is still common for young women to drop out of the labor market permanently after they have children. In fact, the proportion of mothers leaving the labor market has increased in the past few years (ISTAT 2007, 2014c): More than one mother out of five who was working before getting pregnant now has left the labor market or has been fired[13] by 20 months after childbirth, compared with 18 % in 2007 (ISTAT 2007, 2014a). This proportion is significantly higher for mothers who work under an "atypical" contract (50 %) or a fixed-term contract (40 %) or if they if they become mothers before age 25 (40 %) or are less educated (32 %). Women who work in the private sector have double the probability of leaving the labor market compared with women in the public sector. Among mothers of pre-school children, the probability of leaving the labor market is significantly lessened by better job quality, human-capital endowment, and accessibility to childcare (Pacelli et al. 2013). Most importantly, the availability of part-time jobs (33 % of total working women in Italy) reduces the probability that mothers will leave the labor force entirely (Pacelli et al. 2013). It should be noted, however, that part-time employees are more expensive for employers in terms of labor costs, and, therefore, employers are reluctant to allow women (or men) to change from full-time to part-time contracts when they have young children and then change back again.

[13]Actually, the law forbids an employer from firing a woman when she comes back to work after maternity leave until the child is two years old, but the illegal practice of obliging women to sign an undated letter of resignation when hired, to be used by the employer in case a woman becomes pregnant, is far from being abandoned in spite of recent efforts. Moreover, the proliferation of short-term contracts for young women allows employers simply not to renew a contract after childbirth.

Women who do not leave employment after becoming mothers experience a substantial penalty in term of wages, and there are no signs that this gap closes even five years after childbirth[14] (Pacelli et al. 2013). About 40 % of working mothers confirm that they have difficulties reconciling work and family responsibilities due to rigid work schedules (no flexibility in the start or end of the work day or possibility to have short breaks for family reasons), shift work, and non-standard work hours (such as working during the night and/or on the weekend) (ISTAT 2007). These problems are linked to the issue of childcare that will be examined next.

The Childcare Challenge

Balancing work and childrearing in Italy is made more difficult by the limited supply of public childcare for children under age three, both in terms of availability and the number of hours supplied on a day-to-day basis (OECD 2011). This situation, combined with social pressure and expectations, may help explain why Italian parents spend more time caring for their children than parents in other European countries (Pahilé et al. forthcoming; Tanturri 2012).

Several different types of childcare services are available in Italy, varying by the age of the children they serve, the way they are financed, and their degree of flexibility. Starting at age three, children have access to kindergarten, which is practically universally available, public, and almost free (OECD 2007). Nearly all (95.7 %) children age 3–5 attend kindergarten (OECD 2014).

As a whole, the Italian childcare system is mixed. Center-based care of children from age three months to three years is provided mainly by *asili nido* (crèches) that are not part of the state educational system. Only 24.2 % of children age 0–2 attend a crèche, and less than 12 % attend a public childcare center, up only slightly from 9 % in 2004 (Fig. 5). The regional differences are very large, with fewer than 5 % of children in this age group attending a public childcare center in the south (Fig. 5).

This disparity in enrolment rates between crèche and kindergarten can be partly explained by the difference in fees. Most kindergartens are part of the state educational system and are almost free.[15] By contrast, the crèches can be either public —managed by local municipalities—or private, but often even the private crèches

[14]Women unable to reduce their working hours after childbirth have an actual or perceived lower productivity on the job and face a negative wage gap with respect to otherwise similar childless women. A recent empirical study shows that Italian women experience a non-negligible wage penalty when they become mothers. This gap amounts to about €15 (US$16 as of 4 Aug 2015) a week for an average weekly wage of €360 (US$392) before childbearing. The average yearly wage growth is about 3 % lower for women after they become mothers (Pacelli et al. 2013).

[15]Parents are required to pay a small fee (less than €100 (US$109) a year) at enrollment plus the cost of meals for children attending kindergarten on a full-time basis.

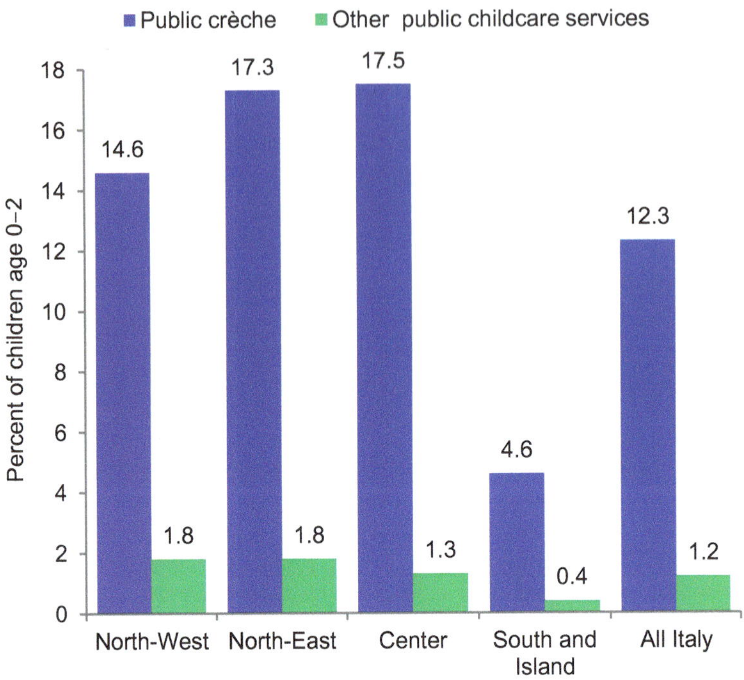

Fig. 5 Percentage of resident children age 0–2 attending a public crèche or other public childcare facility by geographical area, Italy, 2012 (ISTAT 2015c)

are operated through agreements with local administrations (PERFAR 2015). Public crèches are only partially subsidized, and they vary widely among different locations in terms of availability and cost.[16] Local municipalities may also reserve a number of places in private crèches, pay part of the fees, and/or create rules for access.

The rules, the criteria for access to public crèches, and the fees are set by the municipalities, but standards for quality are set by national law—fixing, for instance, a maximum of six children per caregiver for children under three. The number of places is limited, and the unmet demand is high. Interestingly, it is higher in regions with a larger supply of childcare, suggesting that a relatively large supply, in itself, creates demand. Priority of access is usually given to disadvantaged families such as

[16]Overall, only one-half of municipalities offers childcare centers, and the regional differences are very large—from 22.5 % of municipalities offering childcare centers in the south to 76.3 % in the northeast. The proportion of the cost paid by parents also varies widely—from more than 22 % in the north to less than 9 % on the islands. The proportion of children attending a public childcare center varies from 2 % in Calabria to 27 % in Emilia Romagna.

families with a disability (of the child or of a parent), single mothers, mothers who are newly pregnant, families in which both parents have difficult job arrangements (e.g., a long distance between home and work or long work hours), and families with additional children. The presence of close and capable grandparents is also taken into account.

Families are required to pay a monthly fee for childcare services, which varies according to household income and the timetable selected. Some municipalities provide free (or very inexpensive) access to public daycare centers for families with incomes below a certain threshold. Bradshaw and Finch (2002) found that as of about 2000, the average monthly cost for full-time childcare for a two-earner couple (average male wage plus one-half the average female wage)[17] was about €187 (US $203) in Italy, similar to the cost in France, more than the cost in Sweden (€151 or US$164), but less than the cost in Germany or the United Kingdom (€225 or US $244).

In addition to *asili nido*, a 1997 law made it possible for families or groups of families to organize "baby-parking" facilities that provide occasional childcare for a fee on an hourly or daily basis. The same law incentivized private companies to organize their own crèches. On the whole, the results of this policy have been modest. A very small minority of children under age three (1.2 %) attend these alternative childcare services (Fig. 5), and this proportion has halved since 2004.

All in all, Italian public childcare centers have very high quality standards but are also very expensive (Dalla Zuanna and Weber 2012). The highest-fertility area in Italy, the autonomous province of Bolzano, provides additional, more flexible childcare options at lower costs, such as *tagensmutter,* who are mothers on an approved list who provide childcare in their homes to a small number of children according to parental needs. Crèches are usually very rigid in their schedules and the procedures and timing for enrolling (sometimes immediately after the birth of a child). Open hours are usually from 8:00 a.m. to 4:00 p.m. (full-time) or 8:00 a.m. to 1:00 p.m. (part-time) from Monday to Friday, with no accommodation for parents, such as shop keepers, who have non-standard work schedules.

For primary-school pupils age 6–10, school schedules differ, and a full-time schedule (40 h over five days per week) is not available for everybody, but only on demand for a limited number of pupils. Other pupils attend school for 23 h a week, distributed over six days, or 27 h a week, distributed over five mornings and two afternoons. For children age 11–13, standard school hours are from 8:00 a.m. to 1:00 p.m. six days a week, without any lunch service. Before- and after-school care facilities are offered only sporadically, and families (mothers, in particular) are mostly responsible for taking their children to extra-curricular activities such as sports or music lessons.

---

[17]For the most common form of childcare in each country after direct and indirect subsidies but before taxes and benefits.

Grandparents are usually the main care providers when both parents work, according to a long tradition of intergenerational solidarity (ISTAT 2007). In 81 % of families where both parents work, non-coresident grandparents are the primary and secondary caregivers for children age 0–13, and the proportion is even higher for pre-school children (OECD 2014). Childcare by grandparents may be in line with Italian familist culture, but, as a side effect, it may reduce the pressure on fathers to become more involved in childcare and on the government to increase the supply of childcare centers. Care by grandparents is generally preferred to institutionalized childcare because crèches are quite expensive, there are often long waiting lists for places, or the quality of the care provided is perceived—often erroneously—as inadequate (ISTAT 2011). It is interesting that the norm of care by grandparents is so rooted that in many municipalities parents have to declare whether their parents live in the same municipality when they apply for a place in a crèche. It is taken for granted that if the grandparents live nearby they should care for the grandchildren regardless of their willingness or the condition of their health.

Recent studies confirm that in southern Europe the availability of grandparents is often a critical factor in an individual's decision to have children (Aassve et al. 2012). In addition, several studies in Italy show that the presence of a grandmother is a factor strongly linked to the probability that a mother will work. Pagani and Marenzi (2008) show that the informal help received from older relatives strongly increases the probability that Italian women will be engaged in paid work. Arpino et al. (2014) found that the effect of grandparental childcare on the laborforce participation of mothers is positive, statistically significant, and economically relevant. The benefit of grandparental child care is stronger for mothers with low education and those living in northern and central Italy. One may doubt the future sustainability of this care system because grandmothers will be more likely to be working themselves, both because they belong to cohorts where women are more likely to work and because economic reforms have delayed the retirement age for women (Tanturri 2010; Battistin et al. 2014).

The Slow Gender Revolution and the Role of Men in Family Life

Lack of gender equality has been put forward as a possible cause for the persistence of low fertility in some societies (McDonald 2000a, b), and Italy seems to be a case in point. Over the past two decades, Italian women have greatly improved their educational attainment and have raised their labor-market participation. Today, they work more than they did in the recent past, but their employment rate is still low by European standards, and gender gaps in employment and unemployment rates remain among the highest in the EU27. An abundant literature shows the persistence of traditional gender roles in Italy, especially in the south. If we balance the production and consumption of family goods and services, Italian men appear to play the role of free-riders most of their lives, remaining net consumers of family time until age 50, while women become net producers of family goods and services in their twenties. In other words, women produce more than they consume most of their lives, while men only become net producers at an advanced age (Zagheni and Zannella 2013).

The traditional male-breadwinner family model still prevails on the whole, but among the younger generation dual-earner couples are becoming more common. Italian women still spend much more time on unpaid household work, however, than women in countries such as Sweden or France, and they spend more time on childcare than men, even in dual-earner households (Anxo et al. 2011; Mills et al. 2008). This situation is likely to be reinforced by strong family ties (Reher 1998) and by familism (Livi Bacci 2001; Dalla Zuanna and Micheli 2004) that enhances expectations regarding women's household duties. Moreover, the high expectations for total household production in Italy (more services and goods are produced at home rather than out-sourced) and for standards (services and goods must be of high quality), together with a limited supply of household products and services available on the market or supplied by the government (such as care services), mean that a great deal of time is taken up by household labor. Just to give an example, to maintain a household with at least one pre-school child a couple in Italy spends about 64 h a week, compared with 48 h a week in Sweden (Anxo et al. 2011). Moreover, in Italy domestic duties are less equally distributed, with women providing 80 % of household work and family care, compared with 60 % in Sweden. Overall, an Italian woman spends more time on family-related activities (care and household tasks) than both members of a couple in Sweden. When children are grown up, Italian women continue to dedicate a great deal of time to family tasks, double the hours contributed by women in Sweden (Anxo et al. 2011). That means that Italian men, despite the importance given to family life, spend about the same amount of time on childcare and house work as men in Scandinavia, while Italian women contribute much more.

This results in a particularly asymmetrical gender division of labor. Italian men contribute the least household labor among Europeans, whereas Italian women who are employed have the longest work days, including both paid and unpaid labor (Anxo et al. 2011). Childbearing tends to increase this already heavily unbalanced division of household labor, which has the effect of discouraging fertility (Cooke 2003; Mencarini and Tanturri 2004; Mills et al. 2008). The experience of parenthood often exacerbates gender roles, with an increase in women's time spent on housework and childcare and a decrease in leisure time. This situation is obviously worse for working mothers, who are subject to a "dual burden" or "second shift." Indeed, in Italy when a child is born, men typically increase the time devoted to paid work (this effect has not been observed in France, Sweden, or the United States; see Anxo et al. 2011), while women reduce their work hours or even exit the labor market (ISTAT 2007; Mencarini and Tanturri 2004). Paihlé et al. (forthcoming) show that the presence of children reduces the free time of their parents (leisure plus personal time, such as for sleeping or self-care), but the squeeze is much tighter for women, especially when they have three or more children or an infant under age three. Other things being equal, the reduction of free time for women ranges from a minimum of one hour and 20 min a day when they have one child at school age to two hours and 50 min a day when they have three children and the youngest is under age three. For men, the maximum reduction of free time is two hours a day. There is considerable documentation on the low level of Italian fathers' involvement in childcare (Ruspini and Tanturri 2015; Tanturri and Mencarini 2009; Neilson and Stanfors 2014; Smith Koslowski 2008; Tanturri 2012; Mencarini and Tanturri 2004), with mothers carrying, sometimes almost exclusively, the main responsibility.

Table 2 provides an idea of the average time that Italian men and women in families devote to childcare, unpaid work (childcare plus domestic tasks), and paid work (including commuting and breaks), according to the number children and the age of the youngest child. The first column for each sex shows the average daily hours spent on a certain activity calculated from the whole sample during a typical day of the week,[18] while the second column shows the average calculated only for those doing a certain activity on the interview day. The third column shows, for each sex, the proportion of people performing a certain activity on the interview day. Regardless of family typology, virtually all women in couples perform some unpaid work, while among men the participation is not universal. About one man in four does not perform any domestic or care activity at all, and the proportion is even higher for men with three children if the youngest child is over age three (Table 2). Men who do some household work spend much less time on domestic tasks than women—about 2.5 h a day for men compared with 6.5 h a day for women. In general, men's participation and time devoted to paid work changes very little as family composition changes. By contrast, mothers reduce their labor-force participation considerably compared with childless women, but those who remain in the labor market still work long hours (around seven hours a day, compared with eight for childless women) (Table 2).

This unbalanced gender system of family labor clearly has a negative effect on fertility and fertility intentions (Mencarini and Tanturri 2004; Cooke 2003; Del Boca et al. 2009; De Rose et al. 2008). Active, consistent gender policies might help accelerate the trend toward gender equality by promoting an active role for fathers and reducing the burden of motherhood for women.

[18]This means that it is a weighted average with weekdays counted as 5/7 and weekend days as 2/7. To estimate weekly average working hours, we multiply the daily average by seven. For instance, working men spent 64 h and 52 min at work (including commute time and lunch and coffee breaks), while working women spent 52 h and 9 min.

Table 2 Number of hours spent performing childcare, childcare plus domestic work, and paid work by women and men, in an average day, 2008–2009

Number of children and age of youngest child	Childcare			Childcare and domestic work			Paid work		
	Average time spent (entire sample)	Average time spent (performer)	Percent who performed	Average time spent (entire sample)	Average time spent (performer)	Percent who performed	Average time spent (entire sample)	Average time spent (performer)	Percent who performed
Men									
Entire sample	00:41	01:28	46.5	01:59	02:33	78.0	06:57	09:16	75.1
Childless	00:00	–	–	01:26	02:07	68.1	06:54	09:28	72.9
1 Child, 0–2	01:16	01:42	74.0	02:38	03:00	87.6	06:59	09:19	75.0
1 Child, 3–5	01:01	01:28	69.4	01:59	02:18	85.9	07:14	09:14	78.3
1 Child, 6–12	00:37	01:12	51.5	02:02	02:34	79.2	07:10	09:01	79.5
2 Children, 0–2	01:34	01:56	81.4	02:42	02:58	91.2	06:57	09:13	75.3
2 Children, 3–5	00:55	01:26	63.8	02:19	02:57	78.7	06:32	09:10	71.3
2 Children, 6–12	00:33	01:07	49.2	01:51	02:24	77.1	07:02	09:16	76.0
3 Children, 0–2	01:10	01:45	66.9	02:08	02:43	78.8	07:28	09:47	76.3
3 Children, 3–5	01:03	01:37	65.5	02:20	02:58	78.6	07:20	09:55	74.0
3 Children, 6–12	00:19	00:57	32.8	01:43	02:32	67.9	06:03	08:18	72.9
Women									
Entire sample	01:37	02:31	64.3	06:26	06:33	98.2	03:04	07:27	41.2
Childless	00:00	–	–	04:28	04:36	96.9	04:12	08:04	52.0
1 Child, 0–2	03:13	03:19	96.8	07:16	07:20	99.2	02:32	07:32	33.7
1 Child, 3–5	02:07	02:15	94.3	06:32	06:40	97.9	02:33	07:47	32.7
1 Child, 6–12	01:24	01:45	79.6	06:09	06:16	98.3	03:27	07:15	47.7
2 Children, 0–2	03:50	03:58	96.3	08:30	08:30	99.9	01:55	06:34	29.2

(continued)

Table 2 (continued)

Number of children and age of youngest child	Childcare			Childcare and domestic work			Paid work		
	Average time spent (entire sample)	Average time spent (performer)	Percent who performed	Average time spent (entire sample)	Average time spent (performer)	Percent who performed	Average time spent (entire sample)	Average time spent (performer)	Percent who performed
2 Children, 3–5	02:31	02:41	94.3	07:47	07:48	99.9	02:25	06:34	36.8
2 Children, 6–12	01:18	01:38	79.6	06:42	06:48	98.4	02:57	07:04	41.7
3 Children, 0–2	03:28	03:40	94.5	09:09	09:09	100.0	01:12	07:13	16.6
3 Children, 3–5	02:27	02:52	85.3	08:16	08:44	94.7	01:59	07:14	27.5
3 Children, 6–12	00:54	01:30	60.2	05:49	05:59	97.3	03:43	07:23	50.3

Note Average based on the whole sample (first column) or only based on those who performed the activity in the interview day (second column); proportion of people performing a certain activity (third column)
Author's calculations based on data from 2008–2009 ISTAT Time Use Survey

Policy Deficiencies and Inconsistencies

The Familist Welfare Regime and the Taboo that Affects Demographic Policy

Italy occupies a rather peculiar position among Western countries in terms of social policy in general and family policy in particular. In Italy, it has been almost impossible to discuss demographic policies to counter low fertility because the explicitly pro-natalist measures adopted under Fascism in the 1930s have made the issue taboo. Moreover, as Naldini and Saraceno (2008) observe, the "longstanding Italian perception of itself as a country with excessively high fertility" was persistent until the 1990s, although even then fertility levels were among the lowest ever recorded in the world.

With this background, public discourse in Italy focuses on family-friendly, rather than pro-natalist, policies, and over the past few decades the conversation has been characterized by a strong ideological debate on the definition of "family." There is little shared consensus on priorities and a high degree of political and ideological divisiveness with regard to issues concerning the family between political parties on the right and left and between Catholic and non-Catholic visions of society. For instance, parties on the right and Catholics usually want to offer public aid only to families founded on marriage, while parties on the left have a broader definition of family, including cohabiting and homosexual couples. These unresolved issues have probably contributed to impeding the planning and implementation of consistent family-friendly (and gender) policies.

At the same time, the characteristics of the Italian welfare system do not favor a strong state intervention in family life. The historic development of the Italian welfare state was not based on a coherent policy line or recognizable cultural matrix, as argued by Trifiletti (1999). The original liberal and later corporatist welfare state was politically discredited in the years following World War II but was never replaced with a coherent model. While the state does not take responsibility for guaranteeing a family wage, for example, it allows nuclear or extended families to pursue strategies to ensure that at least one member has a well-protected job (Petmesidou 1996). Saraceno (1994) argues that "the Italian familist welfare regime is not exclusively nor even primarily based on a strong breadwinner model, but on the family as perceived as a unit of income and resources, to which everyone contributes according to his/her opportunities, although they may differ by gender. What is assumed is not the figure of breadwinner but family solidarity—including kin—and the primary responsibility of women—married and mothers—in the provision of care."

Thus in Italy, as in other southern European countries, families are expected to support their members (family responsibilities and obligations extend beyond the nuclear family) with only limited help from the state. Family policies are scarcely developed in comparison with many other European countries.

The Italian welfare system is also characterized by a preference for income transfers (particularly pensions) over transfers in kind (e.g., care services), by a dualistic protection system that distinguishes between "insiders" and "outsiders," and by the marginality of family policies in general (Saraceno 2003). In 2009, Italy spent only 1.58 % of GDP on family benefits, as compared to the OECD average of 2.61 % (OECD 2014). In 2013, Italy spent 30 % of GDP on public social expenditures, but pensions accounted for more than one-half of the total (ISTAT 2015c). Expenditures related to the family, maternity, and childhood are only 4.1 % of total social expenditure, and this proportion has decreased slightly over the years. Intergenerational transfers to young people occur mainly within families, which can be a source of social inequity. It can also lead to a pattern of long residence by young people in the parental home.

This "unsupported familism" (Saraceno 1994) implies poor development of childcare services and insufficient measures to help parents reconcile work and family life. Both features have a negative impact on the reshaping of gender relations. Hence, Italy scores poorly on gender-equality indicators both in the public (labor-force and political participation) and the private (share of unpaid work) realms. Given this situation, couples find it difficult to make the transition toward the "dual-earner model," in which both adult members of a family are in paid employment (León and Migliavacca 2013, p. 26). Familist values reinforce the male-provider role by encouraging women to reduce their employment hours when they become mothers and by not supporting a larger family role for men when they become fathers.

Another impediment to the development of family policies is Italy's huge public debt, which has been a structural characteristic of the national economy since the end of the 1980s. In this context, the 2001 constitutional reforms delegated responsibility for social services entirely to the regions, but without clarifying the role of the state. This constitutional change paralyzed reorganization of social services, as previously envisaged by Law 328/2000 (Naldini and Saraceno 2008). Without a clear framework, any enhancement of social services is very difficult.

Leave Policies: Still a Mother's Affair

Maternity leave is legally mandatory for employed mothers both on temporary and permanent contracts. This obligation has recently been extended to mothers working on most atypical contracts. In Italy, maternity leave is quite long (21 weeks), and well paid (at 80 % of previous earnings, 100 % for civil servants). Maternity leave can be taken by fathers only in very specific cases: when the mother did not make use (or made only partial use) of maternity leave, when the mother became seriously ill or died, when the mother abandoned the family, or when the father has sole custody in case of separation or divorce. Until a child is 12 months old, women who are employees are entitled to work reduced hours (one hour less per day if working six hours a day or less; two hours less per day if working longer) for breast feeding, with full compensation of earnings.

In response to the 1996 EU directive on parental leave, new legislation (Law 53/8 March 2000) was enacted that provides parents, including fathers, with the right to take parental leave up to a maximum of six months if only one parent takes leave or 10 months if each parents take some of the leave. In addition, if a father decide to take leave for at least three months (even if not consecutive), the couple gets an additional "bonus" month. Thus in total, parents can take up to 11 months of leave, for example, six months for the mother and four months for the father, which becomes five months thanks to the "bonus" month. Parental leave is not well compensated, providing only 30 % of salary, but it does provide an option for fathers to be more involved with their children.

Fathers' use of parental leave has been very low. Only 7.5 % of entitled fathers with a child under eight took parental leave in 2005, rising to 8.6 % in 2010, and fewer than one out of five of these fathers took at least one month of leave (ISTAT 2011). Many more mothers took parental leave, 45 % in 2010, and most of these mothers (70 %) took off from work for at least one month (ISTAT 2007, 2011). The reasons most often reported by fathers for not using parental leave were: (1) they did not need it because their partner or another person cared for their children (27 %); (2) they preferred working as a personal choice (21 %); (3) their partner used the entire leave (13 %); or (4) they were not entitled (20 %) (ISTAT 2011). Only 4 % of fathers reported financial reasons for not taking parental leave. As in other countries, public-sector workers in Italy are more inclined to take parental leave than those working in the private sector: Around 50 % of fathers in the civil service take parental leave. As Baker et al. (2011) explain, in Italy there is no fiscal incentive to take parental leave, and the concept of fathers taking time off from work to look after children remains stigmatized (see also Mazzucchelli 2011). While 65 % of Italian fathers are aware of their right to take parental leave, the vast majority of these fathers (87 %) show no intention of exercising that right (Mazzucchelli 2011).

Italian fathers have only been entitled to paternity leave (one day with 100 % salary compensation) since 2012. Following a request from the EU Parliament, the Italian Parliament began a debate in June 2010 regarding the introduction of a compulsory and fully paid paternity leave. A recent law (Law 92/2012) introduced an important innovation on a trial basis over the period 2013–2015 and recently prolonged up to 2016: Starting in January 2013, employees who become fathers are entitled to one day of compulsory, fully paid paternity leave and two days of voluntary leave, which can be used as an alternative to the mother's compulsory maternity leave with her consent. In other words, fathers can take two additional days if the mother agrees to transfer these days from her maternity leave allocation. These leave days should be used within five months after the child's birth, and an employee must notify his employer of his intention to take leave at least 15 days in advance. Compensation for this leave is paid by INPS (Instituto Nazionale della Previdenza Sociale, the Italian Social Security Institute) (Addabbo and Giovannini 2013). The measure has not been implemented in the public sector and has not been monitored in the private sector, so there are no data on take-up rates. It is evident that the introduction of paternity leave was purely symbolic in response to the request from the EU Parliament. The fact that the trial period will terminate in 2016, while the measure has not yet been implemented for civil servants, reveals that this policy is not considered a priority.

Support for Childrearing

In Italy, there is no universal children's allowance, and the tax system takes children into account only minimally (Naldini and Saraceno 2008). Tax deductions apply to individuals who pay income taxes and have dependent family members [i.e., a spouse, a child, or another cohabiting family member with no income or with an annual income of less than €2,840.51 (US$3096)] and last for as long as the family member is dependent. The amount is inversely proportional to household income and becomes null over a certain income threshold, depending on the number of children (SSEF 2008). The size of these tax deductions depends on the number of dependent family members, on whether a dependent family member is disabled, and, in the case of children, on their ages. Thus, the amount increases with the number of dependent family members, and especially members who are disabled or are under age three.

Low-income families are eligible for additional family allowances (*assegni al nucleo familiare*) based on income and the number of family members. In order to be eligible, the household annual income must be lower than an amount fixed annually by law, and 70 % of this income must come from non-self-employed work (PERFAR 2015). Minor children for whom allowances are claimed must be resident in Italy. Allowances are paid until the child (assuming he or she is not disabled) is 18 years old. They are higher for single-parent families with at least three dependent members and for families with members who are disabled (i.e., incapable of work).[19]

Over the past 15 years, there has been a debate about whether benefits to families with children or other dependents should be means tested—as they are at present—and whether they should be offered as tax deductions (as at present) or as cash payments. Positions in this debate differ according to whether the goal is income redistribution or fertility support. The debate is still open, but over the past 20 years family allowances for low-income families have remained at quite low levels, while tax deductions for dependent family members have increased. These measures may discourage low-income, low-skilled women from participating in the official labor market, and the poorest families are often excluded (Naldini and Saraceno 2008).

[19]For instance, in 2014, the monthly family allowance varied from €258 (US$281) for a family of four with an annual net income of less than €14,534 (US$15,806) to €0.03 (!) for a family of four with an annual net income of €77,625 (US$84,417).

A recent, temporary measure entitles dependent working mothers and atypical workers to receive a "baby-sitting voucher" of up to €600 (US$655) per month for a maximum of six months over the 11 months after their mandatory maternity leave, as an alternative to taking additional, elective leave. The voucher can be spent on either babysitting in the parents' home or on public or private daycare services. At the moment, data on take-up rates are not available.

Some one-off measures have been introduced to support childbearing, but without a long-term strategy or clear targets. The purpose appears to be merely symbolic. For example, a one-off baby bonus of €1000 (US$1092) was introduced by the Berlusconi government in 2004 and 2006, but the fact that it was introduced, withdrawn, and then reintroduced probably reduced any impact on fertility levels. The current Renzi government has just introduced a means-tested baby bonus that will be in effect from 2015 to 2018. Families who earn less than €12,000 (US $13,102) a year will receive €80 (US$87) a month for 36 months after a birth at any parity, and families who earn less than €7500 (US$8188) a year will receive twice the amount. This seems more a measure to alleviate child poverty than to promote fertility.

Some Italian regions have been more pro-active than the central government in providing child support. In January 2000, Friuli Venezia Giulia, one of five Italian regions with relatively high autonomy and low fertility, introduced a substantial bonus for mothers at the birth of a child. The bonus was limited by marital status (only married women were eligible) and citizenship (only Italians were eligible), and it increased by birth order, especially for a third birth. It was means tested, but the income threshold was fairly high. Boccuzzo et al. (2008) found that after the bonus was introduced fertility increased among low-educated (hence low-income) mothers, especially among those with two or more children. Between 2001 and 2004, total births increased by 2–3 %, while order-three or higher births increased by more than 20 %. Over the same period, fertility among childless women living in Friuli Venezia Giulia or low-educated women living in other Italian regions did not change.

Conclusions

Italian fertility began a steep decline in the mid-1960s. Today, fertility levels stagnate in the north and continue to decline in the south. Postponement of childbearing is extreme, and levels of permanent childlessness are steeply increasing across birth cohorts. The context for childbearing and childrearing appears particularly difficult in Italy, which is paradoxical in a country where the family institution is still important and family values permeate the culture.

Italian society appears to be particularly rigid, making it difficult to change social and economic structures in the face of new globalization challenges. Barriers persist that create deep inequality between generations (the old vs. the young), genders (men vs. women), and regions (north vs. south).

No single reason explains the persistence of very low fertility in Italy. Rather, a mix of institutional factors and rigidities makes the lives of potential parents more difficult in Italy than in many other countries, and these factors and rigidities occur in combination with very high expectancies of what a good parent should be. One of the key factors is the problematic transition to adulthood for young Italians, who are mostly excluded from the protected labor market, have lower entry salaries than their European peers, and face the risks associated with globalization relying solely on their parental families without any state support. Rental housing is scarce and expensive, forcing young people to try to purchase a first home. They have to pay a high down payment, however, and mortgages are hardly available for young workers—regardless of their future earning potential—so they have to rely on resources provided by their parental families. All these mechanisms act to delay the process of family formation.

The structure of the labor market itself, along with a pervading familist ideology and the lack of women in government institutions, makes it difficult to promote measures that facilitate work-family reconciliation. Italian working women pay a large penalty in the labor market when they become mothers, both in terms of wages foregone and a high drop-out rate. Significant gender inequalities in the division of labor in the home further increase the cost of motherhood, and institutions outside the home offer little support. The scarce supply of childcare, the rigidity of school and childcare-center schedules, the reliance entirely on family to provide extra-curricular activities for children—all these make parenting particularly difficult. The persistence of traditional cultural values that emphasize the family's (and in particular, the woman's) obligation to provide high-quality care and domestic services makes it difficult for parents (especially for mothers) to outsource childcare or domestic tasks and probably constrains the demand for public services that has led to policy change in other European countries.

Nevertheless, until now, the Italian social and economic system has found a sort of equilibrium, with low fertility as one key component. It is questionable, however, whether this system will be sustainable in the future. Many issues might compromise the current balance, including a growing demand for care for older people, women's aspirations that contrast with traditional family models, and developments that put the strong intergenerational transfer system into question. What might be the role of policies?

Today, Italy lacks a coherent system of policies to support childbearing and to facilitate work-family reconciliation. There are some positive measures (the system of parental leave, for instance), but their usefulness is limited by a social context that remains quite rigid in the face of changes linked to globalization and the gender revolution. Family policies—long absent in Italy—should be designed with the main aim of reducing rigidities that make steps in the life course, such as obtaining a home or having a child, particularly hazardous. The problem is not only the paucity of family policies, but also their inconsistency with policies in other areas, such as labor or pension reform. For instance, the age at retirement has recently been raised to 65 for both men and women, without taking into account that retired women often perform an important caregiving role for both the older generation and for grandchildren. This reform, which rightly recognizes the equality between men and women as workers, has not been accompanied by other reforms to respond to the needs of families, for example an increase in the supply of care services for both children and the elderly or an extension of school schedules to match the typical work day.

It is possible that a more inclusive and simplified labor market would foster a more rapid transition to adulthood, making it easier for young people to move away from their parents and start families of their own. In the past few years, several reforms have tried to reduce labor-market rigidities, but they are usually harshly condemned by trade unions that want to maintain protection for their members. Meanwhile, labor-market opportunities for young men and women have not greatly improved. The current Renzi government has just approved a Jobs Act (2015) that aims to lessen dualism in the labor market by reducing the inequalities between insiders and outsiders and introducing an increased level of social protection according to the length of work experience. Renzi's Jobs Act replaces the plethora of temporary and atypical contracts—which have been viewed as vehicles for employers to avoid risk while keeping workers in a precarious position—with a single, uniform contract that provides gradually increasing job protections over three years leading to a permanent position. While job protections are supposed to slowly rise the longer a worker remains under the new uniform contract, new staff are effectively on probation during those three years and can be dismissed as in previous atypical contracts.

One important target for family policy is to reduce the level of unintended childlessness among people in their 30s that may easily become irreversible. To achieve this goal, it will be important to invert the public transfer system that now heavily favors the old in order to increase the resources available for supporting young people. Policies to speed up the transition to adulthood could be useful as well as policies to reduce financial uncertainty, such as a minimum wage, greater protection for precarious workers, "flexicurity" measures that combine labor-market flexibility with security for workers, easier access to credit, and public (social) housing. Subsidized ART might also help involuntarily childless couples have children. At the same time, a campaign to provide correct information on the limit of biological fecundity should be promoted, because people frequently seem not to realize that the probability of conceiving decreases sharply after age 35.

A second target should be to increase the probability of having a second child. Effective work-family reconciliation policies should be implemented, not only for mothers but also for fathers. These would include more flexible work schedules, reversible part-time work for parents of young children, school schedules, including extracurricular activities, that match work schedules, and more daycare centers for children under three at low cost and with flexible schedules. It is important that such policies do not have a "boomerang effect" by increasing discrimination against women in the work place. To avoid such unintended consequences, bold gender policies should be adopted that promote and support the role of active fathers and lessen discrimination against working mothers. Policies addressing gender inequalities in the home will only be effective in the long run, but promoting gender sensitivity in school curricula could be a start.

To encourage Italians to have large families—a third important target—more generous financial support will be necessary, both in terms of family allowances and also as subsidies for the cost of raising children. For example, special tariffs could be offered for public transport or support for the cost of school books and materials.

A special effort should focus on sustaining fertility in the southern region by promoting economic development. To raise fertility in the south, it is essential to reduce unemployment rates among young people in the region. At the same time, special support for women's workforce participation might include a network of childcare services that are accessible, affordable, and of good quality.

To conclude, examples of good policies may be found not only abroad, but also within Italy. Indeed, there are two Italian "autonomous" provinces that have higher fertility levels than the EU average—Bolzano and Trento.[20] As of 2013, TFR was 1.64 births per woman in Bolzano and 1.60 in Trento, compared with an average of 1.55 for 28 EU member countries and 1.39 for Italy as a whole. These relatively high fertility levels are due not to any single policy measure, but rather to a "family-friendly" society as a whole. A combination of very good economic development, a sense of security, high women's labor-market participation, generous family policies at the local level, work flexibility in the public sector, an effort to promote work-family reconciliation through audit services for enterprises, and a solid network of childcare services, not only standard crèches, but also the more flexible *tagensmutter*—all these are behind the demographic success. In addition, these two provinces usually rank among the first in terms of quality of life, measured by a mix of indicators including safety, the environment, facilities, and cultural spaces. The extension of these good practices to other parts of the country would require long-term, consistent, and courageous policies combined with the appropriate investment of public resources. In a country with a large public debt and an old electorate, it will not be easy to find the financial resources and political support for the programs required to increase fertility. The future costs of inertia, however, will surely be greater.

[20]Trentino-Alto Adige/Südtirol constitutes a special case of home rule guaranteed by the Italian constitution to five regions, acknowledging their independence in relation to legislation, administration, and finance, in order to take into account cultural differences and protect linguistic minorities. The region as a whole is nearly powerless, however. The powers guaranteed by the constitution are mostly exercised by the two autonomous provinces within the region, Provincia Autonoma di Trento and Provincia Autonoma di Bolzano- Südtirol, with regional institutions limited to a coordinating role. The two provinces have their own budgets (mainly based on taxes from their residents) to support education (from kindergarten through university), healthcare, social affairs, and infrastructure.

Acknowledgments This chapter is based on research funded by the EU's Seventh Framework Program (FP7/2007-2013) under grant agreement no. 320116 for the Research Project on Families and Societies and from the University of Padova's 2013 Research Program under grant agreement no. CPDA139158 for the Research Project on Italian Families between Tradition and Innovation: New Types, New Challenges, and New Opportunities. I acknowledge the valuable help of Antonella Guarneri who provided me with the most recent estimates of fertility indicators computed by ISTAT and also with useful suggestions. I also acknowledge the valuable contribution of Marcantonio Caltabiano who allowed me to use his updated estimates of fertility trends in northern and southern Italy in Fig. 2.

References

Aassve, A., Billari, F. C., Mazzuco, S., & Ongaro, F. (2002). Leaving home: A comparative analysis of ECHP data. *Journal of European Social Policy, 12*(4), 259–275.

Aassve, A., Cottini, A., & Vitali, A. (2013). Youth prospects in a time of economic recession. *Demographic Research, 29*(36), 949–962.

Aassve, A., Iacovou, M., & Mencarini, L. (2007). Youth poverty and transition to adulthood in Europe. *Demographic Research, 15*(2), 21–50.

Aassve, A., Meroni, E., & Pronzato, C. (2012). Grandparenting and childbearing in the extended family. *European Journal of Population, 28*(4), 499–518.

Addabbo, T., & Giovannini, D. (2013). Italy country note. In P. Moss (Ed.), *International review of leave policies and related research 2013*. London: International Network on Leave Policies and Research. http://www.leavenetwork.org/fileadmin/Leavenetwork/Annual_reviews/2013_annual_review.pdf. Accessed August 6, 2015.

AISP (Italian Association for Population Studies). (2007). *Rapporto sulla popolazione 2007: L'Italia all'inizio del XXI secolo* [Population report 2007: Italy at the dawn of the 21st Century]. Bologna: Il Mulino.

Alesina, A., & Ichino, A. (2009). *L'Italia fatta in casa: Indagine sulla vera ricchezza degli italiani*. Milano: Mondadori.

Anxo, D., Mencarini, L., Pailhé, A., Solaz, A., Tanturri, M. L., & Flood, L. (2011). Gender differences in time use over the life course in France, Italy, Sweden, and the United States. *Feminist Economics, 17*(3), 159–195.

Arpino, B., Pronzato, C., & Tavares, L. P. (2014). The effect of grandparental support on mothers' labor market participation: An instrumental variable approach. *European Journal of Population, 30*, 369–390.

Baker, S., Miller, T., Bosoni, M. L., & Rossi, G. (2011). *Men, work and family life: A study of policy and practice in the UK and Italy*. https://radar.brookes.ac.uk/radar/file/e1fe167b-69c6-5f77-8615-66e3d73407cd/1/British_Academy_Fatherhood_literature_review%20May_2012_SBfinal.pdf. Accessed August 6, 2015.

Barbagli, M., Castiglioni, M., & Dalla Zuanna, G. (2003). *Fare famiglia in Italia: Un secolo di cambiamenti*. Bologna: Il Mulino.

Barbieri, P. (2011). Italy: No country for young men (and women). In S. Buchholz & D. Hofaecker (Eds.), *The flexibilization of European labor markets: The development of social inequalities in an era of globalization*. Cheltenham: Edward Elgar.

Battistin, E., De Nadai, M. & Padula, M. (2014). *Roadblocks on the Road to Grandma's House: Fertility Consequences of Delayed Retirement*. CEPR Discussion Papers 9945. C.E.P.R. Discussion Papers. London: Centre for Economic Policy Research.

Bernardi, F., & Poggio, T. (2004). Home ownership and social inequality in Italy. In K. Kurtz & H.-P. Blossfeld (Eds.), *Home ownership and social inequality in comparative perspective*. Stanford: Stanford University Press.

Billari, F. C., & Dalla Zuanna, G. (2008). *La rivoluzione nella culla: Il declino che non c'è*. Milan: Università Bocconi Editore.
Blossfeld, H. P., Klijzing, E., Mills, M., & Kurz, K. (Eds.). (2005). *Globalization, uncertainty, and youth in society*. London: Routledge.
Boccuzzo, G., Caltabiano, M., Dalla Zuanna, G., & Loghi, M. (2008). The impact of the bonus at birth on reproductive behaviour in a lowest-low fertility context: Friuli-Venezia Giulia (Italy) from 1989–2005. In A. H. Gauthier & D. Philipov (Eds.), *Vienna yearbook of population research* (pp. 125–147). Vienna: Austrian Academy of Sciences.
Bonarini F., Castiglioni, M., & Rosina, A. (1999). Infecondità, sterilità e tempi di attesa del concepimento. In P. De Sandre, A. Pinnelli, A. Santini (Eds.), *Nuzialità e fecondità in trasformazione: Percorsi e fattori di cambiamento*. Bologna: Il Mulino.
Bordone, V. (2009). Contact and proximity of older people to their adult children: A comparison between Italy and Sweden. *Population, Space. and Place, 15*(4), 359–380.
Bradshaw, J., & Finch, N. (2002). *A comparison of child benefit packages in 22 countries*. Research Report 174. London: Department for Work and Pensions, Social Research Division.
Caltabiano, M., Castiglioni, M., & Rosina, A. (2009). Lowest-low fertility: Signs of a recovery in Italy? *Demographic Research, 21*(23), 681–718.
Cooke, L. P. (2003). *The South revisited: The division of labor and family outcomes in Italy and Spain*. IRISS Working Paper Series no. 2003–12. Luxembourg: CEPS/Instead.
D'Alessio, G., & Gambacorta, R. (2007). *L'accesso all'abitazione di residenza in Italia*. Occasional Paper no. 9. Rome: Banca d'Italia.
Dalla Zuanna, G. (2001). The banquet of Aeolus: A familistic interpretation of Italy's lowest low fertility. *Demographic Research, 4*, 133–161.
Dalla Zuanna, G., & Micheli, G. (2004). *Strong family, familism, and lowest-low fertility*. Dordrecht: Kluwer Academic Press.
Dalla Zuanna, G., & Weber, G. (2012). *Cose da non credere*. Torino: Laterza.
de Mouzon, J., Goossens, V., Bhattacharya, S., Castilla, J. A., Ferraretti, A. P., Korsak, V., et al. (2012). Assisted reproductive technology in Europe, 2007: Results generated from European registers by ESHRE. *Human Reproduction, 27*(4), 954–966.
De Rose, A., Racioppi, F., & Zanatta, A. (2008). Delayed adaptation of social institutions to changes in family behavior. *Demographic Research, 19*, 665–704.
De Santis, G. (2004). The monetary cost of children: Theory and empirical estimates for Italy. *Genus, 60*(1), 161–183.
De Santis, G., & Livi Bacci, M. (2001). *Reflections on the economics of the fertility decline in Europe*. Paper presented at the EURESCO Conference on the Second Demographic Transition in Europe, Bad Herrenalb, Germany, 23–28 June.
Del Boca, D. (1997). Rigidità del mercato e costo dei figli. *Polis, 11*(1), 51–65.
Del Boca, D. (2003). *Low fertility and labor market participation of Italian women: Evidence and interpretations*. OECD Labor Market and Social Policy Occasional Paper no. 61. Paris: OECD.
Del Boca, D., Pasqua, S., & Pronzato, C. (2005). Employment and fertility in Italy, France, and the UK. *Labor, 19*(4), 51–77.
Del Boca, D., Pasqua, S., & Pronzato, C. (2009). Motherhood and market work decisions in institutional context: A European perspective. *Oxford Economic Papers, 61*(1), 147–171.
European Social Survey. (2008). *Integrated file Round four*. http://www.europeansocialsurvey.org/. Accessed September 14, 2015.
Eurostat. (2015a). *Eurostat: Your key to European statistics: Births and fertility*. http://ec.europa.eu/eurostat/web/population-demography-migration-projections/births-fertitily-data. Accessed September 15, 2015.
Eurostat. (2015b). *Women in the EU gave birth to their first child at almost 29 years on average*. Eurostat News Release 85/2015. http://ec.europa.eu/eurostat/documents/2995521/6829228/3-13052015-CP-EN.pdf/7e9007fb-3ca9-445f-96eb-fd75d6792965. Accessed August 6, 2015.
Facchini, C. (2002). La permanenza dei giovani nella famiglia di origine [The permanence of Italian young adults in the family]. In C. Buzzi, A. Cavalli, & A. de Lillo (Eds.), *Giovani del*

nuovo secolo: V Rapporto IARD sulla condizione giovanile in Italia (pp. 159–186). Bologna: Il Mulino.
Garibaldi, P., & Taddei, F. (2013). *Italy: A dual labor market in transition: Country case study on labor market segmentation.* Employment Working Paper no.144. Geneva: ILO.
ISTAT. (2007). *Essere madri in Italia.* Statistiche in breve: Famiglia e Società. Rome: Istituto Nazionale di Statistica.
ISTAT. (2011). *La conciliazione tra lavoro e famiglia: Anno 2010* [The balance between work and family: Year 2010]. Statistiche report, 28 dicembre 2011. Rome: Istituto Nazionale di Statistica.
ISTAT. (2014a). *Avere figli in Italia negli anni 2000: Approfondimenti dalle indagini campionarie sulle nascite e sulle madri.* Rome: Istituto Nazionale di Statistica. http://www.istat.it/it/files/2015/02/Avere_Figli.pdf.
ISTAT. (2014b). *Generazioni a confronto: Come cambiano i percorsi verso la vita adulta.* Rome: Istituto Nazionale di Statistica. http://www.istat.it/it/archivio/131369. Accessed August 6, 2015.
ISTAT. (2014c). *Natalità e fecondità della popolazione residente 2013.* Rome: Istituto Nazionale di Statistica.
ISTAT. (2014d). *Rapporto annuale: La situazione del paese nel 2013.* Rome: Istituto Nazionale di Statistica.
ISTAT. (2015a). *Demografia in cifre.* Rome: Istituto Nazionale di Statistica. http://demo.istat.it. Accessed September 15, 2015.
ISTAT. (2015b). *Indicatori demografici: Stime per l'anno 2014.* Rome: Istituto Nazionale di Statistica.
ISTAT. (2015c). *Noi Italia: 100 statistiche per capire il Paese in cui viviamo.* Rome: Istituto Nazionale di Statistica. http://noi-italia.istat.it/. Accessed September 15, 2015.
ISTAT. (2015d). *Tavole di fecondità regionali; Iscritti in Anagrafe per nascita.* Rome: Istituto Nazionale di Statistica. http://demo.istat.it/fecondita/index.html. Accessed September 15, 2015.
Kohler, H. P., Billari, F., & Ortega, J. A. (2002). The emergence of lowest low fertility in Europe during the 1990s. *Population and Development Review, 28*(4), 641–680.
León, M., & Migliavacca, M. (2013). Italy and Spain: Still the case of familistic welfare models? *Population Review, 52*(1), 25–42.
Livi Bacci, M. (2001). Too few children and too much family. *Daedalus, 130*(3), 139–156.
Livi Bacci, M. (Ed.) (2006). *Famiglie, nascite e politiche sociali.* Proceedings of International Conferences no. 224. Rome: Accademia Nazionale dei Lincei.
Livi Bacci, M. (2008). *Avanti giovani alla riscossa: Come uscire dalla crisi giovanile in Italia.* Bologna: Il Mulino.
Matysiak, A., & Vignoli, D. (2013). Diverse effects of women's employment on fertility: Insights from Italy and Poland. *European Journal of Population, 29*, 273–302.
Mazzucchelli, S. (2011). The impact of Law 53/00 (Regulation of Parental Leaves) on fathers: A good law disregard in daily life. In M. Cortini, G. Tanucci, & E. Morin (Eds.), *Boundaryless careers and occupational wellbeing* (pp. 241–255). Basingstoke: Palgrave Macmillan.
McDonald, P. (2000a). Gender equity in theories of fertility transition. *Population and Development Review, 26*(3), 427–439.
McDonald, P. (2000b). Gender equity, social institutions, and the future of fertility. *Journal of Population Research, 17*(1), 1–16.
Mencarini, L., Solaz, A., Paihilé, A., & Tanturri, M. L. (2010). *Two generations at home: The time cost of young adults living with their parents in France and Italy.* Carlo Alberto Notebooks no. 179. Moncalieri: Collegio Carlo Alberto. http://www.carloalberto.org/files/no.179.pdf. Accessed August 6, 2015.
Mencarini, L., & Tanturri, M. L. (2004). Time use, family role-set, and childbearing among Italian working women. *Genus, 60*(1), 111–137.
Mencarini, L., & Tanturri, M. L. (2006). Una casa per diventare grandi: I giovani italiani, l'autonomia abitativa e il ruolo della famiglia d'origine. *Polis, 3*, 405–430.

Miettinen, A., Rotkirch, A., Szalma, I., Donno, A., & Tanturri, M. L. (2015). *Increasing childlessness in Europe: Time trends and macro determinants.* FamiliesAndSocieties Working Paper no. 33. http://www.familiesandsocieties.eu/?page_id=131. Accessed August 6, 2015.
Mills, M., Mencarini, L., Tanturri, M. L., & Begall, K. (2008). Gender equity and fertility intentions in Italy and the Netherlands. *Demographic Research, 18*(1), 1–26.
Modena, F., Rondinelli, C., & Sabatini, F. (2014). Economic insecurity and fertility intentions: The case of Italy. *Review of Income and Wealth, 60*(S1), 233–255.
Mortelmans, D., Pasteels, I., Régnier-Loilier, A., Vignoli, D., & Mazzuco, S. (2015). *Analysis of determinants and prevalence of LAT.* FamiliesandSocieties Working Papers no. 25. http://www.familiesandsocieties.eu/wp-content/uploads/2015/01/WP25MortelmansEtAl.pdf. Accessed August 6, 2015.
Mulder, C. H., & Billari, F. C. (2010). Homeownership regimes and low fertility. *Housing Studies, 25*, 527–541.
Naldini, M., & Saraceno, C. (2008). Social and family policies in Italy: Not totally frozen, but far from structural reforms. *Social Policy and Administration, 42*(7), 733–748.
Nielson, J., & Stanfors, M. (2014). It's about time! Gender, parenthood, and household divisions of labor under different welfare regimes. *Journal of Family Issues, 35*(8), 1066–1088.
OECD. (2007). *Babies and bosses—reconciling work and family life: A synthesis of findings for OECD countries.* Paris: Organization for Economic Cooperation and Development.
OECD. (2011). *Doing better for families.* Paris: Organization for Economic Cooperation and Development.
OECD. (2012). *OECD employment outlook 2012.* Paris: Organization for Economic Cooperation and Development.
OECD. (2014). *OECD family database.* Paris: Organization for Economic Cooperation and Development. http://www.oecd.org/social/family/database. Accessed August 6, 2015.
Ongaro, F. (2001). Transition to adulthood in Italy. In M. Corijn & E. Klizing (Eds.), *Transition to adulthood in Europe.* Dordrecht: Kluwer Academic Publishers.
Pacelli, L., Villosio, C., & Pasqua, S. (2013). Labor market penalties for mothers in Italy. *Journal of Labor Research, 34*, 408–432.
Pagani, L., & Marenzi, A. (2008). The labor market participation of sandwich-generation Italian women. *Journal of Family and Economic Issues, 29*(3), 427–444.
Paihlé, A., Solaz, A., & Tanturri, M.L. (forthcoming). *The time cost of raising children in different fertility contexts: Evidence from France and Italy.* Families and Societies Working Papers.
PERFAR. (2015). *Population Europe resource finder and archive.* http://www.perfar.eu/. Accessed August 6, 2015.
Petmesidou, M. (1996). Social protection in Southern Europe: Trends and prospects. *Journal of Area Studies, 9*(4), 95–125.
Poggio, T. (2011). The housing pillar of the Mediterranean welfare regime: Relations between home ownership and other dimensions of welfare in Italy. In R. Ronald & M. Elsinga (Eds.), *Beyond home ownership: Housing, welfare, and society* (pp. 51–67). London: Routledge.
Reher, D. S. (1998). Family ties in Western Europe: Persistent contrasts. *Population and Development Review, 24*(2), 203–234.
Rossi, G. (2009). Development and dynamics of the family in the southern Europe. In O. Kapella, C. Rille-Pfeiffer, M. Rupp & N. F. Schneider (Eds.), *Die Vielfalt der Familie: Tagungsband zum 3. Europäischen Fachkongress Familienforschung* (pp. 365–89). Opladen: Verlag Barbara Budrich.
Ruspini, E., & Tanturri, M. L. (2015). Father involvement with young children in contemporary Italy. In M. A. Adler & K. Lenz (Eds.), *Father involvement in the early years: An international comparison of policy and practice* (pp. 96–126). Bristol: The Policy Press.
Santini, A. (1995). *Continuità e discontinuità nel comportamento riproduttivo delle donne italiane del dopoguerra: Tendenze generali della fecondità delle coorti nelle ripartizioni tra il 1952 e 1991.* Working Paper no. 53. Florence: Department of Statistics "G. Parenti."
Saraceno, C. (1994). The ambivalent familism of the Italian welfare state. *Social Politics, 1*(1), 60–82.

Saraceno, C. (2003). *Mutamenti della famiglia e politiche sociali in Italia* (2nd ed.). Bologna: Il Mulino.

Sironi, E., & Rosina, A. (2012). *The problematic transition to adulthood in Italy: Comparison before and after the beginning of the global crisis.* Paper presented at the Conference on The Transition to Adulthood after the Great Recession. Milan: Bocconi University, 25–26 October. http://transitions.s410.sureserver.com/wp-content/uploads/2011/08/Rosina-_The-Problematic-Transition-to-Adulthood-in-Italy.pdf. Accessed August 6, 2015.

Smith Koslowski, A. (2008). *Who Cares? European fathers and the time they spend looking after their children.* Saarbrücken: VDM Verlag.

SSEF (Scuola di formazione del Ministero dell'economia e delle finanze). (2008). *Libro Bianco: L'imposta sul reddito delle persone fisiche e il sostegno alle famiglie.* http://www.ssef.it/sites/ssef/files/Documenti/Rivista%20Tributi/Suppleme. Accessed September 15, 2015.

Tanturri, M. L. (2010). Demografia e lavoro femminile: Le sfide della conciliazione [Demography and female labor market participation: The work and family balance challenges]. In M. Livi Bacci (Ed.), *La demografia del capitale umano* (pp. 100–122). Bologna: Il Mulino.

Tanturri, M. L. (2012). How much does a child cost its parents in terms of time in an aged society? An estimate for Italy with time-use survey data. In G. De Santis (Ed.), *The family, the market, or the state? Intergenerational support under pressure in ageing societies.* International Studies in Population Vol. 10. Berlin: Springer/IUSSP.

Tanturri, M. L., & Mencarini, L. (2008). Childless or childfree? An insight into voluntary childlessness in Italy. *Population Development Review, 34*(1), 51–77.

Tanturri, M. L., & Mencarini, L. (2009). *Fathers' involvement in daily childcare activities in Italy: Does a work-family reconciliation issue exist?* ChilD n. 22/2009. http://www.child-centre.unito.it/papers/child22_2009.pdf. Accessed September 16, 2015.

Tomassini, C., Wolf, D. A., & Rosina, A. (2003). Parental housing assistance and parent-child proximity in Italy. *Journal of Marriage and the Family, 65*, 700–715.

Trifiletti, R. (1999). Southern European welfare regimes and the worsening position of women. *Journal of European Social Policy, 9*(1), 49–64.

Vignoli, D., Rinesi, F., & Mussino, E. (2013). A home to plan the first child? Fertility intentions and housing conditions in Italy. *Population, Space, and Place, 19*, 60–71.

Zagheni, E., & Zannella, M. (2013). The life cycle dimension of time transfers in Europe. *Demography, 29*(35), 937–948.

Zanini, G. (2011). Abandoned by the state, betrayed by the church: Italian experiences of cross-border reproductive care. *Reproductive BioMedicine Online, 23*(5), 565–572.

Transition from Anti-natalist to Pro-natalist Policies in Taiwan

Meilin Lee and Yu-Hsuan Lin

Abstract Taiwan experienced and completed a demographic transition during the twentieth century. In 1964, the government introduced a family planning program aimed at reducing the birth rate in order to slow down Taiwan's rapid population growth. Fertility reached the below-replacement level, generally defined as 2.1 births per woman, in 1984. After this, fertility decline accelerated, bringing Taiwan into the list of ultra-low-fertility countries. This chapter examines how fertility changed in Taiwan and how new policies were formulated in an effort to counter low fertility and bring about a fertility increase.

Keywords Fertility rates · Pro-natalist policies · Taiwan

Taiwan experienced and completed a demographic transition during the twentieth century. The death rate started to decline in the 1920s (Barclay 1954; Chen 1979; Wang and Chen 1986). After that, the growing gap between birth rates and death rates brought about accelerated population growth. After World War II, the annual birth rate reached a peak of more than 40 births per 1000 population in the 1950s and then began a steady decline that has persisted until the present.

The government initiated a nationwide family planning program in 1964 aimed at controlling the number of births. Under the government birth-control policy, the birth rate declined to about 20 births per 1000 in the early 1980s. Population growth remained high in the 1980s, however, due to the extremely low death rate, at around 4 deaths per 1000 population, and the large number of women in the population at reproductive age (Sun and Chang 1989). Concerned by the apparently growing pressure of population growth, the government announced yet another, stronger wave of family planning programs in 1983. Ironically, in the next year, 1984, the total fertility rate (TFR) dipped to 2.05 births per woman, below the replacement

M. Lee (✉)
Department of Social Work, Asia University, Taichung, Taiwan
e-mail: mlleej@gmail.com

Y.-H. Lin
Health Promotion Administration, Ministry of Health and Welfare, Taipei, Taiwan

R.R. Rindfuss and M.K. Choe (eds.), *Low Fertility, Institutions, and their Policies*, DOI 10.1007/978-3-319-32997-0_10

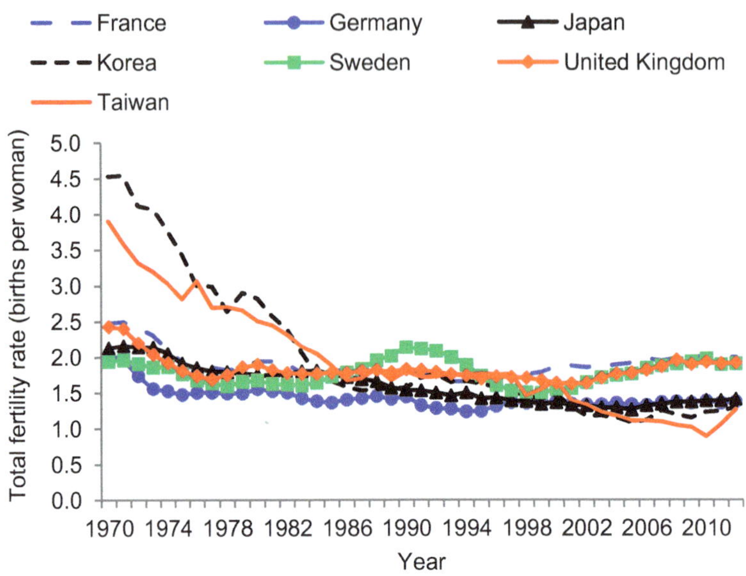

Fig. 1 Total fertility decline in Taiwan and other countries, 1970–2012 Ministry of Interior (2013), Population Reference Bureau (2015)

level of 2.1. During the same year, however, the natural increase in population still maintained a moderate rate, at 14.8 per 1000.

The Demography of Low Fertility in Taiwan

Steep Fertility Decline

Fertility decline occurred in Taiwan during the second half of the twentieth century. The TFR reached a peak of 7.04 births per woman in 1951, and then declined to 4.0 by 1970 and to below-replacement level by 1984. Between 1986 and 1997, Taiwan's TFR stagnated at around 1.75, moderately below replacement level, but then it started another period of decline. In 2003, the official TFR published by the government was 1.23 births per woman, which defined Taiwan as one of the lowest-low fertility countries (defined as a TFR of 1.3 or less) in the world (Kohler et al. 2002). In the 2000s, other advanced economies in East Asia also experienced lowest-low fertility, but Taiwan's fertility rate was even lower than that of Japan or South Korea. Taiwan's TFR was 0.895 in 2010, supposedly the lowest recorded value for any country with a non-urban population that is more than one-quarter of the total[1] (Fig. 1).

[1]Urban is defined as a settlement with a population of more than 20,000 and a population density of more than 300 per km^2. According to this definition, 26.8 % of Taiwan's population is non-urban (DGBAS 1980).

Table 1 Age-specific fertility rates (births per 1000 women age 15–49) and total fertility rates (lifetime average births per woman) in Taiwan, 1960–2010 (Ministry of Interior 1950–2013)

	Age-specific fertility rates								
	Women age 15–19	Women age 20–24	Women age 25–29	Women age 30–34	Women age 35–39	Women age 40–44	Women age 45–49	TFR	Share of TFR for women age 30 and above
1950	61	246	297	269	191	112	30	6.03	50
1960	48	253	333	255	169	79	13	5.75	49
1970	40	238	293	147	59	20	3	4.00	29
1980	33	180	200	69	16	4	1	2.52	18
1990	17	100	159	68	15	2	0	1.80	24
2000	14	72	132	90	24	3	0	1.68	35
2010	4	23	55	65	28	4	0	0.90	54
2013	4	22	62	80	39	6	0	1.07	59

Reduced and Delayed Childbearing

Taiwan's fertility decline since 1950s was composed of two distinct periods, characterized by different fertility behaviors. Before the 1980s, there was a large reduction of fertility among women at all reproductive ages, particularly at higher ages, which contributed to a drop in TFR from 6.0 births per woman to near the replacement level of 2.1 births per woman. After the 1980s, fertility dropped to below replacement level, and the age pattern of childbearing showed a dramatic reduction of fertility among women under age 30 and a widespread delay of childbearing until age 35–39.[2] Table 1 shows that the share of fertility among women age 30 and above increased from 18 % in 1980 to 24 % in 1990, 35 % in 2000, 54 % in 2010, and 59 % in 2013. The mean age of childbearing increased from 25.4 in 1980, to 27.0 in 1990, 28.2 in 2000, 31.6 in 2010, and 32.6 in 2013. Since 2010, the prime age of childbearing has shifted from 25–29 to 30–34, and fertility among women aged 35–44 has actually increased.

Changing Marriage Patterns and Fertility Decline

Both marriage patterns and marital fertility have changed in Taiwan. Several demographers have applied a decomposition technique to discern the relative effect of nuptiality and marital fertility decline, making an assumption that the decision to

[2]In an era of ultra-low fertility, astrological concerns also affect fertility rates in specific years. The drop in fertility in 2010 and the jump in 2012 were due to the inauspicious Tiger year followed by the favorable Dragon year in the zodiac cycle of the Chinese calendar.

marry comes before the decision to have children. Chang (2005) found that during 1965–1980, about two-thirds of the decline in Taiwan's crude birth rate (CBR) was a result of the decrease in marital fertility, and the other one-third was due to a decrease in nuptiality. In contrast, the effect of nuptiality has exceeded that of marital fertility since 1980, accounting for almost the entire fertility decline.

Chen and Yang (2005) found that before 1986, both nuptiality and marital fertility affected the TFR, as older women stopped having children. Then after 1986, nuptiality and marital fertility operated in opposite directions. Nuptiality declined significantly due to the increasing higher education and labor participation of young women, while marital fertility was actually rising. This increase in marital fertility was a result of conscious decisions among young adults—those who chose to marry planned to have children. Chen and Yang (2005) concluded that child-bearing has become a functional cause of marriage among young women. In many cases, marriage seems to be initiated by women who are cohabiting with their partners and become pregnant. According to Taiwan's 1998 KAP (knowledge, attitude, practice) survey, 54.5 % of married women age 20–24 were pregnant before they married (Lin et al. 2002). Among women age 25–29, the proportion was 34.4 %, among women age 30–34, it was 30.1 %, and among women age 35–39, it was 22.6 %.

Looking at women age 20–29, Luoh (2007) found that the proportion who were married declined during the entire period from 1965 to 2005, while marital fertility decreased during 1975–1985 and then increased during 1985–1995 and again during 1995–2005. For the most recent years, 1995–2005, the decline of nuptiality had a greater effect on the TFR than the increase in marital fertility. Thus, Taiwan's TFR would be even lower due to nuptiality decline if the trend had not been compensated to some extent by an increase in marital fertility. For the 25–29 age group, Luoh concluded that nuptiality decline contributed about 70 % to the decline in fertility.

These studies assume that couples decide to marry after they have decided to have children. It might be the case, however, that marriage and fertility decisions are made jointly or even that couples who want to postpone childbearing decide to postpone marriage so that they do not experience pressure from others to have a child soon after marriage. Until there is better evidence on these causal issues, the decomposition studies need to be interpreted with caution.

Marriage in Taiwan used to be early and universal compared with the pattern in Western countries (Hajnal 1965). Nuptiality has undergone tremendous change over the past decades, however. The singulate mean age at marriage was 20–21 in 1960, and then increased from 22.1 in 1970 to 23.8 in 1980 and from 25.8 in 1990 to 29.2 in 2010. Thus marriage has typically been postponed by about eight years in the half century since the 1960s and by about six years just since the 1980s.

The proportion of women currently married at ages 15–19 and 20–24 declined sharply between 1980 and 2010, from 5.0 to 0.4 % and from 39.9 to 4.4 %, respectively. For ages 25–29, the proportion currently married decreased from 78.9

to 23.8 % over the 30-year period. For ages 30–34, the group that currently has the highest fertility, the proportion currently married has dropped by 37.4 % points, from 90.0 % in 1980 to 52.6 % in 2010.

Low Extramarital Fertility

The effect of the nuptiality decline on fertility levels has not been mitigated by an increase in extramarital births. In many Northern and Western European countries, non-marital births contribute 20 % or more to maintain a post-transition, moderately low fertility (Suzuki 2005). In Taiwan, however, extramarital births are considered disgraceful, and there is strong social pressure against childbearing among cohabiting couples or single persons. Atoh et al. (2004) attribute the low incidence of extramarital births in Japan, South Korea, Taiwan, and Singapore to the persistence of the patriarchal family system and cultural heritage of Confucianism, which strongly censors childbearing among unmarried women. Given these attitudes, a nuptiality decline affects fertility in a direct way and with full force.

From 1998 to 2010, the proportion of extramarital births in Taiwan fluctuated at around 3.6–4.2 %, higher than in earlier decades when the proportion was about 1.0 % but still very low by international standards. The small proportion of extramarital births suggests that in the post-transition era, Taiwan's nuptiality decline exercises an important and direct impact on fertility.

Proximate Determinants of Fertility

The decline in nuptiality does not fully explain fertility decline, however, indicating that there are other, proximate determinants associated with a drop in marital fertility (Bongaarts 1978). The use of contraception among married women has remained very high for decades. In 1980, 82 % of married women age 22–39 had ever used contraception, increasing to 93 % in 1985 and 95 % in 1992, and then declining to 90 % in 1998. In 1980, 70 % of these women were currently practicing contraception, increasing to 78 % in 1985 and 81 % in 1992, and then declining to 75 % in 1998 (Lin et al. 2002). A 2012 survey of the pregnancy histories of married women showed that, on average, 25.8 % of pregnancies were wasted, so that 2.2 pregnancies led to only 1.5 live births. Table 2 shows that among women age 20–24, 38.6 % of pregnancies were terminated by induced abortion, compared with only 17.2 % of pregnancies for all women. Of course, some suspect that Taiwan's fertility decline could also be attributed to either a lack of sexual intercourse or an increase in sterility as a result of the rising stress of modern life.

Table 2 Lifetime pregnancy histories, outcomes, and wastage rates, 2012 (Health Promotion Administration 2014)

Ages	Pregnancies	Live births	Still births	Miscarriages	Induced abortions	Pregnancy wastage (%)	Sample size
20–24	1.81	0.96	0.00	0.04	0.70	40.92	21
25–29	1.73	1.45	0.00	0.13	0.32	26.96	169
30–34	2.00	2.02	0.02	0.13	0.32	24.09	453
35–39	2.48	2.44	0.01	0.21	0.41	25.92	588
Total	2.15	1.54	0.01	0.16	0.37	25.77	1333

Socioeconomic Determinants of Fertility

Ideal Number of Children

To explain the very low fertility in Taiwan, it is necessary to examine people's attitudes toward childbearing. Figure 2 shows changes in the ideal number of children and the average number of live births among married women age 22–39 from 1965 to 2012. Although the ideal number of children has been declining, it was still 2.04 in 2012, considerably higher than the actual fertility rate. This discrepancy points to the importance of obstacles that people experience in trying to fulfill their desire for children.

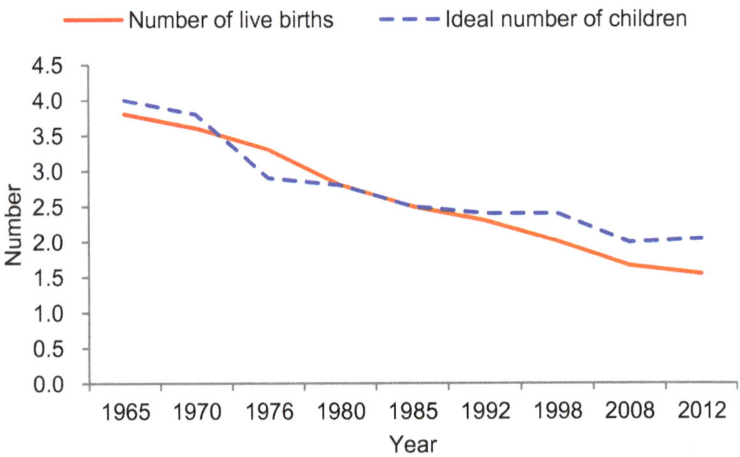

Fig. 2 Ideal number of children and average live births in Taiwan, 1965–2012 (Taiwan Provincial Institute of Family Planning 1992; Health Promotion Administration 2014)

High Direct Cost of Children

The rising cost of educating children is thought to be a crucial factor in explaining Taiwan's fertility decline. Increases in national gross domestic product (GDP) and family income cannot offset these rising costs.

The trade-off between quality and quantity of children has become a prominent concern for the whole society. College enrollment rates illustrate this trend in rising expectations. Figure 3 shows that net college enrollment rates were 11.86 % for men and 10.25 % for women in 1980, rising to 66.02 % for men and 74.11 % for women in 2012 (Ministry of Education 2014). This impressive expansion of enrollment rates signifies a universal expectation of higher education, with a university or college degree seen as a basic requirement for young people. The expansion of higher education has attracted tremendous private and public investment during this period. In 2012, around 70 % of college students were attending private institutions, where tuition is, on average, three times higher than in public colleges or universities.

Parents also incur significant education costs due to the widespread reliance on private cram schools. It is quite common for students to attend cram schools for extra instruction—either in the evening after school, on weekends, or during school vacations—in order to gain acceptance to a good high school or university. Students might be choosing to attend cram schools themselves, or they might be forced by their parents. In many cases, students spend one full year in a cram school in order to get good test results and gain admission to their preferred university. Tuition costs for cram schools are higher than for ordinary schools because they employ well-known teachers with skillful methods and they focus on preparing for important tests.

In recent years, the number of cram schools has increased, but the applicant pool has shrunk due to long-term low fertility, so the schools have expanded into new

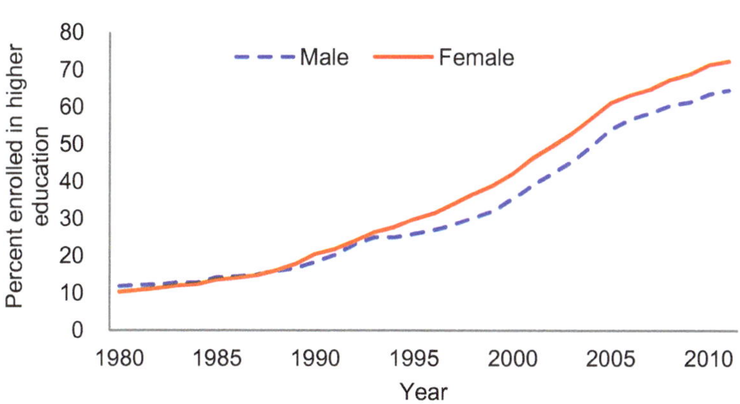

Fig. 3 College enrollment rates for males and females in Taiwan, 1980–2012 (Ministry of Education 2014)

markets, helping university graduates pass professional examinations for a variety of occupations, including government service. Considering all the educational levels and services now required to get a good job, obtain financial self-sufficiency, and enjoy a satisfying life, the cost of children has become very high, imposing a serious burden on Taiwanese parents.

Another aspect of the increasing cost of raising children is the income that women forego if they leave the labor market to become mothers. This has become a more important issue in Taiwan as economic development has increased occupational opportunities for women and women are spending more time in the labor force. Not only has there been an increase in the opportunity cost of childcare as more women have the option to be employed outside of the home, but the persistent gender-based division of labor within the home has made marriage less attractive to women and promoted an increase in the divorce rate.

Female labor-force participation among the major reproductive age groups increased substantially between 1980 and 2012. Figure 4 shows that growth in labor-force participation has been greatest for women age 25–29, doubling from 41.6 % in 1980 to 89.2 % in 2012. Over the same 32-year period, labor-force participation increased from 39.7 to 78.1 % among women age 30–34 and from 43.0 to 74.0 % among women age 35–39 (Statistical Bureau 2014). For women age 20–24, labor-force participation first increased and then decreased, mainly owing to expanding enrollment in higher education, which stood at 54.7 % in 2012.

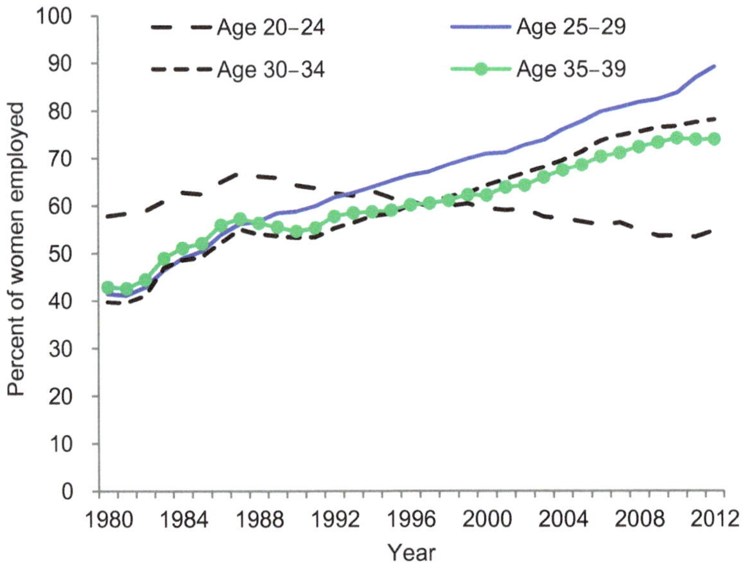

Fig. 4 Female labor-force participation rates in Taiwan, 1980–2012 (Statistical Bureau 2014)

The effect of female labor-force participation on fertility can be linked directly to an incompatibility between work and childcare. This role conflict results in women leaving the labor market after marriage or after childbirth and resuming employment after their children are older. In many places, such behavioral practices can be verified by an M-shaped curve in the age pattern of female labor-force participation. In Taiwan, the age pattern of female labor-force participation showed a pronounced M-shaped curve in 1980, but a much weaker curve in 2012, when labor-force participation reached very high levels among women in their mid-20s and then declined gradually among older age groups (Fig. 5). Compared to 1980, the 2012 pattern not only demonstrates a large increase in labor-force participation but also illustrates a greater attachment to employment with less interruption by marriage and childbearing. Not marrying or postponing marriage might be one way for employed women to ease the conflict between working and bearing or caring for children, therefore creating a tempo effect that reduces fertility. Among women who work and also have pre-school-age children, another important question is how they manage to balance their work and family responsibilities.

Finally, one key factor that adds to the expense of marrying and having children is the difficulty of obtaining housing. Housing costs have soared out of reach for young workers, not to mention post-graduate students without regular incomes, particularly in urban areas where institutes of higher education are usually located. No graduate school, neither public nor private, is capable of providing housing for adult students with dependent families. Rental prices have also risen in major cities, making it difficult for young adults to move out from their parents' households if they wish to marry or even cohabit.

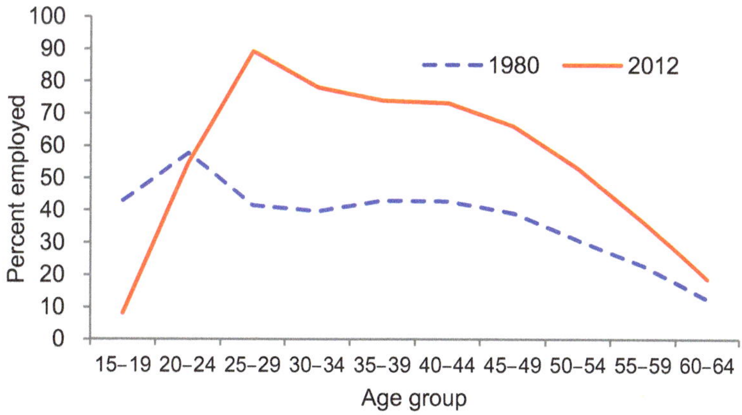

Fig. 5 Age pattern of female labor-force participation in Taiwan, 1980 and 2012 (Statistical Bureau 2014)

Table 3 Major caregiver for children under age three, 1980–2013 (%) (DGBAS 2013)

Year	Major caregiver (%)					
	Child's parents	Relatives	Babysitters	Foreign servants	Childcare centers	Total
1980	82.75	14.64	2.41	–	0.20	100.00
1990	69.72	24.15	5.94	–	0.19	100.00
2000	67.78	23.90	7.72	0.20	0.40	100.00
2010	54.90	34.74	9.37	0.30	0.70	100.00
2013	51.82	38.08	9.07	0.27	0.76	100.00

Little Use of Non-family Childcare

According to a series of Women's Marriage, Fertility, and Employment Surveys in Taiwan, most children under age three are cared for by their own parents, primarily by their mothers. Table 3 shows that 82.8 % of children were cared for by a parent in 1980. Although this proportion has declined over the past 30 years, in 2013, more than one-half (51.8 %) were still cared for by their own parents. Relatives, and in particular the child's grandparents, are usually the second most important option for childcare. In fact, grandparents' role in childcare has become more important, increasing from 14.6 % in 1980 to 38.1 % in 2013. Together, parents and grandparents account for 90 % of childcare for children under age three.

Only 9.1 % of children in this age group were cared for by babysitters in 2013, including babysitting at the child's home or at a family nursery or babysitter's home. Most parents who choose to entrust a child's care to non-relatives are taking their children to a babysitter's home. This is for financial reasons, as it is less expensive than employing a babysitter in the child's home. The enrollment rate of children under three in daycare centers is very low in Taiwan. While enrollment has increased recently, it has never exceeded 1 %.

Comparing the utilization of childcare services in Japan and South Korea with levels in other Organization for Cooperation and Development (OECD) countries, Suzuki (2013) pointed out that the much greater development of non-parental childcare services and higher rates of utilization in Northern and Western European countries improve the compatibility between work and family. This helps these countries avoid lowest-low fertility even with post-modern economic and social changes. In 2010, enrollment rates in non-parental, early-childhood care services were only 28.3 % in Japan and 37.7 % in South Korea (Suzuki 2013, p. 28). They are lower still in Taiwan.

The underdevelopment of early-childhood care services in Taiwan deserves further investigation. In addition to a lack of public investment, another factor might be cultural values that emphasize strong family ties, favoring maternal care for children supplemented by relatives if mothers are working.[3]

[3]The strong family ties characteristic of cultural values in Taiwan emphasize reciprocity between generations. This reciprocity leads to grandparents taking care of small children for their employed

Gender Equity in Public and Private Life

In the process of industrialization and modernization, there have been significant improvements in the status of women. Progress has been made in a number of areas: considerable increase in the number of female college students, higher female labor-force participation, a growing number of female professional and technical workers with high incomes and prestige, shrinking of gender wage differentials, improvements in legal protection for gender equality in employment,[4] and improvements in legal protection from family violence.[5]

In 2013, Taiwan scored 0.055[6] on the United Nations Development Program (UNDP) Gender Inequality Index (GII),[7] which is lower than the scores of its Asian neighbors, Japan (0.138), South Korea (0.101), and Singapore (0.090) (UNDP 2015). This suggests that women in Taiwan enjoy a higher status than women in the neighboring countries, particularly in public life.

Although working mothers often get help from co-resident relatives, they still face substantial difficulties in combining employment, housework, and childcare. Among married couples, dual-earner families prevail as women have become more educated and more likely to hold full–time jobs. Among married women age 25–34, more than one-half live in dual-earner families, and this has been the case since 2006. Yet the division of labor between men and women is quite unequal. Time-use surveys show that employed women work an average of 7.9 h per day and employed men work an average 8.4 h. However, these surveys also show that men spend an average of 0.5 h per day on family work, while women spend 2.4 h (DGBAS 2008a).

One effect of the difficulty women face in balancing work and family responsibilities might be to lower the attraction of marriage and motherhood, particularly as women enjoy a higher status in the public sphere. The Survey of Social Development Trends asked women and men age 35–44 who were unmarried their reason for remaining single (DGBAS 2002). Both men and women mentioned a

---

(Footnote 3 continued)

daughters or daughters-in-law. It is also represented in the pattern of living arrangements for the elderly. The Elderly Person's Living Conditions Survey in 2009 showed that 68.5 % of the elderly were living with a son or daughter, 18.8 % were living as part of a couple, and 9.2 % were living alone. Only 2.8 % lived in an institution (Ministry of Interior 2009). Thus, stem family households still remain prevalent, not yet replaced through the forces of industrialization and urbanization.

[4]The Act of Gender Equality in Employment was enacted in 2002.

[5]The Domestic Violence Prevention Act was enacted in 1998.

[6]Since Taiwan is not a member of the United Nations, the index is calculated by the Taiwan government's Directorate-General of Budget, Accounting, and Statistics (DGBAS 2008b) following technical instructions from UNDP.

[7]The Gender Inequality Index (GII) is a composite measure reflecting inequality between women and men in three dimensions: reproductive health, empowerment, and the labor market. It measures the human-development costs of gender inequality. The GII values range from 0 to 1, and the higher the GII value, the greater the disparity between the status of women and men.

major cause as "not met the ideal mate." In addition, women mentioned "satisfied with present unmarried condition" or "afraid of unhappy marriage," while men tended to mention an economic reason such as "afraid I might be incapable of filling the bread-earner's role."

McDonald (2000), in his theory of gender equity and fertility transition, suggested that the combination of low gender equality within the family and high gender equality outside of the family may lead to low fertility. The disparity between women's public and familial status may lead them to postpone marriage or not marry at all. This pattern strongly affects childbearing behavior in Taiwan, where educated, working women stay single longer and rarely dare to have an extramarital birth. Women in other Asian countries, such as South Korea and Japan, show similar patterns with similar effects on fertility (Suzuki 2005).

Population Policies Over the Years

Slow Shift Away from Anti-natalist Policies

Starting in 1964, the Taiwanese government began introducing family planning programs aimed at lowering the birth rate and slowing population growth. The benefits of small families were advocated through various information, education, and communication programs. Family planning workers were employed in health stations in every township, making door-to-door visits and disseminating contraceptive services. Contraceptive use soon became universal among reproductive-age women in both rural and urban areas and across all education levels. Periodic knowledge, attitude, and practice (KAP) surveys have consistently shown a very high level of contraceptive acceptance and use. In 1987, the World Watch Institute ranked Taiwan's level of contraceptive use at the top among 95 developing countries (World Watch Institute 1987).

Taiwan first reached below-replacement fertility in 1984. At this point, demographers became concerned about population aging and called for a modification of the birth-control policy (Tu and Chen 1989). Among demographic researchers, there was a paradigm shift from a concern about fertility to worries about population aging. Beginning in 1988, Taiwan's national population goals were reassessed. The 1992 Guideline for Population Policy stressed a revision of policy goals from reducing population growth to maintaining a reasonable growth rate.

This 1992 revision of population policy reflected an academic concern but did not induce any practical social reform. A climate of birth control with an anti-natalist emphasis still prevailed among the general public, justified by the link between Taiwan's family planning program and rapid economic progress. Between 1984 and 1996, the TFR remained stagnant at around 1.8–2.0. Then in 1997, 13 years after the TFR reached below-replacement level, fertility entered a new phase of accelerating decline.

Decomposition analyses found that the major component of this new fertility decline was the postponement of marriage. At this point, government policy had favored the encouragement of marriage for some years, but no concrete measures had been put forth that could be considered effective. Since 1980, the behavioral patterns, such as cohabitation, postulated by the theory of the second demographic transition (Van de Kaa 1987) had become more prevalent in Taiwan and in other advanced East Asian countries, but without any increase in extramarital births (Lesthaeghe 2010).

The population-aging issue gradually gained public attention in the mid-1990s, particularly in 1993 when the proportion of elderly in the Taiwanese population first exceeded 7 %, a signpost that the United Nations uses to define a population as aging. Then in 1997, the fertility level, which had stagnated at slightly below replacement, resumed its decline. Low fertility and population aging problems sparked public discussion. Proposals to introduce a universal pension system and to adopt a pro-natalist policy were both hot topics, but the pension plan was viewed more favorably than the pro-natalist proposal.

Specifically, the government's pro-natalist proposals confronted opposition from environmentalist and feminist groups. The experience of rapid industrialization on a highly populous island has led the Taiwanese people to identify overpopulation as a serious social problem. Some degree of depopulation was even viewed as a favorable relief from the long-term accumulated pressure of resource over-exploitation and environmental destruction. Any intention to boost fertility that might imply another wave of population increase was closely scrutinized and criticized by environmentalist groups afraid of further worsening Taiwan's crowded environment.

Feminist groups were not happy with pro-natalist policies in general and with some policy measures in particular. Feminist critics argued that pro-natalist reasoning overstates the economic consequences of labor-force shortages without a gender perspective. Discussions organized by feminist activists and scholars forcefully contended that pro-natalist government interventions would work against gender equality (FWRPD 2000). In fact, any policies that tried to target birth numbers or birth rates, either anti-natalist or pro-natalist, were viewed by feminists as utilizing women's reproductive function to fulfill the government's objectives, humiliating women and depriving them of autonomy. Any fertility goal set in terms of quantity implies that women will have to undergo a certain amount of childbearing to meet the goals of a patriarchal state (FWRPD 2003, 2006). With support from international colleagues (Martin-Matthews 2000; Mitchell 2000), activists in Taiwan managed to slow the progress of pro-natalist policy implementation in the late 1990s and early 2000s. In general, the influence of feminist groups on social policies gained momentum during this period.[8]

---

[8]Some feminist groups supported the Democratic Progressive Party (DPP) in the 1990s. When the DPP won the presidential election in 2000, ending the Nationalist Party's half century in power, these feminist groups gained a strong influence on the government's social policies. A Committee for the Promotion and Development of Women's Rights was set up in 2000 and played an active role during the years of the DPP regime.

Introduction of Pro-natalist Policies

Fertility in Taiwan has dropped to a new record low every year of the 21st century. The TFR was 1.40 births per woman in 2001, 1.34 in 2002, 1.23 in 2003, 1.18 in 2004, 1.12 in 2005, and 0.895 in 2010, supposedly the lowest ever recorded in the world. Despite opposition, this trend eventually led the government to plan the introduction of new population policies (Hsieh 2004).

A Population Policy Guideline was revised in 2006, with active participation from feminist groups. The Guideline rejected conventional quantitative indicators but stressed the qualitative aspects of population development including ecological equilibrium and social justice. Issues covered included the equitable sharing of childcare by men and women, relief of women's traditional burdens in the household, and support for women's participation in the labor force. Direct measures, such as a universal child allowance that transfers cash to families with young dependent children, were disputed because they implied a family wage for women who stay at home and thus reduced women's equal status in the labor force. Other measures, such as a proposal to introduce pre-abortion counseling to reinforce pro-life considerations, were rejected as threatening to women's autonomy.

In March 2008, the government introduced a Population White Paper that tried to incorporate the concerns of feminists, demographers, and economists. The White Paper consists of three distinct parts—child policy, elderly policy, and immigration policy. The first part addresses the problem of ultra-low fertility with countermeasures to halt further fertility decline, mitigate problems associated with population aging, and ease the extent of depopulation in the future. The second part includes measures to meet the needs of a nearly quadrupling elderly population in coming decades. The third part addresses the abrupt rise in the number of cross-border migrants with measures such as multicultural adaptation, social security, and sensitive political issues regarding Taiwan's relationship with mainland China. The White Paper was amended in 2012 and 2013, without altering the original framework but laying out more specific measures and performance indicators (Lee et al. 2007; Ministry of Interior 2008, 2013).

The first version of the White Paper did not state any specific quantitative fertility target, but rather expressed a policy direction for countering the trend toward further fertility decline. In the 2013 revision, the government set a goal of 180,000 births per annum over the next decade, the number required to maintain a natural population increase. This number corresponds to a crude birth rate of around 75 per 1000 population.

The measures put forward to counter the trend toward lower fertility are organized as seven strategies: (1) improving marriage opportunities and rebuilding family values; (2) improving the system for reproductive care; (3) constructing affordable, quality-assured, and accessible early-childhood care and education facilities; (4) providing economic support for families with children; (5) building a family-friendly work environment; (6) implementing a maternity and parental leave allowance; and (7) improving the system for child protection. In sum, a slogan of "happy to marry, willing to have children, and able to raise them" was constructed as the fundamental concept for a pro-natalist policy. Table 4 summarizes the development of pro-natalist policy measures in Taiwan.

Implementing Pro-natalist Policies

Taiwan's experience with pro-natalist policy measures resembles that of other advanced countries that have taken similar policy initiatives (McIntosh 1981; Chamie 1994; McNicoll 2001; Sleebos 2003; McDonald 2006). Below-replacement fertility seems to be a normal response to socioeconomic conditions in the post-industrial era. Specific fertility trends, however, are likely to be dependent on each country's pattern of socioeconomic change, underlying culture, and changes

Table 4 Development of fertility policy measures in Taiwan, 1954–2014

Year	Policy measures
1954	Non-governmental Planned Parenthood Foundation founded in Taipei
1959	Pre-Pregnancy Health (PPH) services initiated in public hospitals
1961	Started employing PPH workers in township health stations; "Lippes Loop" IUD introduced into family planning program
1964	Maternal and Child Health Association founded with responsibility for contraceptive delivery and training program; Department of Health initiated first of a series of midterm Family Health Programs
1965	First wave of national family planning knowledge, attitude, and practice (KAP) surveys conducted
1967	Oral contraceptives introduced into family planning program
1970	Condoms introduced into family planning program
1983	Government advocated strengthening family planning program
1992	Policy to maintain reasonable population growth modified
2002	Gender Equality Employment Act enacted
2008	Pro-natalist Population Policy White Paper approved
2009	Employment Insurance began providing six-month's basic salary for parental leave
2010	Early Childhood Education and Care Act introduced; free preschool tuition introduced nationwide for 5-year-olds
2011	Protection of Children and Youths Welfare and Rights Act amended
	National Pension Act amended to include childbirth benefit
2012	Income tax reform increased tax relief for families with children under age 5; benefits provided to non-employed parents (mothers) with children age 0–2; public-private partnerships for non-profit nanny centers initiated
2013	Childcare subsidy provided to working mothers with children age 0–2; regulations for early discharge from the military through substitute services amended
2014	Population Policy White Paper amended (2nd version); registration system introduced for home-based nanny services

within the family system. Policies represent government interventions into a country's family system, and the effects need to be evaluated and interpreted in each country's cultural and political context.

Rebuilding Family Values

When a population experiences ultra-low fertility, it is a sign that families are losing their reproductive function. Demographic analysis has indicated that Taiwan's declining marriage rate is a crucial factor causing the extreme level of fertility decline. At the same time, the values of Confucianism still have an influence, family ties are strong, and both the government and the older generation have expressed anxiety about the number of young people who are not marrying or whose marriages end in divorce.

Below-replacement fertility emerged earlier in Northern and Western European countries, and the second demographic transition theory interpreted declining fertility as a sign of a value change from an emphasis on the family to greater individualism. According to this theory, the decrease in the marriage rate represents a weakening of family ties, not merely a change in numbers. Indeed, the 2012 Taiwan Fertility and Family Survey showed that Taiwanese attitudes about the importance of marriage have been changing. More than one-half of women age 20–49 disagreed with the statement that "getting married is better than staying single in one's life" (Health Promotion Administration 2014). Younger and more highly educated women were particularly likely to reject the traditional value of marriage.

At the same time, cohabitation is becoming more acceptable. More than 70 % of women age 20–34 disagreed with the statement that "unless they get married, a man and a woman should not live together" (Health Promotion Administration 2014). Yet extramarital births are still extremely rare in Taiwan, suggesting that policies designed to boost fertility must somehow increase the marriage rate.

Specific measures to improve marriage rates include altering the normative life course. The usual "ideal" sequence of events is to finish one's education, become employed, and then marry and start a family. For men, the life course also includes nearly two years of obligatory military service before employment. In general, a man would not be accepted for employment or for marriage until he has completed his military service. To encourage marriage, the military service regulations were amended in 2013 to allow a man to take early discharge with substitute services for family reasons.[9] Another policy change was introduced in recent years to allow military personnel to be stationed near their families (Ministry of Interior 2014).

[9]The amendment states that a draftee may be eligible for early discharge if he "...has two or more children under the age of 12, or has one child under the age 12 and the spouse is more than six months pregnant."

The expansion of higher education over the past 30 years has significantly postponed all of the sequential activities that lead up to family formation. During this period, the Population White Paper proposed that young people be encouraged to "respect marriage, family, and parenting values" by improving education on gender equity, housekeeping, and home economics in schools at all levels. The goal is to provide family-life education that is gender neutral. Yet there has been little progress in providing practical help that will enable young-adult students or workers to marry and start a family.

Improving Childcare Services

The family lost its position as the primary unit of economic production in the course of industrialization. Since then, various family functions have been taken over by the public and market sectors. Childrearing, considered the most basic function of the family, has been the last area of public intervention in Taiwan. The government has introduced compulsory primary and secondary education but has tended not to intervene in early-childhood care. Rather, childcare relies heavily on family and market provisions (Fong 1997; Wu 2006; Wong 2007). As Table 3 shows, few children under age three are enrolled in daycare centers. Parents and relatives provide nearly 90 % of care for young children.

Public investment in early-childhood care was limited in Taiwan until new pro-natalist policies were discussed, with additional pressure from feminists. In recent years, developing an affordable, high-quality, and accessible early-childhood care and education system has been accepted as a top priority. In order to expand early-childhood care and education services, the Early Childhood Education and Care Act was passed in 2010, and the Protection of Children and Youths Welfare and Rights Act was modified in 2011. These two acts allow government to allocate a budget and initiate management of various types of daycare and pre-school education for children age 3–5 and nursery care for children age 0–2. Since 2011, preschool for five-year-old children has been provided free of charge nationwide. A registration system was introduced in 2014 to provide oversight and quality control for live-in nanny services and administer a government subsidy for the cost of nannies. Since 2012, the number of non-profit kindergartens, daycare centers, and after-school care services has been increasing, encouraged by the introduction of public-private partnerships. The Council of Labor Affairs has added pre-service training for childcare personnel (nannies) through its system of vocational training centers.

Economic Support for Families with Children

The rising cost of childrearing has always been considered a crucial factor contributing to fertility decline. The cost has continued to rise, however. Over the years, the government has made a major financial commitment to the education system, starting at age six. The number of years of compulsory schooling was extended to nine in 1967 and is currently being extended to 12. Yet parents have remained responsible for preschool education, thus creating a boom in private kindergartens and nursery schools over the past 30 years. The cost of preschool education has soared, and social surveys have indicated that many people list the cost of preschool education as the most important reason for not having children or not having any more children.

A proposal to provide a child allowance to families with dependent children under age six or under age three, included in the 2008 Population White Paper, was withdrawn because it did not gain support from feminist groups or the Ministry of Finance. Then, prompted by the introduction of childbirth benefits in some municipalities, a measure providing "Parenting Benefits for Children under Age Two" was introduced in 2012. Initially, the benefit was only provided to single-earner families with a consolidated income tax rate of less than 20 %. The aim was to compensate for the lack of a second income due to childcare responsibilities. The exclusion of dual-income families from parenting benefits was criticized as being unfair to employed women, since mothers tend to be the primary caregivers in families even when they are working. Many even argued that the allowance could have a side effect of discouraging women from labor-force participation. As a result, an amendment was passed to help working mothers by providing a subsidy for 0–2-year-old children who are cared for in the home by licensed nannies or a family member (most often a grandmother).

In 2012, the Income Tax Act was modified to include special tax deductions for parents with preschool-age children. Taxpayers with children under age five can receive an annual deduction of TWD25,000 (US$810 as of 10 Jun 2015), about 10 % of the annual minimum wage, with a means test.[10]

Maternity Leave and Parental Leave Allowance

The 2008 White Paper pointed out that maternal benefits were unequal for women employed in different sectors of the economy. The Bureau of Labor Insurance provided much lower benefits for private-sector employees compared with benefits for government employees, teachers, and military personnel. To lessen this inequality, Taiwan's labor employment insurance now stipulates that private-sector employees receive additional maternal benefits equal to three months' salary.

The Gender Equality Employment Act of 2002 provides a maximum of two years' unpaid leave for a parent of a child under three years old. Applications for parental leave have been minimal, however, since this legislation was introduced.

[10]Those taxpayers paying annual consolidated income tax at a rate of more than 20 % or with a basic income of more than TWD6 million (US$19,433) are not eligible for the deductions.

The majority of applicants have been female employees serving in government jobs and female teachers working in public schools. The limited number of applications for parental leave can be explained from both personal and corporate perspectives. From a personal standpoint, income interruption during parental leave would affect family finances, and the working environment in most private-sector establishments would not be favorable to employees who ask for parental leave. From a corporate perspective, most employers are reluctant to provide parental leave unless compelled by law because of the disruption to the flow of work.

To reduce the income interruption incurred during parental leave, an amendment to the Employment Insurance Act of 2008 provides a subsidy of 60 % of a woman's previous salary during the first six months of parental leave. Not surprisingly, working women who give birth tend to take advantage of the paid six months of leave but not the additional 18 months that is unpaid.

Concluding Remarks and Future Prospects

In the half a century between 1960 and 2010, fertility policy in Taiwan shifted from an anti-natalist to a pro-natalist emphasis. This shift came in response to the drastic change in Taiwan's total fertility, which decreased from a high of 7.0 births per woman to the world's lowest recorded level, at less than 1.0.

Taiwan enjoyed a demographic bonus beginning in the 1960s, but this favorable situation ended recently (Mason 2001). The fast and dramatic fertility decline has brought about rapid population aging, along with a concern that the increase in the elderly dependency ratio (the population age 65 and above as a percentage of the working-age population age 15–64) will overwhelm Taiwanese society. According to medium-variant fertility projections, Taiwan's elderly dependency ratio will rise from of 35.8 % in 2010 to 56.1 % in 2030 and 77.7 % in 2060 (CEPD 2012). Expressed differently, the elderly population exceeded 7 % of Taiwan's total population in 1993 and is projected to exceed 14 % by 2018 and 20 % by 2025, making Taiwan a so-called "super-aged society."

The government's White Paper on Population, originally introduced in 2008, marked the beginning of a pro-natalist policy shift, with a variety of measures that were eventually enacted after meeting the objections of environmentalist and feminist groups. The slogan "Happy to marry, willing to have children, and able to raise them" symbolizes the underlying concepts of this pro-natalist policy.

The goal of Taiwan's policy in terms of fertility level is still unclear. Many people think that the TFR is bound to rise from the low of 0.895 in 2010, as no other country has ever experienced such a low fertility rate. Recent official population projections are based on three fertility assumptions. The lowest assumes that the TFR remains constant at 1.05 children per woman until 2035, the medium variant assumes that fertility recovers gradually to 1.30 in 2035, and the high fertility variant assumes that Taiwan's TFR will increase to 1.60 in 2035 (CEPD 2012).

There are several obstacles affecting young people's decision to marry or have children that policymakers need to face. One major problem is the insecure and uncertain economic status of recent graduates. According to earnings and productivity statistics published by the government's Directorate-General of Budget, Accounting, and Statistics (DGBAS), annual real earnings decreased during seven[11] out of the 13 years between 2001 and 2014. At the same time, housing costs soared beyond the means of salaried workers, particularly in urban areas. Starting from a base of 100 in 2009, the housing price index in seven urban areas stood at 116 in 2011 and then shot up in just three years to 137 in 2014 (Taiwan Reality 2015). The government's pro-natalist efforts cannot ignore these critical economic issues that affect young people. Proposals have been made to provide publicly subsidized social housing that will enable young adults to live independently from their parents, but no reasonable plan has yet been carried out.

To be effective, Taiwan's pro-natalist policies also need to meet a challenge in the area of social psychology—the contradiction between the individual's or family's interests and the collective or social interests. Unlike the family planning movement in the 1960s and 1970s, when the interests of individuals and families coincided with the interests of society as a whole, pro-natalist policies today need individuals and families to think more about the collective benefits of higher fertility, which might actually conflict with motivations to maximize career development in a competitive milieu.

Hsinchu City, in the central north of Taiwan, provides an encouraging example of what might be achieved with the right policies. Hsinchu has been famous since the 1980s for its high-tech industrial park, which has served as a gathering place for young engineers and technicians. The Hsinchu municipality enacted a pro-natalist policy in the 1990s, much earlier than the national government. This policy was simply to provide a generous childbirth gift[12] to parents. Through the years since this policy was enacted, Hsinchu has maintained the highest TFR of all Taiwan's cities and counties, about 15 % higher than the national average every year since 2001.

At the national level, it is difficult to assess the effects of pro-natalist policies on fertility given the short history of the government's various policy measures. Since pro-natalist polices were first introduced, the TFR in Taiwan has ranged between 0.90 and 1.27 births per woman. The average TFR over the period 2008–2013 was 1.06. As Sleebos (2003, p. 5) concluded from a multivariate analysis of policy effects on fertility behavior in OECD countries, "...no single bullet is likely to reverse recent declines in fertility rate.... What is required is coherent application of a range of well-designed interventions, applied consistently over time. Also, measures should be directed to families, children, labor markets and society at large, with the aim of supporting those couples who accept the responsibility to

[11]The annual change in real earnings was negative in 2002 (−0.83 %), 2004 (−0.15 %), 2005 (−0.15 %), 2008 (−3.46 %), 2009 (−4.10 %), 2012 (−1.72 %), and 2013 (−0.63 %).

[12]In 2014, Hsinchu municipality provided the following amounts as childbirth gifts: TWD15,000 (US$484) for first births, TWD20,000 (US$646) for second births, TWD25,000 (US$807) for third births, TWD50,000 (US$1,615) for twins, and TWD100,000 (US$3,230) for triplets.

have children because of the collective benefits that stem from their decision." For Taiwan, these observations provide a thoughtful yardstick for assessing policy changes and fertility behavior in the future.

References

Atoh, M., Kandiah, V., & Ivanov, S. (2004). The second demographic transition in Asia? Comparative analysis of the low fertility situation in East and South-East Asian countries. *The Japanese Journal of Population, 2*(1), 42–75.

Barclay, G. (1954). *Population and colonial development in Taiwan*. Princeton: Princeton University Press.

Bongaarts, J. (1978). A framework analyzing the proximate determinants of fertility. *Population and Development Review, 4*(1), 105–132.

CEPD (Council for Economic Planning and Development). (2012). *Population projection for the Republic of China: 2012–2060*. Taipei: Council for Economic Planning and Development (in Chinese).

Chamie, J. (1994). Trends, variations, and contradictions in national policies to influence fertility. *Population and Development Review, 20*, 37–50.

Chang, M. C. (2005). *Taiwan's transition from high fertility to lowest low level*. Paper presented at the International Conference on Lowest Low Fertility and Response: The French Experience and East-Asian Realities, Taipei, October 28, 2005.

Chen, H. H. (1979). *Population changes and social changes in Taiwan*. Taipei: UDN Publications (in Chinese).

Chen, K. J., & Yang, C. L. (2005). *Nuptiality effects on fertility: A compositional analysis*. Paper presented at the International Conference on Lowest Low Fertility and Response: The French Experience and East-Asian Realities, Taipei, October 28, 2005.

DGBAS (Directorate-General of Budget, Accounting, and Statistics). (1980). *Table 11: Number and proportion of population by urban-rural residence and district, Taiwan area* (in Chinese). Taipei: Directorate-General of Budget, Accounting, and Statistics. http://www.dgbas.gov.tw/public/Attachment/8431437871.xls. Accessed June 8, 2015.

DGBAS (Directorate-General of Budget, Accounting, and Statistics). (2002). *Survey of social development trends*. Taipei: Directorate-General of Budget, Accounting, and Statistics.

DGBAS (Directorate-General of Budget, Accounting, and Statistics). (2008a). *Social indicators: 2007*. Taipei: Directorate-General of Budget, Accounting, and Statistics.

DGBAS (Directorate-General of Budget, Accounting, and Statistics). (2008b). *Taiwan's gender statistic and women's life situation: International comparative study*. Taipei: Directorate-General of Budget, Accounting, and Statistics.

DGBAS (Directorate-General of Budget, Accounting, and Statistics). (2013). *Women's marriage, fertility and employment survey report*. Taipei: Directorate-General of Budget, Accounting, and Statistics (in Chinese).

Fong, Y. (1997). *Childcare services: An ecological perspective analysis*. Taipei: Main Stream Publications (in Chinese).

FWRPD (Foundation for Women's Rights Promotion and Development). (2000). *The policy on women in Taiwan*. Taipei: Foundation for Women's Rights Promotion and Development.

FWRPD (Foundation for Women's Rights Promotion and Development). (2003). *Report on Taiwan women's status*. Taipei: Foundation for Women's Rights Promotion and Development.

FWRPD (Foundation for Women's Rights Promotion and Development). (2006). *Taiwan women's almanac*. Taipei: Foundation for Women's Rights Promotion and Development.

Hajnal, J. (1965). European marriage patterns in perspective. In D. V. Glass & D. E. C. Eversley (Eds.), *Population in history* (pp. 101–143). Chicago: Aldine Publishing.

Health Promotion Administration. (2014). *Report of the 11th Family and Fertility Survey in Taiwan*. Taipei: Ministry of Health and Welfare.

Hsieh, A. L. (2004). The Effects of childbearing, childrearing, and immigration on population structure in Taiwan. *Studies on Education and Research, 9*, 99–118 (in Chinese).

Kohler, H. P., Billari, F. C., & Ortega, J. A. (2002). The emergence of lowest-low fertility in Europe during the 1990s. *Population and Development Review, 28*(4), 641–680.

Lee, M. L., Wang, H. Y., Chen, Y. H., Cheng, L. J., Lue, J. D., Peng, H. H., et al. (2007). *Research report on social policy planning in response to lowest-low fertility in Taiwan*. Taipei: Ministry of Interior.

Lesthaeghe, R. (2010). The unfolding story of the second demographic transition. *Population and Development Review, 36*(2), 211–251.

Lin, Y. H., Liu, Y. W., & Lin, H. S. (2002). *Changes of fertility attitudes and behavior among Taiwanese women*. Paper presented at the Annual Conference of the Taiwan Population Association, Taipei.

Luoh, M. C. (2007). The appearance and reality of declining total fertility rates in Taiwan. *Journal of Taiwan Studies, 3*, 37–60 (in Chinese).

Martin-Matthews, A. (2000). Intergenerational caregiving: How apocalyptic and dominant demography frame the questions and shape the answers. In E. Gee & G. Gutman (Eds.), *The overselling of population ageing: Apocalyptic demography, intergenerational challenges, and social policy* (pp. 64–79). Toronto: Oxford University Press.

Mason, A. (2001). Population and economic growth in East Asia. In A. Mason (Ed.), *Population changes and economic development in East Asia* (pp. 1–30). Stanford: Stanford University Press.

McDonald, P. (2000). Gender equity in theories of fertility transition. *Population and Development Review, 26*(3), 427–440.

McDonald, P. (2006). Low fertility and the state: The efficacy of policy. *Population and Development Review, 32*(3), 485–510.

McIntosh, C. A. (1981). Low fertility and liberal democracy in Western Europe. *Population and Development Review, 7*(2), 181–207.

McNicoll, G. (2001). Government and fertility in transitional and post-transitional societies. *Population and Development Review, 27*, 129–159.

Ministry of Education. (2014). *Education statistical indicators*. Taipei: Ministry of Education (in Chinese).

Ministry of Interior. (1950–2013). *Taiwan demographic fact book*. Taipei: Ministry of Interior (in Chinese).

Ministry of Interior. (2008). *Population Policy White Paper*. Taipei: Ministry of Interior (in Chinese).

Ministry of Interior. (2009). *The elderly's living condition survey report*. Taipei: Ministry of Interior (in Chinese).

Ministry of Interior. (2013). *Population policy white paper: Fewer children, ageing population, and immigration*. Taipei: Ministry of Interior (in Chinese).

Ministry of Interior. (2014). *Regulations governing the management of alternative military services*. Taipei: National Conscription Agency, Ministry of Interior (in Chinese). http://www.nca.gov.tw/web/pg_laws.php?gr=&kw=&PG=13&ID=88. Accessed June 20, 2015.

Mitchell, B. A. (2000). The refilled nest: Debunking the myth of families in crisis. In E. Gee & G. Gutman (Eds.), *The overselling of population ageing: Apocalyptic demography, intergenerational challenges, and social policy* (pp. 80–99). Toronto: Oxford University Press.

Population Reference Bureau. (2015). *DataFinder: PRB's hub for US and international data*. http://www.prb.org/DataFinder.aspx. Accessed June 24, 2015.

Statistical Bureau. (2014). *National statistics*. Taipei: Executive Yuan.

Sleebos, J.E. (2003). *Low fertility rates in OECD countries: Facts and policy responses*. OECD Social, Employment and Migration Working Papers No. 15. Paris: Organization for Economic Cooperation and Development.

Sun, T. H., & Chang, M. C. (1989). *Demographic transition and fertility control policies in Taiwan.* Paper presented at the annual meeting of the Population Association of America, Baltimore, 29 March–1 April.

Suzuki, T. (2005). Why is fertility in Korea lower than in Japan? *Journal of Population Problems, 61*(4), 23–29.

Suzuki, T. (2013). *Low fertility and population ageing in Japan and Eastern Asia. Springer Briefs in Population Studies of Japan.* Tokyo: Springer.

Taiwan Provincial Institute of Family Planning. (1992). *Family planning KAP survey report.* Taichung: Taiwan Provincial Institute of Family Planning (in Chinese).

Taiwan Reality. (2015). *Analysis of housing, Taiwan area, 2014* (in Chinese). http://www.twhg.com.tw/bhouseprice01.php. Accessed June 11, 2015.

Tu, E., & Chen, K. J. (1989). Effects of population changes on the social security system in Taiwan. *Taiwan Sociological Review, 13*, 169–190 (in Chinese).

UNDP (United Nations Development Program). (2015). *Table 4: Gender Inequality Index.* http://hdr.undp.org/en/content/table-4-gender-inequality-index. Accessed January 12, 2015.

Van de Kaa, D. J. (1987). Europe's second demographic transition. *Population Bulletin, 42*(1), 1–59.

Wang, T. M., & Chen, W. L. (1986). Mortality trends in Taiwan since the Japanese colonial period (in Chinese). In *Collection of papers for the Conference on Taiwan's Population Change during the Twentieth Century* (pp. 57–78). Taipei: Taiwan Population Association.

Wong, S.-Y. (2007). A study on public child care in Taiwan (in Chinese). In Special Issue (Ed.), *On employment and security* (pp. 63–107). Taipei: Taiwan Think Tank.

World Watch Institute. (1987). *Access to birth control: A world assessment.* Population Briefing Paper No.19. Washington: World Watch Institute.

Wu, S. J. (2006). Current situation of childcare in Taiwan. In Y. C. Yeh (Ed.), *Childcare services.* Taipei: Psychology Publications (in Chinese).

Governmental Support for Families and Obstacles to Fertility in East Asia and Other Industrialized Regions

Anne H. Gauthier

Abstract This chapter examines low fertility and government responses in East Asia and other industrialized regions. It does so from two angles: first by examining individuals' perceived obstacles to fertility on the basis of survey data, and second by examining governmental support for families via a series of indicators. Through this two-pronged approach, the aim is to identify possible mismatches between the demand for family support on the one hand and the supply on the other. In other words, we are interested in the divergence between what people perceive as being needed and what governments actually do for families. The data for the first part of the chapter reveal the dominance of the cost of children as a key obstacle to fertility. In contrast, the analysis of governmental support reveals the relatively low level of financial support for families in Japan, South Korea, and Taiwan as compared with levels in some European countries. Results also reveal that although all three East Asian governments have placed an increasing priority on work-family reconciliation measures in recent decades, large obstacles to the combination of work and family, especially for women, nonetheless persist. The implications of these findings for fertility are discussed in the last part of the chapter.

Keywords Family policy · Low fertility · Cost of children

The rapidly falling fertility rates across the globe and the persistence of below-replacement fertility levels have attracted considerable attention in scientific and political circles in the past few decades. For instance, the European Commission (2005) stressed the problems associated with low fertility in a widely discussed Green Paper in 2005, and *The Economist* (2009) published an issue with the heading "Falling fertility" on its cover in October 2009. In most of these documents, the key conclusions were two-fold: first, low fertility was the result of persisting obstacles to fertility—especially financial obstacles and obstacles related

A.H. Gauthier (✉)
Netherlands Interdisciplinary Demographic Institute (NIDI)
and the University of Groningen, The Hague, The Netherlands
e-mail: gauthier@nidi.nl

R.R. Rindfuss and M.K. Choe (eds.), *Low Fertility, Institutions, and their Policies*, DOI 10.1007/978-3-319-32997-0_11

to the combination of work and family life—and second, adequate policies could remove these obstacles and in so doing bring about an increase in fertility.

These conclusions have a definite appeal: By doing more to support families, governments should see an increase in fertility. Numerous studies have shown, however, that this is not necessarily the case. While policies indeed appear to have a positive impact on fertility, this impact tends to be very small and oftentimes temporary (e.g., Gauthier 2007; Thévenon and Gauthier 2011). This puzzle is at the core of this chapter. In particular, we investigate two possible reasons for the absence or limited impact of policies on fertility: First, because the policies in place provide too little support for families to make a difference in people's fertility decisions, and second, because the policies do not adequately target the actual obstacles to fertility. In investigating these possible reasons, we draw from two different sources of data: social and demographic surveys on people's views about fertility obstacles and databases of family-policy indicators. In doing so, we are able to put in parallel people's views on the one hand and governmental support for families on the other. This is rarely done in the literature and thus provides us with a new vantage point to examine the potential effectiveness of government policies. In particular, it allows us to identify possible mismatches between what governments do and what people want.

In this chapter, we focus mainly on Japan, South Korea, and Taiwan: three countries with very low levels of fertility, but also three countries for which we have data on perceived obstacles to fertility. We also provide comparative material from European and other industrialized countries in order to place these three East Asian countries in a broader international perspective.

The chapter is structured in four sections. First, we set the scene by briefly reviewing trends in fertility and government responses. This is followed by an analysis of survey data on people's perceived obstacles to fertility and then by a detailed analysis of governmental support for families including financial support and support for working parents. The chapter then concludes with a discussion of the possible impact of policies on fertility.

Setting the Scene: Low Fertility and Governmental Response

The starting point for this chapter is the sharp divergence between the fertility trends observed in East Asia during the past decades and those observed in some European countries. Figure 1 displays the trends in Japan, South Korea, and Taiwan and contrasts them with trends in France and Norway, two European countries that have maintained fairly high levels of fertility in recent decades. As discussed elsewhere in this volume, some other European countries, notably in Southern and Eastern Europe, have experienced much lower levels of fertility. Still, the contrast displayed in Fig. 1 is remarkable, reaching close to one child per woman.

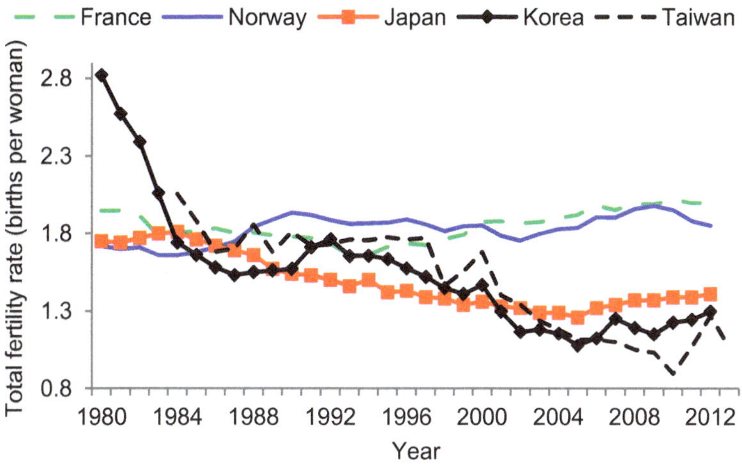

Fig. 1 Trends in total fertility rates, selected countries, 1980–2013 (*Note* Data for France, Norway, Japan, and South Korea from OECD 2015a; data for Taiwan from Republic of China 2015)

Governments in East Asia have not been insensitive to these trends (Frejka et al. 2010). As early as 1991–1992, the Japanese government introduced a series of measures in reaction to rapidly declining fertility (Suzuki 2012). These measures were expanded in subsequent years through new plans and amendments, culminating in 2010 with the adoption of a new action program called "Visions for Children and Childrearing" with, as one of its goals, the achievement of work-life balance for men and women. Instead of being openly pro-natalist, the Japanese government has thus opted for a more comprehensive approach, embracing the well-being of children, parents, and parents to-be.

The policy responses to low fertility in Taiwan and South Korea came much later, even though below-replacement fertility had already been reached in the early 1980s. In Taiwan, the key landmark was the White Paper on Population Policy in 2008, with a wide-ranging set of family policy measures, while in South Korea the key landmark was the governmental action plan of 2006 (Saeromaiji Plan) and its subsequent follow-ups (Chen 2012b; Lee 2009b; Suzuki 2012). Similar to policies in Japan, the various programs and plans of the Taiwanese and South Korean governments all contain elements designed to allow couples to have their desired number of children. In contrast to their Japanese counterparts, however, the South Korean government has formulated in these official documents an explicit fertility target of 1.6 children per woman, to be reached by the year 2020 (Jones 2008; Westley et al. 2010).

The European Commission's 2005 Green Paper, entitled "Confronting demographic change: A new solidarity between generations," was a landmark in that it explicitly portrayed low fertility as a societal problem and identified the return to demographic growth as an essential priority. The document received a great deal of criticism, however, from stakeholders and academics, including reservations about the need to increase fertility as a solution to population aging as well as skepticism about the possible impact of policies on fertility (e.g., EuroHealthnet 2005). A follow-up document, published in 2006, adopted a somewhat more nuanced stance, emphasizing the importance of creating "conditions supportive of those who wish to have children" (European Commission 2006, p. 8). Since then, the objective of better reconciling work and family life has been at the core of the European Commission's stance on demographic issues. In particular, and in the context of population aging, the need to stimulate the economy and female labor-force participation has become central to the Commission's goals. And while some documents continue to refer to the need to close the gap between people's intended and actual fertility, the priorities have shifted to improving support for families as well as encouraging women to join the labor force.

On the basis of this global picture, we now turn in the next section to survey data in order to examine people's perceptions of obstacles to fertility. This will be followed by an examination of governmental support for families.

Perceived Obstacles to Fertility

At first sight, capturing people's perceived obstacles to fertility through survey questions may look like an easy task. In reality, the measurement of people's actual reasons for low fertility, or for not wanting a larger family, can be rather tricky. For one thing, people may answer questions on fertility obstacles in a very general way in terms of reasons why they think people around them have few children, as opposed to the reasons why they themselves do not have more children. Or people may reconstruct in a vague way the reasons why they did not have more children—a decision which itself may have taken place a long time in the past. Moreover, the actual phrasing of the questions on obstacles to fertility and the subgroups of respondents targeted by these questions both tend to differ widely in different countries. Still, the responses to survey questions about perceived obstacles to fertility emerge as particularly interesting, displaying some similarity across countries.

We start with the case of Japan and draw from a series of national fertility surveys that have included one question over the years on why couples do not realize their ideal number of children (Table 1). The survey question was posed to couples whose intended number of children was less than their ideal number. The question was therefore directed to a very specific subgroup of respondents and most likely captures obstacles to higher-order births. Financial reasons, namely "it costs too much to raise and educate children," clearly dominate the results in all three years reported here, 2002, 2005, and 2010. More than 60 % of respondents chose this answer. This result most likely reflects the actual high cost of raising children, especially the high level of private expenditures on education observed in East Asian countries. In contrast, less than 20 % of these respondents mentioned work-family issues as a reason for not having more children. To some extent, this low response is surprising considering the documented difficulties confronting

Table 1 Reasons why couples do not realize their ideal number of children, Japan, 2002, 2005, and 2010

		Percent mentioning each reason		
Broad categories	Reasons	2002	2005	2010
Cost of children and other financial issues	It costs too much to raise and educate children	62.9	65.9	60.4
	House is too small	14.6	15.0	13.2
Work-family incompatibility	Interference with one's job or business	17.1	17.5	16.8
General context and other childrearing issues	Can't mentally/physically bear the burden of childrearing anymore	21.8	21.6	17.4
	Social environment is not suitable for children to grow up without worry	20.4	13.6	7.2
Demographic issues	Hate to bear children at older age	33.2	38.0	35.1
	Want to have a child but can't conceive one	15.7	16.3	19.3
	Health reasons	19.7	16.9	18.6
	Want the last child to grow up before husband retires	9.6	8.5	8.3
Other	Can't get husband's cooperation with household chores and childrearing	12.1	13.8	10.9
	Husband does not want a(nother) child	7.2	8.3	7.4
	Want to cherish life as a couple or as oneself	11.5	8.1	5.6

National Institute of Population and Social Security Research (2011), Table 3.2; Kaneko et al. (2008)

Note The survey question was asked to married women under the age of 50 whose intended number of children was less than their ideal one. The sum of the various items may exceed 100 % since multiple answers were allowed

women in Japan in combining work and family responsibilities. But since the survey question was asked only to married couples, and to a large extent to those who already had children, it could well be that combining work and family was no longer an option for respondents or it was an issue that they had already dealt with.

Questions about obstacles to fertility were also asked in surveys in South Korea and Taiwan, both conducted in 2008. The actual phrasing of the question and the subgroup targeted differed from the Japanese survey, however. In these countries, the question was only asked to respondents who stated that their desired number of children was zero or one and was phrased as: "What is the biggest reason to have a small number of children?" The possible answers also differ from the Japanese ones, but can be grouped in roughly the same broad categories. The data appear in Table 2. The results for Taiwan are to some extent in line with the Japanese ones, especially in identifying high costs as the main reason for having fewer children. More than 30 % of respondents chose this answer. In contrast, the results for South Korea identify unstable economic, political, and social conditions as the dominant

Table 2 Reasons for having fewer children, South Korea and Taiwan, 2008 (Chen 2012a, Table 8)

		Percent mentioning reason	
Broad categories	Reasons	S. Korea	Taiwan
Cost of children	High childrearing expenses	6.8	30.6
Work-life compatibility	Difficulties combining childrearing with work	8.8	15.3
Context of childrearing	Unstable economic circumstances	25.0	29.4
	Unstable political and social conditions	48.6	5.6
	Anxious about the future of children	6.1	11.2
Health and other	Conjugal life or individual accomplishment	3.4	4.6
	Health problems or sterility	1.4	1.2

Note The question was only asked to respondents who stated that their desired number of children was zero or one

reasons for having fewer children, with nearly three-quarters of respondents choosing these answers. Likely this is related to the actual timing of the survey, which was carried out during the recent economic recession. Reasons related to the difficulties in combining work and childrearing received a much lower percentage of responses, as was observed in Japan.

An analysis by Fokkema and Esvelt (2006), based on a survey carried out in 13 European countries in the early 2000s—the Population Policy Acceptance Survey (PPAS), helps put these results in a more international perspective. Like the surveys in East Asia, the PPAS contained a question about the obstacles to fertility but phrased more specifically as reasons for not wanting a (or another) child. It asked: "There are different reasons for not wanting a(nother) child. To what extent are the following reasons important to you personally for (definitely or probably) not wanting a(nother) child?" Results appear in Table 3 and refer to respondents of childbearing age (20–40 years old) who stated in an earlier question that they were not currently pregnant or that they were not intending to have more children. Here we reclassify responses into broad categories in order to facilitate comparison with the earlier tables. Results mirror to some extent the results from Asian countries in identifying concerns about the future as well as the cost of children as the key obstacles to fertility.[1] Reasons related to lifestyle and to the combination of work and family responsibilities receive a lower level of support.

A slightly different picture emerges from a survey carried out in 2008, covering all 27 European Union (EU) member states. The survey question was not phrased in

[1]As in Japan, results related to health also receive a high level of support. We do not focus on these health-related responses because they have no direct connection with government support for families.

Table 3 Reasons for not wanting a (or another) child, average for selected European countries, 2003 (Fokkema and Esvelt 2006, Table 3.3)

Broad categories	Reasons	Percent indicating that the reason was very important
Cost of children and other financial issues	A(nother) child would cost too much	17.7
Work-family incompatibility	My job and professional activities would not allow it	9.4
General context and parenting issues	I am too concerned about the future of my children	27.4
Lifestyles	I want to maintain my present standard of living	11.5
	I would have to give up leisure time interest	4.5
	I would not be able to enjoy life as I have so far	7.4
Demographic issues	I am/my partner is too old	8.3
	My state of health does not allow it	18.6
	I have all the children I want	40.4
	My partner does not want a (nother) child	10.8
	I live alone and do not have a steady partner	9.7

Note Values are the averages across countries of the percentages of respondents age 20–40 who answered that the items were "very important" for not wanting a(nother) child. Results include respondents in Austria, Belgium, Cyprus, the Czech Republic, Estonia, Finland, Germany (East and West), Hungary, Lithuania, Poland, Romania and Slovenia (questions were not asked in Italy). The figures refer to respondents who stated in an earlier question that they (or their partner) were not currently pregnant or that they were not intending to have more children or did not know or were uncertain about it

terms of smaller family size or number of children but instead in terms of difficulties confronted by families with children. The actual survey question was: "I am going to read out a list of difficulties that families could face. In your opinion, from this list, what are the two main difficulties?" The question was posed to men and women age 15 and above. Results appear in Table 4. To facilitate comparison with the earlier tables, responses were reclassified into broad categories. Financial problems, including housing and the high cost of children, dominate these results. Across the 27 EU member states, 32 % of respondents identified the high cost of children and 39 % the high cost of housing as the key difficulties confronting families with children. In fact, the item "difficulties associated with the high cost of children" appeared among the three difficulties mentioned most often in the large majority of member states (European Commission 2008). Problems related to the combination of work and family responsibilities ranked third, with 25 % of respondents selecting

Table 4 Difficulties in daily life faced by families, average for European Union countries, 2008 (European Commission 2008)

Broad categories	Difficulties	Percent mentioning difficulty
Cost of children and other financial issues	High cost of housing	39.0
	High cost of raising children	31.6
	Level of public financial support for families	15.6
Work-family incompatibility	Difficulty combining work and family life	24.7
	Too little support from employers	9.8
	Difficulty arranging good childcare	11.8
General context and parenting issues	Poor quality of school	17.6
	Burden of caring for aging parents or relatives	22.3
	Unequal sharing of household tasks between partners	5.8

Note The figures refer to respondents aged 15 and over (men and women)

this answer. This is in large contrast to the results for East Asia where the issue of work-family balance was less prominent.

It is not surprising that the cost of children appears to be the top obstacle to fertility in East Asian countries. Numerous studies have documented the very high pressures on Asian families to help their children succeed in the education system, especially by gaining entrance to the best schools (Anderson and Kohler 2013). A large percentage of families invest in expensive private schooling and tutoring for their children. Data from the Organization for Economic Cooperation and Development (OECD) on public and private expenditures on education provide further confirmation of this special situation in East Asian countries. While across all OECD countries private household expenditures on education (for all levels of education combined) represented 14 % of total expenditures on education on average in 2011, in Japan and South Korea the figures were 32 and 26 %, respectively. In contrast, the figures in several Western European countries were much lower—11 % in France, for instance, and a mere 1 % in Norway (data not shown). No comparable data are available for Taiwan, but there is evidence of the widespread prevalence of private tutoring and cram schools, also resulting in high education costs for parents (Liu 2012).

If the importance of the high cost of children in the three East Asian countries is not unexpected, the relatively low ranking of work-related issues as key obstacles to fertility is surprising. In South Korea, the reason for this likely lies, at least partly, in the persistence of negative views about working mothers (e.g., Choe et al. 2014). One indicator often used in surveys to assess the acceptance of working mothers is respondents' agreement with the statement: "A preschool child is likely to suffer if

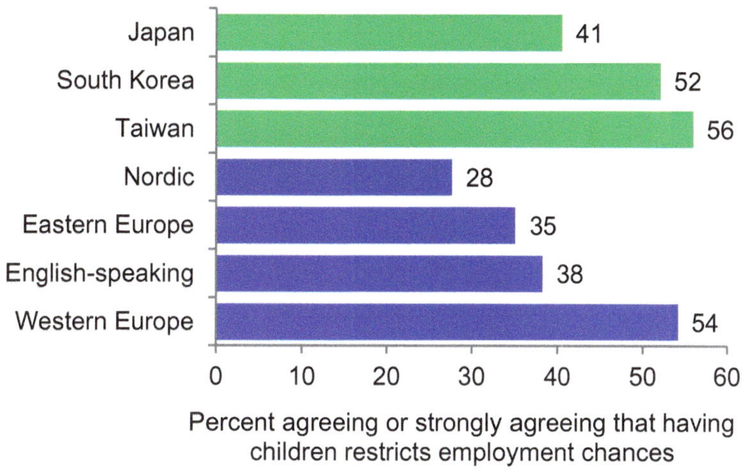

Fig. 2 Percent of respondents agreeing that having children restricts one's career (*Source* ISSP 2012, Question Q7d. Own analysis using the online Zacat/Gesis tool). *Note* The geographical regions are: (1) English-speaking region: Australia, Canada, Ireland, United Kingdom, United States; (2) Eastern European region: Bulgaria, Croatia, Czech Republic, Latvia, Lithuania, Poland, Slovakia, Slovenia; (3) Nordic region: Denmark, Finland, Iceland, Norway, Sweden; (4) Western European region: Austria, France, Germany, Switzerland. Data for Southern European countries are not available for this indicator

his or her mother works." Data on this indicator come from the 2012 International Social Survey Program's Survey on Family and Changing Gender Roles (ISSP 2012) and reveal large differences between the three East Asian countries. While 69 % of respondents in South Korea agreed or strongly agreed with the statement, only 48 % agreed or strongly agreed in Taiwan and only 21 % in Japan. The figure for Japan is, in fact, only slightly higher than that observed in some European countries (e.g., 15 % in Norway) (own computation).[2] That South Korean men and women are less liberal in their attitudes towards women's employment than their Japanese counterparts is, in fact, not a recent trend but was already noted by Lee and Eun (2005) on the basis of older data.

We get a slightly different picture when respondents are questioned about the impact of children on their parents' careers. Again, data come from the 2012 ISSP Survey on Family and Changing Gender Roles. Figure 2 shows the percentage of respondents agreeing or strongly agreeing with the statement: "Having children restricts the employment and career chances of one or both parents." To facilitate comparisons, they are displayed as averages for four geographical regions—Eastern Europe, Western Europe, Nordic countries, and English-speaking countries (the data

[2]The 2010–2014 wave of the World Value Survey provides a similar ranking: 55 % of respondents in South Korea agreed or strongly agreed with the statement "When a mother works for pay, the children suffer." The comparable figures for Japan and Taiwan were 15 and 16 %, respectively, in line with the figures observed in some European countries (own computation).

for Southern European countries are not available for this indicator)—as well as for Japan, South Korea, and Taiwan. This time, Taiwan appears higher in the ranking, with 56 % agreeing with the statement, compared to 52 % in South Korea and 41 % in Japan. Not surprisingly, the Nordic countries, with their high level of support for working parents, have the lowest percentage of respondents agreeing with the statement. As will be seen below, in all three East Asian countries major governmental efforts have been devoted in recent years to improving compatibility between work and family responsibilities. Yet support for working parents continues to lag behind that provided in several European countries, notably the Nordic ones.

Governmental Support for Families

The term "governmental support for families" encompasses a wide array of benefits and services provided to families by various levels of governments. Such benefits and services range from financial support in the form of cash transfers and tax relief to families with children all the way to support for working parents in the form of various leave policies and childcare programs plus support in the areas of education, health, and housing. These measures are rarely governed by a single family policy but are instead under the realm of different ministries and departments.

Total Public Spending on Family Benefits

To obtain a first glance at the level of governmental support in our East Asia countries and other industrialized regions, we used data from the OECD on the total public spending on family benefits as a percentage of gross domestic product (GDP). This indicator does not include all types of support. It is restricted to child allowances and credits, childcare support, income support during leave, and sole-parent payments (see Adema and Ladaique 2009). The results for 2011 appear in Fig. 3. Not surprisingly, Nordic countries rank first, with the highest percentage of GDP devoted to public spending on family benefits. In contrast, Southern European countries are at the bottom of the ranking, together with Japan, South Korea, and Taiwan. In this graph, the ranking for English-speaking countries is high and to a large extent contrary to what one would expect given their liberal welfare state tradition. The average for all English-speaking countries is, in fact, to some extent misleading as it captures wide variations across countries. In particular, while the public spending on family benefits in the United Kingdom[3] (UK) and Ireland

[3]In the UK, the high figure for this indicator represents a deliberate effort by the government to reduce child poverty. Programs tend, therefore, to be largely targeted at low- or medium-income families.

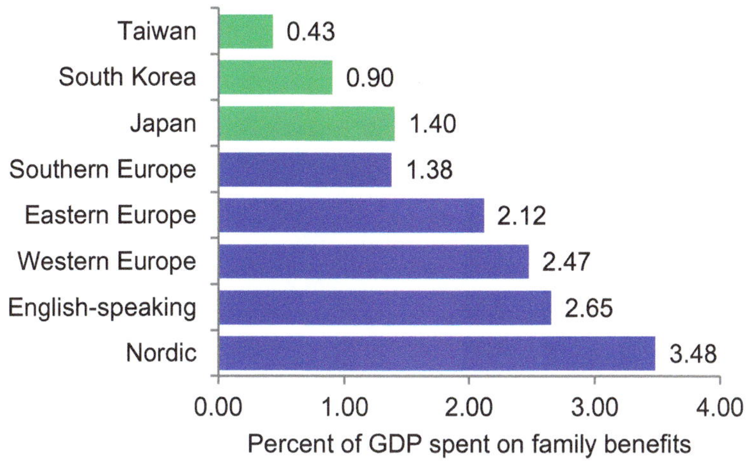

Fig. 3 Public spending on family benefits in 2011 as a percentage of GDP (*Source* OECD 2015b; for Taiwan, ILO 2015). *Note* Public spending on families includes measures such as child allowances and credits, childcare support, income support during leave, and payments to sole (single) parents. The data for Taiwan are for 2009. The geographical regions are: (1) English-speaking region: Australia, Canada, Ireland, New Zealand, United Kingdom, United States; (2) Eastern European region: Czech Republic, Estonia, Hungary, Poland, Slovak Republic, Slovenia; (3) Nordic region: Denmark, Finland, Iceland, Norway, Sweden; (4) Southern European region: Greece, Italy, Portugal, Spain; (5) Western European region: Austria, Belgium, France, Germany, Luxembourg, Netherlands, Switzerland

are high, those in the United States and Canada are very low, comparable to those observed in East Asia.[4]

Financial Support for Families

Financial support for families includes various types of cash transfers and tax benefits, some universal and some means-tested. One way of capturing the overall level of financial support is to compare the disposable income (after taxes and transfers) of families with and without children. The resulting index represents the percentage of additional income available to families with children as compared to that of equivalent childless families. Results appear in Fig. 4 and refer to the case of

[4]Public expenditures for families have increased in recent years in both Japan and South Korea (time-series are not available for Taiwan). For example, in Japan, public expenditures on families increased from 0.5 % of GDP in 1980 to 1.4 % in 2011. In South Korea, the increase was from 0.1 % of GDP in 2000 to 1.2 % in 2012 (OECD 2015b). Despite these increases, the level remains below that observed in most other industrialized countries.

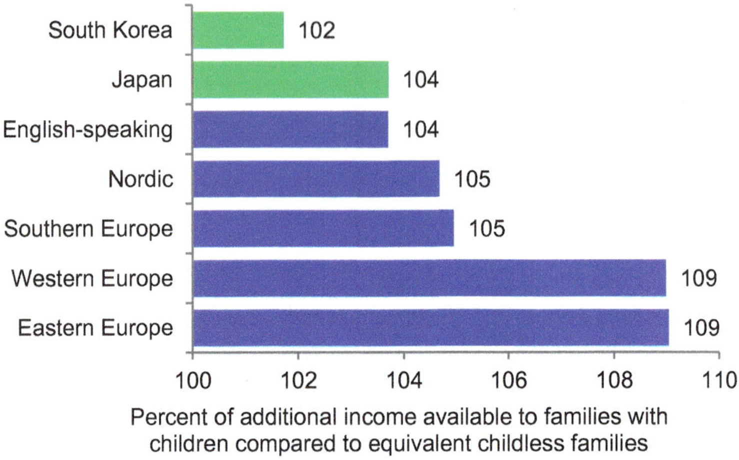

Fig. 4 Index of financial support for dual-earner families with children, 2012 (*Source* own calculation from the OECD online tax-benefit calculator). *Note* Geographical regions are: (1) English-speaking region: Australia, Canada, Ireland, New Zealand, United Kingdom, United States; (2) Eastern European region: Czech Republic, Estonia, Hungary, Poland, Slovak Republic, Slovenia; (3) Nordic region: Denmark, Finland, Iceland, Norway, Sweden; (4) Southern European region: Greece, Italy, Portugal, Spain; (5) Western European region: Austria, Belgium, France, Germany, Netherlands, Switzerland. Data for Taiwan are not available for this indicator

dual-earner couples with two children.[5] They, once again, reveal the lagging position of Japan and South Korea as compared to other industrialized countries. While financial support from government sources adds about 9 % to the disposable income of dual-earner families with children (as compared to their childless equivalent) in Eastern and Western European countries, the comparable figure for Japan and South Korea is less than 4 % (data for this indicator are not available for Taiwan). In other words, families in Japan and South Korea are not largely compensated for the actual cost of children. It has to be said that the data in Fig. 4 refer to families with children age four and six, and thus do not take into account financial support provided by governments to families with younger children. For example, Japan significantly increased the cash benefits for children age 0–2 in 2009 (Suzuki 2012). No internationally comparative figures are available for families with infants or very young children, however.

Cash transfers and tax credits are not the only type of financial support for families. Governments also support families through subsidies and services in the areas of health, housing, and education. Cross-nationally comparable data on these other policy areas are, however, very rare. To our knowledge, the study by Bradshaw and Finch (2002) is the only one that attempted to quantify a broader set

[5]More precisely, one adult is assumed to be earning 100 % of the average wage, and the other 67 %. The children are assumed to be 4 and 6 years old, respectively.

of governmental support for families in a large number of countries. Their results vary depending on the circumstances of each family (i.e., income and number of children) but generally confirm those presented here in revealing the relatively low support for families provided in Japan (South Korea and Taiwan were not included in their study). Moreover, Japan's ranking, already low when based on cash transfers and tax credits only, worsens considerably when also taking into account governmental support in the areas of health, education, and housing. In other words, while the level of financial support provided to families in Japan through taxes and benefits is low by international standards, it is even lower when other sectors are included in the analysis.

Support for Working Parents

In recent decades, governments in industrialized countries have introduced a wide array of measures aimed at better supporting working parents. Among these, the maternity, parental, paternity, and childcare leave schemes occupy a central place. The use of these terms is not consistent across countries, but in general the term maternity leave refers to the period immediately before and after birth, is often of short duration (a few months), and is reserved for the mother. In contrast, the terms parental and childcare leave tend to refer to leaves of longer duration (sometimes a few years) which, in several countries, can be shared (totally or partially) between parents.[6] Finally, the term paternity leave is used for the very short period of leave reserved exclusively for fathers, usually associated with childbirth.

One way to provide comparable measures of governmental support in terms of leave arrangements is to express these schemes in terms of their duration (in number of weeks) pro-rated by the amount of cash benefits paid during the leave. The resulting index should be interpreted as the number of fully compensated weeks of leave (e.g., 12 weeks paid at 60 % of previous earnings is equal to 7.2 weeks full-time equivalent). Results for 2013 appear in Fig. 5. As can be seen, the Eastern European countries have the longest fully compensated leaves, while the English-speaking countries lag far behind. The leading position of the Eastern European countries is mostly explained by their provision of long parental leave—much longer than provided in other countries. These long leaves have, in fact, been the subject of some criticism, especially since they appear to be associated with a negative impact on mothers' long-term earnings (Gupta et al. 2008). Japan, South Korea, and Taiwan fare fairly well in this comparison. Their position reflects policy changes in recent years that have lengthened the duration of leave and increased the amount of cash benefits paid during leave.

---

[6]Some countries draw a distinction between parental leave, which refers to the leave of absence immediately following maternity leave and which can last up to three years, and childcare leave, which in some countries is a subsidy for stay-at-home parents. In most countries, however, the two terms are synonymous.

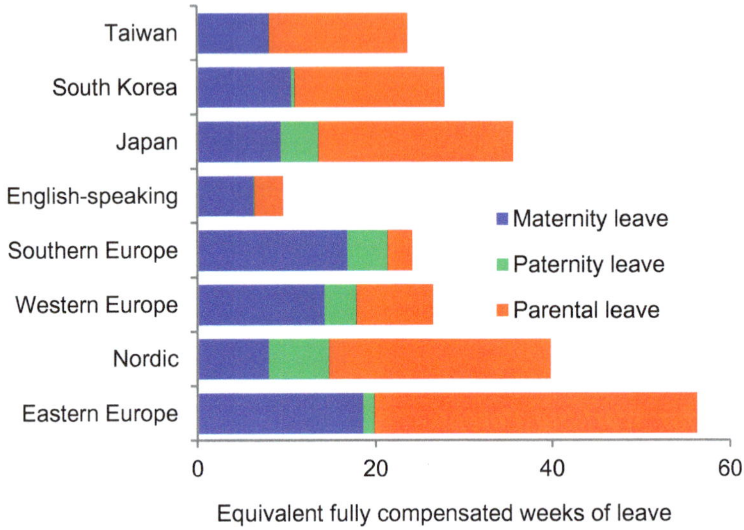

Fig. 5 Provision of maternity and parental leave, 2013 (*Source* Data for OECD countries from OECD (2015a), Table PF2.1.A; data for Taiwan from Feng and Han (2010)). *Note* Duration of leave (in weeks) pro-rated by the percentage of wages paid during leave. See text for an explanation. Geographical regions are: (1) English-speaking region: Australia, Canada, Ireland, New Zealand, United Kingdom, United States; (2) Eastern European region: Czech Republic, Estonia, Hungary, Latvia, Lithuania, Poland, Slovak Republic, Slovenia; (3) Nordic region: Denmark, Finland, Iceland, Norway, Sweden; (4) Southern European region: Greece, Italy, Portugal, Spain; (5) Western European region: Austria, Belgium, France, Germany, Luxembourg, Netherlands, Switzerland

While leave arrangements are a key way of helping parents combine work and family responsibilities, the provision of, and subsidies for, childcare comprise another crucial element. In most countries, the provision of public childcare has increased steadily since the 1980s. The supply, however, continues to lag severely behind the demand in several countries, and the cost remains very high for most families. Figure 6 reports data on enrollment in formal childcare and pre-school for children under age three and for those age 3–5. Enrollment figures for the older children are high in all countries and exceed 80 % in Japan and South Korea. This places Japan and South Korea on par with the Nordic countries and those of Western Europe. The data, however, strictly refer to the provision of childcare and, as will be discussed below, ignore the issue of the quality of care. In contrast, enrollment figures for children under age three are much lower everywhere and reach 50 % only in the Nordic countries and South Korea. There are no comparative data on enrollment in formal childcare in Taiwan, but a 2008 White Paper on Population Policy did call for the introduction of a comprehensive childcare system. Until then, the system was characterized as deficient in terms of provision as well as being expensive (Lee 2009a).

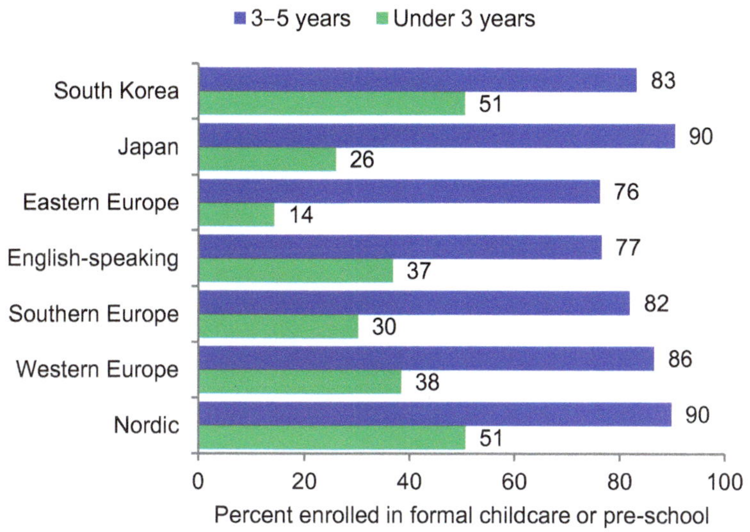

Fig. 6 Enrolment in pre-school and formal childcare among children age 3–5 and under three years, percent (*Source* OECD 2015a, Indicator PF3). *Note* Geographical regions are: (1) English-speaking region: Australia, Canada, Ireland, New Zealand, United Kingdom, United States; (2) Eastern European region: Bulgaria, Czech Republic, Estonia, Hungary, Latvia, Lithuania, Poland, Slovak Republic, Slovenia; (3) Nordic region: Denmark, Finland, Iceland, Norway, Sweden; (4) Southern European region: Greece, Italy, Portugal, Spain; (5) Western European region: Austria, Belgium, France, Germany, Luxembourg, Netherlands, Switzerland. Data for Canada are not available for children the under age three

In Europe, the provision of childcare is seen as a central element to promote female labor-force participation. Actual targets were formulated in 2002 by the European Council, the so-called Barcelona Objectives. They aimed at increasing the provision of childcare by 2010 to cover at least 90 % of children between age three and the mandatory school age and at least 33 % of children under age three (European Commission 2013). These objectives were reaffirmed in subsequent documents and became part of the European Commission's Europe 2020 Strategy to promote employment. As of 2011, only six member states had achieved the childcare objectives for both age groups, while 12 countries (all of them in Eastern Europe) had achieved neither of the objectives.[7] While these objectives are without any doubt important for the reconciliation of work and family life, they have been criticized for ignoring the other components of care, including quality and cost.

The issue of quality of care is, in fact, extremely important but one for which we lack cross-nationally comparable indicators.[8] What we do know is that the

[7]The countries that had achieved both objectives were Belgium, France, Denmark, Slovenia, Sweden, and the UK.

[8]There are data on various indicators of quality, such as staff-to-child ratios, but there is no single comprehensive indicator that allows easy comparison across countries.

favorable position of South Korea noted earlier reflects a very significant expansion of childcare provision in recent years (An 2013) but without a concomitant increase in quality. In particular, numerous observers have pointed to the low quality of care when it comes to areas such as the safety condition of facilities, staff training and salaries, management, and fiscal accountability, as well as large disparities between different types of childcare facilities (Rhee 2007; OECD 2012; Yun et al. 2014).

The cost of childcare remains a particularly large problem, especially for low-income families and single mothers. For example, estimates for the EU member states reveal that in most countries the percentage of children age 0–2 enrolled in formal care is considerably lower among households in the poorest income quintiles (European Commission 2013). Yet we know that both the quality and cost of childcare are important, especially in view of evidence showing the influential role of childcare quality on child development (Marmot et al. 2012) as well as the particularly beneficial impact of high-quality formal care for children from low-income families (Esping-Andersen et al. 2012).

This description of governmental support for working parents is obviously incomplete. A more complete picture would require additional data on the conditions of work (e.g., the possibility of working from home, having flex-time, or opportunities for part-time work), the quality and cost of childcare provision, and legal protection for workers in connection with childbirth and childrearing. Despite these limitations, the overall conclusion is that governmental support for families has increased in recent decades, especially in the field of support for working parents. Support for families in Japan, South Korea, and Taiwan has followed a similar trend, although it tends to remain below levels provided in Europe's leading family-friendly countries.

Policy Mismatch and the Possible Impact of Policies on Fertility

To a large extent, these results point to a mismatch between the demand and supply of family policies. In particular, while the high cost of children is clearly perceived as a major obstacle to fertility, the level of financial support for families remains low in many countries and, consequently, does not match the demand. But while the mismatch between the demand and supply may be hypothesized to be contributing to low fertility, its actual impact on fertility may only be inferred indirectly (see also Ogawa et al. 2009).

More direct evidence regarding the possible impact of policies on fertility can be found in the Population Policy Acceptance Surveys (PPAS), as reported in the first part of this chapter. These surveys asked respondents directly whether or not they thought that governmental support could affect their fertility decisions. They thus provide a unique opportunity to examine the question of policy impact from the point of view of the potential recipients. The questions asked involved three steps. First, the respondents were presented with a series of policy measures and were asked if they were in favor or against them. Second, they were asked which of these measures they would most like to see implemented by their government. Finally, they were asked: "If those [policy] measures which you consider desirable were introduced, would this have consequences for your own personal life? Please indicate whether you agree or disagree with the following statements." The statements themselves ranged from allowing respondents to more easily have the children they intend all the way to probably deciding to have another child.[9]

In order to capture the possible impact of policies, we restrict the results to respondents who stated earlier in the survey that they were not intending to have additional children or were uncertain about it. Among these, 22 % of childless respondents and 35 % of those with one child agreed that they would probably decide to have additional children if their preferred policy measures were introduced (Esveldt et al. 2008, pp. 380–381). These figures are undoubtedly high and likely capture the very hypothetical nature of the survey questions. Responding in a survey that one would have another child may well be very different from actually deciding to have a child. Despite these limitations, these results do provide some evidence that people are not insensitive to their policy environment and that some concrete policy measures could alter their fertility decisions.

These data can also be used to estimate the impact of policies on fertility levels, in this case in terms of total number of intended children. The idea is to estimate, based on the survey, the average number of intended children (by respondents intending to have children) and to add the number of additional children that would result from the implementation of the family policy measures (by respondents who stated that they were not intending to have children or were uncertain about it and who said that they would probably decide to have a(nother) child if their preferred measures were introduced). The result is that the total number of intended children would be higher by about 0.15 child per woman (average across countries) as a consequence of policies (Fokkema and Esvelt 2006). Of course, this result should be interpreted with caution as it likely represents an upper-bound estimate of the possible impact of policies on fertility. Still, it is interesting to note that the estimate is very similar to that obtained some 10 years earlier on the basis of the first round of the PPAS (Kamaras et al. 1999) and is, moreover, quite consistent with results obtained from various econometrics models (see, for example, the review in Thévenon and Gauthier 2011; Gauthier 2007).

[9]The actual statements were: (1) "it would make it easier for me to have the number of children I intend to have;" (2) "It would enable me to have my next child sooner;" (3) "I would reconsider the possibility of having a(nother) child;' and (4) "I would probably decide to have a(nother) child."

Conclusion

The objective of this chapter was to better understand the reasons behind the persistence of very low levels of fertility in East Asia, particularly by examining the possibility of a mismatch between the type of support provided by governments to families and people's perceived obstacles to fertility. In other words, the key question asked was: Have the governments missed the mark and/or should they do more (or differently) for families? Three conclusions seem to emerge. First, we saw that governmental financial support for families is low, especially in the three East Asian countries, and consequently represents a very small fraction of the actual cost of raising a child. The problem is particularly acute when it comes to the cost of education. The share of private (i.e., family) spending on education is much higher in East Asia than in other high-income regions. Not surprisingly, survey respondents mention financial constraints as a major obstacle to fertility. Better financial support for families with children, especially to help cover the cost of education, appears to be an area where current governmental policies and families' needs diverge.

Second, there is evidence that more general concerns about children's future, the overall economic climate, and job prospects are also perceived as obstacles to fertility. These are areas that are usually not covered by family policies but instead come under the realm of economic policies. Addressing these issues could be another way to help reduce obstacles to fertility.

Finally, there is the whole issue of work-family reconciliation that has been the focus of much attention by governments in recent years, both as a way of achieving gender equality and as a way of promoting female labor-force participation. Here we found some contradictory information in terms of people's perceptions. On the one hand, and surprisingly so, we found that constraints on fertility related to work-life balance were not ranked very highly in the three East Asian countries. This was in large contrast with European countries where problems related to achieving work-life balance are more likely to be perceived as important obstacles to fertility. On the other hand, when the survey question was phrased in terms of children restricting one's career (instead of career as an obstacle to fertility), agreement was much higher in Taiwan and South Korea.

What could be happening here is a complex interplay between perceived difficulties in combining work and family responsibilities together with social norms that continue to work against mothers' employment. When it comes to the area of work-family reconciliation policies, there appears to be a good match between governmental support on the one hand and families' needs and wishes on the other. Better leave arrangements and greater provision of childcare facilities do appear to be responding to a real need among the population. In addition, issues related to the quality and cost of childcare also need to be addressed in order to provide more satisfying solutions to working parents.

Societies in East Asia have been changing rapidly over the past few decades, resulting in increasing average ages at first birth, very low levels of fertility, and much higher participation of women in the labor force. At the same time, societal norms have also changed, including a greater acceptance of women's employment, but also increasing pressure on families regarding the educational achievement of their children. The net result points to a clear tradeoff between the quantity and quality of children and also to incompatibility between work and family responsibilities, especially for women.

Government policies, such as those introduced in recent years, are one step to help create a more child- and family-friendly environment. Their impact is likely to be limited, however, and not immediate. Other areas—including issues of gender equality, fathers' role in childrearing, secure employment, workplace culture and work conditions, and housing—will also have to be addressed in order to create a more comprehensive system of support for families. And while there is no denying that the severe fiscal constraints confronting governments in recent years are likely to make progress in these areas very difficult (Jones 2011), creating the conditions for more gender equality and for better work-life balance as well as investing in the next generation of children are arguably essential components for building more sustainable societies.

References

Ademea, W., & Ladaique, M. (2009). *How expensive is the welfare state? Gross and net indicators in the OECD Social Expenditure Database (SOCX).* OECD Social, Employment and Migration Working Papers No. 92. http://dx.doi.org/10.1787/220615515052. Accessed June 17, 2015.

An, M.-Y. (2013). Childcare expansion in East Asia: Changing shape of the institutional configurations in Japan and South Korea. *Asian Social Work and Policy Review, 7*, 28–43.

Anderson, T., & Kohler, H.-P. (2013). Education fever and the East Asian fertility puzzle: A case study of low fertility in South Korea. *Asian Population Studies, 9*(2), 196–215.

Bradshaw, J., & Finch, N. (2002). *A comparison of child benefit packages in 22 countries.* Department for Work and Pensions Research Report No. 174. Leeds: Her Majesty's Stationery Office.

Chen, F. -L. (2012a). *The changing attitude towards children and elderly arrangement after financial crisis—A comparison study of Taiwan and South Korea.* Paper presented at the Joint East Asian Social Policy Research Network and the UK Social Policy Association Annual Conference 2012. http://www.social-policy.org.uk/lincoln2012/Chen%20P7.pdf. Accessed June 17, 2015.

Chen, Y.-H. (2012b). Trends in low fertility and policy responses in Taiwan. *The Japanese Journal of Population, 10*(1), 78–88.

Choe, M. K., Bumpass, L., Tsuya, N. O., & Rindfuss, R. R. (2014). Nontraditional family-related attitudes in Japan: Macro and micro determinants. *Population and Development Review, 40*(2), 241–271.

Esping-Andersen, G., Garfinkel, I., Han, W.-J., Magnuson, K., Wagner, S., & Waldfogel, J. (2012). Child care and school performance in Denmark and the United States. *Children and Youth Services Review, 34*(3), 576–589.

Esvelt, I., Fokkema, T., & Miettinen, A. (2008). Anticipated impact of family policies on fertility behaviour among the childless and among one-child parents. In C. Hohn, D. Avramov, & I. E. Kotowska (Eds.), *People, population change and policies: Lessons from the Population Policy Acceptance Study* (Vol. 1, pp. 369–390). New York: Springer.

EuroHealthNet (2005). *EuroHealthNet response to the communication from the commission on confronting demographic change: A new solidarity between the generations.* COM (2005) 94 final. http://eurohealthnet.eu/sites/eurohealthnet.eu/files/publications/eurohealthnet_response_to_demographic_change.pdf. Accessed June 17, 2015.

European Commission (2005). *Confronting demographic change: A new solidarity between the generations.* Green Paper COM/2005/0094 final. Brussels: European Commission.

European Commission (2006). *The demographic future of Europe—from challenge to opportunity.* COM (2006) 571 final. Brussels: European Commission.

European Commission (2008). *Family life and the needs of an ageing population.* Flash EB Series #247. Brussels: European Commission.

European Commission (2013). *Barcelona objectives: The development of childcare facilities for young children in Europe with a view to sustainable and inclusive growth.* Report from the Commission to the European Parliament, the Council, the Economic and Social Committee, and the Committee of the Regions. Luxembourg: Publications Office of the European Union.

Feng, J. Y., & Han, W.-J. (2010). Maternity leave in Taiwan. *Family Relations, 59*(3), 291–312.

Fokkema, T., & Esvelt, I. (2006). *Child-friendly policies.* Population Policy Acceptance Study (PPAS) Dialogue Working Paper No. 7. http://www.bib-demografie.de/SharedDocs/Publikationen/EN/Research/DIALOG/dialog_ps_no7.pdf?__blob=publicationFile&v=4. Accessed June 19, 2015.

Frejka, T., Jones, G. W., & Sardon, J.-P. (2010). East Asian childbearing patterns and policy developments. *Population and Development Review, 36*, 576–606.

Gauthier, A. H. (2007). The impact of family policies on fertility in industrialized countries: A review of the literature. *Population Research and Policy Review, 26*(3), 323–346.

Gupta, N. D., Smith, N., & Verner, M. (2008). The impact of Nordic countries' family friendly policies on employment, wages and children. *Review of Economics of the Household, 6*(1), 65–89.

ILO (International Labor Organization) (2015). *Social security expenditure database.* http://www.ilo.org/dyn/sesame/IFPSES.SOCIALDBEXP. Accessed July 14, 2015.

ISSP (International Social Survey Program) (2012). *Survey on family and changing gender roles IV.* http://www.gesis.org/issp/modules/issp-modules-by-topic/family-and-changing-gender-roles/2012/. Accessed November 25, 2015.

Jones, R. S. (2008). *Public social spending in Korea in the context of rapid population ageing.* OECD Economics Department Working Papers. No. 615, Paris: OECD Publishing. http://dx.doi.org/10.1787/241545746547. Accessed June 19, 2015.

Jones, R. S. (2011). *Education reform in Japan.* OECD Economics Department Working Papers. No. 888, Paris: OECD Publishing. http://dx.doi.org/10.1787/5kg58z7g95np-en. Accessed June, 19 2015.

Kamaras, F., Kocourkova, J., & Moors, H. (1999). The impact of social policies. In R. Palomba & H. Moors (Eds.), *Population, family and welfare: A comparative survey of European attitudes* (Vol. II). Oxford: Clarendon Press.

Kaneko, R., Sasai, T., Kamano, S., Iwasawa, M., Mita, F., & Moriizumi, R. (2008). Marriage and fertility in Japan today: Overview of the results of the thirteenth Japanese National Fertility Survey, married couples. *The Japanese Journal of Population, 6*(1), 51–75.

Lee, M. (2009a). Transition to below replacement fertility and policy response in Taiwan. *The Japanese Journal of Population, 7*(1), 71–86.

Lee, S.-S. (2009b). Low fertility and policy responses in Korea. *The Japanese Journal of Population, 7*(1), 57–70.

Lee, Y., & Eun, K. (2005). Attitudes towards married women's employment in Korea and Japan: Implications from latent class analysis. *Development and Society, 34*(1), 125–145.

Liu, J. (2012). Does cram schooling matter? Who goes to cram schools? Evidence from Taiwan. *International Journal of Educational Development, 32*(1), 46–52.

Marmot, M., Bell, R., Bloomer, E., & Goldblatt, P. (2012). WHO European review of social determinants of health and the health divide. *The Lancet, 380*(9846), 1011–1029.

National Institute of Population and Social Security Research (2011). *The Fourteenth Japanese National Fertility Survey of 2010: Highlights of the survey results on married couples.* www.ipss.go.jp/site-ad/index_english/nfs14/Nfs14_Couples_Eng.pdf. Accessed June 17, 2015.

OECD (Organization for Economic Cooperation and Development) (2015a). *OECD Family Database.* www.oecd.org/social/family/database.htm. Accessed June 18, 2015.

OECD (Organization for Economic Cooperation and Development) (2015b). *Social Expenditure Database (SOCX).* http://www.oecd.org/social/soc/expenditure.htm. Accessed June 17, 2015.

OECD (2012). Sustaining Korea's convergence to the highest-income countries. In *OECD Economic Surveys: Korea 2012* (pp. 45–86). Paris: OECD Publishing. http://dx.doi.org/10.1787/eco_surveys-kor-2012-4-en. Accessed June 19, 2015.

Ogawa, N., Mason, A., Chawla, A., Matsukura, R., & Tung, A.-C. (2009). Declining fertility and the rising cost of children. What can NTA say about low fertility in Japan and other Asian countries? *Asian Population Studies, 5*(3), 289–307.

Republic of China (2015). *National Statistics: Population and Housing: Table 14 Fertility rates for women of childbearing age.* http://eng.stat.gov.tw/public/data/dgbas03/bs2/yearbook_eng/y014.pdf. Accessed June 17, 2015.

Rhee, O. (2007). Childcare policy in Korea: Current status and major issues. *International Journal of Child Care and Education Policy, 1*(1), 59–72.

Suzuki, T. (2012). Low fertility and governmental intervention in Japan and Korea. *The Japanese Journal of Population, 10*(1), 60–77.

The Economist (2009). Demography, growth, and the environment: Falling fertility. *The Economist.* http://www.economist.com/node/14744915. Accessed June 17, 2015.

Thévenon, O., & Gauthier, A. H. (2011). Family policies in developed countries: A 'fertility-booster' with side-effects. *Community, Work and Family, 14*(2), 197–216.

Westley, S. B., Choe, M. K., Retherford, R. D. (2010). *Very low fertility in Asia: Is there a problem? Can it be solved?* Asia Pacific Issues No. 94. Honolulu: East-West Center.

World Value Survey (2010–2014). *Online data analysis.* http://www.worldvaluessurvey.org/WVSOnline.jsp. Accessed June 19, 2015.

Yun, H., Kim, I., Kwon, H. (2014). *Nine observations on Korea child care support and their policy implications.* KDI Focus No. 34. Sejong City: Korea Development Institute.

Kolibri 360 GmbH
Ferdinand-Jühlke-Straße 7
99095 Erfurt, Deutschland
produktsicherheit@kolibri360.de